TELLING LIVES IN INDIA

Telling Lives in India

Biography, Autobiography, and Life History

edited by

DAVID ARNOLD

&

STUART BLACKBURN

Indiana University Press
Bloomington and Indianapolis

This book is a publication of

Indiana University Press
601 North Morton Street
Bloomington, IN 47404-3797 USA

http://iupress.indiana.edu

Telephone orders   800-842-6796
Fax orders   812-855-7931
Orders by e-mail   iuporder@indiana.edu

The paper used in this publication meets the minimum requirements of
American National Standard for Information Sciences—Permanence of Paper
for Printed Library Materials, ANSI Z39.48-1984.

Cataloging information is available from the Library of Congress.

ISBN 0-253-34486-7 (cloth : alk. paper) — ISBN 0-253-21727-X (pbk. : alk. paper)

1 2 3 4 5 09 08 07 06 05 04

Contents

Acknowledgments

This volume of essays grew out of a "Life Histories" project established at the School of Oriental and African Studies (SOAS) in London, during the period when Stuart Blackburn was Chair of the South Asia Centre, and where the first workshop was held in November 1998. Further meetings and discussion took place in collaboration with other South Asianists, principally at the London School of Economics (LSE) in London, at Oxford (where a second meeting was held in June 1999), and at Cambridge. The main workshop was held in London on May 15–17, 2000, at the British Library, which kindly made its splendid conference facilities available for this purpose. In all some twenty-five scholars presented papers, from a range of very different disciplines and perspectives, and the editors are grateful to them all for their invaluable contributions.

The editors wish to thank the British Academy and the Research Committee at SOAS for their help in funding the project, and to acknowledge the help of David Washbrook (in hosting the Oxford meeting), of Johnny Parry (at LSE) and Sudipta Kaviraj (at SOAS) for their help in planning the London conference and commenting on the draft introduction, and of Barbara Lazoi for her assistance as executive officer at the South Asia Centre at SOAS. The editors are also indebted to Rukun Advani at Permanent Black and Rebecca Tolen at Indiana University Press (IUP) for seeing this volume into print and to the two anonymous reviewers for IUP, whose knowledgeable and constructive comments enabled us to revise and reframe the Introduction to this volume.

DAVID ARNOLD AND STUART BLACKBURN

Notes on Contributors

David Arnold is Professor of South Asian History at the School of Oriental and African Studies, London. His published work has ranged extensively over India's colonial history and includes *Colonizing the Body: State Medicine and Epidemic Disease in Nineteenth-Century India* (1993) and *Gandhi* (2001). His current research is on colonial science, landscape, and travel in early-nineteenth-century India.

Stuart Blackburn is Research Associate at the School of Oriental and African Studies, London, and Director of the ESRC project, "Tribal Transitions: Cultural Change in Arunachal Pradesh." His recent publications include *Moral Fictions: Tamil Folktales from Oral Tradition* (2002) and *Print, Folklore and Nationalism in Colonial South India* (2003). Currently he is working on oral literature and material culture in tribal societies in Arunachal Pradesh.

Sudipta Kaviraj is a Reader in the Department of Political Studies at the School of Oriental and African Studies, London. His research interests include Indian politics and theories of the state. His published work includes *The Unhappy Consciousness: Bankimchandra Chattopadhyay and the Formation of Nationalist Discourse in India* (1995). He has also edited *Politics in India* (1997) and, with Sunil Khilnani, *Civil Society: History and Possibilities* (2001).

Barbara D. Metcalf is currently Alice Freeman Palmer Professor of History at the University of Michigan, Ann Arbor. A specialist in the history of South Asian Muslims, she is the author of *Islamic Contestations: Essays on Muslims in India and Pakistan* (2003) and *Islamic Revival in British India: Deoband, 1860–1900* (2nd edition, 2002); co-author of *A Concise History of India* (2002); and author and translator of *Perfecting Women: Maulana Ashraf 'Ali Thanawi's "Bihishti Zewar"* (1990).

Kirin Narayan is Professor of Anthropology and Languages and Cultures of Asia at the University of Wisconsin–Madison. She is the author of *Storytellers, Saints and Scoundrels: Folk Narrative in Hindu Religious Teaching* (1989), and (in collaboration with Urmila Devi Sood) *Mondays on the Dark Night of the Moon: Himalayan Foothill Folktales* (1997). She has also published a novel, *Love, Stars and All That* (1994). She is currently working on a book about her fieldwork on women's songs and life stories in Kangra.

Francesca Orsini is University Lecturer in Hindi at the Faculty of Oriental Studies, University of Cambridge, and the author of *The Hindi Public Sphere: Language and Literature in the Age of Nationalism* (2002). She is currently editing a book on love in South Asian traditions and working on a project on commercial publishing in nineteenth-century North India.

Jonathan P. Parry is Professor of Anthropology at the London School of Economics. His recent publications include *Caste and Kinship in Kangra* (1979); *Death in Banaras* (1994); and the edited collections *The Worlds of Indian Industrial Labour* (with J. Breman and K. Kapadia 1999) and *Institutions and Inequalities* (with R. Guha 1999). He is currently studying industrialization and industrial life in the Chhattisgarh steel town of Bhilai.

Jean-Luc Racine is Senior Fellow, Centre for the Study of India and South Asia, CNRS–Ecole des Hautes Etudes en Sciences Sociales, Paris. In addition to the life history of Viramma, and several essays on cultural geography in South India, he is the editor of *Les Attaches de l'homme: Enracinement Paysan et Logiques Migratories en Inde du Sud* (1994; English edition, 1996); *Tiers Mondes: Figures d'incertitude: Autonomies et Dépendances* (1991); and *Rural Change in Karnataka* (1989).

Josiane Racine researches popular culture in Tamil Nadu, South India. In addition to the life history of Viramma, she has published several essays on various aspects of Tamil culture and literature, especially singing traditions and Dalit identity.

David Shulman is Professor of Indian Studies and Comparative Religion at the Hebrew University, Jerusalem. Among his recent publications are (with V. Narayana Rao and S. Subrahmanyam) *Textures of Time: Writing History in South India, 1600–1800* (2001) and (with V. Narayana Rao) *Classical Telugu Poetry: An Anthology* (2002). His current research topics are Telugu poetry and poetics; South Indian Saivism; and the history of the imagination in South India.

Sylvia Vatuk is Professor Emeritus of Anthropology at the University of Illinois at Chicago. She is the author of a book and many articles on Indian kinship and family, gender, aging, and intergenerational relations. Her essay in this volume is an outgrowth of research on the history of a prominent South Indian Muslim family, and she has recently completed a field study in Chennai and Hyderabad on Muslim personal law.

CHAPTER 1

Introduction

Life Histories in India

DAVID ARNOLD AND STUART BLACKBURN

Life histories have a wide, if not universal, appeal. Nearly all of us have at some stage been fascinated by other people's lives. Life stories[1] of one kind or another have been told to us from childhood; we have heard them or read them for ourselves or seen them enacted on stage or screen. They may have been the lives (however edited or embellished) of historical men and women, or, no less influentially, characters in folktales, novels and myths. They may have been intended to entertain or admonish us, to encourage emulation or inspire repugnance and fear: we may even have contemplated the prospect, some day, of publishing a life history of our own. But if life histories are so omnipresent and central to human experience, how might they nevertheless differ in content, form and intention from one society to another, or from one age to another? Given this volume's focus on India, do different societies, or even part-societies, articulate life histories in distinctive ways? Are there, moreover, significant differences in the ways in which scholars from different disciplines approach life-historical material, and what can they profitably learn from each other's techniques?

1. Why Life Histories?

India provides a critical site for the discussion of life histories. It might, at least until recently, have been remarked that scholars of India, and of South Asia more generally, have been neglectful, at best wary, of the life-history form compared to scholars of other regions.[2] That the life-history approach has not been entirely absent can readily be demonstrated by referring to David G. Mandelbaum, the anthropologist whose pioneering essay, thirty years ago, drew upon the life of Mohandas Karamchand Gandhi as a case study and argued that the task of life-history studies was to emphasize "the experiences and requirements of the individual—how the person copes with society rather than how society copes with the stream of individuals" (Mandelbaum 1973: 177). It was perhaps significant, however, that Mandelbaum chose to discuss the life of the most famous—and most widely written about—individual in modern India, though his life-history approach was sub-sequently taken up by other scholars looking at very different subjects, including James M. Freeman in his 1979 account of Muli, an Untouch-able in Orissa. Despite something of a hiatus in life histories thereafter, recent years, especially since the mid 1990s, have seen the publication of a number of "person-centered" studies, not just for India alone but almost the entire South Asia region from Sri Lanka to Nepal, and from a variety of different (if predominantly anthropological) perspectives.[3] Despite this, however, it might still be maintained that historically there has been a reluctance to regard India as suitable territory for an approach that has long gained wide acceptance for many other regions and (especially with regard to autobiographical narratives) in such well-developed fields as women's studies and black studies (Olney 1980: 13–17).

One explanation for this general reluctance might be that in South Asian scholarship a paradigm of "collectivity" has tended to prevail. In the anthropology of the 1960s and 1970s, as in many related fields of study (history, politics and religious studies), it was frequently assumed that caste was one of the essential attributes of Indian society and that identities founded on caste and religion dominated to such a degree that individual agency and a sense of selfhood (and hence life histories and other individualistic modes of expression) were marginal to South Asian thought and behavior. To cite a perhaps extreme case, McKim Marriott argued that Indians were best understood as "dividuals" rather than individuals, the person in South Asia being a less discrete, less bounded and more permeable entity than a person in Europe or North America (Marriott 1976). A few privileged individuals might be sufficiently exceptional—or Westernized—to be deemed worthy subjects for conventional biographies by historians or political scientists; or, like Gandhi, Nehru and Nirad Chaudhuri,[4] be able to compose their own self-narratives. But nineteenth-century Orientalist scholarship and colonial ethnography, as much as the post-Independence anthropology of scholars like Marriott and Louis Dumont (for all their differences of perspective), seemed to uphold the dominance of caste identities and the hierarchical ideas and practices that accompanied it (see Inden 1990 for a critique of these ideas). To put it starkly: in India society was valorized; the individual was not (Dirks 2001: 57).

Such an extreme emphasis upon caste-based identities and collectivity may now have been overturned, but it has left a long and lasting impression on the way in which scholars approached the study of India and the kinds of sources considered appropriate to their enquiries. Moreover, a regional identification of India with the exclusivity of caste was reinforced by wider presumptions about the unique historical legacy and cultural specificity of the West. It was confidently assumed that articulate individuality was a hallmark of the West, at least since the *Confessions* of St Augustine, and latterly of its modernity, as it evolved through Renaissance Humanism and Rousseau-style "confessions," through Enlightenment histories that gave prominence to individual acts and achievements, through self-reflexive travelogues, and finally to Freudian analysis (cf. Taylor 1989; Porter 1997). And all of this, so evident in the West to the West, was seen by contrast to be absent from "the East." In recent years, however, scholars of India,[5] as well as those of the Middle East and South East Asia, have begun, sometimes indignantly, to reject the idea that a developed sense of selfhood has existed only in the West, even if the forms that that individualism has taken have been influenced by the history and culture of the specific region.[6] Life histories in India do not necessarily conform to Western conventions and modes of expression (some do, many don't), nor should one expect to find the peculiar forms of individualism that emerged in the West replicated in India (in fact, these essays show how much diversity there was and continues to be). One of the appealing possibilities opened up by examining life histories across several disciplinary fields and situating them comparatively, side by side, is not only to show the variety of forms life histories can take within a single region, but also to shed fresh light on the way we perceive and analyze Indian society.

Despite the partial move away from the polished biographies and autobiographies of the "great and famous" toward the investigation of more marginalized and subaltern sections of society, for which few such literary self-narratives are available, historians of India have generally been inclined to consider life histories as *sources*, of varying degrees of utility and trustworthiness; they have seldom paused to consider them as *genres* worthy of systematic analysis. In descending the social scale from elite to subaltern, an emphasis upon individual lives, and attempts to interrogate their meaning, is often seen by historians to display a "romantic" tendency, attributing to individuals an agency and consciousness, even an "Enlightenment rationalism," they could not plausibly possess (see O'Hanlon 1988). Even anthropologists, who are among the primary users and theorizers of life histories, have sometimes considered the life-histories approach as problematic, in danger of merely replicating, without duly analyzing or contextualizing, personal stories in which the auditor has become too personally

ne reason for the broad appeal of life histories, to the ider public, is precisely that they straddle the elusive rsonal narrative and objective truth. Derived from this double identity are two dominant assumptions about life histories as they appear in both earlier and current research. The first relates to veracity. Life stories, far from being mere fabrications, are seen to be imbued with an extra dose of "truth." Narratives, in this view, are not just entertaining fictions but meaningful explorations of life which reveal emotional and social realities that otherwise elude identification and explanation. As the psychologist Jerome Bruner (1986) puts it, narratives represent an alternative way of knowing and a basis for understanding human action. If narratives in general are imbued with this oracular quality, then stories of individual lives are seen to be capable of disclosing the deepest secrets, those buried deep in the human experience of their subjects and creators. A further reason for attributing an underlying veracity to life histories is that, even when written, they seem to speak directly to us, without the distorting mediation of an author, without editing or censorship (though, as these essays themselves attest, the process of eliciting and recording life histories is never entirely free from outside mediation). As Sandra Stahl (1989) points out, the autobiographical element in many life histories can endow them with the added authority of the speaker, though this might also make us wary of the partisan telling and selective recollection of events and experiences.

A second dominant assumption informing much current life-history research is that these accounts of personal lives reflect culture-specific notions of the person or self. Here written texts, primarily biographies and autobiographies, as well as oral histories and stories, are viewed as valuable sources for understanding the emergence of a modern sense of self, of individualism and self-consciousness as opposed to collective identity. As already observed, one of the purposes of these essays is to explore life histories in order to counter the perception of India as essentially a society composed of castes, religious communities and kinship networks, in which, as a consequence, a sense of selfhood, of personal identity and agency, is muted and subsumed within larger social and cultural domains. However, as discussed in the conclusion to this Introduction, such a mutually exclusive dichotomy between collectivity on the one hand, and individuality on the other, is not fully borne out by these essays: indeed, they show India as a field of constant interaction and negotiation between the two.

It is certainly not the purpose of these essays to present life histories as self-evident statements of social or historical "truth."[8] Contributors to this volume are well aware that biography, in whatever form it is presented, is from a scholarly perspective "anything but innocent." As John and Jean Comaroff have expressed it, "the diary and the life history are culturally specific," and can be "patently ideological modes of inscription" (Comaroff and Comaroff 1992: 26). But such indeed may be precisely their value as social documents, as insights into the ways in which individuals (or the societies around them) sought to present their version of "truth." Whatever the limitations of this approach, it would be reckless to discard life histories as being only "an instrument of bourgeois history-in-the-making" (Comaroff and Comaroff 1992: 26), or as merely valorizing the "cultural logic of late capitalism" by keeping "the myth of the autonomous individual alive" (Goodson 1995). It has also been noted that the recent upsurge of interest in life histories has followed from a growing distrust of "meta-narratives," a new-found skepticism toward sweeping generalizations and grand theories of social change, and hence a move toward a more nuanced, multi-stranded understanding of society and a greater recognition of the heterogeneity of human lives and lived experience, even under overarching systems of patriarchy and colonialism (Raheja and Gold 1994; Lamb 2000: 4–7; Fay 2001: 2–4). But in the context of India, life histories should not be seen as therefore a narrowing down or even a disavowal of grand themes, even if the immediate source material and subject content are more focused. Rather, life histories enable us to render more intelligible precisely the complex of forces at work in modern societies and to reflect further, and from more solid foundations, on many of the major themes that dominate the subcontinent—gender, modernity, colonialism and nationalism, religion, social change, family and kinship, and interrelationship between self and society.

In this book we argue that, as a cultural category, the life-history form is too important to be lightly dismissed or ignored. We hope to demonstrate that life histories reveal insights not just into the experiences and attitudes of the individuals directly concerned, but also of the wider society, or social segment, of which they are a part. This is of particular value in seeking to understand and analyze groups that are socially marginalized and hence not normally heard, such as women and Dalits ("Untouchables"). As many of the titles in this type of scholarship attest, finding the "voice" of the otherwise apparently voiceless has a force propelling the investigation of life histories as a whole, and not least in South Asia; in this way, the life-history approach is a means of breaking the silences imposed by society and history. We would add, however, that it is of no less value in allowing us to stand back from the familiar lives of the "great and famous," of deities, saints and heroes, and to see them as representative of, or creative departures from, established life-historical forms.

Life histories, as they are considered here, show great diversity of form and intent; they also illustrate the power of certain cultural conventions and constraints in the presentation of one's own or others' life histories. As readers will see, there are evident differences between the modern, written life histories discussed in Part One, the more traditional lives presented in Part Two, and the oral lives elicited in Part Three of this collection. But it is one of the objectives of the volume as a whole, and the particular concern of several essays individually (notably Vatuk's account of a life story which was first written as a text but later amplified through speech), to show that these categories overlap and that many life histories are the product of more than one mode of composition and authorial intent.

2. Life Histories in India

Whatever the validity of earlier caste-focused understandings of India, it is certainly true that life histories have been a historically persistent and socially pervasive form of cultural expression in the subcontinent. Many religious traditions (not only Buddhism, Islam and Christianity but also Hinduism in its various manifestations, from Sanskrit texts to popular, devotional bhakti worship), diverse regional cultures, and different social groups (divided by class, ethnicity and gender), have combined to produce a variegated repertoire of life stories. These have circulated and been reworked, by visual, textual and oral techniques, so that both historical and mythological characters are repeatedly drawn upon by individuals as much to give meaning to their own lives as to commemorate the lives of others.

Early Pali and Sanskrit narratives told the life story (or *carita*, a term which also encompasses both "history" and "legend") of Shakyamuni Buddha; Buddha's life, from Boddhisatva to enlightenment, was also represented visually in the didactic iconography of Buddhist temples from the second century AD onward. Accounts of lives were produced in a wide spectrum of forms in pre-modern India. Genealogies, both orally transmitted and written, and horoscopes (again in both oral and written forms) might be considered part of this wider genre, but the great majority of pre-modern life histories were hagiographical— oral and written accounts of the lives of deities, kings, cultural heroes, saints, poets, poet-gods and poet-kings (see the essays by Shulman and Blackburn in this volume). Not all were male or high caste, and several of the best known represented a kind of radical egalitarianism.

While these hagiographies exist in both poetry and prose, and are told from varying points of view, they are characterized by a tendency to praise their subjects and to place the narrative within a mythic framework that is explanatory and not merely ornamental. Events in the life of the poet or hero are often explained by reference to supernatural events, dreams, predictions, vows and divine intercession. Lives of individual poets and poet-saints were often transmitted as part of a self-conscious and explicitly named tradition (*sampradaya*), and many such lives were canonized and anthologized. Defined by literary descent and devotion to guru and god, these communities generated their own life histories, which are sometimes highly dramatic, even humorous. The subject faces dilemmas and makes decisions, but there is little "character development" because, in the end, the course of events is beyond his or her control. Many of these early life histories do contain facts, dates and historical events, but these usually provide context rather than causation.[9]

Another stream of Indian life histories entered with the arrival of Islam and the subsequent elaboration of life-history forms derived from the Middle East and Central Asia (for which see Kramer 1991;

Fay 2001). These included, at a popular level, the "lives" of Sufi *pirs* and *ghazis* (whose tombs often became sites of veneration and the center for the dissemination of tales of their saintly acts or heroic deeds). At the level of court culture and the evolving Indo-Persian tradition, the early Mughal emperors famously penned their own autobiographical memoirs, commencing with the *Babur-nama* early in the sixteenth century and continuing with the *Akbar-nama* (Dale 1996), while (as Barbara Metcalf shows in her essay in this volume) a tradition of religious biography, of "lives as lessons," also began to circulate and develop in Muslim South Asia. From the early nineteenth century, and even earlier in some parts, accounts of the life of Christ and those of Christian saints and heroes, as disseminated by missionaries and their converts, added a further element to the already diverse nature and content of life stories and exemplary biographies.

By the late eighteenth and early nineteenth centuries, as India entered the colonial era, the earlier hagiographical tradition was beginning to be supplemented, and to some extent supplanted, by a new form of biography, in which greater attention was given to complexity of character and personal motivation, to specific places and events, and to their role in shaping and explaining individual lives. In part in response to the protracted encounter with European ideas and education, traditional legend and fable began to yield to "history," in its eighteenth- and nineteenth-century European representations, with a corresponding emphasis upon textual evidence as a kind of scientific "truth."[10]

However, modernity did not replace traditional life histories so much as recast them. As Shulman's essay shows, the eighteenth-century biography of the celebrated South Indian Ananda Ranga Pillai, written in Sanskrit, contained a mixture of both pre-modern and modern features. Commercial printing, which emerged in India in the nineteenth century, stimulated the production and circulation of large numbers of life histories, many of them in the form of brief biographies of real, but usually exemplary, men and women, Western as well as Indian. Often hagiographic in form and style, these too often bore the term *carita* in their titles, as did many of the first Indian attempts at biography and autobiography. But in the sense of a sustained narrative account of one's own life, autobiographical writings began to appear in Indian languages only in the second half of the nineteenth century (exemplified by Sibnath Sastri's Bengali autobiography,

Atmacarit or "self-story," discussed here by Sudipta Kaviraj), and were not common until early in the twentieth (Das 1991). The autobiographies of Gandhi (first published 1927–9) and Nehru (1936)—both discussed by David Arnold in his essay—were among the most celebrated literary works to emerge from the Indian nationalist movement: in becoming models for many other "lives" of the period, they also intertwined the narration of self with the narration of the oppressed or emergent nation. But by the time that the autobiographical genre had fully established its popularity, the Indian cinema had also begun to offer its own influential portrayal of the lives of gods and saints, warrior heroes and political leaders, and even, in more realist vein, of ordinary men and women.

3. What is a Life History?

One of the central issues concerning this volume as a whole is what constitutes a "life history?" The contributors to this volume (and to the discussions preceding it) have taken a broad view of what legitimately falls within this category. They have not sought to confine it to what are clearly biographical or autobiographical texts, for to do so would be to privilege print over orality and to ignore the often fragmentary or allusive nature of many life-historical forms. Following Peacock and Holland, the anthropologists contributing to this volume tend to prefer the use of the term "life story" over "life history," on the grounds that "story" "does not connote that the narration is true, that the events narrated necessarily happened, or that it matters whether they did or did not" (Peacock and Holland 1993: 368). This volume does not adhere to a rigid distinction between the two, partly regarding it as being a matter of disciplinary tradition and preference. In practice, as already indicated with respect to Vatuk's essay, written and spoken forms to some extent converge and interact in the process of making a life history. Indeed, a principal argument informing this project as a whole has been that one form of life history in a multi-stranded society like India can seldom be adequately understood in isolation from others. Hence, despite the obvious differences between, say, a written autobiography, the hagiography of a bhakti saint and a life story elicited by interviews from an illiterate informant, the contrasts can too easily be exaggerated and their linkages overlooked.[11] Rather than draw artificial boundaries, we believe that readers will benefit from looking at diverse forms side by side as part of a wide range of over-lapping and intercepting narrative strategies and presentational techniques.

As for the forms involved, a life history could be a single-authored work, after the manner of the biography of Ananda Ranga Pillai, an eighteenth-century Tamil merchant, or the autobiography of Sibnath Sastri, a nineteenth-century Bengali writer and religious reformer (discussed here by Shulman and Kaviraj, respectively). A life history could also be presented in the rather different style of Maulana Muhammad Zakariyya's *Life*, a twentieth-century Muslim intellectual's memoirs, analyzed in Metcalf's essay. But even these apparently uncomplicated examples are likely to reflect or invoke other life-history forms extant in Indian society,[12] and all deserve to be treated in various ways as partial texts, as much in need as any fable or hagiography of supplementary evidence about their provenance and purpose, and of interest as much for what they omit as for what they declaim. A life history of a more collectively generated and shared kind might be articulated through a popular ballad (as discussed here by Blackburn), or in more elusive fashion by a fragmented account of one's self embedded in a series of sketches ostensibly about other people's lives (the case of the Hindi writer Mahadevi Varma, considered by Francesca Orsini). A life history might be a work of hagiography, of spiritual self-discovery, or a life as reflected in travel or in exile. It might deploy the techniques of a letter-writer, diarist or essayist, or manifest itself (perhaps more safely) through the surrogacy of fiction. It might be put together in an episodic way and essentially for only a family audience (as in the case of the Muslim woman considered by Vatuk), or elicited, as by Kirin Narayan, Josiane and Jean-Luc Racine, and Jonathan Parry in this volume, through interviews, conversations, or by listening in on other people's lives. But, like the more formal texts of the historian or the literary scholar, modes of verbal self-representation also have their cultural models and their self-imposed or authorial silences and omissions.

The lives represented in a life history also come in many shapes and sizes. A life history might record the achievements and opinions of "the great" as well as "the good." Celebrating the virtuous as well as the famous has historically been a primary function of life histories, though in this volume, as in much of the recent life-history literature, we seek to give due attention to "ordinary lives" as well, whether elicited or recorded by the local culture.[13] Life histories can also assume the form of a folk narrative or of an unnarrativized social memory, transmitted through anecdotes or other expressions of popular consciousness, or even through institutional records (as in those for a prison or the army) of those whose stories would otherwise be entirely lost to us. Some life histories reach us as apparently complete and finished entities. They may be subject to an author's revisions, afterthoughts and additions (as with Mahadevi Varma), or to the vagaries of translation (as with Gandhi's autobiography, *The Story of My Experiments with Truth*, first published in Gujarati and later translated into English by Mahadev Desai, Gandhi's secretary). But in the main most printed life histories were clearly conceived and constructed in a recognizable literary form by the person we can, with some confidence, identify as the author. The title page proclaims as much, and the preface or introduction establishes individual ownership (many, not always convincingly, also explain the motives behind the work).

We need, nonetheless, to be aware of the conventions that govern the creation of even the most self-evident life histories. Writing, for instance, of "the rhetoric of the distinctive Indo-Persian cultural and literary tradition," Metcalf emphasizes the need to recognize three major characteristics in this particular life-history genre. First, she notes, "chronology is irrelevant since the essential personality is inherent from the start." Actions and sayings are presented in the life history to show a category of "person" as already defined within society. Second, the person thus documented is seen not as notable for his or her "individuality" but for representing a "timeless pattern." Hence, Metcalf observes, "significance is found in similarity, not difference." And last, the subject of the life history "may well not be imagined as an individual actively conquering and shaping the world independently but as responding to, even being the sport of, outside events" (Metcalf 1995: 476; see also her essay in this volume). How far these conventions *always* applied to Muslim-authored life histories, even in the Indo-Persian tradition,[14] or spilled over into other genres, such as autobiographies written in a more evidently Western form (like Sibnath Sastri's or Jawaharlal Nehru's), remains subject to further investigation. The importance of recognizing differences even between related forms of life histories is clear, just as we should recognize that one form of life history does not necessarily displace another but (as both Shulman and Metcalf show) can coexist and interrelate, one with the other.

For many in South Asia, as elsewhere in the world, to have one's achievements embodied in a life-history text, whatever its form, has been a way to leave "a trace" of oneself, to make a lasting mark on the world and ensure a kind of immortality for one's thoughts and deeds (Desjarlais 2003: 288–9). But not everyone has the ability or authority to tell a complete life history of his or her own, or possesses the verbal or literary capacity to present it as more than a disjointed or elliptical series of events and episodes. In many cases "lives" can be generated only through the musings and recollections of somebody else—the chronicler and the poet, the biographer and the bureaucrat, the oral historian and the anthropologist. But if some people seem to have less than a "life," defined only obliquely in relation to something or someone else, others seem to live different lives simultaneously, without all of these constituent elements combining to form a single, coherent whole. Even when presented in written and published form, the self-authored "life" of an individual is still capable of multiple interpretations and appropriations. Gandhi's autobiographical attempt to define himself through his *Story of My Experiments with Truth* was far from being the only authoring of his "life," including the very different "life" generated by (or perhaps for) the peasants of India with their own magical and millenarian understanding of "Gandhi as Mahatma" (Amin 1984). Authors might attempt through the power of the written word to pre-empt history or to define it in their own terms,[15] but they did not necessarily have the last word on this, and many Indian life histories owe more to ongoing social processes, to popular reinterpretation or the cultural accretions of generations, than to an actual life as lived or defined in a single work.

Of course, many life histories do not reach us in seeming self-explanatory or pre-packaged forms at all. We may have no physical text (not even an incomplete one) or even a coherent body of oral tradition to work from. As scholars, we have to find, or more often construct, the material for ourselves—from snippets of conversations or fragments of correspondence, from personal observation and discreet enquiry. To these "works" we inevitably bring our own obsessions, interpretations and narrative styles.[16] In this attempt to construct a life history (even in a sense "authoring" it) we may be aware that to some extent we are dealing with the shadows cast by other "lives"—by the way our subjects are consciously or unwittingly invoking as a model for their own life that of an authoritative family member, a saint, a guru, or a cinema idol. We may be aware that the telling of a life is pre-structured and formulaic—established by cultural convention or by the expectations of those who commissioned the spoken life, or gave it authority and a public.[17] As Parry remarks in his essay about the illiterate Somvaru's life history, it exists only in his (Parry's) notebooks, as "a kind of patchwork made up of accounts of incidents which were probably triggered by real experiences but which are now represented in wholly conventionalized and formulaic terms; of recollections of previous recollections, and of previously unverbalized memories." We need to understand what these conventions are, but we might also find ourselves looking out for precisely those moments when there is a departure from convention (or from reticence and discretion) that might reveal more about the individuality of our subject or how their own choice of words and idioms sheds light on their social world.

Authors may be very conscious of their medium (of what it will and will not allow) and of their audiences, writing or performing a "life" that they know will please, move or possibly incite their readers or auditors—or at least not overly offend the family circle or the community that will be its principal recipients. In Orsini's essay we learn that a woman writer like Mahadevi Varma could be very conscious of her authorial technique and of how to conceal her own inner identity behind an authorial "I" and conventions of "self-effacement." Other authors in other times and places might seize the opportunities created by the rise of court society, printing, or the modern mass media to project their ideas of personhood to a new and wider audience. They might write less in the interests of "truth" than for money or fame and to advance or defend their professional and political careers. In considering what might be distinctive about Indian life histories, the perceived role of fate or predestination is a recurring theme in several of these essays, though seldom to the extent of denying a degree of individual choice and agency. In some examples, though, a life may be traced as a process of fulfilling what has already been prefigured in one's ancestry (as in the genealogical accounts that preface elite Muslim biographies and autobiographies), or (as Blackburn and Shulman show, in many Hindu folktales and legends) from horoscopes and astrological signs at the time of one's birth, or more generally according to standards of conduct already established as exemplary, kingly, or devout. The lives of kings, heroes and saints form no small part of the Indian life-histories tradition and provide important exemplars for others, much as Gandhi thought of the moral life-story of Harishchandra—the mythological king who sacrificed everything rather than lie—as a suitable model for his own "experiments with truth" (Gandhi 1945). Some life histories are clearly celebratory, but many others (as discussed particularly in Part Three of this volume) are predicated on hardship, suffering and the suppression of individual goals and desires.

Some life histories take the form of "conversion narratives," so common for stories of bhakti saints, but also in biographies of political activists and public figures. A life is thus seen as having little positive meaning or value until, in a moment of revelation or renunciation, through a chance meeting, or a sudden threat or unplanned-for experience, that life is totally transformed, re-routed onto different tracks, sent off in a new spiritual (and/or social) direction.[18] Life histories are often constituted, too, in relation to other people and things. This might most obviously be in relation to a set of traditions or social expectations that prescribe certain ways of writing about one's self and others. Lives can be lived, and hence represented, through the recollections of esteemed and revered others—the guru or *acarya*, the husband and patriarch, the Gandhi-like charismatic political and social leader—rather than as accounts of individual achievement and emancipation. Not infrequently, too, as in the essays by Kaviraj, Vatuk and Shulman, one text (written, oral or in some combination of the two) fashions another. One author sets out to emulate, respond to, or complement the work of another. And so, as in a long hall of mirrors, one life history reflects and informs a multiplicity of others.

4. Silence, Reticence and Privation

As indicated earlier in this Introduction, life histories have often, and increasingly, been used to uncover lives that would otherwise have remained marginal and obscure, and several of the essays in this volume take up and develop that approach. As Josiane and Jean-Luc Racine remind us, there is now an extensive, primarily anthropological, literature about Untouchables, including such person-focused studies as Freeman (1979), Moon (2001), and their own life of a Tamil Dalit woman, Viramma (1995). To these can now be added Parry's account in this volume of a Satnami called Somvaru and his "marital history." (It might be noted in passing that there have, by contrast, been few studies of tribal lives, though presumably their social and physical marginality might equally lend itself to the life-history approach.)

As Vatuk's essay reminds us, the life-history (or life-story) approach has also found favor among historians, anthropologists and feminist scholars writing about women. She cites several examples of this, including books or articles by Geraldine Forbes, Malavika Karlekar, and Tanika Sarkar, as well as her own work and that of the Racines. In this case, given the range (in class terms) of the women involved, written as well as oral testimony is often available (at least to those scholars determined enough to search it out and bring it to critical attention), though it may require particular care in its analysis. But one of the principal reasons for turning to the life histories of women, as with Dalits, is that their lives are not generally accessible by other means, and their individual voices, and the underlying subversive messages they may contain, are too readily silenced in the more familiar, accessible and overtly self-important sources that serve the perspectives of the state or those of the dominant caste and gender. For these reasons, life histories are a way of rescuing or recovering the woman's (or Dalit's) voice, "buried," as Vatuk puts it, "as it often is in the unrecorded past or in the unwritten lives of contemporary non-literate and often oppressed and marginalized peoples."

Even if life histories are seen to be expressions of the self or individual personhood, or of some conception of these cultural constructs, they are subject to the same battery of editorial strategies as other cultural representations. Indeed, several essays in this book, while noting the expressiveness and immediacy of many life histories, also detect a selective silence within and around them, a "reticence" on the part of the writer or speaker, an "awkwardness" and "embarrassment" at the kind of confessional self-revelation that has been seen as a characteristic of Western biography and autobiography since Rousseau, and especially since Freud. Nor, given the conventions that govern self-expression in many parts of the Western world, is this reluctance necessarily surprising.[19] The silences attending life histories are variously explained in this volume. Even seemingly frank and confessional writing can provide well-known figures with an opportunity to win public sympathy and confidence without necessarily revealing all. This is certainly true of Nehru's autobiography, in which, as Sunil Khilnani has put it, he "gave away virtually nothing of himself," especially with respect to the shadowy figure of his wife Kamala.[20] A reluctance to speak openly about emotions and feelings is mentioned, too, in Parry's account of a Dalit's life story and, in a very different social context, in Kaviraj's analysis of Sibnath Sastri, whose autobiography he terms "un-emotional" and "un-psychological."[21]

Gender is offered as one further explanation for the silences in several of these life histories, especially those self-revelatory writings and stories written or related by women. Whether a renowned Hindi author, a highly educated Muslim in Hyderabad, or villagers in north-west India, women are found to use silences and ellipses as a protect-ive strategy. Vatuk, for example, explains that an autobiographical text written in Urdu, and only circulated within the family, by a Muslim woman in the 1950s is full of elliptical references to events that might have caused considerable offense if more fully explicated. Self-censor-ship is also at work, in the context of the Kangra village discussed by Narayan, where women exchanged life histories told in such a way as to "withstand communal scrutiny" and maintain "familial respectabil-ity." Noting the local "prohibition on speaking the names of elders," Narayan draws attention to other linguistic means—ellipsis, abbrevia-tion and coding—in the stories she collected, one of which she herself suppressed because it was too painful to allow the teller to share with the outside world. When the teller is a famous writer, like Mahadevi Varma, the censorship is more likely to be self-imposed. This best-known of women writers in Hindi between the wars described other people in her lively sketches but maintained a resolute silence about herself, creating, as Orsini puts it, a "scintillating circle around a hol-low centre."

These gendered, generational and historical explanations of silence in life histories add to our understanding of the forces that shape ex-pressions of the self in India, but strategies of avoidance may also be linked to another feature of life histories already mentioned—their perceived truth-value. Silence is not, of course, a strategy or condition peculiar to life histories: all language, spoken and written, is edited and molded to some extent to suit intended audiences. But those forms of language imbued with truth, those stories which threaten to reveal, call forth extra effort—psychological and linguistic—to prevent embar-rassment and worse. Here we should keep in mind the widespread belief that life stories are exemplary stories and, whatever the exact manner of their presentation, are perceived to have an inner core of social, moral or spiritual veracity. Among Muslims in the late nineteenth century, Metcalf notes, written histories of the Prophet and his followers gained special value as guides to a true and righteous life. In the very different context of Hindu South India, Blackburn points out, legends of local heroes are also seen as truth-disclosing narratives. The question of how far "lives" are necessarily "true"—to the extent that they can provide reliable forensic evidence—or have a kind of inner truth sustained by a familiar cultural motif (the dying man, rescued from the cremation grounds, who becomes a wandering sadhu, but later returns to reclaim his inheritance) is an issue that has recently been explored by Partha Chatterjee in connection with the claimant to the Bhawal zamindari in early-twentieth-century Bengal (Chatterjee 2002). The definition of these diverse truths established by and through life-history narratives is, of course, culturally contingent and the narratives are accordingly shaped by different conventions and formulae. The eighteenth-century biography of Ananda Ranga Pillai invokes a set of mythic and genealogical references that differ widely from those used in the North Indian Islamic tradition by Maulana Muhammad Zakariyya in the 1970s, and even more from those self-consciously employed by Nehru in the 1930s to frame his autobiography.

The avoidances and perceived veracities observed in these essays show us that the telling of lives is caught up in a tension between the desire to tell the truth and an equally intense desire to regulate it. Silences, as several of the essays demonstrate, are strategies of protection, whether for the speaker or writer, for the people in the story, or for their relatives. These avoidance strategies indicate that the cultural stakes are high in autobiographies, biographies, legends, and even diaries. In short, silence is a feature of life histories precisely because they are, potentially, dangerous. On the other hand, while the experience of oppression and deprivation may be among the factors that discourage the telling of one's *own* life story, the recounting of the lives of others might, in such a context, acquire additional significance, as a source of inspiration and defiance, or perhaps of comfort and solace. For many subordinated and marginalized groups, telling—through the singing of devotional songs or the recounting of legends—the lives of those who defied feudal or patriarchal authority or exemplified a lost age of justice and prosperity, might serve, however modestly, as a "weapon of the weak" (cf. Mukta 1994). And there is also another kind of silence, a stony silence or deafness, in the reception of these life histories of the poor and illiterate.

As an apparent motivation for telling life histories, suffering and deprivation are not restricted to marginalized people; it is not just village women and Dalits but also middle-ranking Muslims in Hyderabad and Muslim intellectuals in North India who want to tell their story of privation. As Metcalf points out, the term *aap biitii*, usually glossed as "autobiography," actually means something closer to "an account of one's sorrows," and Zakariyya's life history follows this tradition in presenting a series of episodes in his life as "trials of affliction." When upper-caste women in Kangra gather and tell each other about their lives, they are "performing sorrows and joys," a phrase which (Narayan notes) significantly inverts the normal sequence of these contrasting conditions, by placing suffering before happiness. Deprivation, or at least physical confinement in prison cells or in exile, has also played a role in motivating well-placed political activists to write their life histories, as Arnold shows with respect to prison narratives.

If suffering and deprivation provide one narrative trigger for telling lives in India, other kinds of motivation or cultural preconditions operate as well. Many life histories discussed here owe their expression to larger processes of historical and cultural change. In contrast with a rather idealized notion of Indians as rooted in a particular town or village, life histories frequently relate to more complex and shifting notions of place—this is especially true for "narratives of displacement" in which the experience of pilgrimage, soldiering, imprisonment, exile and migration provide a personal impetus and a narrative structure for thinking, speaking and writing about one's self or one's family.[22] Moments of rapid historical and cultural change also appear to be a powerful stimulus. The growing European influence on India had an impact on the eighteenth-century biography discussed by Shulman, and more especially on husband and wife, and father and son, in the late-nineteenth-century autobiography described by Kaviraj, just as the authoritarian figure of the colonial state lies behind Arnold's prison narratives. More recent changes—the transformations arising from Independence, Partition and postcolonial politics—have likewise stimulated, albeit in very different ways, the life histories written by the Muslim woman (in Vatuk's essay) and the Islamic scholar (in Metcalf's). Social change also appears to have played a part in encouraging young, media-savvy girls in Kangra (discussed by Narayan) to speak out in a way that their parents and an older generation did not. Even the domestic alterations induced by modernity can lie behind the telling of life histories: the enjoyment of new private spaces for married couples in late-nineteenth-century Calcutta is linked, Kaviraj argues, to a new sense of self and its literary expression as autobiography. Similarly, as Parry shows, emergent social and economic forces in today's India are to be counted among the many cultural conditions and contexts that influence the telling of other lives. A room of one's own, whether a marital bedroom or a prison cell, can engender a story of one's own.

5. Conclusion: The Self-in-Society

As stated earlier, a central objective behind the project from which this volume has emerged was to examine life histories in order to question the view that Indian society is dominated by collectivities. Life histories, the organizers argued, might demonstrate the significance of individual agency and of notions of self in a region of the world where people have historically been seen to identify themselves in terms primarily of caste, but also kinship and religion. However, from the essays brought together in this volume, we now see that life histories, or at least the sample represented in this book, do not consistently or unambiguously reveal the isolated, autonomous, individual self. What they do reveal is a formulation of self-in-society that is more complex and subtle than a mutually exclusive opposition between an all-subsuming collectivity on the one hand, and a rampant individuality on the other. Some of these life histories do, in fact, present novel articulations of the individual and of autonomous selves acting "on their own," but nearly all of them, in one way or another, demonstrate that Indians present individual lives within a network of other lives and that they define themselves in relation to larger frames of reference, especially those of family, kin, caste, religion, and gender.

Perhaps the most individualistic expressions of a self are found in the twentieth-century prison narratives discussed by Arnold, in which the social isolation of incarceration seems to have prompted a new kind of introspection that in turn resulted in the autobiographies of many political leaders and activists.[23] Another novel sense of self, with redefined life goals, is apparent in the Bengali autobiography analyzed by Kaviraj; and the use of the poetic "I" by the Hindi woman writer in the 1930s, in Orsini's essay, represents yet another sort of innovation in self-representation. These three essays, accordingly, appear in Part One of this volume, as representing, each in rather different ways, protracted engagement with both modernity and selfhood. New selves, or their novel expressions, are not quite so evident in the three other written life histories, which are discussed in Part Two, where many more traditional elements surface in the manner of presenting and representing a life, and yet all three exhibit a degree of new sensibility about the individual or authorial self. Thus, the eighteenth-century biography of Ananda Ranga Pillai is not, Shulman notes, a full-blown expression of a modern self, but it does portray an image of an individual who is "whole and singular, strikingly separate from other individuals." The two twentieth-century autobiographies, both written serially by Muslims, might not present radical notions of a self, but they, too, demonstrate how a life history can be employed in the pursuit of individual goals. An educated housewife, in Vatuk's essay, wrote about herself in a family journal in ways that helped define her life purpose; and in Metcalf's piece, a leading Islamic scholar broke new ground by writing his own story in response as much to contemporary events as to an awareness of a specific life-history tradition.

Nevertheless, even in these instances of innovative self-representation, the lives of individuals are not presented in isolation: the story is not that of a single self battling against society, overcoming obstacles and thereby achieving a new, autonomous identity for himself or herself. Rather, the commonality among these life histories, even those of twentieth-century selves, is that they present the life of the individual in active conjunction with the lives of others. Only perhaps in the loneliness of prison writings do we find anything approaching an agonized and isolated self; and even Gandhi's autobiography, now the most famous of all Indian life histories, is primarily concerned (in Arnold's words) "with the pursuit of spiritual salvation, and the moral instruction his life may provide for others, not with unlocking his unconscious." Similarly, the radical self-identity expressed in Sibnath Sastri's autobiography contributes to the "invention of a private life" (in Kaviraj's apt phrase), and yet it, too, is defined through a series of relationships with family, friends and fellow Brahmo Samajists. Likewise, the autobiographical self revealed in a Muslim family magazine (in Vatuk's essay) is framed within a close network of family and kin relations. In some cases, the network of relations is charged with moral purpose, as in the Islamic theologian's use of exemplary lives, from his friends to the Prophet, to construct his own story; in others, the individual life possesses an "ancestral logic," as with the genealogical frame invoked by the eighteenth-century biographer of Ananda Ranga Pillai. Mahadevi Varma is more reticent about relations, but she nonetheless creates a surrogate family, with bonds and responsibilities for herself, in her biographical sketches.

We should also note that the individual lives embodied in these Indian life histories are inflected not only through family but also through a broader network of relations and identities, involving caste, religion and gender. In the written life histories of Part One and Part Two, the role of religion in defining the individual life is variously evident in the Brahmo Samaj concept of a "self," in Hindu notions of individuals and their ancestry, and in Sufi ideals of self-discipline. When we turn to the oral stories and spoken lives discussed in Part Three, we see even more unambiguously how the individual life is expressed in terms of kin, caste, and religious identities. Family relations are thus fundamental to the life stories told by Viramma in Tamil Nadu, Somvaru in Bihar, and the women in Kangra. However, Viramma also speaks of herself as a member of her Untouchable caste (or sub-caste) and its neighborhood, the *ceri*. High-caste women in Kangra similarly speak of female ancestors and relations as extensions of themselves "on a continuum of selfhood," and the caste code of honor makes them reluctant to speak openly of conflicts; the life stories told by younger, low-caste women, on the other hand, hide nothing and openly defy restraints on telling the truth. Caste identity and genealogy also inform the biographies contained in Tamil folktales and legends, which, as Blackburn explains in the closing essay of Part Two, represent collective tellings of a life history. And finally, gender identity is a salient element in many women's life histories recounted in this volume, from sophisticated literary self-representations to colloquial recollections. These stories of "growing up female," the struggle to develop a personal id[...] cultural definitions of gender, illustrate the elusive bal[...] self and society that underlines many of the life histories[...]

Even though life histories focus on individual lives, they are firmly located in social experience. A life history often begins with a personal memory, but (as Halbwachs reminds us) such recollections are always made by a person as part of a social group. Thus, the life histories in this volume do not entirely turn away from collectivity and open a window onto a hitherto unknown vista of Indian individualism; nor do they support the view that in India individual identities are largely subsumed within monolithic categories of caste, kin, and religion. The lives represented here are neither entirely autonomous nor altogether anonymous; the individuals, whether public figures or ordinary villagers, are neither isolated, willful egos nor flattened into collective conformity. Instead, life histories in India are a means for negotiating the irreducible dichotomy of the self-in-society; they are a narrative form for expressing and imagining an individual's existence, which includes group identities and relations with others. The image of a network— an individual (not necessarily at the center) linked to many others, through alliances of varying intimacy and intensity—enables us to visualize the predicament presented in these life histories.

Many forms and idioms are available for making sense of the welter of human experience, but it is worth stressing that among them the life course stands out as a biological universal. Life history, with its ready-made narrative template, and its built-in chronology, is easily adapted to storytelling. When people tell their stories or those of others, the focus on the individual life typically involves a more personalized sensibility than is found in other narrative forms, but the life-history form does not thereby lift the individual life out of its social surroundings. For Indians, as for anyone else, life histories are a narrative strategy for the representation of a person's social experience; and as the essays in this book make clear, life histories present those individual lives within a network of wider social relationships.

We have emphasized the variety of life histories found in India, and readers will find that reflected in these essays. Some life histories are widely circulated in print to readers or recounted to listeners as moral models; others are handwritten in personal journals or revealed verbally only to a trusted outsider. Literary or oral, in Sanskrit or in colloquial speech, they may be instructive or reticent, ambitious or contemplative; they may have no more than a private circulation or they may be addressed to the entire nation.

Whatever their form or intent, life histories offer unique—and still relatively underexplored—perspectives on Indian society. They are not intrinsically more or less valuable than any other cultural form, from temple sculptures and cinema screens to festivals and novels, for all these contain clues to social and or individual practices and intentions. In the case of life histories, however, those practices and intentions are filtered through the patterning of a life or lives, a sequence of events that is perceived to have an extra degree of immediacy and truth-value. Through life histories we can learn something of the impact of large-scale forces (such as industrialization and urbanization, the spread of literacy and the rise of the nation state) and the imprint of collectivities on individuals. The generational shifts in intimacy felt by Sibnath Sastri in Calcutta and Somvaru in Bihar, the Dravidian politics experienced by Viramma and her family in Tamil Nadu, as well as the socialization of females within a joint family in Hyderabad, plus the influence of television and film on young women in Kangra—all these are just a few of the instances when wider forces impinge on individual lives. However biased and incomplete these personal reflections may be (and in that they are not so different from other kinds of histories), life histories open up an experience of the self-in-society unrecorded elsewhere.

S Story: gives that opportunity.

REFERENCES

Amin, S. 1984. "Gandhi as Mahatma: Gorakhpur, Eastern UP, 1921–2." In R. Guha (ed.), *Subaltern Studies III*, pp. 1–61. Delhi: Oxford University Press.

Banerjea, S. N. 1963 [1925]. *A Nation in the Making: Being the Memoirs of Fifty Years of Public Life*. Bombay: Oxford University Press.

Bonarjee, N. B. 1970. *Under Two Masters*. Calcutta: Oxford University Press.

Butalia, U. 1998. *The Other Side of Silence: Voices from the Partition of India*. New Delhi: Viking Penguin.

Bruner, J. 1986. *Actual Minds, Possible Worlds*. Cambridge: Harvard University Press.

Callewaert, W., and R. Snell (eds). 1994. *According to Tradition: Hagiographical Writing in India*. Wiesbaden: Harrassowitz.

Chakrabarty, D. 2000. *Provincializing Europe: Postcolonial Thought and Historical Difference*. Princeton: Princeton University Press.

Chatterjee, P. 1993. *The Nation and Its Fragments: Colonial and Postcolonial Histories*. Princeton: Princeton University Press.

———, 2002. *A Princely Impostor? The Strange and Universal History of the Kumar of Bhawal*. Princeton: Princeton University Press.

Colley, L. 2002. *Captives: Britain, Empire and the World, 1600–1850*. London: Cape.

Comaroff, J., and J. Comaroff, 1992. *Ethnography and the Historical Imagination*. Boulder: Westview Press.

Crapanzano, V. 1984. "Life-histories." *American Anthropologist* 84: 953–60.

Dale, S.F. 1996. "The Poetry and Autobiography of the*Babur-nama.*" *Journal of Asian Studies* 55: 635–64.

Daniel, E.V. 1996. *Charred Lullabies: Chapters in an Autopography of Violence.* Princeton: Princeton University Press.

Das, S.K. 1991. *A History of Indian Literature, VIII, 1800–1900. Western Impact: Indian Response.* Delhi: Sahitya Akademi.

Desjarlais, R. 2003. *Sensory Biographies: Lives and Deaths among Nepal's Yolmo Buddhists.* Berkeley: University of California Press.

Dirks, N.B. 2001. *Castes of Mind: Colonialism and the Making of Modern India.* Princeton: Princeton University Press.

Fay, Mary Ann (ed.). 2001. *Auto/Biography and the Construction of Identity and Community in the Middle East.* New York: Palgrave.

Freeman, J. M. 1979. *Untouchable: An Indian Life History.* London: Allen and Unwin.

Gandhi, M.K. 1945. *An Autobiography: The Story of My Experiments with Truth.* Ahmedabad: Navajivan Publishing House.

Goodson, I. 1995. "The Story So Far." In J.A. Hatch and R. Wisniewski (eds.), *Life History and Narrative*, pp. 89–98. Washington D.C.: Falmer Press.

Halbwachs, Maurice. 1992 [1950]. *On Collective Memory*, edited, translated, and with an Introduction by Lewis A. Coser. Chicago: University of Chicago Press.

Inden, R. 1990. *Imagining India.* Oxford: Blackwell.

Kramer, M. (ed.) 1991. *Middle Eastern Lives: The Practice of Biography and Self-Narrative.* Syracuse: Syracuse University Press.

Krishnadas, 1951. *Seven Months with Mahatma Gandhi.* Ahmedabad: Navajivan Press.

Lamb, S. 2000. *White Saris and Sweet Mangoes: Aging, Gender and Body in North India.* Berkeley: University of California Press.

Langford, J.M. 2002. *Fluent Bodies: Ayurvedic Remedies for Postcolonial Imbalance.* Durham: Duke University Press.

Mandela, N. 1994. *Long Walk to Freedom: The Autobiography of Nelson Mandela.* London: Little, Brown and Co.

Mandelbaum, D.G. 1973. "The Study of Life History: Gandhi." *Current Anthropology* 14: 177–96.

Marriott, M. 1976. "Hindu Transactions: Diversity without Dualism." In B. Kapferer (ed.), *Transaction and Meaning: Directions in the Anthropology of Exchange and Symbolic Behavior*, pp. 109–42. Philadelphia: Institute for the Study of Human Issues.

Metcalf, B.D. 1995. "Narrating Lives: A Mughal Empress, a French Nabob, a Nationalist Muslim Intellectual." *Journal of Asian Studies* 54: 474–80.

Mines, M. 1994a. *Public Faces, Private Voices: Community and Individuality in South Asia.* Berkeley: University of California Press.

———. 1994b. "Conceptualizing the Person: Hierarchical Society and Individual Autonomy in India." In R.T. Ames (ed.), *Self as Person in Asian Theory and Practice*, pp. 317–34. Albany: State University of New York Press.

Moon, V. 2001. *Growing Up Untouchable in India: A Dalit Autobiography.* Landham (Maryland): Rowan and Littlefield.

Mukta, P. 1994. *Upholding the Common Life: The Community of Mirabai.* Delhi: Oxford University Press.

Narayana Rao, V., D. Shulman and S. Subrahmanyam. 2001. *Textures of Time: Writing History in South India, 1600–1800.* New Delhi: Permanent Black.

Nehru, Jawaharlal. 1936. *An Autobiography.* London: Bodley Head.

O'Hanlon, R. 1988. "Recovering the Subject: *Subaltern Studies* and Histories of Resistance in Colonial South Asia." *Modern Asian Studies* 16: 110–20.

Olney, J. 1980. "Autobiography and the Cultural Moment: A Thematic, Historical and Bibliographical Introduction." In J. Olney (ed.), *Autobiography: Essays Theoretical and Critical*, pp. 3–27. Princeton: Princeton University Press.

Ostor, A., L. Fruzetti and S. Barnett (eds). 1983. *Concepts of Person: Kinship, Caste and Marriage in India.* Delhi: Oxford University Press.

Peacock, J.L., and D.C. Holland. 1993. "The Narrated Self: Life Stories in Process." *Ethos* 21: 367–83.

Porter, R. (ed.). 1997. *Rewriting the Self: Histories from the Renaissance to the Present.* London: Routledge.

Raheja, G.G., and A.G. Gold. 1994. *Listen to the Heron's Words: Reimagining Gender and Kinship in North India.* Berkeley: University of California Press.

Sax, W. 2003. *Dancing the Self: Personhood and Performance in the Pandav Lila of Garhwal.* New York: Oxford University Press.

Stahl, S.D. 1989. *Literary Folkloristics and Personal Narrative.* Bloomington: Indiana University Press.

Taylor, C. 1989. *Sources of the Self: The Making of Modern Identity.* Cambridge: Cambridge University Press.

Tucker, J.E. 2001. "Biography as History: The Exemplary Life of Khayr al-Din al-Ramli." In Fay (ed.) 2001, pp. 9–17.

Viramma, J. Racine and J.-L. Racine. 1995. *Une Vie Paria: Le Rire des Asservis. Inde du Sud.* London: Verso.

Watson, C.W. 2000. *Of Self and Nation: Autobiography and the Representation of Modern Indonesia.* Honolulu: University of Hawaii Press.

NOTES

1. For the distinction between "life histories" and "life stories," see section 3 of this Introduction.
2. As for instance in the use of "slave narratives" in African-American history, or more recently in discussions of history and society in the Middle East: see Kramer 1991.
3. Notably Ostor, Fruzetti and Barnett 1983; Mines 1994a; Viramma, Racine and Racine 1995; Daniel 1996; Butalia 1998; Moon 2001; Desjarlais 2003.
4. Nirad C. Chaudhuri's widely read *Autobiography of an Unknown Indian* was first published in 1951.
5. For two recent but very different examples of how ideas of self and selfhood might be investigated in the Indian context, see Langford 2002 and Sax 2003.
6. For the Middle East, see Fay 2001: 2; Tucker 2001: 9–11. But for a more ambivalent position, see the essays in Kramer 1991. For South East Asia, see Watson 2000, who remarks (134–5): "To any anthropologist who has worked in non-European societies, the proposition that non-European peoples lack a sense of self is absurd. Anthropological literature is full of discussions of questions of identity in other cultures, and we find that debate on categories of self in other societies turns not on a denial that a sense of self exists, but on the recognition of the different perceptions that obtain among different cultures concerning the relations—psychological, moral, spiritual—between self and others within society." For India, one of the most effective responses to both the caste-focused and Eurocentric views is Mines 1994b.
7. See Crapanzano 1984.
8. A distinction is sometimes made between the use of life histories to provide "facts" and hence "a veridical record of events," and a more "subjectivist" approach in which the life-history text is investigated for its insights into the subject's social or psychological condition (Peacock and Holland 1993: 369–70; Watson 2000: 10–15). In this volume the contributors' interests lie much less in establishing "facts" than in showing how life histories (or life stories) can be deployed to reveal underlying social situations or are themselves a distinctive and polyvalent cultural form, subject to the varying influences of tradition, continuity and change.
9. On the Indian hagiographical tradition, see Callewaert and Snell 1994.
10. "Myth and history," however, do not exhaust the possibilities of writing about the past, at least in early modern South India (Narayana Rao, Shulman and Subrahmanyam 2001).

11. Desjarlais 2003 provides a fascinating illustration of how life stories might be elicited not merely from illiterate subjects but also from those whose perceptions and forms of self-expression have been informed by their visual sense, including the written word.

12. There has been no attempt in this volume to discuss the life histories of Europeans in colonial India, though as both biography and autobiography this has long been, and remains, one of the principal and most characteristic genres of writing about India. For a recent attempt to recover the life histories of "white subalterns" in early colonial India, see Colley 2002.

13. Interesting work is currently being conducted by Richard M. Eaton into less famous men and women in the Deccan between 1300 and 1750 whose life histories help inform the social and political history of the period.

14. For a rather different discussion of the factors informing Arab life histories in the Middle East, see Tucker 2001.

15. As elsewhere in the world many Indian autobiographies were attempts to defend or rationalize an individual's career. This was perhaps especially so during and immediately following the colonial era, with those bureaucrats and politicians who were accused of being too close to the British or too moderate for an age of militant nationalism (e.g., Banerjea 1963; Bonarjee 1970).

16. For an exploration of these issues, see the essays by Narayan and Parry in this volume; also Crapanzano 1984: 957.

17. For the "commissioning" of a "life" by one of its subjects, see Daniel 1996: 105.

18. Bhakti provides many such examples: the sixteenth-century Rajput princess Mirabai, who rejected marriage to become a wandering devotee of Krishna; and the eleventh-century Kannada poet Mahadeviyakka, who did the same and "married" Shiva. But even in more "ordinary" lives, the sudden social and locational changes involved in marriage might have a similar effect on a woman of being "startled into alertness" (Desjarlais 2003: 118). There are also echoes of a conversion narrative in nationalist discourse, especially in association with Gandhi (e.g., Krishnadas 1951).

19. Such an autobiographical "reticence," especially in relation to intimate family and sexual matters, is by no means confined to India, but has been noted with respect to several other parts of Asia, for instance Indonesia (Watson 2000: 51, 109).

20. Sunil Khilnani, "Nehru's Nehru: The Uses of Autobiography," paper presented to the conference on South Asian Life Histories, London, 2000.

21. On the silences and omissions in Bengali autobiography, see also Chatterjee 1993: 137–40 and Chakrabarty 2000: 35–7.

22. Daniel 1996: 154–93 and Desjarlais 2003 are both very informative about the importance of movement and disruption to the telling of life stories.

23. This is, however, a not uncommon feature of autobiographical writing in many colonial and postcolonial societies in Asia and Africa: see Mandela 1994; also Watson 2000: 70–105, for the 1940s autobiography of the Indonesian Communist leader Tan Malaka, entitled *From Prison to Prison*.

CHAPTER 2

The Self and the Cell

Indian Prison Narratives as Life Histories

DAVID ARNOLD

The prison figured prominently in the Indian middle-class imagination and experience between the 1890s and 1940s. This arose in part from the centrality of jail-going in the civil disobedience movements led by M.K. Gandhi, but it also reflected the extensive British recourse to imprisonment to combat opposition of all kinds, and even before the 1920s the prison had widely come to symbolize the oppressive nature of colonial rule in India. The purpose of this essay is not to try to provide an objective account of prisoners' lives and the conditions in which they were confined, but to examine the self-perceptions of middle-class prisoners and to present the narratives they produced as a significant sub-genre of modern South Asian writing about the self, and as an important contribution to the production of Indian life histories.

Although a large number of what can broadly be described as prison writings were produced during the freedom struggle and in its immediate aftermath, there was no standard format by which authors' diverse impressions and experiences were transformed into written texts. They range from "jail diaries" kept during imprisonment (and not always intended for a wider audience) to polemical narratives of prison life written up for publication, sometimes as newspaper articles, shortly after the event, and autobiographies in which a large part of the author's account is devoted to jail experiences or in which the time spent in prison is represented as being of particular personal or political significance. The prison also found its way into many novels and plays, though no attempt will be made to examine them here.

It might be argued that any connection between the prison and autobiography was largely fortuitous: certainly, the taste for autobiographical writing was well established in India, in English and in the vernaculars, long before Indians began to write about their prison experiences in the 1890s and 1900s. But, while prison may not in itself have generated the Indian urge to autobiography, it surely gave it a significant impetus. The prison was the birthplace of some of India's most celebrated autobiographies, notably Jawaharlal Nehru's *Autobiography*, first published in 1936 and originally to have been entitled *In and Out of the Prison*. Gandhi also began *The Story of My Experiments with Truth* at Yeravda Jail near Pune in the early 1920s, and a number of other nationalist autobiographies were written largely or entirely in jail, though they do not necessarily thereby give prominence to prison experiences (e.g. Prasad 1957). It became as much a nationalist convention for political prisoners to write their prison memoirs as it was a patriotic duty for newspaper editors and book publishers to put them into print. It is indicative of the popularity of the genre, the breadth of its intended readership as well as its diverse authorship, that prison memoirs were written not just in English (like Nehru's) but in virtually every major Indian language from Gujarati and Marathi to Hindi, Bengali and Malayalam. Some of these vernacular works, like Upendranath Bandyopadhyay's *Nirbaster Atmakatha* ("The Autobiography of an Exile"), recounting his experiences of imprisonment in the Andaman Islands, enjoyed considerable popularity and had passed through several editions by the 1970s. Prison narratives were written to inspire as well as inform. Prison elicited many life histories that would not otherwise have been written. It could provide the time as well as the incentive for autobiographical writing, though it should be noted that conditions in jail were not always so conducive for middle-class prisoners, some of whom (like M.N. Roy) were deliberately denied ink, pen and paper as well as access to books and newspapers. For others, it was only following their release that writing became emotionally as well as physically possible. After a long and grueling period of confinement, writing about jail experiences might be a kind of necessary self-purging, answering a therapeutic need to "imprison" the ordeal of incarceration on paper and so to come to terms with the humiliation and suffering involved (cf. Keenan 1992: xiv).

It is one of the arguments of this essay that prison constituted more than just the occasion for autobiographical writing. Despite the often deadening routine and isolation, for many political activist-authors the months and years spent in prison were among the most meaningful periods of their lives, and they left it very different from when they entered. For others the experience, while certainly testing, was less transforming, and their memoirs tend more to political polemic than psychological self-analysis. Even so, incarceration forced many writers to strengthen or redefine their sense of identity and purpose, particularly in relation to the prison's other inmates, the officials, warders and convicts who differed so markedly from the jailed but who, nonetheless, appeared illustrative of the nature of state and society under colonial rule. The writers of prison narratives were almost invariably middle class, though not, after 1930, exclusively male (e.g., Mirabehn 1960: 156–71; Pandit 1979: 101–14). They therefore represented only a minority of prisoners, even during the civil disobedience campaigns, and even in the Andamans—the penal colony whose brutal practices they helped publicize through their own struggles (Sen 2000; Scott-Clark and Levy 2001). Despite their authors' middle-class origins, these narratives turn the prison into a significant site for the observation and representation of the subaltern classes. In an institutional arena where the individual identity of the majority of inmates was almost lost in a sea of regulations and statistics, subsumed within colonial categories of race, caste and religion, and the only "life history" was that manufactured by the state for its own administrative needs, political prisoners often authored life stories for those "common criminals" who left no written record of their own.

"An Unknown Place"

"Prison," wrote Nehru of his first term of incarceration in 1921–2, "was still an unknown place, the idea of going there still a novelty" (Nehru 1936: 79). However, as Nehru acknowledged later in his autobiography, imprisonment for political offenses was not in fact so new. Since the 1890s the Maharashtrian Bal GangadharTilak and a number of Bengali revolutionaries had been imprisoned, and Gandhi had been jailed several times between 1908 and 1914 in the course of his satyagraha (civil disobedience) campaign in South Africa. But what was different for Nehru in 1921 was that middle-class Indians had begun systematically to court imprisonment in support of the nationalist cause (Nehru 1936: 90). Even so, the jail was not such an "unknown place" in 1921. The prison had been a site of contention in India for more than fifty years, going back to the protests against common messing in the jails of Bengal and the North-Western Provinces in the 1840s, the liberation of prisoners during the 1857 rebellion, and periodic controversy from the 1870s over the treatment of both male and female prisoners. Prison issues gained fresh intensity with the imprisonment of Surendranath Banerjee in 1883, followed by Tilak in 1897 and again in 1908, and reports of the systematic abuse of prisoners at Port Blair in the Andamans from 1906 onward.

In nineteenth-century India the prison was one of the most visible manifestations and menacing symbols of colonial rule, and part of the contentious history of the prison and the array of penological practices that surrounded it was authored not by the middle classes but by popular rumor and report. A site of pollution as well as physical pain, a place where caste was reputedly broken and religious taboos violated, where men and women from all castes and classes were subject to cruelty and deprivation, the prison held a deep and troubling significance for Indian society. The number of prison inmates might be small relative to the size of the total population, but from debt or disloyalty, from alleged infanticide or conspiracy to murder, few even of the higher castes and most privileged classes could feel safe from its clutches. If the prison was a common target for peasant insurrection and tribal revolt, it was also from the 1870s a subject for numerous tracts and plays, especially those produced by the Bengali intelligentsia (Mukhopadhyay 1996: 265–81). As Nehru put it from the perspective of the early 1920s, the middle classes viewed prison with "repugnance." "In our minds the place was associated with isolation, humiliation, and suffering, and, above all, the fear of the unknown" (Nehru 1936: 90).

One of the first impulses of the middle classes was to seek to expose the secretive life of the prison and open it up to public accountability, to transform it from a "hell on earth" to a place of humane detention and rehabilitation. In the late 1890s the editor of the Bengali weekly *Hitavadi* wrote a series of articles based on his recent prison experiences, calling for the reform of jail conditions while simultaneously revealing some of the more sensational aspects of convict sub-culture (*Bengal Native Newspaper Reports*, January 1898). Commenting on these articles, another Bengali paper, *Samay*, described British rule as resting on two instruments of coercion—the police and the jails. The police were bad enough, with their repeated acts of "cruelty, barbarity and injustice," but what went on in the jails was "a thousand times more dreadful, more cruel and more fiendish." It was not only the lower classes who suffered:

> Educated people belonging to the higher classes are not infrequently imprisoned with or without reason. But none of them ever care to write a book or a pamphlet describing what goes on in the Indian jail . . . Englishmen have written books on jail life in England, and have thereby improved the condition of the inmates of English jails. The condition of Indian jails is miserable, because no one has written anything about it (*Bengal Native Newspaper Reports*, January 1898).

Gandhi's "Jail Experiences"

Although it was to be another twenty years before conditions in India's jails were extensively publicized, Gandhi's first experiences of imprisonment in South Africa effectively initiated a new phase in the middle-class discovery of the prison. Between January 1908 and December 1913 Gandhi was imprisoned four times, totalling nearly seven months in all: his longest period of confinement was in Pretoria Jail, from February to May 1909. Imprisonment for Gandhi was a necessary part of the struggle to defend Indian rights against racist laws and discrimination in South Africa. As he told an audience in Johannesburg in May 1909, "If you go to gaol, you will be assured of victory" (*CWMG* 9: 219). But the experience of imprisonment contributed—to an extent Gandhi did not anticipate and historians have seldom recognized—to his personal and political evolution in these years. Although his metamorphosis from anglicized lawyer to incipient mahatma had begun several months earlier, the impact of the "education" he received in prison supports the view that Gandhi's emerging political identity owed at least as much to his South African experiences as to his Kathiawari upbringing or his student days in London.

Curiously perhaps, Gandhi made only passing reference to his South African jail experiences in *The Story of My Experiments with Truth*, written in the mid 1920s and begun in jail, but he had already given a more extensive account of them in *Satyagraha in South Africa*, much of which was also written during his imprisonment at Yeravda in 1923–4. He also wrote about his initial jail experiences at the time and at considerable length, in both Gujarati and English. His articles in *Indian Opinion* were intended to be "useful to others" (*CWMG* 8:

134) by accurately informing the Indian community about prison conditions and so, by overcoming their nightmares, encouraging them to participate in civil disobedience. They also chart Gandhi's personal transformation. His experience of jail proved to be extremely traumatic and as such can be taken as indicative of the wider capacity of the colonial prison to transform the lives of its inmates, and even to force them to radically rethink their identity.

Despite the prior determination to endure prison hardships as part of the self-sacrifice demanded by satyagraha, Gandhi's first experience of jail in 1908 threw him back on many of the antipathies of class and religion that made prison such a place of fear and loathing for the Indian middle class. Moreover, in South Africa there was the additional factor of racial repugnance at being confined with those whom Gandhi habitually called "Kaffirs." To be treated, in terms of food, dress and accommodation as no better than black Africans, when one of the primary motives behind the struggle in South Africa was precisely to establish equality with whites, was deeply galling to Gandhi. This, he reflected in March 1908, was an "experience for which we were perhaps all unprepared" (*CWMG* 8: 120), and yet being "classed with Natives" was bitter confirmation of the "degradation" Indians were subjected to in South Africa: "We could understand not being classed with the whites, but to be placed on the same level with the Natives seemed too much to put up with. I then felt that Indians had not launched on passive resistance too soon. Here was further proof that the obnoxious law [the Asiatic Registration Act] was intended to emasculate the Indians" (*CWMG* 8: 135).

Being threatened, taunted and abused by "Kaffir" prisoners and warders further convinced Gandhi that the "separation" of Indians and Africans was a "physical necessity." Indian prisoners, he declared, had nothing in common with Africans and everything to fear from them. "Kaffirs," he wrote, "are as a rule uncivilized—the convicts even more so. They are troublesome, very dirty and live almost like animals . . . The reader can easily imagine the plight of the poor Indian thrown into such company!" (*CWMG* 8: 135) Deep offense was felt, too, at being denied European or Indian food and being obliged to eat "Kaffir" food—maize meal. African and European prisoners received food "suited to their tastes," Gandhi protested, while Indian needs were ignored. The prescribed diet was "totally unsuitable" for Indians, who were "either in the habit of taking European food or mostly so"

(*CWMG* 8: 39). He protested, too, at the inclusion of animal fat in food served to Indian prisoners, as being unacceptable alike to Hindus and Muslims, and demanded rice, pulses and ghee instead. Though Gandhi was apparently unaware of it, his struggle in South Africa re-enacted many of the scenes of dietary confrontation that had been staged in India's own prisons over the previous sixty years.

Gandhi saw himself as leading a largely successful struggle against such injustices and winning a number of important concessions from the jail authorities (*CWMG* 24: 56). But the prison changed Gandhi more than Gandhi changed the prison. The experience of incarceration profoundly affected his evolving political ideas and overturned many of the conventional beliefs and assumptions he had hitherto shared with other middle-class, high-caste Indians. In this sense Gandhi's "jail experiences" have something of the flavor of a conversion narrative. While at times comparing his ordeal to that of Daniel in the lion's den, Gandhi could declare with all the zeal of a recent convert that prison was also a place of instruction, conducive to self-purification and moral regeneration. He described the hardships of jail life as "mostly imaginary" and encouraged Indians to think of prison as "a holy and happy place," a "palace," even a "paradise" (*CWMG* 8: 160; 9: 93, 96, 182). Citing Bunyan and Tilak as examples, he presented prison as a place where "conscientious men" had "achieved great things" (*CWMG* 8: 160). At a more mundane level, prison food, so loathed at the outset, came to signify a duty to curb indulgence. The sparseness of jail diets was a reminder that back in India there were millions of people who had far less to eat. Even "mealie pap," judged inedible in January 1908, had within a year become "a sweet and strength-giving food," which "with some adjustments" could be made a "perfect diet" (*CWMG* 9: 123). And while remaining staunchly opposed to mixing with "Kaffirs," the prison, which confronted Gandhi with the many troubling divisions in Indian society—between Hindus and Muslims, high castes and low—encouraged him to see the camaraderie of prison life as helpful in countering such "false distinctions" (*CWMG* 9: 180–1).

Despite his growing disillusionment with modern civilization (proclaimed in *Hind Swaraj* in 1909), Gandhi identified the prison as a model of sanitation and hygiene from which Indians might profitably learn. Stung by allegations that Indians were "uncivilized" and "dirty," and that their insanitary practices spread plague and other epidemics, Gandhi approved of the "excellent" sanitary regime he found in jail. While doubting that the ventilation in the cells quite met "modern requirements," he invoked the authority of "medical science" in support of hard beds and the liberal use of disinfectant and white-wash. He even asked, for health's sake, to have his hair cropped and moustache shaved off, though prison regulations did not require it (*CWMG* 8: 138–41). Prison labor, for all the undoubted hardship and humiliation involved, caused Gandhi to reflect positively on "the great Ruskin" and his revelation that the life of labor was the "life worth living" (*CWMG* 9: 140–1, 181). Even cleaning out latrines and carry-ing buckets of urine—in caste terms extremely offensive and a repeated cause of protest among political prisoners in India in the 1920s—was ascribed moral as well as sanitary value and set Gandhi thinking about the inequities of Untouchability. It was wrong, he wrote, "to think of any work as humiliating or degrading" (*CWMG* 9: 146).

For Gandhi, who had begun his experiments in *brahmacharya* (celi-bacy) less than two years before his incarceration, the constraints of prison life and control of his "animal desires" became closely linked. Twenty years later, in one of the few direct references to jail experiences in his autobiography, he observed: "I saw that some of the regulations that the prisoners had to observe were such as should be voluntarily observed by a brahmachari, that is, one desiring to practise self-res-traint" (Gandhi 1940: 245). Prison was free from sexual temptation (though not, to judge from his encounters with African and Chinese prisoners, from sexual menace), just as it denied other indulgences, like rich food and idleness. In prison "all of one's bad habits fall away. The mind enjoys a sense of freedom . . . The body is held in bondage, but the soul grows more free" (*CWMG* 9: 182).

Gandhi undoubtedly found prison life in South Africa harsh, brutal and inhumane, especially when he was kept in virtual isolation in Pretoria Jail in 1909. Even from the vantage point of 1932 he recalled his time in South African jails as his "real imprisonment," harsher than anything he had experienced subsequently in India (Desai 1953: 12–13). And yet, for all the hardships, the experience paradoxically pro-vided Gandhi with a model of how Indian society might be purged of some of its most undesirable and harmful practices. Prison life in South Africa taught him to think and feel differently not only about society, but also, crucially, about his own body. Through the ordeal of imprisonment he came to regard his body with a peculiar detachment, as an object to be disciplined not indulged, ordered not obeyed. This process had begun earlier (during his days with the Indian ambulance corps during the Zulu Rebellion of 1906) but was accelerated and intensified by the prison experience. Still in many ways shy and acutely conscious of his physical frailty, Gandhi sought to compensate for this through strict physical as well as mental self-control. Jail-going required "a well-disciplined body": "a physical wreck" would "not be able to bear gaol life." A satyagrahi, he added, "knows that his body is lent to him on hire. He should prove a worthy tenant by keeping it clean and glowing with health" (*CWMG* 9: 236–7).

In coming to terms with prison's hardships and humiliation, Gandhi came to see his body as a potent symbol, a vehicle by which to convey, even without words, what he suffered, believed in or aspired to. While being transferred from Johannesburg to Volksrust Jail in November 1908 Gandhi was seen at the railway station in his prison clothes by some Indian passengers (who, aptly, happened to be tailors). "Of course, talking was not allowed," but seeing his prison clothes "some of them were filled with tears. Since I was not free even to tell them that I did not mind my dress or anything else, I merely remained a silent spectator"—an onlooker, as it were, to the spectacle of his own body (*CWMG* 9: 164). Gandhi learned through such episodes that the body, even that of the prisoner, disheveled and clad in convict clothes, could be extremely eloquent, without needing any verbal appeal for sympathy or solidarity. Aided by his jail experiences, he learned to use his clothing, his body and the marks of physical suffering as symbols of great potency and communicative power (Tarlo 1996: 67–77).

Gandhi's prison experiences were further reflected in other aspects of his personal and political metamorphosis. Some writers have sought the origins for the Phoenix Settlement, begun in 1904, and Tolstoy Farm six years later, in a creative reworking of Indian tradition or in the influence of Ruskin or Christian monasticism. All these doubtless played a part, but Gandhi himself acknowledged the importance of prison to the evolution of his ashrams. In particular, Tolstoy Farm, set up to support satyagrahis and their families, was intended to harden them for civil disobedience and imprisonment. Life on the farm borrowed the prison's strict disciplinary regime and time-regulated working day, its common messing and the minimizing of personal needs and privacy. As in prison, the food was basic but wholesome, and "served in a single dish . . . a kind of a bowl such as is supplied to prisoners in jail." "We had all become laborers and therefore put on laborers' dress but in the European style, viz., working men's trousers and shirts, which were imitated from prisoners' uniform." Work at Tolstoy Farm, Gandhi recalled, "was certainly harder than that in jail." The "inmates" ate, dressed, even shaved their heads like prisoners, and a well-known picture of Gandhi as a satyagrahi in 1913 shows him with his hair cropped and clothed like a convict (*CWMG* 29: 222–4).

After leaving South Africa in 1914 Gandhi partly abandoned the prison model, identifying more strongly with peasant life instead, but the experience of prison was not entirely forgotten. Indeed, it was re-inforced by the collective experience of nationalist jail-going in India over the next thirty years. Significantly, in 1915 his new commune was located close to Ahmedabad's Sabarmati Jail, which he dubbed "our other ashram" (Pyarelal and Nayar 1991: 17), and in 1931, during his meetings with the viceroy, Lord Irwin, he insisted on eating with the utensils he had saved from Yeravda Jail (Mirabehn 1960: 122). That Gandhi continued to regard his "jail experiences" as critically impor-tant to himself and others is also evident from his efforts to maintain a jail diary in 1922–3, and the subsequent publication of a second series of articles about prison, and from Mahadev Desai's detailed ac-count of his 1932 imprisonment. When Desai died in detention in August 1942, Gandhi insisted that his physician, Sushila Nayar, take over responsibility for keeping an "authentic" record of his daily prison life (Nayar 1996: 75, 176). But if his prison experiences were so crucial to Gandhi, why was so little said about them in his autobiography? One reason is that *The Story of My Experiments with Truth* is a highly selective account of Gandhi's life, which, rather than attempting to give a complete account of his life, uses certain personal episodes to il-lustrate moral "truths" and weaknesses. Further, Gandhi probably felt no need to discuss his early prison experiences in the autobiography, having only recently described them in *Satyagraha in South Africa*. The autobiography ends in 1920, and by the time he wrote it his positive perception of his jail life had been overshadowed by the very different experience of his two years of "solitude and introspection" (*CWMG* 23: 196) at Yeravda. Although Gandhi liked to regard himself as "a seasoned jail-bird" (*CWMG* 23: 130), this had ended in February 1924 with his release following an operation for appendicitis, but also in his virtual mental and physical collapse. His first taste of prison in India left Gandhi appalled at the intransigence of the authorities and their determination to starve him of the "oxygen of publicity," but also at the conduct of his fellow Indians—convicts and officials alike. Prison was no longer "paradise," or even a convenient model for how Indian society might reform itself. On the contrary, he now saw prisons as "hot-beds of vice and degradation," full of violence, corruption, and a depth of moral depravity he had not expected to find among Indians (*CWMG* 23: 507). Yet, deeply troubling though the Yeravda experience undoubtedly was for Gandhi, none of this anger and disgust was allowed to infiltrate the uplifting story of his "experiments with truth."

India: "A Vast Prison"

It was a common convention among middle-class nationalists in the 1920s and 1930s to assert that under colonial rule India was itself a prison. Thus, the Congress leader C.R. Das declared in 1921 that, while technically free, he felt "the handcuffs on my wrists and the weight of iron chains on my body . . . The whole of India is a vast prison" (Nehru 1936: 79). It was further claimed, in the manner of Henry David Thoreau more than half a century earlier, that under an unjust government "the true place for a just man is also a prison" (Thoreau 1962: 245). Thus Gandhi, who only read Thoreau in South Africa after developing his own theory of civil disobedience, declared at his trial in 1922, that "[u]nder tyrannical rule, the jail will always remain a gateway to freedom," and, following his release from Yeravda two years later: "[a]s long as the entire country remains imprisoned, we can take no rest or peace" (*CWMG* 23: 6, 383). In similar fashion Nehru remarked in 1933 that "the whole country seems a vast prison" (*SWJN* 5: 494), and in his autobiography he quoted (or rather paraphrased) Thoreau as saying that "[a]t a time when men and women are unjustly imprisoned the place for just men and women is also in prison" (Nehru 1936: 394).

The view that colonial India was in effect a prison, and hence that being in a real prison could be no worse and even a more honest place to be, was loyally repeated by many nationalists of the period. C. Rajagopalachari, the Tamil Congress leader, imprisoned in Vellore Jail from December 1921 to March 1922, confided to his diary after only a few hours' confinement, that prison was "a delightful place." The next day he mused: "Have I really become so free that Government have to lock me up if they wish to keep me? For the first time in my life I felt I was free, and had thrown off the foreign yoke" (Rajagopalachari

1941: 5). A few days later, the experience of being locked up every evening led him to comment: "Why do not people realize the fact that the nation is locked [up] and imprisoned like this, not at 6 p.m., but every hour day in and day out, so that it is one long night of slavery. Realizing this, one feels free when one has actually to be shut up like this by the tyrant's arm that holds the country" (7).

Rajagopalachari was far too guarded about himself and too wily a political campaigner to reveal much in his (published) diary about his inner self, but he did reveal for the benefit of his middle-class readers some of the hardships of jail life—the physical discomfort, the unwholesome food, the crude sanitation, the bug-infested hospital, the constant lack of privacy, and the resentment at being treated like a "common criminal." "Our food is the same as that of the ordinary criminals," he wrote in December; "we are locked in and let out at the same hours, we have to eat on the filthy ground, standing, or sitting on our toes, and hurrying it off the plate, like beggars being fed." But, as a loyal Gandhian, this merely confirmed him in the need to suffer stoically for freedom's sake. Nationalist prisoners were not going to be broken by such treatment. "Government does not know that this merely enhances our sacrifice, and strengthens our determination. Special comforts would undermine our strength in a subtle manner" (5–6). If he "hungered" it was not for better food, but for more nationalists to join those already in jail (55). "Nothing," he wrote, "has so strengthened the nation as the cheerful manner in which numbers of the most cultured classes have undertaken to suffer, and are undergoing the rigours of the worst forms of jail life" (129). As his term came to a close, he declared that his three months in jail had been "one of the happiest periods" of his life. Almost uninterrupted communication with other Congress prisoners had made it like "a college hostel," so reminding him "of the happy days of youth" that he "hardly felt that it was a prison" at all (139). Even toward the warders and officers, whose conduct he had railed against during his first weeks of imprisonment, Rajagopalachari now felt more mellow, if only from the belief that Gandhian humility and the satyagraha spirit had won them over and generated a new respect for political prisoners. That he had ever felt bitterly toward them was presented as evidence of the authenticity of his "jail experiences" (139–40).

It was also one of the conventions of prison writing to claim that in many respects political prisoners were freer than those set to guard over them. As Rajagopalachari remarked in his diary: "The life of the warder is little better than that of his fellow inmate, the convict . . . His life is on the whole a miserable one, though he takes unconscious vengeance for it by brutality toward the . . . convicts" (47). Similar observations surface in a number of other prison narratives, as in V. D. Savarkar's account of his imprisonment in the Andamans, first published in Marathi in 1927. Sentenced to life imprisonment for involvement in terrorist activities, Savarkar served thirteen years in prison (from 1911 to 1924), almost all of it in the notorious Cellular Jail at Port Blair. In a narrative of more than five hundred pages, Savarkar is almost entirely silent about his earlier life: the jail experience seems to encompass his entire existence. Like Rajagopalachari, he is hardly concerned with his inner self, concentrating instead on the brutal experience of imprisonment and his politically inspired observations of fellow convicts and warders. The prison becomes the nation, or rather the nation in the making, populated by heroes as well as plagued by demons. Prison exemplifies the callous brutality of the colonial regime as well as the defiant suffering of India's imprisoned youth, but it is also a place of ambiguity, in which the dividing line between the prisoner and the jailor is not always as absolute as might at first appear.

In Savarkar's narrative one of the principal antagonists is an Irish jailor called David Barrie, whose abusive banter and violent conduct mark him out as a renegade who has betrayed the cause of the freedom struggle in his native Ireland by becoming a jailor for the British in India (Savarkar 1950: 380). As the story unfolds, Barrie is revealed as being almost as much a prisoner as the Indians he torments. Savarkar tells Barrie, "the whole of India is a vast prison-house, as much as Ireland" (330). But the barely literate Irishman is worn out by more than twenty years at Port Blair and the unremitting struggle to control his prisoners, while Savarkar increasingly strives to educate and lead them: he is ready, on his release, to return to India and fulfill the mission to advance Hindu nationalism that prison life has served only to intensify.

Given the extensive reliance within the Indian prison system on convict warders—convicts given some measure of responsibility as warders and rewarded with certain privileges and improved status— it is not surprising that these figure prominently in most jail narratives. They are often represented as being particularly cruel and rapacious and responsible for much of the corruption and brutality, including the sexual violence, occurring inside the prison. But in some narratives the warders are given an even more hated role than that of the British themselves, and thus serve to typify the problems that beset the aspiring nation. Apart from Barrie, Savarkar's other main antagonists at Port Blair are the Muslim warders, especially the Pathans, whom he describes as "bigoted Mohomedans" with a "fanatical hatred of the Hindus," led by Mirza Khan, the "Chota Barrie" (90–1, 200). The Muslims serve to reinforce Savarkar's identity as a Hindu nationalist in opposition to the followers of a rival faith, who latch on to the power of the British by seeking to convert Hindu prisoners and who want to turn the prison into a "jail-masjid" (277–8). There are perhaps parallels here with Gandhi's antithetical "Kaffirs," for both sets of adversaries serve to represent the uncivilized but threatening Other against which the Hindu prisoner sharpens his own threatened sense of identity.

But, like Irish jailors, convict warders have a liminal quality that makes them both part of the tyrannical regime of the prison and part of the nation envisioned through the prison. While Gandhi clearly loathed much of his time in Yeravda in the early 1920s, and implicated convict warders in many of its brutal torments, he also wrote series of sketches—in effect potted life histories—of the convict warders assigned to watch over him. As if deliberately to remind him of his South African ordeal, or perhaps simply to minimize communication and empathy, Gandhi was assigned a Somali Muslim, named Adan, jailed for being an army deserter. Although Adan knew no English, nor any Indian language apart from a smattering of Urdu, Gandhi apparently won over this "devout Mussalman" by his kindness (including, by one account, sucking out the poison when he was stung by a scorpion). Having developed a "deep personal attachment" for Gandhi, there was "a sad parting" when Adan was transferred to another part of the prison (*CWMG* 24: 366–7; Kalelkar 1960: 101–2). The almost mythic quality of this encounter is echoed in the succession of convict warders who attend Gandhi—a Punjabi Hindu, a Muslim, a Mahar, a caste Hindu from Maharashtra, a Gurkha, and a Kanarese—who seem almost deliberately to have been chosen to illustrate the inclusiveness of the Indian nation and the Mahatma's universal appeal. No wonder Gandhi remarks that "Yeravda was to us a whole world, or better still, the whole world" (*CWMG* 24: 368).

In the course of his imprisonment in 1923, Gandhi declared that satyagraha required a prisoner to "obey all reasonable prison regulations, and certainly to do the work given. Like a prisoner of war, resistance ceased once he was in prison" (*CWMG* 23: 156). Rajagopalachari similarly maintained that it was the duty of prisoners to obey jail regulations: non-cooperation was to cease on entering prison (1941: 90). "It is to suffer unjust punishments without protest or complaint that we have come here, and we would be destroying our own foundations if we attempt, when inside jail, to agitate, protest or offer Satyagraha against the hardships imposed on us here" (94). In theory, then, Gandhians rejected any idea of trying to reform the prison from within, whether for their own benefit or on behalf of the rest of the prison population. It would do "great injury to the movement and impede its progress," Rajagopalachari remarked, if nationalists did anything to make the world believe that prison life was hard. "We have gone in for a great cause on which we should concentrate our thoughts and efforts and not fritter them away in the reform of Jail administration and the purification of subordinate officials" (78).

In practice, however, as with Gandhi's own tussles in South African and Indian jails, political prisoners of all persuasions engaged in sustained and often bitter struggles with the prison authorities over such matters as diet, work regimes, the nature of punishments, access to newspapers and books, and the receipt of letters and visitors. In part, this was because they were so outraged by what they experienced, or by what they saw and heard, that (whatever their principles) they felt compelled to protest and try to effect change. But it was more than that. Prison narratives are paradoxically replete with a powerful sense of individual agency. Believing in their ability to confront colonial oppression and injustice even in prison was vital to middle-class prisoners' sense of their own ability to survive the prison ordeal and to their belief that even in jail they were neither powerless nor irrelevant to the political struggle outside. One reason for Gandhi's near collapse in 1923–4 was his frustrating sense of powerlessness in trying to influence the prison authorities or control the conduct and maltreatment of other political prisoners, despite threatening to fast to achieve his goals. Some of the most protracted and hard-fought episodes of defiance were, in fact, carried out not by Gandhians but by other political prisoners, like the Bengali revolutionary Jogesh Chandra Chatterji, who spent twenty-four of the thirty years from 1916 to 1946 in jail.

His prison struggles, which included lengthy hunger strikes countered by brutal and painful forced feeding, were vital to the self-representation of his life as one of unremitting revolutionary struggle (Chatterji 1967). As with Savarkar's Andamans "story," such accounts were also intended to show the major contribution revolutionaries had made to India's freedom struggle and the extent to which their and their comrades' suffering in prison (encompassing exhaustion, torture, madness and death) gave them as great a claim to national leadership and political authority as the more widely publicized but much milder jail experiences of Gandhi and his followers.

Despite such efforts at resistance and reform, in general the experience of prison, as represented in the narratives, seems to have accentuated social difference, in particular highlighting the gulf between "ordinary convicts" and political prisoners. The entry of middle-class prisoners after 1890, and more especially from 1920 onward, forced major changes in India's prison regime. Against their inclination, and only as a result of repeated prison protests and outside pressure, the authorities were forced to recognize political prisoners as a separate entity, deserving better treatment than that meted out to ordinary convicts. They were placed in separate cells or barracks (sometimes in parts of the prison formerly reserved for Europeans), given better food and lighter work regimes (or no labor at all), allowed access to books, newspapers and visitors, and even permitted forms of dress and recreation unthinkable for most prison inmates. Political prisoners were often themselves acutely aware how their own sanity and sense of self were saved through the award of such hard-won privileges. As Gandhi remarked of his testing time in Pretoria Jail, "My books saved me" (*CWMG* 9: 241), or as Nehru put it in similar circumstances in the 1930s, "books, books—what would we do without them to escape from ennui and depression?" (*SWJN* 5: 402; cf. Chatterji 1967: 87–8). But, by the same token, being able to read and write, to remain effectively part of their middle-class world and its accomplishments, accentuated the distance between political prisoners and ordinary convicts.

It was often hard for men like Rajagopalachari not to adopt a superior attitude to prisoners who were "felons and degraded characters" (1941: 33). For the socialist Nehru, writing in the mid 1930s, the ordinary convicts, especially the "lifers," occupied a more positive place and he could write about learning from them and their far harsher experience of life, inside and outside the jail (1936: 96). Their entry into his prison narrative parallels his introduction to the peasants earlier in the *Autobiography*. Both bring him closer to the "real India," the India of the masses that he is slowly discovering under Gandhi's tutorship and which he wants to identify with and understand. Like many other middle-class prisoners of the time, Nehru seeks to refute the crude colonial sociology of "criminal types" and "criminal classes" that has become so powerfully entrenched in colonial policing and in juridical and penological practice. These, he insists, are human beings with individual identities of their own. They are, besides, not "really guilty" men and women at all, but have been driven to crime by material need or by fits of anger and despair. "A more sensible economic policy, more employment, more education would soon empty out our prisons," he concludes. But under colonialism, "Not the least effort is made to consider the prisoner as an individual, a human being, and to improve or look after the mind." Yet, while empathizing with convicts as the victims of colonialism and capitalism, Nehru can never lose his class distance from them or his hegemonic desire to educate and lead them. He cannot avoid pitying them for not being more like himself. It seems particularly oppressive that such prisoners are cut off from the outside world by their illiteracy and their difficulty in maintaining contacts through letters and interviews, precisely the kinds of links that keep Nehru alert and alive in prison (1936: 219–23).

Nehru goes only so far in his sociological and sentimental investigation of non-political prisoners. M.N. Roy, jailed in 1931, went rather further along the path of representing the prison as a meaningful site for social observation and analysis. For Roy, so long an exile, the prison almost becomes India. After five years spent continuously in jail, he can see a central prison as "a fairly representative replica of the entire country" and hence a suitable basis for generalizing about India as a whole (Ray 1997: 517). What fascinates and yet perturbs Roy is that, although many crimes are committed either under the pressure of economic necessity or as a result of the constraints imposed by Hindu society, many prisoners accept their fate rather than strive to resist it. In this way, "the law of karma reinforces the laws of the Imperialist State" (516). Intent on making the subalterns speak, and to give them a kind of agency by authoring brief life histories on their behalf, Roy recounts six "typically Indian" life stories of prisoners he has encountered and the "crimes" that have led them to jail and to the gallows— the incestuous brother who kills his widowed sister; the peasant widow who strangles her illegitimate baby at birth; the old man who murders his erring young wife; the family who slay the village moneylender; the "madman" who kills his "witch" wife; the young man who bludgeons to death the religious mendicant who has sexually exploited him. In each of these sociological vignettes, gender, sex, and psychology reinforce the central message that "crimes are symptoms of social malady" (531). That prisoners should nonetheless meet their fate with "supine resignation" is seen by Roy as evidence of India's "moral degeneration" and the "shameful psychological state of the Indian masses" (537).

There is little direct testimony about the prison experiences of the subaltern classes themselves: what we do have is tantalizing but fragmentary (Arnold 1994). To a large extent the only record of their lives is that to be found in the institutional record—in the crude statistics of prison numbers or in accounts of trials, transportation and executions (Anderson 2000). As far as the prison bureaucracy was concerned, the essential information was that recorded on the wooden tags prisoners wore, though even these "histories" could be singularly inaccurate (Rajagopalachari 1941: 8). Paradoxically, then, the life histories of many ordinary prisoners survive only in the second-hand narratives compiled by middle-class prisoners like Gandhi, Nehru, and Roy, and their observations are often too infused with their own social and political concerns to constitute an impartial record.

Prison and the Psyche

During his second term of imprisonment, in Lucknow District Jail in 1922–3, Nehru found himself confined in a barrack with nearly fifty other prisoners. Most he already knew, some he counted as friends, but Nehru was dismayed by "the utter want of privacy," day and night, which became "more and more difficult to endure." There was "no escape. . . . We bathed in public and washed our clothes in public . . . and talked and argued till we had largely exhausted each other's capacity for intelligent conversation." It was, he remarked, "the dull side of family life, magnified a hundred-fold, with few of its graces and compensations." The "great nervous strain" of being imprisoned so intimately with others left him yearning for solitude (Nehru 1936: 93).

By contrast, at Naini Central Jail in 1930 Nehru encountered the "novel experience of being kept by myself" (219). His months of solitary confinement, which continued intermittently for the next five years, told heavily on Nehru, but at least he had access to books and could devote his time to voraciously reading and writing. In many ways he preferred this self-absorbed solitude to the crowded life of the prison barrack. Free to pursue his own thoughts, he felt far removed from political infighting in the Congress and the troubles and responsibilities of his home life in Allahabad. He was still very conscious of his isolation and subject to "prison humors," but without a regime of physical labor to grind him down, Nehru (as revealed in his prison diary, even more than in his autobiography, polished for publication) showed an intense preoccupation with a "care of the self" which included physical exercise, keeping a careful record of his weight and temperature, and making notes on his mental and emotional state. At one level Nehru wondered why he bothered to keep a diary at all, as there was little worth recording in the dull routine of prison life (*SWJN* 5: 381), but at another he saw its value in keeping himself alert and preventing him from going "to pieces" (Nehru 1936: 348). Michel Foucault unwittingly described Nehru's prison life when, in describing the time spent in "application to oneself," he wrote:

This time is not empty; it is filled with exercises, practical tasks, various activities. Taking care of oneself is not a rest cure. There is the care of the body to consider, health regimens, physical exercises without over-exertion, the carefully measured satisfaction of needs. There are the meditations, the readings, the notes that one takes on books or on the conversations one has heard, notes that one reads again later, the recollection of truths that one knows already but that need to be more fully adapted to one's own life . . . [I]t is a sustained effort in which general principles are reactivated and arguments are adduced that persuade one not to let oneself become angry at others, at providence, or at things (Foucault 1990: 51).

It was in part to counter loneliness and incipient depression that Nehru began his autobiography in 1934. His extensive reading and writing during this and subsequent periods of incarceration did as much as Gandhi's initiation into prison life in South Africa to shape the man Nehru became. Through his intensive bouts of reading and writing in prison Nehru developed his distinctive "facility with words" (King 1997: 153): this was to form an important element not only in his growing political stature as a speech-maker and writer in India but also his standing as one of India's leading (and most intelligible) spokesmen in the West. Nehru was fortunate to be imprisoned in relative comfort. At times the colonial authorities seemed remarkably willing to accommodate the personal needs of middle-class political prisoners, allowing them reading and writing materials, and even, on occasion, entertainments. In 1920 J.C. Chatterji and his fellow inmates in Rajshahi Jail were allowed to play badminton and successfully petitioned the authorities to allow them to celebrate the Durga Puja festival, during which they were shown films, albeit war documentaries (Chatterji 1967: 119). But at other times isolation and the withholding of books, newspapers, and writing materials were deliberately used to augment punishment and crush prisoners' spirit. In his five years in jail between 1931 and 1936, Roy was often held in solitary confinement and for a time (in 1934) was denied access to pen and ink. He nonetheless contrived to write political tracts and smuggle them out of jail through his "secret allies"—fellow prisoners and sympathetic warders. He also managed to write letters about his prison experiences, and these, despite the censors, reached the outside world and testified to the ordeal of his prison years.

In 1934, at a time of extreme physical and mental exhaustion, Roy began to write the *Memoirs of a Cat*. This was possibly a literary device borrowed from Bankimchandra Chattopadhyay's *Kamalakanta* (Kaviraj 1995: 27–71), but, like Nehru and Gandhi, Roy was fascinated by the liminality of prison cats, creatures able to observe human behavior intimately while remaining in the world of animals, critically detached from it, living within the confines of the human jail but free to slip at will through the prison bars. Perhaps for Roy, still a dedicated Marxist, to write directly about himself (in the grand Nehruvian manner) would have been too bourgeois an indulgence. Seeing the world through a cat's eyes allowed him to stand outside himself, yet still see Indian society with feline insightfulness: "Unfortunately, I have not lived in a human home [the cat observes]; but prison is also an interesting place. Here . . . the beast in man creeps out of his human skin; and one, with a keen power of cynical observation, possessed by my species, encounters all sorts of amusing and illuminating mental phenomena" (Ray 1997: 464).

By the time Nehru and Roy came to write and reflect on their prison thoughts and experiences they had access to a new language of the self, informed by psychology and psychoanalysis. That the discourse of psychoanalysis should surface in prison narratives was in part simply a reflection of wider intellectual trends and fashions, but for Nehru in particular there was a sense in which the "unknown" of the prison, with all its torments and terrors, summoned up a need to explore the "unknown" within himself and those about him. Nehru, who claimed to have been "saved" by his habit of "introspection" in prison (1936: 204), presented the whole of his autobiography as a piece of extended self-analysis, an exploration of his conscious and unconscious self and hence a means to understand (and thereby free himself from) his inner turmoil. For him its "primary test" was its ability to give "a certain psychological insight into the mind and soul of our national movement" (*SWJN* 7: 140).

In keeping with this psychoanalytical vein, Nehru's autobiography is also about his struggle with the two dominant personalities in his life (by contrast, and not unlike the reticence observed in other life histories in this volume, his wife, Kamala, makes only a shadowy appearance and, apart from the book's dedication, is not even named until more than halfway through the work). These commanding figures are his father Motilal, branded an "extrovert," and Gandhi, labeled an "introvert." Motilal, who died a few years earlier, in 1931, he seems to have the measure of, but the younger Nehru repeatedly invokes the language of psychoanalysis to try to pin down the "paradox" that is Gandhi (and thus India's and his own). He deploys psychoanalysis as a science that can dispel superstition and help establish his own claim to modernity, while decrying Gandhi's utter denial of the modern world, and to explain his own feelings of both repulsion and attraction toward the Mahatma. In a critical passage reviewing Gandhi's attitudes to sex, Nehru confesses to finding his views on celibacy "unnatural and shocking," adding that "if he is right, then I am a criminal on the verge of imbecility and nervous prostration." He continues:

> In these days of the Oedipus complex and Freud and the spread of psychoanalysis this emphatic statement of belief [by Gandhi about the necessity of sexual abstinence] sounds strange and distant. . . . I think Gandhiji is absolutely wrong in this matter. His advice may fit in with some cases, but as a general policy it can only lead to frustration, inhibition, neurosis, and all manner of physical and nervous ills. . . . I presume I am a normal individual and sex has played its part in my life, but it has not obsessed me or diverted me from my other activities. . . . Essentially, his attitude is that of the ascetic who has turned his back to the world and its ways, who denies life and considers it evil (1936: 512–13).

These ideas are echoed in Roy's prison writings, where they serve even more cogently (but perhaps paradoxically in a Marxist) to stress the importance of understanding the inner self rather than accepting socially determined norms of caste and religion. Speaking through his cat persona, Roy observes that man has not "lived down his animal self." "Modern psychology," he adds, "has scant respect for the vanity of man. Psychoanalysis . . . demonstrates that human behaviour, base as well as noble, is determined by purely animal motives." This provides her (the cat is a female as well as feline *alter ego*) with an opportunity for a scathing attack on Gandhi's *brahmacharya*: "Modern psychology has discovered that active suppression or subconscious inhibition of the sex impulse is the cause of grave mental derangements." The cat then launches into a textbook discussion of how a human being is dominated mentally as well as physically by his (or her) unconscious,

> which is the accumulated store of natural impulses. The heritage of the whole animal ancestry is deposited in that store. The mental or spiritual aspect of a human being is like an iceberg: only a small part appears above the level of consciousness, the rest remaining submerged in the Unconscious. . . . What is called conscience acts as the censor, and would not permit civilized human beings to act according to the impulses inherent in their very existence, unless they are dressed up in the glittering garb of hypocrisy and falsehood (Ray 1997: 469, 478–9).

Although for Roy, as for Nehru, the prison necessarily represents backwardness, repression and a denial of progress, it does at least allow the middle-class author the freedom to explore his prison-based observations of self and society through a modernity of the mind. This is all very different from Gandhi's own approach to autobiography a decade earlier. Although Gandhi had seen aspects of the prison regime in South Africa in 1908–9 as modern, scientific and even sanitary, by the time he wrote his autobiography in the mid 1920s his attitudes to both prison and modernity had changed. In the Introduction to *The Story of My Experiments with Truth*, he relates a conversation with a friend who observes that "[w]riting an autobiography is a practice peculiar to the West. I know of nobody in the east having written one, except amongst those who have come under Western influence." To this Gandhi replies that he is not writing a *real* autobiography: "I simply want to tell the story of my numerous experiments with truth, and as my life consists of nothing but those experiments, it is true that the story will take the shape of an autobiography." He then adds: "What I want to achieve—what I have been striving and pining to achieve—is self-realization, to see God face to face, to attain *Moksha* [salvation]" (Gandhi 1940: ix–x). Although Gandhi refers to having gone through "deep self-introspection" and having "searched myself through and through, and examined and analysed every psychological situation" (1940: x), this exercise is clearly far removed from the kind of quasi-Freudian self-analysis indulged in by Nehru or Roy's feline *alter ego*. Gandhi's primary concern is with the pursuit of spiritual salvation, and the moral instruction his life may provide for others, not with unlocking his unconscious.

Conclusion

Among the many books Nehru read in the mid 1930s was *Letters from Prison* by the German socialist Ernst Toller. After Toller had praised Nehru's autobiography, the latter replied that "those who have been in prison and have not finally broken down under the ordeal, develop some kind of common outlook and a bond which unites them invisibly. When I read your beautiful *Letters from Prison* again and again they brought pictures of my own moods and thoughts in prison to me and your book occasionally became a mirror of myself" (*SWJN* 7: 153).

It might be argued that all political prisoners share similar experiences and learn to cope with—even to write about—them in not dissimilar ways. In other words, the genre of the prison narrative, far from being specific to India or anywhere else in the modern world, has a universal signification and appeal. But, while this may be largely the case, it is important not to lose sight of what may have been Indian and/ or colonial about the narratives discussed here and the circumstances of their production. The nature as well as the number of Indian prison narratives testify not only to the exceptional role of jail-going in the Gandhi-led movements in South Africa and India from the 1900s to the 1940s but also to the extensive recourse to imprisonment to counter political movements of all kinds in British India. The exact nature and conditions of that imprisonment varied very widely (as between, say, Chatterji and Nehru or Gandhi and Savarkar), but intense political activism over a period of roughly fifty years from the mid 1890s to the mid 1940s brought a relatively large number of educated and articulate middle-class men and women into the jails of British India. It gave them exceptional opportunities to observe state and society through the prism of the prison and even, in many cases, the freedom to read and to write about their jail experiences from within the walls of the prison itself. The highly influential precedents of Gandhi and Nehru's prison writings cannot be ignored as factors in stimulating the rise and dissemination of this particular form of life history in India. To argue further that colonial prison, with its systematic assault upon social convention and cultural taboo, was a site of particular revulsion to Indians, more especially to Hindus, would be harder to demonstrate, except perhaps through a lengthy exercise in comparative penology, but it might be that in this lies an additional reason why so many middle-class Indians felt impelled to record their jail experiences, whether for themselves or for posterity.

REFERENCES

Anderson, C. 2000. *Convicts in the Indian Ocean: Transportation from South Asia to Mauritius, 1815–53*. Basingstoke: Macmillan.

Arnold, D. 1994. "The Colonial Prison: Power, Knowledge and Penology in Nineteenth-Century India." In D. Arnold and D. Hardiman (eds), *Subaltern Studies VIII: Essays in Honour of Ranajit Guha*, pp. 148–87. Delhi: Oxford University Press.

Bengal Native Newspaper Reports, Oriental and India Office Collections, British Library, London.

Chatterji, J.C. 1967.*In Search of Freedom*. Calcutta: Firma K.L. Mukhopadhyay.

CWMG: Collected Works of Mahatma Gandhi, 90 vols, 1958–84. Delhi: Government of India Publications Division.

Desai, M. 1953. *The Diary of Mahadev Desai, Volume I*. Ahmedabad: Navajivan Publishing House.

Foucault, M. 1990. *The Care of the Self*. Harmondsworth: Penguin.

Gandhi, M. K. 1940. *An Autobiography, or the Story of My Experiments with Truth*. Ahmedabad: Navajivan Publishing House.

Kalelkar, K. 1960.*Stray Glimpses of Bapu*. 2nd edition, Ahmedabad: Navajivan Publishing House.

Kaviraj, S. 1995. *The Unhappy Consciousness: Bankimchandra Chattopadhyay and the Formation of Nationalist Discourse in India*. Delhi: Oxford University Press.

Keenan, B. 1992. *An Evil Cradling*. London: Hutchinson.

King, R. D. 1997. *Nehru and the Language Politics of India*. Delhi: Oxford University Press.

Mirabehn (Madeleine Slade). 1960. *The Spirit's Pilgrimage*. London: Longmans.

Mukhopadhyay, A. 1996. "Legal and Penal Institutions from a Middle-Class Perspective in Colonial Bengal, 1854–1910." PhD thesis, University of London.

Nayar, S. 1996. *Mahatma Gandhi's Last Imprisonment: The Inside Story*. New Delhi: Har-Anand Publications.

Nehru, J. 1936. *An Autobiography*. London: Bodley Head.

Pandit, V. 1979. *The Scope of Happiness: A Personal Memoir*. London: Weidenfeld and Nicolson.

Prasad, R. 1957. *Autobiography*. Bombay: Asia Publishing House.

Pyarelal and Sushila Nayar. 1991. *In Gandhiji's Mirror*. Delhi: Oxford University Press.

Rajagopalachari, C. 1941. *Rajaji's 1920 Jail Life*. Madras: Rochouse and Sons.

Ray, Sibnarayan (ed.). 1997. *Selected Works of M.N. Roy, Volume IV, 1932–1936*. Delhi: Oxford University Press.

Savarkar, V.D. 1950. *The Story of My Transportation for Life*. Bombay: Sadbhakti Publications.

Scott-Clark, Cathy, and Ardian Levy. 2001. "Survivors of Our Hell." *Guardian Weekend*, June 23, 2001.

Sen, Satadru. 2000. *Disciplining Punishment: Colonialism and Convict Society in the Andaman Islands*. Delhi: Oxford University Press.

SWJN: Selected Works of Jawaharlal Nehru. 1973–5. New Delhi: Orient Longman.

Tarlo, E. 1996. *Clothing Matters: Dress and Identity in India*. London: Hurst.

Thoreau, H.D. 1962. *Walden, and On the Duty of Civil Disobedience*. New York: Collier Books.

CHAPTER 3

The Reticent Autobiographer
Mahadevi Varma's Writings

FRANCESCA ORSINI

The title of this essay is admittedly contentious: not every writer may want or be expected to write an autobiography, and most writers (and critics) will argue that one should only consider the text and not the writer. The question why Mahadevi Varma (1907–87) was reluctant to speak about herself in any direct or specific way in any of the many genres she practiced is, nonetheless, significant. It is significant because Mahadevi trod a thin line between the poetic, the authorial and the real self: in her poetry she chose to speak in the first person, she pioneered the genre of life sketches and wrote *other* people's life stories, and she was the first woman intellectual who lived on her own in the Hindi literary sphere. For poets of her generation, writing was both a question of self-expression and a form of public address; the autonomy of the literary field had invested individual writers with a new dignity as original intellectuals and put them in the limelight, while the role assigned to literature in the economy of the nationalist movement entrusted literary people with the responsibility of "writing for the nation." This made the position of young and educated women writers like Mahadevi particularly difficult. Her resolute attempt to exploit the possibilities of the poetic "I" while shielding her own privacy was bound to meet with great difficulties. As she wrote in 1936:

> The very mention of ability in a woman never fails to create amusement. . . . When a woman enters the literary field . . . she is greeted with astonishment and disbelief. . . . The existence of a few women who do is seen as a mere exception to the general stupidity of the female

species. . . . Today's men are incapable of relating to women outside their family in the sympathetic, respectful and natural way they relate to their mothers and sisters at home. . . . Women writers are misunderstood and held in disrepute by the male literary community. . . . The misunderstanding and problems by which women writers are surrounded nowadays are enough to demoralize any writer. . . . If a woman writes a story about a woman's unhappy experience, it is taken to be autobiographical, and attempts are made to use it against her. . . . If she writes a poem about love, hundreds of love poems come raining down on her in reply. . . . If she speaks out against these things, all manner of cruel and indecent charges are made against her. . . . A woman in literature is to men primarily a source of humor and entertainment.[1]

The danger of autobiographism must be universal and across the gender divide, but it held particular dangers for a lone woman writer in conservative north India in the 1920s. One way to defuse this tension was, as Mahadevi's case shows, to call poems of intense longing "mystical" poems; Mahadevi could then be comfortably accepted as the "modern Mira." In other ways, too, Mahadevi shielded her private self while consigning it to the page through various strategies: irony, distance, abstraction, and through a careful and controlled arrangement and rearrangement of her poems. Thus, while in her poems, sketches and essays she emerges as a modern writer who seriously engaged with the possibilities of subjective expression and asserted the right of every individual to develop freely, she also embodied the tensions that being a public intellectual and an independent woman entailed. Artistically, she was able to create an oblique style that lovingly detailed the daily foibles of individuals around her while steering clear of her own self. While, generally speaking, the autobiographical mode is one that extends outward, from a self solidly placed at the center to the people that the self comes in contact with, in Mahadevi's case we have the opposite. She concentrates on people around her while leaving herself, at the center, obfuscated: the result is a scintillating circle around a hollow center.[2] At a more general level, strategies of obliqueness and the reluctance to speak directly about oneself must come as necessary points of reflection within any discussion centered on narrating life histories. What cannot be narrated, and why, are surely questions that must accompany us.

1. Poems and the Inner Life

The choice of a subjective voice, a poetic "I," was in keeping with the poetic movement that Mahadevi was identified with, Chhayavad. This was a poetry based on emotions which, in the wake of Rabindranath Tagore, superseded the didactic and narrative Hindi poetry of the first decade of the century (Schomer 1983). Mahadevi's poems, which started to circulate from 1922–3 in Hindi literary magazines and were first published in book form in 1930, when she was only twenty-three, were a hundred per cent Chhayavadi in diction, imagery, and in the use of a poetic "I". In relation to diction, she made use of new meters and rich-sounding words from the Sanskrit poetic tradition. In relation to imagery, she spanned the whole Chhayavadi spectrum of natural images—night, dawn, ocean and waves, flowers and pollen, and birds and bees were often personified and laden with allusions to the Indian religious and literary heritage. Dawn scenes, for example, were Rigvedic echoes. This web of concepts, images and themes in Chhayavadi poems made the past meaningful in a personal way and characterized the poet's attitude to, and appropriation of, the cultural heritage (Schomer 1983: 41, 43). As with the other Chhayavad poets, most of Mahadevi's poems were written from the perspective of a poetic "I," often in dialogue with a non-specified "You" (*tum*).

This first-person voice of Chhayavad poets took the Hindi reading public by surprise (see Schomer 1983). Early readers and critics tended to identify the poetic "I" with the real poet, so much so that poet Jayshankar Prasad, when asked for an autobiographical statement, wrote the following poem, denying that there was any point in talking about the real self:

What bee hums its own story?
So many leaves withered today
and fell.
Life stories, numberless in this deep, infinite blue,
fret their time away in self-mockery!
And yet you ask me to speak of my frailty!
What pleasure will it give you
To see my water jar empty? [. . .]
Why look at the stitches in my loincloth?
What great tales in this small life of mine?
Better for me to listen quietly to what others say,

What will you do with my innocent life story?
Besides
There is no time—look! My silent anguish, weary,
Fell asleep!

(Prasad 1964 [1933]: 11)

The poetic "I" of Chhayavad was thus different from the "real self" and allowed for the construction of a poetic persona that transcended the boundaries of reality. This persona allowed for directness of expression, intensity of feeling, and "made it possible to express a conception of reality that differed from what was dictated by tradition or generally accepted" (Schomer 1983: 59). Subjective poems made extensive use of natural imagery, majestic or personified, to convey a sense of the individual being "grounded in a greater cosmic reality," and they did the same with traditional religious and philosophical concepts (Schomer 1983: 51). The individual and the cosmos, *vyashti* and *samashti*, were, as we shall see, two coordinates of Mahadevi's thought.

In Mahadevi's first collection *Nihaar* ("Dew," 1930), the poetic "I" evolved into two distinct sets of configurations. There were poems of intense feeling and yearning which mapped the inner world (e.g. "Beyond", "My Solitude", "My Longing", "My Reign", "Pride", "Emptiness"). And there were poems in which emotions of longing were ascribed to a poetic persona, that of the *virahini*, the woman waiting and pining for her absent lover; this would later take further shape in the figure of the "woman with the lamp" of her collection *Deepshikha* ("*Lamp Flame*," 1942).

In the first set of poems, the "I" is indeterminate. The setting of emotions is the night with its solitude and quiet, where yearnings can be both expressed and contained:

Of this private reign of solitude
I am the spirited queen.
Like an oil-lamp I offer my life
for an endless Divali.

("Mera Rajya," July 1927; Varma 1962 [1930]: 21)

In this "reign of solitude" (*sunapan, ekant*), yearnings for "crazy love" and "dormant sighs" shake "my crazy life, my stubborn tiny life" ("Abhimaan" and "Meri saadh," both January 1929; Varma 1962

[1930]: 28, 32). Strong, unspecified feelings become personified and acquire a life of their own, while the setting for their exuberance is also the space that contains and neutralizes them. In the poem "My Solitude," for example, solitude resists the onslaught of sensuous and turbulent emotions. Her solitude is a woman whom "excited winds" try to awaken; she is an ascetic forest (*tapovan*) which the sensuous flowers of the grove try to distract; a cenotaph which waves try to wash away; and a "desert forest" which a charming spring tries to arouse ("Mera ekaant'" August 1927, Varma 1962 [1930]: 52–3). Poetic allusions to renunciation and to Krishnaite eroticism are cleverly juxtaposed, with the former winning over the charms of the latter.

The emotional inner landscape of these poems is therefore a troubled one of yearnings and emotions which the poetic "I" leaves unspecified, at times even unvoiced. To contain and neutralize them, this "I" juxtaposes images of an enfolding space of quiet achieved through renunciation. In "Us paar," we find fear, confusion, emotional turmoil, real hardships, hopes for a brighter world "on the other side": all this is contained in the image of the tiny boat tossed about by the stormy sea.

> Dreadful darkness, shadows all around.
> Menacing clouds gather thickly,
> Mighty winds hurl against me,
> Mountains shudder,
> Roars the ocean,
> Who will steer me
> to the other side?

The night tells the poetic "I": give to the sea as an offering the flowers of your cherished wish. Another voice whispers: take the boat midstream, only if you drown will you reach the other side ("Us paar," July 1924, Varma 1962 [1930]: 30–1). *Visarjan*, the sacrifice of life by consigning it to water, is the message of the poem, one which Mahadevi specifically named as expressing her basic orientation toward life (see Schomer 1983: 188). Sacrifice should be glossed here not as passive self-sacrifice—nothing could be further from Mahadevi's life—but as an active movement of renunciation, something encouraged by Gandhian nationalism.

The other poems from *Nihaar*, also written from the subjective position, belonged to the fictive persona of the *virahini*, the woman who pines and waits for her absent lover. This is a hallowed figure in the Indian poetic tradition, both folk and classical, and one to which Mirabai had in the sixteenth century lent religious significance and extraordinary power. Mahadevi brought to this figure all the subtle web of correspondences and multiple dimensions of Chhayavad poetry. Indeed, she became so identified with the persona of the *virahini* that Hindi literary critics of the 1920s started calling her the "modern Mira" and interpreting all her poems in a mystical light (Schomer 1983: 241). In doing this they were helped by the dual meaning of the Hindi word *rahasya*, which means both "mystery" and "mystical." In the introductory statements to her collections Mahadevi pointed out again and again that whatever *rahasya* there was in her poems, it was not mystical, and that her spirituality had nothing to do with religion but rather with her sense of the "subtlest" aspect of things (Varma 1962 [1940]: 37). However, she confirmed attributions of *all* her poems to the poetic persona of the *virahini* when she rearranged them in the collection *Yama* (1938), illustrated with her own remarkable artwork. The motifs of the lamp and of the beautiful *virahini* were applied even to poems like "My Solitude" which did not need such attribution. Similarly, "Us paar" was illustrated in a much more literal way which consigned it to a world of fantasy.

In her introduction to *Yama* Mahadevi spoke of the four collections included as successive "periods" of her inner life that marked a progression from emotional anguish to balanced harmony (Varma 1951 [1938]: 6).

> At the time of *Nihaar*, the feelings that surged within me were a blend of wonder and anguish, like those which arise in the heart of a child when it first sees the golden dawn or the heavy rain-clouds but finds it impossible to reach out and touch them. *Rashmi* took form at a time when I preferred reflecting about emotional experience to the experience itself. But *Niraja* and *Sandhya-geet* express a mental state in which I began to spontaneously experience a sense of harmony in the midst of both joy and sorrow (Varma 1951 [1938]: 6; transl. Schomer 1983: 284).

The emotional turmoil of the poems quoted above was thus downplayed as childish wonder, a stage left behind, while emotional stability and serenity were explicitly valued as goals.

By creating a clearly demarcated poetic persona, that of the *virahini*, which gradually subsumed all subjective poems; by only partly expressing, and immediately containing, emotions and projecting them on to the fictional figure of the *virahini*; and finally by going along, to some extent, with a mystical, certainly metaphorical, reading of her poems, Mahadevi managed to neutralize the potential exposure that poetic subjectivity entailed while exploiting its expressive possibilities. Poems, she wrote, expressed her "inner world." Yet already from her first collections she seems to have used poems, written generally in the quiet and solitude of night hours, as a bounded space in which turbulent emotions could be safely vented, while her stated position remained that detachment and harmony were the goals to which she aspired. The obliqueness of Chhayavad poetry was eminently suited for this kind of strategy, of voicing personal yearnings through a poetic "I" and within a safely unspecified and circumscribed space, and many women poets at the time followed her on this path. Thus, despite exploring intense inner emotional landscapes, Mahadevi's poetry succeeded in not exposing too much of the author.

2. Essays and Reflections

If poetry expressed Mahadevi's inner world through a veiled subjectivity, for her moments of reflection she chose prose. It was through essays, editorials and public addresses that Mahadevi gained increasing recognition as an intellectual of profundity and stature in the Hindi public sphere. She emerged as a person of remarkable intellectual clarity and with a confident and committed public voice. As an orator she could make "her audience resonate with her at the deepest levels of Indian cultural identity" (Schomer 1983: 205). Her 1952 nomination to the Uttar Pradesh (UP) Legislative Assembly testifies to her public recognition as an intellectual of stature (Schomer 1983: 238). Rather than the thematic content of her essays, what I am concerned with here is her authorial voice and the way she presented her position. Even when talking about poetry or womanhood—in other words aspects of her own predicament—she chose to do so not through subjective statements and her own experiences, but rather through objective, general and abstract reasoning.

The most striking thing about Mahadevi's essays is their lapidary quality: as if setting words in stone, the impersonal and detached third-person authorial voice proceeds from general definition to general definition by way of well-constructed and balanced arguments and by a deft use of mostly impersonal verbs and carefully balanced sentences. If she uses the first-person subject, it is never "I" but "we;" and then, too, even in her essays on women it is rarely "we women" but rather "Indian society." The contrast with polemical writers on the woman's question, such as her contemporary Chandravati Lakhanpal (1904–69) in her book *Striyon ki sthiti* (1932); or with Ramrakh Singh Sahgal (her predecessor as editor of the women's journal *Chaand*, which Mahadevi edited in the 1930s), is remarkable.

As an example of her strategy and style, we may take her long introductory essay to the first anthology of her poems, in the series *Aadhunik kavi* ("Modern Poets," 1962 [1940]), within which she replied to critical attacks on Chhayavad by the emerging "Progressive" critics. Instead of directly defending herself and her own practice, in the way Nirala would have done, Mahadevi did so obliquely, by speaking about poetry and humanity in the most abstract terms. At the same time, even these oblique arguments tell us a lot about her own position within the Hindi literary field and within north Indian society of the time: they speak of her views about individual self-development, and of her anxiety about her position as a poet and member of the educated, middle-class community of writers within the nation-in-the-making.

In her Introduction she begins by discussing the difference between man (*manushya*) and all other living species in terms of man's craving for something beyond "the things of the external world"—which had for man both a practical and also an aesthetic function. She then discusses the part heart and intellect play in the development of man's inner world in the guise of intelligence (*buddhi*) and emotions (*bhaav*). Excessive emphasis on one at the expense of the other has resulted in a harmful imbalance. Excessive emphasis on the intellect made intelligence self-enclosed and detached from the world, while excessive reliance on emotions gave impetus to life but deprived it of direction. These two concepts, of intelligence and emotion, were used by Mahadevi in her subsequent arguments about literature and life. Always proceeding on an abstract, general level of discussion, she argued that life and literature needed emotions in order to break free of the intellectualism and emotional dryness of the present age, for only emotions bring dynamism to life. Poets, like everyone else, live at the level of individuality (*vyashti*) and collectivity (*samashti*) and need both emotions and intelligence for their development in order to live in harmony with life at the collective level (17). Poets and artists, then, had to "go beyond the inactive intellectualism and inert realism to reach active emotions" (17).

Mahadevi's defense of Chhayavad is thus couched in philosophical terms. So is her statement on the predicament of the modern poet. Though this closely mirrored her own position, it is expressed in general, impersonal terms:

> A poet is surrounded on the one side by the vast knowledge of a handful of people, divided into many groups and sub-groups, and on the other side by the wealth of ignorance of humankind, lumped together inertly by superstitions. The ones are eager to buy the poet's voice for spreading their own particular brand of ideas, the others make as much meaning out of the poet's words as out of a crow crowing in the courtyard. On the one side, politicians think poets are useless, on the other side social reformers consider them infantile (Varma 1962 [1940]: 33).

Under the present circumstances, and faced with such a tall order, according to Mahadevi, poets had to walk out of their artificial life of study, forsake the nourishment of ideologies and mix uncompromisingly with life: "Today's poet must be a citizen and yet hospitable to the world, detached from himself and yet affectionate to all, a *sannyasi* [renouncer] but a *karmayogi* [one who pursues the path of action] to everybody else, because today he must find himself by losing himself" (Varma 1962 [1940]: 34).

Only at the end of this long general discussion about poets and society did Mahadevi come to talk, albeit reluctantly, about herself as a poet, and in terms very similar to those just mentioned above: thus she used general arguments to make a personal point. Mahadevi's restrained authorial voice and measured style of argumentation mirrored her own attitude, and her balanced sentences reflected her need for harmony and balance between different positions. In the essay quoted above, it was balance between intellect and heart. In her editorials for the journal *Chaand*, which were later collected in a book called *Rings of a Chain* (*Shrinkhala ki kariyaan*, 1942), it was between tradition and modernity. The book won Mahadevi the most prestigious literary prize for women writers in Hindi, became a textbook in women's schools and colleges, and has earned her a feminist tag with some Western scholars (see Schomer 1983). I would argue that her position is somewhat different from that of feminism and makes the success of this book all the more significant.

The categories these essays work with are those of *vyakti* and *samaj* (individual and society), and of *prakriti* and *vikriti* (nature and the distortion of nature). The universal, gender-neutral category of "the individual" is significant here, and consistent with Mahadevi's writings on society.[3] Thus, instead of speaking from the position of "we wronged women" (like Chandravati Lakhanpal in *Striyon ki sthiti*), Mahadevi used the general category of "the individual" for a similar radical purpose—of asserting gender equality—but without the polemical edge. *Rings of a Chain* thus meant two things: the chains that bind Indian women's feet, but also the fact that Indian women are necessary links in the chain of Indian society, and that they need to develop freely in order to become full-fledged citizens (19–20). In her argument, the free development of every individual is necessary for the good functioning and progress of society, and thus the fact that Indian women have not been allowed to develop freely has been detrimental to all: "Everybody needs free individual development, because without it a human being cannot say that will-power and resolve are really his own nor weigh any of his own actions on the scales of justice" (Varma 1958 [1942]: 11).[4] The gendered effects of such a distortion proceed from this general postulate about justice: women have led lives of duty and self-sacrifice (*tyaag*), but not out of conscious choice; and when values are passed on and followed blindly, Mahadevi further argues, all their value is lost. Thus, women's blind devotion has made them neither strong nor more respected by men. Unsupported by individual resolve, their most "natural" and praiseworthy quality, softness, has become their weakness (see "Naritva ka abhishap," 1958 [1942]: 39–44). All Indian women are mothers, but without the "natural dignity of motherhood;" all are wives, but those "who know the recesses of their companions' hearts are rare" (15).

The same categories of "individual" and "collectivity" also allowed Mahadevi to develop another side of the argument she cared about: the predicament of educated women like herself within north Indian society. More than other contemporaries writing on the "woman's question" in the Hindi public sphere, she sought to temper women's demands for individual independence: education and self-development must carry some commitment to the collectivity, she argued, and individual choices must be made intelligible to, and be accorded due respect by, society. To this effect, she was critical of educated women doctors and teachers who had formed their own separate society and looked at housewives with little sympathy (26). Writing in the 1930s, Mahadevi was keen that women's self-development and work should be seen in a favorable light. Thus, the fact that those educated women who had taken up responsibilities both at home and outside the home were not viewed with respect concerned her, and felt "it is paramount that it be made clear that they have accepted their new, independent lives not out of helplessness but because of their talents" (26). "The first and greatest necessity in life is to create a favorable environment for the free development of social beings. In the same way as it is true that society is made up of and transformed by individuals, it is also true that the individual is born not just with, but within society. Therefore an individual should develop in a way that will safeguard and transform common social principles" (17–18). Once again, she chose to make her point through a general argument, in this case about the gendered nature of the individual. Here two other concepts, of *prakriti* and *vikriti* , came into the frame. For men and women were different and complementary by nature (*prakriti*), and "natural" qualities should be nurtured by education and self-development.[5] *Vikriti* was the term Mahadevi used to cover any unjust or objectionable practice or attitude, with the implication that it was a distortion of its proper nature. Thus, when Mahadevi came to contemplate—rather critically—the situation of Indian women in her time, she distinguished between women who blindly followed tradition and had been prevented from developing their own personalities, and those modern women who wanted at all cost to be like men: "In short, on the one hand there is meaningless conformity, on the other senseless emulation" (14). To be like men was a *vikriti* for the modern woman because it meant losing those qualities of affection, softness and compassion, qualities that are central also to Mahadevi's characters in the life sketches discussed below: "The rebellious woman of today is more hard in her practical life, more inflexible and unemotional at home, more independent from the economic point of view, more free socially, but she is a prisoner of her own narrowly-defined lines" (15). These are words that could have come out of a conservative woman-basher of the day, if they did not reveal, behind the detached, third-person tone, an anxiety about Mahadevi herself as a modern Indian woman. The image of the modern, independent woman as hopelessly Westernized was a well-established object of contempt, and Mahadevi was no exception in describing Western women and suffragettes as selfish, tough and un-feminine (clearly *vikrit*: 49). The anxiety that transpires here as well as in other essays and sketches is one that called for a balancing act: between individual freedom and social expectations, between individual dignity and social respect, between self-development and the need to relate and contribute to society. A balancing act that was all the more difficult for women.

Returning to the subject in a series of editorials about "modern woman," Mahadevi distinguished between three kinds of modern Indian women: (a) Those who were taking part along with men in the political movement, defying age-long constraints; they gave proof of great strength and sacrifice, earned well-deserved respect and benefited all women by dispelling false notions of women as being weak and emotional beings. (b) Then there were "some educated women who, despite their favorable conditions, could find no solution to social ills and turned their education and awakening into a source of livelihood and into public service" (52). Mahadevi would probably have put herself in this category. (c) Finally, there were those fashionable and wealthy women with a little education who had refashioned their home life under the influence of Western modernity.

Although sympathetic to their predicament, Mahadevi was none-theless critical of *all* of these. Women nationalist activists had "gained something precious but lost something precious": by becoming heroic fighters they had acquired a toughness that was fit for fighting but not for ordinary life. Rebellion, Mahadevi reminded them in one of her lapidary sentences, "is not the marker of a social individual but the ex-pression of discontent" (54). Thus, the criticism of those who felt that modern women were characterized by "an independence that borders on recklessness, a disregard for any tie, be it good or bad . . . and undue harshness" was extreme, but not unfounded (55).

The voice we hear in these essays is that of the editor preaching to her flock, but the anxiety mentioned above and her urge for balance are also evident. In a more reflective mood, she praised women's ability to adapt their lives to whatever circumstances, but also their inner urge to hold on to their "natural qualities." "This is why Indian woman has been able to preserve her particular qualities better than Indian man"

(26). It was these concerns, of individual dignity versus social predicament, of women's nature *versus* modern culture, of writing *versus* living, of how to be a modern Indian woman, that we find expressed in Mahadevi's life sketches, and it is there that we may look for some answers.

3. Life Sketches

The life-sketches form the third component of Mahadevi's oeuvre and the final segment in the configuration of her creative personality. Unlike her poems, Mahadevi had no literary precedent when she started writing sketches of the people around her—according to her own dating, in 1920. As she wrote in the Preface to the first collection, published in 1941, the sketches were not initially meant for publication but rather to preserve in her memory those "*individuals who gave movement and direction to my thinking and my sensibility.* [. . .] the subjects of these memoirs, rather than being objects of exhibition, have been the objects of my imperishable affection. Rather than test whether others would accord equal veneration to them, it seemed preferable to wait and defer publication" (Varma 1994 [1941]: xxii, emphasis added).[6] Compared with her essays, here Mahadevi's emotional involvement in the people she wrote about is unmistakable: these are not sociological observations but moving life stories. And despite the fact that the author's mistrust of publicity initially shielded her cherished characters, the sketches quickly became Mahadevi's most celebrated work and were followed by three further collections.[7] Published in a decade dominated by realism-oriented "Progressive" writing and criticism, these sketches of menial servants, laborers and child-widows were greeted with enthusiasm, and no doubt the class angle of "middle-class author representing the subaltern" could be fruitfully examined. What concerns us here, however, is that the sketches are also a more direct source for Mahadevi's life and personality than her poetry or essays: though the sketches are composed in very tightly controlled prose, they are by their own nature revealing. First, the characters are inscribed in Mahadevi's own life and touch upon it in several, if tangential, ways—the circumstances of their meeting and Mahadevi's relationship with them. Second, her *reactions* to as well as *reflections* about them—hence both her raw, emotional response as well as her reflective thinking about them and about what they taught her— reveal more of her personal attitudes than the abstract essays ever do.

Thus some of the concerns voiced in her essays come back in the sketches but fleshed out and charged with emotion. This is particularly clear in her sketches about women: here we see Mahadevi comparing her own life with theirs and voicing all her scorn at the way society allowed them to be mistreated. The characters in the sketches form a ring around Mahadevi herself; turning the spotlight on them she deflects attention from herself, as we shall see, and thus the effect is that of a dark, private core in an otherwise fairly public life. That this was itself possible for a woman alone, to have a *private* life, live independently and remain respectable, must have been one of the most significant things that Mahadevi taught Hindi readers as well as her fellow women litterateurs in the 1930s.

At the time of publishing *Ateet ke chalchitr* ("Sketches from the Past") in 1941, thirty-four-year-old Mahadevi was already the principal of a nationalist girls' school, Prayag Mahila Vidyapith, in Allahabad, and was living in a small bungalow in the school compound. After her father had, against family pressure, backed her refusal to live with the husband she was married to as a child, and after she fleetingly considered becoming a Buddhist nun, in 1930 Mahadevi settled for graduate studies in Sanskrit at Allahabad University, and the protected but relatively free environment of the hostel in a girls' college. Some of the sketches written about that time already show an independent and forceful woman who divided her time between studying, writing poetry and teaching children in two villages across the Yamuna as her form of Gandhian "constructive work." In 1933 she moved to the Mahila Vidyapith and remained its principal until retirement (Schomer 1983). Given the times, she wrote, "there was never any question of devoting myself exclusively to poetry" (Varma 1962 [1940]: 61). Although she did not directly engage in political activity, her work in the field of education stemmed from her commitment to nationalist ideals and to her concern that women in particular should be educated in order to become full-fledged citizens. She described herself as "one with a multiplicity of occupations" (quoted in Schomer 1983: 202).

Education was one of the first accepted career choices for women who refused to marry and lived independent lives, and hostels quickly became alternative families. Mahadevi found herself not only in charge of her students but also of the school's many permanent and casual workers, and of the strangers, hawkers and mendicants who frequently called in on her. As she pointed out in the case of a young child-widow and her illegitimate child whom she accepted as her ward, "at the age of 27 I had to accept the burden of an 18-year-old daughter and a 22-day-old grandchild" (Varma 1994 [1941]: 57). The sketches show her as willful, organized and always surrounded by people, hardly ever alone. The theme of "strangers who become companions" is a key motive: the "disposition" (*samskara*) that she inherited from her mother, who had at home been surrounded by needy neighbors and itinerant beggars, prevented her from ever turning anyone away emptyhanded. But, in line with her shift from "blindly inherited values" to "individually held convictions," I argue that, in embracing this retinue of what she refused to call "servants," Mahadevi found a way out of the impasses of the modern woman and modern writer outlined in her essays. She could be independent and yet caring, leading an autonomous life yet respected for her charitable attitude, a sophisticated middle-class intellectual who could be approached by, and who respected, illiterate menials as individuals. This fulfilled both a social and an individual exigency. By positioning herself in the midst of this alternative family Mahadevi showed that she accepted , while refashioning, customary ties of family and responsibility—this time not as a bride in a patriarchal family but from a position of authority as a woman householder and a hostel warden.

The urge to write the first sketch came from witnessing an act of injustice: a lady acquaintance had turned an old servant out of the house for a "negligible offense;" the old man, denied reacceptance, would later be found waiting to catch a glimpse of the children, who were his former wards, and plying them with humble presents. This episode reminded Mahadevi of their old servant, Rama, who had looked after Mahadevi and her siblings when they were children. The life of Rama served as a template for subsequent sketches, which all display a common structure: (a) memory, (b) the first meeting, (c) physical description, (d) the life story and (e) the character's disappearance or death.

(a) The sketches generally begin with a memory. Indeed, musings on the peculiar ways in which memory works provide a running theme through the sketches, inscribing the characters as part of Mahadevi's life and mind. Childhood memories do not preserve the exact circumstances of the first meeting. Rama was

> as much part of our childhood as father's desk, which was covered with bits and pieces, and beneath which the world of our toys dwelled in the quiet of the afternoon. Rama's presence was as comforting as the huge

poster bed with iron springs on which we sprawled, looking like reincarnations of Lord Vishnu as a tortoise and fish. He was as omnipresent during our childhood as the deity in Mother's prayer room, in whose solemn presence we used to stand like white cranes with our eyes half shut, surrounded by conches and bells, patiently counting each stroke of the bell while waiting to gobble up the offerings intended for the deity. In much the same way we had known the short, dark-skinned and strongly-built Rama from the tips of his massive toes to the edge of his top-knot (Varma 1994 [1941]: 3).

(b) Sketches about other characters stress the casualness of the first meeting: Bitto, the young and withered bride of a middle-aged widower, caught Mahadevi's attention during a chance meeting with a long-lost childhood friend (Varma 1994 [1941]: 46–7). Mahadevi's housekeeper "Bhaktin," the Chinese peddler, and Alopi the blind vegetable seller, planted themselves on her doorstep demanding attention. The young widowed mother of an illegitimate child who sent for Mahadevi in the dark and stormy night was a perfect stranger.

(c) The account of the first meeting is followed by a brisk and scintillating physical description of the character. Here metaphors drawn from mythology and poetic tradition pile one upon another to elevate the subject, often somewhat ironically. It is not just the poet's brush and keen eye at work, but also the attempt to turn these figures, who would seldom receive a second glance, into veritable *nayakas* and *nayikas* by honoring them with "head-to-toe" descriptions. Rama's "immensely bushy eyebrows on [his] narrow forehead," his "tiny eyes," "thick, pudgy nose, like the final error of a tired sculptor," his lips "bursting from unrestrained laughter," and the "row of crowded white teeth which reminded one of yogurt stored in a black stone bowl" cannot be called beautiful, yet the description makes them so. The Nepalese coolies whom she befriends on one of her Himalayan journeys are affectionately called "Shiva's wedding guests" and their description elaborates the initial metaphor of monkeys, prefaced by the observation that while Shiva's guests were only ugly, the coolies were rather poor than ugly (Varma 1994 [1943]: 30–1).

Incessant tramping on mountain rocks and paths had broken his toenails and sandals of coarse wild grass had splayed apart his injured toes, as if mocking God for having turned men into animals without giving them hooves. Jangiya's trousers, made of several cotton and woollen pieces stitched carefully together, hung only down to his knees and jeered at man's modesty. His jacket, given to him long ago, had become threadbare, exposing a filthy lining, and made its wearer seem more like an animal. His rough hair, popping out of the holes of a cotton cap of unidentifiable form and color, reminded one of seaweed sticking out here and there from muddy water. Beneath thick eyebrows his face was somewhat broad, and his nose was slightly rounded. His unfailingly grinning lips almost reached out to his ears. . . . Hemmed in by a narrow forehead and a stunted round chin, the small watery eyes in his broad face glimmered like oases in the desert . . . (Varma 1975 [1943]: 34–5).

Because suffering often becomes a sort of ornament, the faces of people who suffer inevitably mesmerize the beholder. The attractiveness of Radhiya's face was clearly due to her suffering, because if one looked closer at her features her face was a little too broad. Her nose drew a sharp line between her eyes and got rounder above her lips. Her eyes, surrounded by dark patches, looked like somebody had pressed them down with a finger and buried them in kajal [blackener]. Her shriveled lips were pursed together as if always pressed against a cup of bitter medicine. The attractive harmony of those irregular features could only stem from Radhiya's anguished heart (Varma 1994 [1941]: 117).

Such elaborate descriptions serve a precise purpose: they train readers to look for beauty even in ugliness, or rather to measure their standards of beauty against that of the character's inner qualities. "To call Munnu's mother a beauty would be untrue, yet to call her ugly is difficult. Her beauty lies actually not in her features but in her sentiment: that is why the eyes fails to find it but the heart feels it without effort. There is nothing special about her face . . ." (Varma 1975 [1943]: 47). This is made even more explicit in Rama's case through some general philosophical considerations:

Truly, life is the essence of beauty. But beauty finds embodiment more readily in symmetrical rather than in asymmetrical lines. As we become sophisticated and more preoccupied with appearances, we tend to lose sight of the substance of life. Unlike the adult, the child is not specially acquainted with life's coarse superficialities, which is why the child recognizes and responds only to what is sincere in life. Where the child finds rays of affection and goodwill bursting forth, it overlooks the outward irregular shapes. But where life is covered with the smoky cloud of jealousy and hatred, the child will not accept even the appearance of harmony. (Varma 1994 [1941]: 5)

(d) The description of the first meeting and of the physical appearance of each character is followed by his or her life story. This is where the writer's imagination is most at work, transforming the fragments of information she must have received over time into coherent narratives, complete with dialogues, time sequences and, in Bhaktin's case, even chapters. This is what Mahadevi never did about her own life, yet there is no reticence on her part here. It is through these short life histories that their characters who people the margins of established middle-class existence acquire a dignity and pathos of their own: Rama the house servant, Bibiya the washerwoman, Bhaktin the housekeeper, the sweeper woman, Alopi the vegetable seller, Badlu the potter, the Chinese hawker who hardly speaks any Hindi, and all the others.

Rama, for example, collapsed on Mahadevi's mother's doorstep in Indore after escaping the brutality of his stepmother. He was then put in charge of the children and took care of their daily needs with affectionate roughness; he became their "most splendid companion," who scolded them for their pranks unless danger befell them (as when Mahadevi got lost at a fair) and cured them devotedly in times of illness, as when he saved her from the plague and almost died himself. The happy life with them lasted until Mahadevi's mother urged him to start his own family; he brought back a young bride who, behind her veil, became the object of much childish hostility and rivalry, until in the end Rama was advised to settle down independently. News of his illness was the last they ever heard of him.

(e) Death or disappearance mark the sombre ending of these sketches: characters disappear without leaving any trace other than in the author's memory. Thus, from the beginning to the end, these characters are inscribed within Mahadevi's life.

When narrating women's lives, Mahadevi's pen becomes more pungent, almost vitriolic, and passionate at the same time. The contrast with the controlled and detached reflections of her essays on women could not be more striking. With an irony that borders on sarcasm she evokes the social expectations that govern and enclose women's lives and which are described in everyday language: sisters-in-law "initiate the bride in the dharma of service;" when fathers marry off their young daughters they "earn fame by walking two steps ahead of the Shastras;" *panchayats* do not hesitate to marry a raped girl to her rapist as the only way of "purifying the sin of Kaliyug;" and it is "only proper" that the women in the family will show contempt for a bride who only produces daughters (Varma 1993 [1943]: 71, 10, 12, 11).

The act of comparing and contrasting the characters' lives with her own is, as we shall see, integral to the project of writing these sketches, and it is even more marked in the case of women characters. For example, one of the qualities Mahadevi most admires in her women is their industriousness, generally for the benefit of others, and in their life stories they are shown struggling to survive and to maintain their family and dignity through sheer hard work. The four chapters in her maid Bhaktin's life all see her battling against difficult circumstances with hard work and dignity: first as the young bride married into a poorer family of cowherds by an overzealous father and cheated out of her inheritance when he dies; then as a hardworking daughter-in-law who, after producing only daughters, sets up a separate house and defends it strenuously after the death of her husband. In the third chapter of her life she manages well with her widowed daughter, who has come back to live with her, until her in-laws set a plot to entrap her daughter with a complacent, good-for-nothing nephew. After he locks himself in a hut with her, the *panchayat* resolves that they must be married and Bhaktin is once again cheated out of her property. "This insult became the biggest black mark on her industriousness," and rather than being dependent on them Bhaktin goes to the city and becomes Mahadevi's most loyal and idiosyncratic companion (Varma 1993 [1943]).

In Arail village, where she goes to teach children, Mahadevi encounters Munnu's mother. The orphaned daughter of a storyteller, she spent the first years of her life accompanying her father on his rounds; his death left her at the mercy of a pandit friend of his, who thus acquired a hardworking servant. Mahadevi here makes ample use of the imagination while describing the young child's hardships and her quiet acceptance of traumatic events: the girl is given thought and dialog, and even dramatic scenes are introduced. She is finally married to the good-for-nothing son of a poor Brahmin and quickly becomes the sole earner in the family. Indeed, the first part of her life story is devoted to her daily search for food and work, which requires "as much intelligence as playing chess" (Varma 1993 [1943]: 47). She could have an easier time working in the Mahila Vidyapith and caring for her son but is reluctant to leave her husband and father-in-law, and returns to work as a day-laborer on the river bank.

But nowhere do sparks of irony and tragedy fly more than in Bibiya's story, the washerwoman who washed Mahadevi's clothes, liked nice clothes, and had too much self-dignity for her own good. A child-widow even before she could realize it, sharp and hardworking, Bibiya was married off a second time by her brother. When she reappeared after some time, everybody suspected that it was because of some fault on her part. Unwilling to believe in rumors, Mahadevi later found out that Bibiya's husband was a lazy drunkard and gambler, and that tension between them had started on the first night after Bibiya had castigated him for addressing her in an improper way and then threatened him with kitchen tongs. Hurt in his male pride and prodded by his gambling companions, who believed that such a proud and sharp-tongued bride could not be a virtuous wife, her husband had finally rejected her (Varma 1993 [1943]: 90). Back at home, life with the sister-in-law and without dignity was hard for Bibiya, but she worked hard and fought tooth and nail when she was packed off again to another husband, this time a man already twice widowed. When she reappeared a second time, she was a broken woman who would not show her face in public. Once again, rumors spread, but it slowly transpired that she had been the innocent victim of her own stepson, who, after repeated attempts, had finally managed to rape her. There was no possible dignity left for the once-proud and industrious Bibiya, and one day she vanished forever: but whereas according to rumor she had fled with a lover, an anguished and indignant Mahadevi preferred to think she had drowned herself in the river. "Bibiya was a rebellious flame that burned without ashes. The world had insulted her dignity without reason . . . The motivation the world gave to Bibiya's disappearance was according to its own preference; but I am not obliged to accept its conclusion as a conclusion" (Varma 1993 [1943]: 100).

Even in sketches which revealed aspects of her private life, Mahadevi was keen to deflect attention from herself.

My own life has inevitably stepped in as an integral part of these recollections. That was only natural. After all, we are able to see objects lying in the dark only after we bring them into the dim or bright circumference of light. However, the element of self-publicity that comes from proximity to the characters has no more significance than the ash that keeps the embers covered in an effort to keep the fire alive. Whoever is unable to recognize that my presence in these memoirs is truly incidental is not capable of reaching the heart of these sketches (Varma 1994 [1942]: xxii).

Despite the warning, let us nonetheless explore the ways in which Mahadevi allowed aspects of herself to be revealed in these sketches, and the strategies by which she tried to reveal as little as possible, since they are both relevant to the issue of "reticence."

Besides acting as the frame which contained and linked the life stories, Mahadevi featured indirectly in the sketches in chiefly two ways: either self-mockingly, or as the "civilized" (*sabhya*), middle-class witness and counterpart to working-class characters. Either she laced her presence with self-irony, inviting mockery on herself as a child and on her foibles as a young adult, or else urged herself and her readers to reflect on the difference between "them" and "us," the so-called "civilized society."

Irony here worked a strategy of self-screening, of pre-empting further curiosity by invoking an amused response: we are to laugh at her childish innocence when she wondered if the child-widow whose eyes peep out behind the curtain was the princess of her fairytale, or at her skirmishes with the feared Maulvi Sahab who came to teach her Urdu. Her resolution to open a school under a tree in the villages of Jhunsi and Arail is self-professed "madness," and so is her fondness for collecting stray animals as pets. The irony, often marked through high-sounding sanskritized Hindi, deflects attention from her willfullness and independence, and from her ability to actually do what she likes. How this strategy works is shown in her sketch on Thakuri Baba. The strangeness of her decision to spend the month of January, a young woman on her own, in a makeshift hut on the banks of the Ganges during the Magh Mela (also called Kalpavaas, or "live a long time"), is deflected by a lengthy description of her housekeeper's spirited protests; the contrast between Bhaktin's Avadhi dialect and the narrator's lofty Hindi is part and parcel of the comic description.

> Bhaktin already knew that to speak against my resolution is only to make it firmer; but she has no control over her tongue. When she saw that I did not waver despite the steady torrent of her questions she pouted—Go when your time for Kalpavaas is ripe. Or have you vowed you'll do all your *nem-dharma* in one day? To explain to Bhaktin that

I don't do it for *niyam-dharma* [religious rituals] could be difficult, therefore, rather than trying in vain to convince her, I confirm her misapprehension by remaining silent. She knows that silence is with me a sign not of defeat but of victory; thus she is far more apprehensive of my silence than of my arguments, because to change one's mind after an argument is easy, but silence leaves no scope for doing so (Varma 1993 [1943]: 59).

Having thus rebuffed her housekeeper's protests, it is easier for Mahadevi to put forward her own motive: "The month by the Ganges attracts me because nowhere else is it possible to acquire such extended knowledge of life, and then, too, perennial curiosity about life has become part of my nature" (Varma 1993 [1943]: 60). Mahadevi knows that such curiosity could be seen as inappropriate and allays Bhaktin's misgivings: as, when writing about her women characters, Mahadevi appears well aware of the social expectations surrounding a respectable woman. Silence, rather than argument, is her weapon. On her part she will take precautions to ensure that the move outside familiar and protected territory will not expose her to anything untoward: she will live not in a tent but in a proper hut; and she will have her as a companion. What the sketch also reveals to the prying reader is the amazing efficiency with which she assembled a household and continued her normal college routine. When a group of village pilgrims sought shelter on her verandahs for the night, she quickly overcame Bhaktin's reservations and welcomed them. They, and their leader, the folk-poet Thakuri Baba in particular, ensured that her *kalpavaas* was indeed exposure to a wealth of life and a rich store of memories.

Apart from self-mockery, the figure under which Mahadevi reveals herself in the sketches is that of contrast. The contrast and difference between her own condition and that of her subjects is brought out again and again. Binda, the child who is paraded before young Mahadevi as a model of good behavior, is nevertheless scolded incessantly by her stepmother for invisible crimes. "I, myself, never had to do any chores, and indeed, I created havoc day and night—yet my mother never cursed me, wished me dead, or threatened to gouge out my eyes" (Varma 1994 [1941]: 38). While at Mahadevi's house children are pampered and well fed, Binda is kept without food and seemed a magician "since I considered the completion of so many chores to be humanly impossible" (Varma 1994 [1941]: 38). The unaffected artistry of Thakuri Baba is contrasted to the arrogant vacuousness of Hindi poets at poetry meetings (Varma 1993 [1943]: 80). The (self-)questioning that comparison and contrast generate acts as a connecting frame across the various sketches: it is one of the functions that these life stories are meant to have for Mahadevi and for the readers, and it continues the reflections of her women's essays. The way Mahadevi articulates the contrast is however a far cry from "Progressivist" positions. Despite her eagerness to help, meditating on contrast first of all leads Mahadevi to recognize the distance between her characters' lives and her own "civilized society" and the impossibility of bridging that distance in any simple way. About Thakuri Baba she muses: "I have seldom met a more sensitive man than him. I have often come to wonder what he would have been like if this old man had lived among us . . . but the study of life has taught me that it is not simple to erase the difference between these two societies" (Varma 1993 [1943]: 81). And after realizing the potential of some of the village children she teaches, Mahadevi drops her intention of taking them to study in the city when she realizes that they are the sole support of their mothers.

Unsurprisingly, the contrast is generally expressed in terms of urban, middle-class artificiality *versus* rural, lower-class naturalness. Thakuri's sensitivity is that of his community:

Their outward life is poor and our inner life is empty. In their society deficiencies are in the individual, and goodwill is in the community. On the contrary, our [middle-class] weaknesses are in the community and strength is to be found in individuals (Varma 1993 [1943]: 81).

The life of this stratum of society is like an open book, so to narrate its story from the beginning to the end, not just on important occasions but also on petty ones, is quite easy. On the contrary, our increasingly complicated inner world and increasingly artificial life inevitably lead to a situation in which our holier-than-thou, white-as-heron exterior comes to rely for its whiteness on the fish rotting inside. Thus, our disconnected story becomes more and more incommunicable and the simple affecting qualities of joy and sorrow become more and more lifeless. We are unable to tell our tangled story in a simple way. And when we set out to tell it, each and every string of imagination resonates with reverberations which sound true but only complicate truth further (Varma 1994 [1941]: 102).

Once again, the act of contrast is more marked and more personal in the case of women characters. It is also a gradual process of self-awareness. As a child, comparing her own childhood with that of Binda or the neighboring child-widow, Mahadevi had been struck by the much greater freedom she had. As a young woman, she questioned patriarchal norms and, turning attention on herself, mused on the arbitrary basis of her own respectability.

That [Munnu's mother], a Brahmin, should carry earth on her head did not please either her caste or her family; but she paid heed to no one. . . . If this woman, forged in the furnace of hard work, preferred carrying earth on her head to Brahminical begging it was out of personal necessity. But if society, which revels in following the tracks of custom, were to allow its pretensions to be washed away, none of its tracks would be left. Thus, the Brahmin wife-laborer was like grit in the eye of the glorious community of Brahmin beggars (Varma 1993 [1943]: 55–6).

The sight of the child-mother and her illegitimate child fills Mahadevi with scorn at the "fraudulent society" which would rather she gave up her child and "motherhood" so that, "after fasting, penance, and prayers, she could disguise herself as a chaste widow and have the freedom to commit similar oversights." It is perhaps out of its fear of the "power of motherhood," she muses, that society seeks to deprive the illegitimate mother of her child; it "strips her of her maternal armor, leads her inside the *chakravyuha* [in the *Mahabharata*, a trap from which one cannot escape] and, by shooting arrows, makes a sieve out of her . . . For eons man has been punishing woman, not for her strength and defiance but for her forbearance" (Varma 1994 [1941]: 71, 72).

The "unfortunate woman" who comes to seek work to pay for her husband's illness is the daughter of a courtesan who

without holding an entry permit from society . . . had sought to join the ranks of chaste women. She did not realize that society holds that magic wand with which only the woman whom it touches and declares to be virtuous can have the good fortune of being considered a virtuous wife [*sati*]. Women ordered by society to stand outside the row of virtuous women should consider the privilege of being there, for themselves and their successive generations, as life's greatest boon. If, out of perversity, [women] seek to defy social sanctions, their offense is bound to be deemed unpardonable. . . . That naive woman who had appropriated [lit. stolen] "wifehood" was definitely incapable of understanding society's complex code of ethics. Her questioning glance silently asked me in an achingly pitiful manner, "Am I not pure?" (Varma 1994 [1941]: 94–5).

Unlike her essays, in which Mahadevi reflected in abstract terms on the condition and challenges of women, the life sketches show her directly confronting the reality of their lives. Hence, her reflections too take a more direct and personal quality.

As I sat there, the contrast between our respective situations became painfully clear. On the one hand, here was a woman whose mother had been denied even the right to be a mother. On the other hand, here I am, whose mother, grandmother, and great-grandmother, and all other female ancestors on both paternal and maternal sides have earned the certified designation of pious wives, not only for themselves but also for my sake. And they have done that by accepting as their sacrament the dirt that washed off from their husband's feet, and some even by entering the funeral pyre while still alive. Throughout my life I have been addressed by everyone as a venerable mother or respected sister. But what unfortunate soul would risk being defiled by calling this woman a mother or sister? (Varma 1994 [1941]: 95).

Despite, or perhaps on the strength of, such contrasts, the life sketches reveal how their subjects affected Mahadevi and how they reflected her own concerns. They were her antidote to the excessive "urbanness" she detected and detested about modern life and modern writers, and they reflected her aspiration to live an active, independent-minded and open-hearted life; finally, they helped her define her own position as a lone woman-householder in a patriarchal society.

However conventional Mahadevi's mistrust for the "artificiality of modern life" may sound, the sketches reveal one very concrete form her life took—that is, the attitude toward mendicants. The first sketch, dedicated to the servant from her childhood, Rama, shows us her mother as being particularly dedicated to the idea of *daridra-Narayan*, God who comes in the guise of a beggar, so much so that their house resembled a "veritable zoo" (Varma 1993 [1941]: 13). This passed on as a most enduring disposition to Mahadevi, admittedly "more out of a concern for my own politeness than for the needs of the beggar"

(Varma 1993 [1943]: 76). All the sketches, however, bear witness to how the sudden encounters become occasions for "self-expansion" (*atma-vistaar*) and for forming and accepting new ties that far exceeded the dictates of politeness. The climaxes in these life stories are emotional moments that best reveal what attracted and "bound" Mahadevi to the characters: *mamta* and *sneh*, affection, intimacy, industriousness, natural politeness, and a certain dignified pride in the face of all adversities. It is these words which, reflecting and resonating in the characters, come closest to defining what Mahadevi felt she needed, as a modern Indian woman, in order to maintain her "natural" inner qualities and her ties to the life of society at large. Contact with these characters meant for her contact with life, "stepping out of the fantasy-world of studying . . . and mixing with life," as she had put it in her statement about the poet's predicament (Varma 1962 [1940]: 33).

Further, what she called her disposition—inherited from her mother—which entailed accepting fictive kin relations with servants (Varma 1993 [1943]: 84), became for Mahadevi a way of creating an alternative living environment to that of the patriarchal family. In fact, she refused to call them servants, and relations with them generally ended only when they died. Even pets were part of her "family" (*Mera parivaar*, Varma 1972). As she put it:

> To describe the relationship between Bhaktin and me as one of master and servant would be difficult; because there can hardly be a master who cannot dismiss his servant even if he wants to, and it is unheard of for a servant to laugh dismissively at the master's order to leave. To call Bhaktin a servant (*naukar*) would be as inappropriate as to consider as servants the rotation of night and day and the roses and mangoes growing in my courtyard. To the same extent that they have a separate existence, and while fulfilling it give us joy and sorrow, Bhaktin has her own independent personality, and while developing it she has shared my life (Varma 1993 [1943]: 18).

By accepting the terms of kinship with the washerwoman, the vegetable seller, the Nepali coolies and the Chinese hawker, Mahadevi was able to make her choice of independent life intelligible and acceptable to society. Just as by becoming a "sister" to male Hindi writers she was able to entertain relationships with them and carve an acceptable and respectable place in the Hindi literary community, by creating a network of fictive kinship ties with those who became the subjects of her sketches, she was able to find an acceptable and respectable way of living as a woman alone.

Conclusions

If some educated ladies, afflicted by the plight of women, set out with dignity and spend their lives finding and removing the causes of the degradation of women, will anybody dare laugh at them? Never! But in order to gain that admiration they will have to weigh every act on the balance of sacrifice and selflessness; their stature will not be judged in terms of self-indulgence and satisfaction (Varma 1952 [1942]): 26).

Mahadevi Varma was well aware of the predicament that educated working women like her were in. She succeeded—despite her unconventional life and her choice never to live with her husband—in being taken seriously and not being laughed at. Reticence, the reluctance to reveal oneself in writing or in public life in general, was her strategy. Thus, at a time when other litterateurs and freedom fighters took to autobiographical writing as a way of recording the political in the personal and the personal in the political, Mahadevi chose to write as little as possible about herself. She never wrote about her feelings in anything but an anecdotal way, and she shrouded her whole emotional life in silence. It was not my aim here to pierce this veil of reticence, but rather to understand its roots and ramifications. For this reticence reflected as much a cultural, personal and artistic attitude. Culturally, reticence could be read as self-effacement, a much-approved attitude particularly in women; silence was often the only means of protecting one's "private" life in environments which usually made it very difficult, especially for a woman. Personally, Mahadevi seems to have had a particularly acute sense of individual dignity and to have cherished solitude and privacy. Her prolonged period of study apart from her family, the difficult choice regarding her marriage, and her subsequent life as a working woman alone must have made her particularly protective of her own privacy. In her writings, the carefully controlled release of any information about herself in the sketches, the grafting of her subjective and emotional poems on a fictive persona, and the balanced, detached stance of her critical essays are all evidence of her attempt to deflect attention from her private self. Artistically, this attitude of reticence produced peculiar styles of poetry and of prose which privileged *indirectness* and allusion; these are of course familiar to the

Indian poetics of *vyangya* and can provide great aesthetic effect. Thus, reticence could produce remarkable results on the artistic plane as well.

The prism of "reticence" across the various genres in Mahadevi's creative output has further allowed us to grapple with what has been a persistent source of puzzlement for her critics and literary friends, namely the perceived cleavage between her poetry, her sketches, and her "feminist" essays, leading some to believe that one of the two personae she presented to the world in her writings must be false (Schomer 1983: 281). As we have seen, in her poems, she created a poetic "I" and a poetic persona; in the essays, she eschewed a personal voice in favor of general philosophical arguments. In the life sketches, she chose to keep herself deliberately out of focus in the role of eloquent witness, putting the brilliance of her pen at the service of frail and fleeting lives.

These considerations help us understand the peculiar nature of Mahadevi's extraordinary sketches: neither sociological studies nor narratives of oppression, they rather record the debt of the sensitive middle-class artist to the casual inhabitants on the margins of her world. It was, after all, because they gave movement and direction to her thinking and her sensibility that she set out to record their lives.

REFERENCES

Prasad, Jayshankar. 1964 [1933]. *Lahar*. Allahabad: Bharti Bhandar.
Schomer, Karine. 1983. *Mahadevi Varma and the Chhayavad Age of Modern Hindi Poetry*. Berkeley: University of California Press.
Varma, Mahadevi. 1951. *Path ke saathi*. Allahabad: Bharti Bhandar.
———. 1951 [1938].*Yama*. Allahabad: Bharti Bhandar.
———. 1958 [1942]. *Shrinkhla ki kariyan*. Allahabad: Bharti Bhandar.
———. 1962 [1940].*Aadhunik kavi. 1. Mahadevi*. Allahabad: Hindi Sahitya Sammelan.
———. 1962 [1942]. *Deepshikha*. Allahabad: Bharti Bhandar.
———. 1962 [1930]. *Nihaar* . Allahabad: Sahitya Bhavan Limited.
———. [1932]. *Rashmi*. Allahabad: Sahitya Bhavan Limited.
———. 1972. *Mera parivaar*. Allahabad: Lokbharti Prakashan.
———. 1993 [1943]. *Smriti ki rekhaen*. Allahabad: Lokbharti Prakashan. Engl. transl. 1975. *A Pilgrimage to the Himalayas and Other Silhouettes from Memory*, transl. R.P. Srivastava and L. Srivastava. London: Peter Owen.
———. 1994 [1941]. *Ateet ke chalchitra*. Allahabad: Lokbharti Prakashan. Eng. transl. 1994. *Sketches from My Past*, transl. N. Kukhreja Sohoni. Boston: Northeastern University.

NOTES

1. Mahadevi Varma, "Hamare pinjrabaddh sahityik," *Vishal Bharat*, September 1936, pp. 235–8; quoted in Schomer 1983: 247.
2. I owe this point to Sudipta Kaviraj.
3. In her editorial article in the special issue of *Chaand*, dedicated to "society," she was the only one to write uncompromisingly about society in these terms and bypassed other social and gendered groups; "Samaj aur vyakti," *Chaand*, "Samaj ank," November 1937.
4. Page numbers in brackets refer to this book.
5. The list of "natural qualities" of men and women is a predictable one and includes, for men: justice, vengeful anger, dry duty, force; for women, forgiveness, pity, emotional compassion, strength of resolve; men's energy was like electricity, it spurred them to great things; women's was like a water-spring, it could quench thirst; Varma 1958 [1942]: 12, 14.
6. I have quoted the available English translations of the two collections of sketches, but with some alterations. When translations are directly from Hindi, I have cited the Hindi edition.
7. Mahadevi Varma, 1993 [1943], *Smrti ki rekhaen*; idem, 1951, *Path ke saathi*; and idem, 1972, *Mera parivaar*.

CHAPTER 4

The Invention of Private Life

A Reading of Sibnath Sastri's *Autobiography*

SUDIPTA KAVIRAJ

This essay offers an analysis of a single text by a single individual in nineteenth-century Bengal, but it seeks to make a more general point about how concepts and practices travel through history and between societies. It is sometimes stated that all societies share certain common values and that distinctions between public and private (because they center on the universal question of sexual life and how people should relate to their own and others' sexuality) are correspondingly universal. All societies, in this view, have some idea of what is public and what is private. This point of view is well intentioned, but historically lazy and inaccurate.

My general point can be made by an analogy with the phenomena of marriage and kinship. Sexual relations are a biological universal, but kinship is a social construction and its universality is rather like that of human language. All societies have language, but each society has a language of its own. Kinship always centers on relations between the sexes, but *social* relations are configured in startlingly different ways. I wish to argue, similarly, that a distinction between what is accessible—seen, heard, communicated—to others, and what is not, is common to most societies; but exactly where the lines of distinction fall, and where conceptual distinctions are inflected, differs widely between societies. Accordingly, although the sense that the individual has some properties or mental features which cannot be shared by others (and should therefore be socially protected) occurs in many cultures, especially through religious reflections on interiority, the idea of a "private life" is a historical construction of Western modernity.

When this idea travels to other societies, and is accepted by certain social groups, it has to be translated into the different context of that society through two parallel processes. Firstly, the incorporation of these practices requires experimentation with their lives by adventurous individuals. But, secondly, these experiments cannot affect social practice without a discursive accompaniment. Additionally, as many pre-modern cultures possess pre-existing concepts and arguments about interiority, affability of emotions, and associated states of consciousness, the reception of modern Western concepts is inevitably mediated through these intellectual habits.

In the Bengali context, this discursive accompaniment, or a constant reflexive commentary on this mode of social being, is provided by new forms of writing, primarily novels, lyric poetry, and autobiography. Novels provide both description and evaluative commentary on the fictive lives of characters. But in the nineteenth century the literary canon of modernity is composed primarily of realistic novels. The central characters in these must be socially credible and act like ordinary individuals in society, which means that interior reflections and commentaries can apply to actual social life. Lyric poetry, in its characteristically universal, unindexed mode of enunciation of the abstract self, explores the emotional universe associated with a new kind of conjugal relationship. It is striking that, almost universally, the romantic novel is interested in the period in which a relationship is negotiated between two individuals, when their romantic encounter is in its formative stage, and requires a re-education of sentiments and its moral justification. The autobiography, the third distinctively modern literary form, holds a peculiarly significant place in this inauguration of new forms of social life. It describes and reflexively comments on real—not fictive—lives. Novels assert the possibility of modern lives in the abstract; autobiographies have the ineradicable advantage of describing the real. Every autobiography is thus a vindication that such a new kind of life for the individual is not merely desirable, but actually possible.

SASTRI'S *ATMACARIT*

The text taken up here for analysis is an early Bengali autobiography (Sastri 1918), written by Sibnath Sastri, a major Brahmo intellectual in late-nineteenth-century Calcutta. Besides being a major religious reformer, Sastri was a literary writer of considerable repute who composed poetry and wrote social novels, though not of such stature as to be included in the highest canon of modern Bengali. Bengali school students are likely to learn about him in histories of literature as a second-level figure rather than to read his texts. However, much of modern intellectual history has stressed the importance of the "little texts" which surround the great texts and constitute their language and fields of signification. Seeking to understand social history only through great literature can be misleading: individuals who are not leading writers often play a determining role in shaping social norms and in the creation of a modern consciousness. Sastri belonged to the latter type. His reputation rested on his fame as a man of "high character" (*unnata caritra*), as a reformer, an eloquent preacher of the Brahmo religion, and as a person who lived a new kind of intensely moral life. For Bengalis cautiously intending to be modern, his life thus had a double, slightly contradictory, attraction: it was both "saintly" and rationalistically modern. Its central theme was that it was possible to remain religious while acting in impeccably rationalistic ways.

In studying the "translation" of ideas from the West, or just the historical inauguration of modernity, performances in the purely intellectual field are not the only relevant measure. Performances in the translation or transformations in practice are of equal, often greater, significance.[1] Sastri was, in many ways, a heroic figure—not merely in articulating intellectual ideas and arguments, but in his character (his *carita*), in "leading a life" that was exemplary in a modern way. What people admired were not the texts he wrote, but the life he authored, the events that constituted it, the principles that structured it, gave it its peculiar form and direction, and its historic meaning. The *Atmacarit* is his own chronicle of his life. It is called simply *Atmacarit* (*Atmacharit* in the more usual Bengali transliteration), a compound of two well-known words. *Atma* means the self. *Carita* contains the fertile ambiguity of reference to both the character displayed in the events of the life and a recounting of that story. Thus the title and its presentation are as simple and intentionally humble as possible, and there is an almost deliberate gesture of conspicuous humility in the plainness of the title and the invitation it offers to the reader.

This plainness is deceptive, however, not because the humility is insincere, as in many traditional saints who often turn such gestures into a conventionalized excess of inconspicuousness.[2] Nor is it a conventional hyperbole. Yet there is a peculiar irony in the emotion and the gesture itself. The traditional gesture of moral debasement worked through a simple technique. By asserting the extraordinary sinfulness of the devotee, it indirectly enhanced the glory of the redeemer: for the more fallen the sinner, the greater the glory of God who purified him. But Sastri's autobiography follows a modern moral path, which considered such self-abasement unworthy of human dignity. In his ability to shape a moral life for himself, the modern individual moral subject took a much more upright stance. The entire life narrated in Sastri's book continues this ironic relation to ordinariness: because, clearly, to be successful with its intended audience, it must appear as both ordinary and extraordinary. It is a kind of life that Sastri, through the story of his life, and its example, attempts to appear reasonable and socially possible to everybody. But, in his historical context, that required extraordinary effort, dramatic conflict, and social tension. The story of his life is a contest between two models of ordinariness, two contrasting, if not conflicting, forms of what an ordinary life should be. This conflict of two "common senses" spread to every level—one's self-identity, childhood, youth, conjugality, parenthood, friendship, religiosity, rationalism, cosmopolitanism. All these themes, ideas, and practices had their given, ordinary, meanings in customary Hindu life. For nearly all of them Sastri wanted a new definition to make them "ordinary." But that required the substitution of one discourse of "common sense" by another. Thus the title is deceptive in its plainness. By trying hard not to embellish the title or the literary performance in the narrating, the author seeks to convey a sense of commonness. But it is not in any sense a common life. It is a life of great moral achievement, and it is lived with extraordinary deliberateness in a historical world, a language, and a changing sensibility.

The Awkwardness of the Autobiography

The autobiography is a highly specific literary form, and at Sastri's time it was not commonplace, as it would become within fifty years. In *Atmacarit*, the two words which are compounded are both common; but their conjunction is not. *Carita* or *caritra* is a common religious biographical genre. It may appear, anachronistically, that writing an *Atmacarit* is simply transferring the skills from that convention to just another object—one's self. Instead of another person of extraordinary merit, the object of narration is the person who happens to be the writer. But it is not that simple. In fact, some of the well-understood rules of this convention of biographical composition have to be abandoned, at times inverted, when a person starts to write a *carita* about himself. This involves not merely writing about a different subject; the subject forces the writer to engage in a very different kind of writing.

Conventional biographies were written about persons of great religious merit or sometimes about military conquerors, both of whom were clearly claimants to extraordinary lives. Ordinary people do not live the excessively religious, or morally unimpeachable, lives of saints; nor do they have the power and authority to embark on military conquests and glory. It is precisely the extraordinariness of those other lives which made them deserving of the distinction of a narrative. But the connection between ordinary people and this kind of exemplary or extraordinary life is significant. Most people in traditional society would be expected to live their lives according to strict routines of occupation and conduct, which set out their social roles, the criteria for their exemplary performance, and the norms of moral behavior according to the station to which they belonged. Some individuals' lives would be "extraordinary" because they would conform to these standards to an extent not normally achieved by others. Exemplary lives would be exemplary in the literal sense, their devotion to their roles and their internal criteria of excellence would be of such a high degree of perfection as to serve as examples to others. By following these life-story models, ordinary lives would become firmer in their conception of their own roles and modes of meritorious conduct; ordinary lives would tend toward those high ideals without ever reaching their levels of perfection of moral performance. Thus these stories could contribute to the building of "character." Interestingly, there is a necessary relation of non-identity in this narrative arrangement. The saint never recites his own life, his moral achievements: someone less capable of such excellence does. To put it another way, there is a necessary separation between the protagonist and the narrator. This is the concept of *caritra-puja* (character-worship).

Why should there be an implicit rule of disjunction between the character and the narrator? First, the character has a perfection of personality that does not need models of this kind. He is also usually bound by rules of reticence,[3] so that it would become immodest on his part to narrate what he has achieved. His life is seen by a separate, different, lesser eye, which can, precisely because of this difference in the scale of achievement, grasp and admire its greatness. Saints, in any case, are heroes of moral action; they lack the leisure to be writers. Their lives are spent in creating bold acts, showing that such perfect acts are possible, not by preaching them, but by enacting them. In great acts, whether of kindness, compassion, sacrifice, or conquest, it is the doing that convinces, not mere saying. By definition, therefore, they do not have the time to narrate what they have accomplished. It requires a different role—that of the disciple, author, narrator, and litterateur. So every Caitanya has a Krishnadas, every Rama a Valmiki, every Krishna a Vyasa.[4] The author of acts and the author of stories must be different.

It is that combination—the undeniability of the ideal and its simultaneous unattainability—which induces ordinary individuals to a life of virtue. This "building" has two connotations. It connotes the act of combining elements from different sources and giving them a crafted and fashioned coherence, and also of putting things together to make something strong. A true human character needs both: it needs to search for and select elements—dispositions, skills, and capacities—that can be culled from the most wide-ranging and diverse sources to make it rich, complex, and interesting; but it must also be a combination of some fundamental dispositions in which the person would have an immovable faith.

There are dangers in unifying the subject and the narrator. Human beings are naturally prone to self-indulgence; it is too easy and pleasant to be deluded about oneself, and fatally easy to be self-righteous about the course of one's life. Stories told by the self cannot have completeness, because they are not told at the completion of a well-lived life, impartiality—because we tend to rationalize our acts, and because of the utter impossibility of achieving the detachment required in a moral tale. Thus, it is possible to make a strong case for the separation of the liver of the life and its narration, to devise a powerful pre-emptive argument against the autobiographic impulse. An autobiography written by an Indian in this cultural habitus must surmount some of these traditional concerns.

This set of concerns about narratives of the self, which barred their writing,[5] could, however, be dramatically undermined by a new kind of moral thinking framing the individual and his God. Following Weber, it is possible to sketch the most important ideas of this framework of moral life. Individuals always live in the unblinking gaze of God. There might be some escape from human criticism, but none from the ever-present scrutiny of God, particularly because he is not an external witness, but an internal one. He lives *inside* the human heart, inside the Rousseauian moral sentiments instilled in human beings by nature (Taylor 1989). In the Brahmo literature, it is interesting to see how *isvara* (God) is slowly turned into somebody who is *hrdayavasi*, one who resides inside the heart. Thus there is a constant need to be honest and examine one's own actions and the events constituting one's life unceasingly, and to face the challenge, often the mortification, of making them public. This is also why there is such a constant need for penitence: the need to open oneself to God and to his rebukes. The self is thus divided into two parts: it is both the vehicle of the person's experience and its judge. Moral judgment cannot be avoided because the agent of this judgment lives inside, not outside.

There is also another interesting transformation in the nature of God. It is his suspiciously Christian-looking pity and kindness for erring human souls that is constantly evoked in the Brahmo literature, rather than his more Hindu characteristics of infinite power or infinite knowledge. Sometimes, there is a sense of a deep intimacy with one's God, but the quality of this intimacy is vastly different from the *vatsalya* intimacy of the Hindu devotee of Krishna. There is a strange ring to constantly repeated phrases like "God's infinite kindness." The traditional God was also infinitely kind, but not in quite this sense.

Schematically, Sastri's text begins with a brief genealogy, indicating where his family came from—both in the sense of their physical origins in South India and the values it passed on. The original, unreconstructed answer to the question of who they were came in the splendidly rhetorical exaggeration of a verse his grandfather taught him in his childhood:

Yavay merau sthita deva
yavat ganga mahitale/
candrarkau gagane yavat/
tavat viprakule vayam

("as long as the Ganga flows on this earth, and the sun and the moon are in the heavens, have we been Brahmins.") Note here the intended ambiguity of the indescribable tense. There is no way of telling whether it is a reference to antiquity or to unendingness, to the past or the future.

Sastri later decided that he was what he was not because of birth but by choice. He moves from the repetitiveness of the village community and its unchosen vocations to a city where lives are elected by a series of willed decisions. One of his main concerns is about domesticity and conjugality, which creates one of the greatest tensions in his life, and so also in the narrative. Marriage, which was the most passive event in the life of the Hindu adolescent, becomes a matter of the most wide-ranging experiments—of marriage among grown adults, marriage of widows, turning an arranged marriage into something utterly unlike itself, a companionate marriage of love. The autobiography is also tormented by his attempts to produce a defensible code for his two marriages, of doing right in a situation that is inherently wrong—having two wives. The movements and agitations of his life do not cease: he is forced into the upheavals and transformations of the Brahmo Samaj. The conflict between the two principles of kinship and friendship, between given and chosen relationships, is never resolved. The commonness of collective interest or intellectually shared enthu-siasm never produces a thick enough sociality. It constantly, achingly, seeks something like a family; in being different from the ties of kin-ship it constantly mimics it, looks for the warmth, the comfort, the unthinking, assumed trustworthiness and availability of kin, parent, brother or sister. His physical movement into differently signified spa-ces also never ceases: he comes out of his village to Calcutta, to India, and literally to the world, to distant England. Everywhere his culti-vated nature is put to the test—of being collected, civilized, never lost for words, or for acts of grace and kindness in a different milieu. That is the test of character. So, in a sense, what he is writing about is not a single person, but a type, the modern individual, of whom he is an example.

An Outline of Sastri's Life

Sibnath Sastri was born in 1847 in a small village in the southern part of modern West Bengal, close to the Sundarban forests. But in this desolate region the kingdom of the Bengali ruler Pratapaditya had flourished a century earlier and Sastri's ancestors, who came from an unspecified region of South India, were invited to settle there by the king. Sastri gave up the practice of caste as repugnant, but was not en-tirely above a certain sense of pride in his line of *daksinatya* (southern) Brahmins. He was born into a family of renowned pandits. His grand-father enjoyed a great reputation for his erudition in the *sastras*, which he passed on to Sastri's father. The latter received a modern education, but could not acquire a sufficiently advanced English education to be able to enter the wholly modern teaching sector. He led a strangely mixed existence, teaching Sanskrit in the school system run by the government, a situation of some irony and considerable discomfort. Sastri's maternal ancestors were also illustrious. His eldest maternal uncle, Dwarkanath Tarkabhushan, taught at the Calcutta Sanskrit College. He was the editor of *Somprakash*, a leading journal in which Sastri had his writing apprenticeship. Dwarkanath was a close friend of the reformer Iswarchandra Vidyasagar, whom Sastri knew intimately from his childhood. He recounts how, as a child, he avoided meeting Vidyasagar: he had a pot belly, and Vidyasagar had a strange way of showing his affection by pinching his tummy.

Sastri's father lacked the means to send him to the most progressive English-medium schools in Calcutta, and sent him, somewhat regretfully, to the Sanskrit College, which was going through its glorious phase with Vidyasagar as its principal. As was common among *daksinatya* Brahmins, he was married at the age of sixteen to a girl, Prasannamayi, from a family of similarly high descent, though of distinctly less erudite reputation. This caused the most significant revolution in his life. His family, particularly his father, looked down on the background of the new daughter-in-law, and afterward, following a trifling incident, decided to send her back to her parental home. Sastri, as we shall see, ineffectually protested to his father about this, but was forced to marry a second time. He kept regretting his second marriage, apparently on two different grounds. Firstly, by this time he had joined the modern-educated progressive intelligentsia in Calcutta who rejected the polygamous ways of traditional Brahmins; and, secondly, he obviously felt keenly the injustice in the treatment of his first wife. This conflict, he asserts, made him increasingly critical of traditional religious customs and drew him toward the progressivism of Brahmo culture. After joining the Brahmo Samaj, he called his first wife back to live with him in Calcutta, but was irretrievably saddled with his second wife. He had wild and impractical ideas about practicing a form of monogamy within this compulsorily bigamous life, without eventually working out a wholly immaculate solution. Apparently he lived ever after in moderate happiness in this morally messy relationship with his two wives.

Sastri's autobiography is a report on a religious life. He soon gained prominence in the Brahmo Samaj and came close to two of its major figures: Devendranath Tagore, the poet Rabindranath's father, who led the Samaj for some time, and the mercurial Kesabchandra Sen. Sen constantly experimented with both the emotional and philosophical content of the Brahmo religion and its institutional form. This caused him to lead a life of exhausting religious enthusiasm and institutional turbulence. A substantial part of Sastri's autobiography deals with these upheavals. It faithfully chronicles his initial attraction to Kesabchandra, joining him in his experiment with a modern ashram, and his gradual disillusionment with Sen's arbitrary and tyrannical style. Eventually, he became one of the major *pracaraks* (itinerant preachers) of the Sadharan Brahmo Samaj. He gave up his comfortable employment as a head teacher for the uncertainty of the itinerant life of a preacher and organizer, living primarily on charity. In the second part of his active life he traveled widely—first in the immediate Bengali sub-empire of the presidency, but later more widely in northern, western and southern India. A significant part of the autobiography is devoted to his six-month sojourn in England and his exchanges with British religious figures. He spent the rest of his life in the service of the Brahmo Samaj, which was by that time fast losing its radical and revolutionary character and turning into one unremarkable sect among the various strands of modern Hinduism.

Sastri was a writer of considerable range and versatility. His writing career began in his early student days, composing satirical verses on the foibles of anglicized Bengalis. In his maturity, much of his writing was devoted to internal disputes among the Brahmo sects. His sermons to Brahmo meetings were collected in a volume, *Dharmajivan* ("A Life in Religion"), published by the Samaj. He also wrote *Mejobau*, an early social novel, and volumes of poetry, often meant to be set as Brahmo hymns. However, his long-term reputation rests on his *Atmacarit* and his masterful sociological account of Bengal in *Ramtanu Lahiri O Tatkalin Bangasamaj* ("Ramtanu Lahiri and the Bengali Society of His Times"). As often happens, there is a certain inextricability between the two works: the concerns of one work spill over into the other, or themes abandoned in one are taken up and resumed for reflection in the other. One can see a simple division of principle between the two works: *Atmacarit* is more the story of an individual life, and the tone is somewhat more personal, while *Ramtanu Lahiri* is a more general account of society; but the two are also obviously connected. The assumption behind the telling of the life story was not that such a life was incredible, extraordinary, and unrepeatable, but that it was possible and ordinary. If the story was remarkable, it was because it was witness to a society which was equally noteworthy. Even fifty years earlier, a life of this kind would have been unthinkable.

As a result, the autobiography narrates the life of the person and also of the community of which he is a significant part: it tells the story of Sastri's life by telling the story of the Brahmo Samaj, and beyond that of Bengali society. All these conceptions of sociability of different scale and qualities are contained in the altering semantics of the term *samaj*. In the early parts of the story, when Sastri decides to join the Brahmos and reject orthodox brahminical conduct, his father disowns him. This was for two reasons: his father was a sufficiently enlightened modern person to acknowledge the right of the individual to his religious conscience, a right recognized by Hindu polytheism. He disagreed with the Brahmos and disapproved of his son's heterodoxy; but at least in part this was also because he had to lose face in his community, his samaj in the oldest, entirely traditional sense. "Samaj" here invokes the idea of a circle of people joined by birth and kinship, and those to whom one should rightly feel the greatest obligations of sociability. However, the Brahmos also constitute a samaj. In so doing, however, they wish to obliterate the principle that birth and kinship impose the most significant obligations. They emphatically retain the idea of a community, or samaj, infused with obligations, but based, unlike the earlier brahminical community, on choice and intellectual fellowship. Finally, when Sastri wrote about the state of *Bangasamaj* at the time of Ramtanu Lahiri, his friend and contemporary, this signified society in the abstract modern sense.

Formal Aspects of Sastri's Autobiography

Autobiographies clearly exhibit many different styles of writing. In the Western autobiography this is clearly reflected in various ways of presenting the self. Obviously, there is a strong connection between the tone or style of writing and the type of self the author wants to present to his audience. Take the most obvious examples: St Augustine and Rousseau. Taking these two is not entirely irrelevant, because Sastri's Brahmo religious experiences were in deep contact with various strands of Christian thought. Evidently, the tone of personal relationship with God, divested of brahminical ritualism and priestcraft, had an equal measure of debt to Christian, particularly Protestant, examples and rationalist thinking. Though there are no explicit references to St Augustine in his work, the attitude of devotion to God is striking.

Rousseau's thought was widely known and deeply influential among his generation, though there are no significant direct references to him in the text. However, I am using these two examples as forms of writing, and wish to contrast Sastri's writing with them because of its striking difference on some points.

European autobiographies are often personal in two radically different ways. Augustine's confessions are deeply personal, written in a tone which is a mixture of introspective soliloquy and formal writing. Despite the perfection of its formal execution, the tone is of one speaking to himself, or in his case to the self of his self, someone sitting deep inside him. Although this image of God as seated in an inner self is not strictly part of traditional Hinduism (which commonly regarded God as *antaryami*, one who can go inside persons, which is different from residing inside them), by the time Tagore was writing his deeply introspective poetry he could refer to his God as "*ke go antaratara se*," that is, one more inside than the inside. Christian autobiographies often put the inner content of religious life—with its doctrines, emotions, doubts, and states of mind—into the act of writing. Thus, Augustine's *Confessions* turns the recounting of the events of his life into a long prayer. Accounts of even apparently insignificant incidents are turned into an invocation and celebration of God—from his first breaking into inarticulate sociability through a smile, to his being led astray through theft in his boyhood. Augustine's confessions have an unrivaled intensity of introspective attention. It is almost as if, during the laborious composition of this highly literary masterpiece, he does not take his eyes off his inner self. The world exists and comes in only in reports of his unbroken continuous conversation with his self and God sitting inside this self. Augustine's autobiography constantly reports the states of his mind, and of his religious emotion, and in the latter task, naturally, there is a detailed analysis of Christian religious doctrines and their adversaries.

There is a second kind of personal writing in Rousseau, whose *Confessions* is equally intent on his internal emotions: Rousseau is a painter of emotions for himself as much as for others. In addition, in this entirely secular recounting of emotional life, there is a subtle gratification of daring, to be able to talk about personal things and to bring them to public view. There is a combination of both confessional moral courage of a certain kind and the very different courage of causing outrage.

On the formal side, Sastri's autobiography differs sharply from both Augustine and Rousseau. It is written artlessly, without any attempt to bring in literary skills or subtlety. Religious issues and crises are reported, but Sastri never adopts the tone of introspective intimacy, never reports the states of his consciousness psychologically. His text is strikingly unemotional and unpsychological. And, although he often touches on subjects which could be intimate or embarrassing, there is hardly any of the confessional daring of the personal autobiography. The personal is simply hinted at, intimacies are implied, but everything is reported in a tone of unemotional calm and matter-of-fact detachment, as if he is writing about someone else's life. I feel this is because the embarrassment of the autobiography in the Indian context has been overwhelming. It is often the story of a person, but mostly of the public side of his life and of emotions which can be shared in public. Only Gandhi's autobiography, *The Story of My Experiments with Truth*, is able to overcome this reticence about the private. Yet there is something remarkably accomplished in Sastri's book. Without detail about his relations with his wives, or his dealings with his friends, or much psychological reporting of his thinking about God, Sastri records an astonishing phase of change in Bengali social life: the subject of this story, told so unemotionally, is precisely the invention of something called the private life of the individual, an essential part of the invention of a modern self.

The Idea of a Private Life

Family life, surprisingly, was the theatre of some of the greatest changes in early modern Bengal, and this was reflected in contests in the practice of family life and an intense intellectual disputation about the nature of the institution of the family and the role of the family in the structure of social life. To put it simply, there were two sides to the family debate or theoretical disputes about private life. Both thought that the family was at the center of the arrangement of various layers of sociability and their specific structuring in Hindu society. But the two sides' conceptions of the family and its underlying principles were radically different.

Without going into the details of this complex literature, I shall discuss the arguments of two most remarkable participants in this contest over the hearts and minds of modern Bengalis, both exceptionally gifted in intellectual debate, exceptionally convinced of the justice of their views, and interestingly, both equally convinced that what they experienced in their own lives showed, unproblematically, the justifiability of much larger social forms. These two figures are Bhudev Mukhopadhyay and Sibnath Sastri. It is not entirely accidental that they wrote about very similar things, though from opposing (or at least very distinct) points of view. Both of them spent much of their lives searching for answers to some of the central moral questions of their age: what was *dharma* (an ethical life)? What was the place of the family in it? What was the form of a good society in the Indian context? And what was to be learnt from the modern West? Bhudev's answers to these questions about the family are contained in his famous tract, *Parivarik Prabandha*. Sastri's book, *Grhadharma*, was equally central to Brahmo domesticity and is a strikingly coherent and reasoned discourse on the ethics of domestic life.

Parivarik Prabandha is a text of astonishing complexity. What is most remarkable about the book is not what it says, but what is left unsaid. Bhudev's conservatism is utterly different from the conservatism of other Hindu orthodox writers: it gives up an appeal to habitualism and replaces it with rationalist arguments. But in the end Bhudev's treatise on the family was disappointing: it provides, on most matters, a total intellectual justification of conventional Hindu families. Sastri's highly influential *Grhadharma* argues the opposite case. There is no direct reference to Bhudev; but the subjects are common. Both Bhudev and Sastri write about marriage and the nature of conjugality, parents' relation with children, the circle of friends (*bandhu*), the maintenance of the household, cleanliness, and domestic order. What Sastri omits from his discussion of the family is also symptomatic: he does not discuss obligations to various types of kinship— *gnati* and *kutumba*—which loom very large in Bhudev's picture of domesticity. This is a long and intricate argument in itself. Let me show an example of their differences by taking their views on child marriage. Bhudev writes:

> The two who are united in their childhood by parents grow together like two creepers intertwining each other. The kind of permanent affection that is possible among them, how can that affection grow among adults? . . . [Among young people] the senses are irresistible, imagination is powerful, and affection/attraction is intense. The intelligence and patience that is required in testing each other's character

is usually entirely disabled at that stage. Just one arch look, one sweet smile, one peculiarity of movement captures the fortress of the heart at once. It does not allow time for examination of character, disposition or taste (Mukhopadhyay 1884: 2–4).

And Bhudev concludes correctly that in all societies where marriage is based on individual choice there are arrangements for divorce. Sastri's arguments are entirely hostile to child marriage:

> At the root of marriage is love, at the root of love is respect, and at the root of respect lies knowledge of each other. Therefore, the custom of arranging marriage through *ghataks* [marriage brokers] that exists in this country is not the correct path. Young men and women would mix with a lot of others, and from them would nominate one person—this should be the main principle of marriage. Where marriage is based on love it brings an amazing education to the hearts of men and women. First, it binds individuals to the community (*janasamaj*); second it binds them with religion (*dharma*), third it binds them to God (*isvar*) (Sastri 1963: 28).

What did Sastri see as being narratable in his life, so that he could overcome reticence about the self? I think it was his sense that his life showed the transformation of some of the most fundamental definitions of social conduct, the meanings of religion, leading a religious life, and of the everyday activities of living in a marriage, raising children and passing one's life with friends. All these had changed historically, and he thought, correctly, that his life was an excellent example of how it had changed, and what people had to go through to make that change happen.

Before individuals can have and defend private lives, the concept of a private life has to become common in society, a matter of social decision which can give rise to intense public debate because these changes signify a fundamental reorientation of the most inescapable province of conduct and experience for all individuals. Sastri's autobiography is fascinating precisely because it is a chronicle of the unremitting struggles of a man trying to live a private life in a society which still refuses to recognize such an idea, and to take, unmolested by others, what appear to us to be the most inoffensively ordinary decisions. His questions were about how to practice his religion, how to think of God and best to serve him, how to decide about his own career, how to marry, to bring up his children. I shall analyze his story now in terms of three forms of *intimacy*—conjugality, the relation between parents and children, and friendship. But I shall follow the sequences of an ideal biography, starting with relations with parents, because they come first, followed by marriage and the setting up of his own *separate* family, and developing relations of friendship with acquaintances through work and intellectual fellowship rather than kinship and family (Bhudev's *gnati-kutumba*).

The Relation of Parent and Child

One of the most significant strands of his autobiography concerns Sastri's relations with his elders, in particular the very different inflections of intimacy with his father and mother. Sastri receives a classical and exacting traditional education in being a good child. His father is unable to stay with his family and has to teach in government schools, but his values and personality traits determine some of the outlines of their domestic life. He is obviously a man of learning and great honesty; but despite his straitened financial circumstances he defies the power of the local landlords in sending his daughters to the village girls' school. There is, also, an interesting distinction at the heart of Hindu Brahmin domesticity: several incidents clearly demonstrate that inner religious life is considered both sacred and, in the traditional way, personal. A son wishing to follow the Shakta form of worship might cause a Vaishnava father some displeasure, but he would not normally interfere in these matters of belief. Turning Brahmo was, in one sense, simply changing religious conviction within the broad Hindu fold. Yet clearly becoming a Brahmo was treated as an act of a different kind. In traditional Hindu conduct, the liberty of inner attachment to God in any of his usual Hindu forms is counterbalanced by a strong emphasis on orthopraxy, the acceptance and performance of suitable conduct for a caste and associated occupation. If Brahmo doctrine had been associated with religious beliefs or doxa, it would not have been different from earlier Hindu sects; but its revolutionary heteropraxy was intolerable to traditional Brahmins.

In the traditional system of beliefs, childhood implied two things: only the first and evident part of it is the inability of the child to perform grown-up activities, his inability to feed or look after himself. Far more important, theoretically, was the principle of hierarchy, the son giving way to the father's wishes, whatever their age. Children outgrew the first kind of dependence, but never the second. In extreme cases, when the father might become senile and wish something clearly unreasonable, the son might uphold the appearance of accepting his father's wish while in fact doing what is socially reasonable. But this external appearance of obedience, even when it is utterly formal and unreasonable, was considered an act of great merit. Sastri's conflict with his father centered on these principles of heteronomy and unreasonable hierarchy, the idea that whatever the case, and whatever their age, the son must always submit to the will of his father.

His childhood and early youth did not see any conflict with his father: in many respects, Sibnath was an ideal child—obedient, gifted, highly successful in education. He also looked on his father's character with considerable filial pride. But the first and vital clash concerned the question of family life. Sastri was married very early to Prasannamayi, and she came to stay in their household, although Sastri was still mainly in Calcutta at the Sanskrit College. Sastri's own account of the critical incident gives us some significant pointers:

> When I was immersed in the enjoyment of the pleasures of poetry, an unfortunate family incident took place. For some particular reason, my father became angry with my first wife, Prasannamayi, and her family, and sent her back to her father's house. He said she would never be welcomed back. When it was decided to reject her finally, the question arose how, since I was an only son, the family line could be maintained. Thus it was decided that I was to be married again. By that time, I had grown up enough to know that polygamy was reprehensible. It was not that I had a particular affection for Prasannamayi. However, I felt that she and her family were being given a severe punishment entirely disproportional to their lapse. My mind became agitated thinking about how I could possibly assist in such a ruthless [heartless] act. However, from childhood I was in such fear of my father that it was impossible for me to oppose his resolve. Still, I let him know myself, and through my mother, that I did not consent to such a [second] marriage (Sastri 1918: 67).

Sastri recalls that, on a journey to the village, he took courage in both hands and told his father, to his face, that he objected to these plans. His father, with characteristic vehemence, which he consistently confused with the legendary brahminical force of character (*tejas*), threatened to beat him with his slippers and told him to return to

Calcutta. Sibnath persisted in accompanying him to the village, complained to his mother, but his mother pleaded inability to dissuade his
father. Sibnath was duly married for the second time to Virajmohini;
but he was so little involved he was unsure if it happened in 1865 or
1866. Sastri thought in retrospect that this was the most significant
event of his life: and the two sections in the *Atmacarit* are tellingly entitled "consequences of the second marriage" and "the beginnings of
religious life." His own record is highly suggestive:

> Immediately following this marriage, my mind was ravaged by a ter-
> rible sense of guilt [*anutap*: regret felt after a wrong act]. A punishment
> was wrongly inflicted on an innocent woman, and despite my unwill-
> ingness, I became the central figure in that wrongful act; at this
> thought I was overwhelmed by shame and sorrow. Before going out to
> marry at my father's command, I had prepared my mind by thinking
> that Ramachandra had gone through fourteen years of exile in a forest
> to obey his father's command; I might have to undergo suffering
> throughout my life. But at this moment of crisis, that thought failed
> to give me [moral] strength. I began to think, individuals are responsi-
> ble for their own actions; even with a thousand parental commands,
> no one takes a share of one's guilt [*pap*]. My mind was tormented by
> self-condemnation. When I think of that intense self-hatred, I tremble
> even today. I used to be a happy, humoros, friendly character; my sense
> of humor and happiness disappeared. I was drowned in deep gloom.
> While stepping forward, it seemed I was stepping into an abyss. When
> night arrived, it seemed better if morning never came (Sastri 1918:
> 68).

"In this state," Sastri says, "I took refuge in, and sought succor, from
God" (1918: 68). His father, in an apparent attempt to help him solve
his moral dilemmas, engaged him in discussions of atheistic doctrines
from Hindu philosophy and sometimes indicated that Vidyasagar was
an atheist. But Sastri had never liked atheism. Previously, he had never
thought deeply about the relation between God and the individual
soul; he did not have a habit of serious prayer. One of his friends sent
him Theodore Parker's *Ten Sermons and Prayers*, and these prayers gave
him "a new life." "While praying, I observed two changes in my mind.
First I got strength in place of weakness: I decided 'I shall fearlessly act
on what I would see as my duty, even if it led to sacrifice of wealth,
prestige or life.' I prepared myself to follow the commands of dharma

[moral truth], and of God who lives inside our heart" (1918: 69). The external manifestation of this resolve was to attend the prayer congregations of the Bhawanipore Brahmo Samaj, in which he was initially somewhat shamefaced, but slowly acquired conviction.

His immediate worry, as he recalls decades afterwards, was his slow but decisive alienation from his father. Sastri explains: "I had said before that prayers gave me strength, which meant that my mind gradually became free of the fear of other human beings, and the inclination to act according to my own beliefs became stronger." His father heard of his visits to the Brahmo congregations and asked him to stop:

> I said calmly, "Father, you know I have never disobeyed your commands. I am willing to obey all your wishes. But do not interfere with my religious life. I cannot give up joining the worship at the Brahmo Samaj." My father said nothing in the rented house I shared with others, but he found this answer so novel and terrible that I heard he wept inconsolably that day (Sastri 1918: 70).

When his father returned to his village, as his mother asked for news of their son the cryptic answer came back "He is dead." It took his mother some time before she realized this "death" was metaphorical. Sastri took recourse to prayers at this point of moral crisis, greatly aided by Parker's humorous and optimistic devotion. He faced "severe struggles" now. Earlier, when he returned home during his holidays, he used to perform the domestic worship, *puja*, in place of his father. That summer, Sastri went home and told his mother of his resolve not to perform the household worship ceremony. His father was initially furious, and took up a wooden plank to beat him with. But when Sastri, once again "calmly" refused, he did not insist and performed it himself. Even in his village, Sastri began to join a few Brahmo friends for daily prayers. His conversion to the Brahmo faith could not now remain an internal family secret and became a scandal for the joint family. When he returned to Calcutta he joined the Brahmo social reform movement with enthusiasm and played a leading role in negotiating one of the first widow remarriages in Calcutta. His father was eventually so enraged that he engaged a gang of thugs to beat his son. After many years he relented slightly and simply left home when his son came back to meet his mother; still later he contented himself with being around but not speaking to him. Sastri's father apparently kept his vow of never speaking to his son until the very end. There were only two exceptions: once when Sastri was seriously ill in Calcutta, he took his mother to nurse him back to health—but as a man of honor, accomplishing this rather complex task without exchanging words. At the time of his death, when Sastri went to Benaras to see his father, there was a brief final reconciliation.

Sastri's account shows with great clarity that it was possible to respond to the new ideas of the Brahmo faith in two radically different ways. His parents responded to his conversion very differently. His father's sense of brahminical piety was strongly intellectual, with a deep pride in devotion to knowledge and acceptance of a life of high-minded poverty; but it was, in consequence, utterly inflexible. When Sastri gave up idolatry, abandoned his sacred thread, and joined Brahmoism (entailing non-observance of caste practices), his father resolved never to speak to him again, i.e. never to take up a rational dialogical stance. Throughout his life he stuck to this high-minded, peculiarly principled inflexibility as a mark of his brahminical "character." From his point of view, it would have been cheating if he disapproved of his son's conduct and carried on as usual in their father–son relationship. Sastri himself expresses admiration for this devotion to principles and claims he learnt his sense of moral rectitude from his father, though he used it in the service of different religious principles.

Yet, inside the family, his mother's response to his conversion was radically different. She did not express consternation when he joined the Brahmos, and her only concern on his announcement that he would not do the household worship was that her advice would have no weight with his father. She did not respond in this way because her religious conviction was less intense. When his father debated *nastika darsana* (atheistic schools) with his son, she strongly disapproved and feared this would lead to his moral ruin. She regarded her relationship as a mother as morally more important than her duties as a Hindu, and worked out a rational trade-off between the two. She often also performed the role of a highly sensitive and skilled intermediary between childishly and insensitively inflexible intellectual men—a common theme in Bengali novels.

Sastri's autobiography moves on at a fast, hurried pace, without pausing to reflect on the principles involved in the social changes he was enacting in his personal life. He gives us little information about his relations with his children, and whether in his own life he worked out fundamentally different moral relations with the next generation.

But the conflict with his father can be analyzed to yield some points on which his sense of correct relationships was "new and terrible." His father, despite a modern education and proximity to people like Vidyasagar and Dwarkanath Vidyabhusan, clung to the traditional principles of hierarchy and an unreasoning continuity of religious conduct. In all such cases, continuity of conduct involves the added Hindu principle of submission to authority. In these moral systems, acting on one's own views, however considered, is regarded as willfullness and a kind of ethical egotism. Ability to submit to the will of "elders" is similar to selflessness. In that moral world, too, there was a difference between "being a Brahmin" well or badly; but "being a Brahmin" was not itself subject to rational choice. More importantly, Sastri thought it right to give children a right to choose their own religious orientation. Given that freedom of choice, the relation between parents and children could continue to be intense and intimate. But the most important principle, to which others were subordinate, was the one of individuality and autonomy. For Sastri, religion was nothing without autonomy; it was a dull, repetitious routine, without the thrill of acting well. For his father religion was nothing if autonomy was brought into it. Yet, in the way Sastri paints his mother's reactions to his religious crisis, it is clear he believed that there was a possible solution of this problem from within the traditional repertoire of moral conduct. His mother's response was not due to a weaker sense of religious conviction, but a different kind.

Relationships of Conjugality

Sociologically, parent–child relationships are intrinsically related to alterations in the central notions about conjugal life. Modern occupational life disrupts the structural form of the joint family based on common agricultural labor, and the replication of occupation across generations which gives individuals a fund of skills they absorb easily through their close family context. Training for an occupation was internal to the traditional caste-based family system, rather than externally arranged through schools or academies. In early modern Bengal conjugality changed fundamentally through a combination of intellectual and social influences. Sibnath Sastri's family was typical of the first wave of social groups who benefited from, and were deeply affected by, institutional changes brought in by early modernity. His grandfather had lived a life of the traditional pandit in the local context of the village; but his father received an education that was modern in spirit, though his specific qualification was in the traditional discipline of Sanskrit. Harananda Bhattacharyya, Sibnath's father, was placed in a strangely mixed position: his learning was traditional but his occupational position was drastically different from his ancestors'. He did his teaching in government-funded schools, for a regular salary, independent of the earlier system of village support, usually supplemented by some ownership of land. Sastri does not tell us very much about his family's finances, but it is clear that his father's family survived mainly on his small salary, and the smooth running of the household depended on his mother's intelligent ability to manage on such meager means.

Despite the insufficiency of the pay, the *structural* difference was enormous. In a single generation, Sastri's family had exchanged the older, village-bound, caste-based, localized occupational system for the life of the salaried professional. Since salaried people often had to move from place to place on government jobs, this had an immediate impact on the way the family ran. Harananda arranged his family in the traditional manner: he did not leave his ancestral seat in the village, the spatial center of his existence. He kept his wife and young children in the ancestral home, and moved himself to his places of work. The distances were manageable, and he was able to spend time with his family over weekends or holidays. But this made life difficult for his wife. She had to run the household entirely on her own, as well as fending off unwelcome attention from amorous males, like her son's primary schoolteacher. For his entire life, Harananda maintained this dual existence—of the family seat as the principal home (*badi*) and an insubstantial, rented residence at the place of work for the single male (*basa*). In fact, both in everyday thinking and in high literary discourse, there was much play on these two forms of residence. For Harananda, Calcutta was the place of learning, with occasional visits to family members or valued friends, but nothing more.

In Sastri's generation successful people commonly took up government employment, which immediately altered all the circumstances of intimacy in their lives and the kinds of people with whom they spent most of their time, in the closest emotional relationships. Usually, these jobs came with high salaries and associated perks. These salaried individuals had to leave their ancestral homes, take up residence in often large, luxurious government accommodation; but the most significant change in their lives was sociological. They had to live permanently away from their circles of intimate relatives in the village or towns; thus a traditional existence surrounded by close kin—siblings, cousins, in-laws, etc.—was impossible. Increasingly, however, both their salaries and their mental orientation allowed them to take their wives to live with them—a structure of conjugal life radically different from the village-centered world of Sibnath's father. In many of these cases, particularly for the financially fortunate ones, this left a couple of relatively young people of comfortable income in the unaccustomed intimacy of each other's unobstructed company. They lived in large, spacious, fashionable homes, which invited decoration as their intimate living space. Decoration accorded to this space a special individuality and marks of intimacy. It marked the space off as "their space," separated from others'. The private character of this space was marked by objects of personal taste, conjugal photographs, even the double bed. Till fairly recently, traditional people regarded these as a vulgar display of sexuality: as a shameless display of selfish indulgence.[6] The private space could be filled with furniture and household things which not merely declared their relative level of opulence, but also a space for the display of taste and a material culture of owning things of sophistication and delicacy. Material objects came to have a role that was different from, and beyond, the dry functionality of objects in the rural household.

Traditional conjugality had to develop in the context of the joint family, and from both novelistic and biographic evidence it can be clearly seen that those circumstances produced a peculiar ethic of good conjugal behavior. Young couples felt shame at being together in the presence of others: for both males and females there was a peculiar ethic of demonstrative attention toward others, to show to members of the joint family that they were not given to a selfish, and probably carnal, attentiveness to their spouses. For women, especially, this ethic of inattentiveness encompassed a demonstration of love for children other than one's own. The internal ethic of the joint family enjoined a rule of equality with respect to children, and a good mother was the woman who treated all the other children as her own.

Spatial relocation away from the ancestral seat of the joint family altered this sociological context radically. There were no relatives, particularly elders, to enforce the ethic of conjugal shame. More substantially, since elders and other close kin were not around for constant influence and consultation, the husband's main ally and adviser became his wife. This resulted in a tendency toward greater equality in their relationship, not in terms of power, but because they were subjected to the same experiences and had to find their joint way through problems, opportunities, and decisions. Excessively unequal relationships became unhelpful for men. It was a seriously inconvenient situation if the wife did not have the education to share the husband's tastes and concerns. Evidently, this did not lead to a sudden era of women's empowerment; but husbands found it in their own interest to give education to their wives and make them culturally more their equals. As couples went through their lives in situations of mutual dependence, and as no one in their joint family could share this joint memory and experience of life, this tended to cement the bond between the spouses and mark them off from others. Thus a new form of intimacy developed between married men and women living a modern life, driven by material circumstances of sharing occupational experience and ideological power of rationalistic doctrines of autonomy, assisted by the moral imagination of romantic novels. Many marriages did not start as romantic, but were made so retrospectively.

Sibnath initially regarded his village home as the spatial center of his existence, the central point from which all spatial relations radiated outward toward his increasingly expanding universe of experience; and whenever he had the chance, on short or long holidays, he went back to the village. His life with Prasannamayi began in highly fraught circumstances. He was married very young, and when his father decided to send her away he confesses he did not feel great attachment to her. He began to think seriously about her out of a sense of moral responsibility rather than emotional attachment, and only when he was driven into his second marriage. He requested his uncle to call Prasannamayi to his house and went there to meet her and apologize to her. She stayed in his uncle's house, and he went there every Saturday—to set up a new, partially autonomous relationship with her. His father was initially furious at this disobedient action but subsequently accepted it and even relented, accepting her back into his own family. Eventually, when his father threw him out for becoming a Brahmo, Sastri had to set up home in Calcutta. He brought Prasannamayi to Calcutta to set up his own nuclear family. This, however, left the question of his second wife very unsatisfactorily unresolved. When he set up a base in Calcutta with a friend whom he supported in marrying a widow, he had some "wild designs" (Sastri 1918: 79). "At this time, all kinds of absurd projects entered my mind, all kind of projects for the deliverance of India," among which, he retrospectively recognized, were his designs about his second wife.

He was sharing a house in Calcutta with his friend Yogendra, who had lost his wife and married a widow. Sastri used to teach her English and Bengali, while "at this time, reading John Stuart Mill's works, Yogendra temporarily turned into an atheist" (1918: 79).

We three people had become such great "reformers" that we decided that we would bring my second wife Virajmohini and marry her off a second time. I had not yet taken Virajmohini as a wife. In the year 1868 I once went to bring her. She was a girl of 11 or 12 years. Probably, they [Virajmohini's family] refused to send her down with me because I had gone without my parents' permission. I did not treat her as my wife because it would have been wrong to live with someone I was intending to marry off a second time (1918: 79).

On this occasion the problem passed, as her parents did not allow her to accompany him, and he could not put his reforming ideas of marrying his wife to a second husband into practice. By 1872, however, her parents and siblings had died in a cholera epidemic. Her uncles accepted her unwillingly and asked Sibnath to take responsibility for her. He accepted his responsibility to look after her, but his Brahmo friends pointed out: "A Brahmo living with two wives is a detestable idea. One of our major principles is to protest against the practice of polygamy. If you live with two wives, how would you protest against polygamy?" (1918: 112). Sastri replied: "But I am not going to fetch her with the intention of living with two wives. What is her guilt that I shall not offer her refuge after her parents passed away? The guilt of this bigamy rests with me, not her. I am going to bring her here because I will educate her; if she agrees, I will give her in marriage a second time" (1918: 112). Sastri and his friends had obviously overlooked some problems in their state of moral enthusiasm: it would mean bigamy for his second wife, a far more problematic status for Hindu women, and also the small matter—for ideological supporters of moral autonomy—of the choice of the woman herself. Faced with this moral conflict, Sastri sought advice from Kesabchandra Sen, his religious leader at the time. Sen gave him the practical advice of bringing in his second wife, saying to Sastri: "In a society that practices child marriage, how can women be held guilty in cases of bigamy? If a man marries ten women and then becomes a Brahmo, it is his moral duty to give shelter to these ten women. In fact, if he refuses to take care of them, and any of these women goes astray, he is responsible for that" (1918: 112).

Sastri reports that he had some difficulty persuading Prasannamayi to accept this high-minded scheme of bringing in the second wife, and giving her an education until she could be remarried. But the greater oversight in this was that no one considered the possible views of the woman herself. When she was brought to Calcutta, Sastri explained to her two possible courses of action: the first was for her to grow up and marry someone else when she came of age; the second was for her to get an education, so that she could take care of herself. To both these high-minded proposals she responded, not surprisingly, with horror. "She was startled by the first proposal [of remarriage], and exclaimed, 'My God, how many times can a woman marry?' On seeing her reaction, and her deep repugnance for the idea of a second marriage, the genie I had kept in my head for so long left at once. I realized that it was the second proposal that I had to turn to practice" (1918: 112).

Understandably, this led to a serious domestic crisis:

> From another angle, I faced a further severe test. When Prasannamayi and Virajmohini began to live under the same roof, I did not treat Virajmohini as my wife and I began to feel that it was morally right for that period to live apart, away from Prasannamayi. By then we had a long conjugal relationship, and Hemlata, Tarangini and Priyanath had been born. But inside the ashram there were no outside rooms except for the schoolroom and Kesabchandra's office. Where do I sleep at night, if not in Prasannamayi's room? To live apart became a great struggle for me. It was also very distressing for Prasannamayi. Eventually, I managed to convince Prasannamayi, and took her leave, and started sleeping wherever I could. By chance, an expedient came to light. On the verandah of the Hindu College, there was an empty table [that] . . . lay empty at night. After dinner at night I took a book with me, and placing my head on that book, I slept soundly on that table.

He added, somewhat incongruously, "I spent my time wonderfully" (1918: 112–13).

However, both his wives got to know of this unorthodox arrangement and became disconsolate. Soon afterwards, Sastri was called by his uncle to take charge of his highly respected journal, *Somprakash*, and went to live in a small town, Harinabhi, leaving his two distressed wives in Kesabchandra's ashram in Calcutta. Again, not surprisingly, Kesabchandra expressed concern about the untenability of the arrangements, and said he feared Virajmohini might commit suicide. Eventually, Sastri decided on an ingenious plan which combined domestic peace with moral rectitude: "When I found that Virajmohini did not want to be separated from me, I decided to take the following course: when she would be with Prasannamayi, I would live apart from both of them. When they would live in different houses, I would unite with them as their husband. We started acting accordingly. For a long time, as long as Prasannamayi lived, this is how it went on" (1918: 113).

By this strange device, Sastri saved his conscience and turned his bigamous life into discrete monogamies with two wives. Strange times need strangely imperfect moral solutions.

Apart from the peculiarity of this marital story, what is interesting is the unfolding of the principles of conjugality in Sastri's autobiography. Several types of conjugality figure in the social universe around him. Conventional orthodox relationships, of course, abounded: many Brahmos or progressive Hindus practiced their progressivism in strictly segmented spheres. They lived a life of friendship and work with male friends who shared their world, but retained a totally orthodox relation with their wives. But most of Sastri's intimate circle experimented with a different flavor of conjugal relationship. A few who married widows were fortunate to have as wives women who were comparatively older, more mature, usually educated, from cultivated, liberal families. These women shared the interests of their husbands' lives more fully, and apparently controlled the domestic sphere, which included considerable freedom of financial expenditure. Others married wives who were too young, and usually less educated than themselves, but they quite often spent considerable effort in getting such wives educated, and often succeeded.

In most cases the huge moral ideal of the romantic novel, of a companionate relationship with one's wife, based on love, could not be translated into reality easily or entirely. The women were rarely independent, nor free to choose their partners at the time of their marriage; nor did the circumstances favor pre-marital courtship. But after marriage, when the wives came to maturity, progressive men often tried very hard to graft a quasi-romantic relation on that heteronomous arrangement. And although women never enjoyed complete equality within those relationships, they often earned a great deal of autonomy of action and respect. Sastri's own short sketch of Prasannamayi is a wonderful example of such respect, expressed with great dignity and restraint. But the moral imaginary of the novel is of great significance: it was always one step ahead of social practice, drawing social conduct toward that ideal by the most intangible and powerful enticement. Novelistic plots painted, as it were, a picture of a completely ideal conjugal relationship, and although reality usually fell far short of such exhilarating and ennobling emotion, they constantly stretched the margins of possibility, legitimizing in the sacred language of literature a mode of conduct which real life could not sustain.

Relationships with Friends

Another significant new development was the emergence of a new sociability of friendship. This should not be taken to mean that before the arrival of modern influences Indians did not know what friendship was. But with the advent of modernity, the recasting of social norms leads to two kinds of changes in patterns of friendship. First, the range of people from whom friends can be selected is vastly widened, though we should be careful in recognizing its limits as well. Secondly, the place of friendship among other types of sociability changed fundamentally in a general reorganization of relationships of intimacy. It would be grotesque not to observe the existence of mythological and literary models of friendship in the traditional literature, not least because, even after the new form of friendship flourished, traditional literary examples remained powerful models. Friends were made traditionally either in the pursuit of a common caste profession or within the circle of kinship. Caste made friendship outside of common professions improbable and difficult to sustain, and it was usually disapproved of by society. The functional interdependence so central to the operation of the caste system disallowed intimacy and friendships across the boundaries of caste and kin, which were related in any case.

This order was decisively broken with the arrival of the forms of modern sociability. Some economic and structural changes played a central role in this transformation. Evidently, these changes affected only the more upper-class elements in Bengali society, residing in urban centers, and living their lives on the plane of a new kind of professional space spanning the whole of the British imperial domain. Bengalis monopolized administrative posts, and a doctor or an inspector of schools—such as Bhudev Mukhopadhyay—could be posted to distant reaches of the empire. This process of constant relocation affected the structure of sociability of such people deeply. As it loosened the ties with the paternal family and kin, it compelled people to seek out others who could provide them with a social life in unfamiliar areas. Modern professionals therefore developed strong friendships with people from similar stations and professions in life, and who had similar ideas about social norms. Groups like the Brahmos provided a much-needed structure of social sustenance in this sense, apart from their more explicit doctrinal norms. Among the Brahmos, precisely because they rejected conventional Hindu customs, there was a strong urge to codify the rules of a new domesticity, and Sastri's *Grhadharma* played an important role in the standardization of domestic conduct. In his own life the importance of friendships of the new kind was inestimable. As his family refused to give him sustenance, he depended increasingly on his friends.

At an early stage, his friends come primarily from college mates, or students studying in Calcutta and forced to mess together in rented houses with common living space and servants. There are also touching examples of Sastri providing support to others in need, such as his attempt to support a friend who married a widow at his instigation. As they advance in life, these examples of youthful frenzies of idealistic enthusiasm abate somewhat, but the close relations with friends continue. Friends made in early life, at college or through common enthusiasm for Brahmo reform, mostly grow into successful professional men, because, in the colonial dispensation, once a person became part of the modern education system, he could hardly fail. This imparts a certain homogeneity to the social group—financially and ideologically—among whom this was practiced. But evidently, prosperous friends tended to support less fortunate ones, as evident from the life of the poet Michael Madhusudan Dutt, who led a peculiarly difficult life. In Sastri's case, the relationship with friends was slightly different: although prosperous friends sometimes paid for his needs, he was in the morally superior station of the religious preacher.

What is remarkable in his autobiography is the total absence of intimacy with his kin, and the complete dominance of relationships with friends. This demonstrates the social possibility of a new kind of life for the reformed Hindu of intense sociability without the kinship circle. There is always an underlying theoretical argument. Influenced by some contemporary Western theories, the new individuals in effect assert that traditional friendship and sociability limited to kin becomes morally unjustifiable if they accept a process of individual differentiation. Even close kin, like brothers or sisters, might not share an individual's temperament or intellectual enthusiasms and, as economic modernity unfolded, his occupational culture. Relations with friends are based, by contrast, on similarity of temperament and intellectual inclination: these are, therefore, more intense and reliable. In any case, it seems clear that, in the life of socially mobile upper-class Bengalis, relationships of friendships became more important over time than kin-based intimacies. In literary writing, particularly in the novels of Tagore and Saratchandra Chattopadhyay, there is a constant and searching reflection of the nature of friendship—its various possible forms and intricate structures. Instances of strong friendship are very central to novelistic narratives, and, in some striking cases, intellectual bonds survive serious misunderstandings. In some instances there is also a suggestion of complementarity, as in the case of Binoy and Gora, both in terms of character and intellectual arguments in Tagore's novel, *Gora*. Literary narratives also speculate about the possibility of a "friendship" between men and women which is distinct from (and does not constitute simply) the early stages of romance.

The Self and Intimacy with God

The autobiography is, after all, the story of a self. What kind of sense of self is portrayed in Sastri's work? Is this sense of self different from more traditional ones? Is there a connection between these redefined intimacies and the exact nature of religious life Sastri valued? I think there is a strong connection between the redefinition of intimacies and the particular conception of the moral self that was central to Brahmo doctrine. Although these doctrinal arguments are oddly absent from the *Atmacarit*, Sastri presented them with great theoretical clarity in some of his regular Brahmo sermons. In a sermon entitled "God resides in the heart," he first rejects several conventional Hindu conceptions—of a God declaring moral rules through the infallible verbality of the Vedas, a God available to men as *avatara*, and a God of idolaters.

The common fault with all these conceptions of religious life is that it makes moral rules into something to be laid down from outside, and therefore experienced as constraining, rather than discovered from inside, and thus experienced as fulfilling. In all these pictures of moral life, God appears intermittently and suddenly to light up the true path. True religiosity yearns for an intimate and incessant contact with God. Unlike the Hindu belief in God's externality, God resides inside the human heart, and his commands are not written in external tablets of religious instruction but are whispered by the utterings of our conscience. In the deeper self, human beings are in contact with the divine. In accordance with this view, Brahmo temples have to reject the noisy chaos of Hindu worship, and, most important of all, every Bengali home must replicate the peace and domestic order Sastri had found in the homes of the English middle class. What he admired most in English homes was the designation of a private space, however small, for each individual, where every person could enjoy undisturbed solitude, where he could develop an intimacy with himself, and listen to God speaking through his heart. In the usual distractions and clatter of everyday life, these whispers are stilled (Sastri 1933, 2: 73–84). It requires peace and silence to listen to the God sitting inside us and speaking through the untrammeled language of conscience. Sastri develops a theory of a particular relationship with one's self which is also couched, in a sense, in a language of intimacy.

In the intense debates about the nature of religious life, and the two crucial concepts at its very center—God and the self—essential social practices were being redefined. But it is characteristic that these social themes figure in a religious debate. Sastri's religion is radically different from Bhudev's. It rejects and disconnects itself from the Hinduism which values external manifestations and ritualism. It is radically critical of caste and its dual commitment to predestination and hierarchy. And it reorders the picture of the universe by placing God inside men rather than in an inaccessible part of the world—creating a deep moral impulse toward an intellectual and religious individualism. Intense religious and intellectual individualism was a precondition for individualist social practices. Precisely because these reorientations of practical conduct touched some of the fundamental moral values of Hindu society, they needed not just the force of economic change to secure them but a language of moral legitimation to impart to them something close to sacrality. The creation of privacy was not just an arrangement of convenience, but part of a moral order.

Just as Weber saw in Protestant loneliness in the world the sanctifying language for capitalist conduct, Sastri produces through his religious ideas the essential moral arguments for the new institution of the Bengali individual's privacy. The Bengali individual could from now on become different from his father in his profession, keep his deepest thoughts from his family, value his friends more than his kin, seek from his wife companionship rather than subjection, use his affection for children to let them develop as individuals—all unthinkable infringements of traditional Hindu conduct. This is the historical invention of a private sphere, of a private life for individuals, a conceptual space in which they are sovereign, subject to some rules of sociability. Sastri's religious teaching seeks to make this private sphere more than just intellectually acceptable. He wants to make it sacred. The modern individual, he believes, needs this space, literal and metaphorical, not just to escape from everyday aggravation, but to meet himself, and his "more than inner" (*antaratara*) God.

REFERENCES

Eisenstadt, S.N. (ed.). "Multiple Modernities." *Daedalus,*, Winter, 2000.
Mukhopadhyay, Bhudev. 1884. *Parivarik Prabandha*. Calcutta.
Sastri, Sibnath. 1918. *Atmacarit*. Calcutta: Prabasi Karyalaya.
———. 1933. *Dharmajivan*. 3 vols. Calcutta: Sadharan Brahmo Samaj.
———. 1963. *Grhadharma*. Calcutta: Sadharan Brahmo Samaj.
Tagore, Rabindranath. 1970. *Gitabitan*. Calcutta: Visvabharati.
Taylor, Charles. 1989. *The Sources of the Self*. Cambridge: Cambridge University Press.
Wagner, Peter. 1994. *A Sociology of Modernity: Liberty and Discipline*. London: Routledge.

NOTES

1. A similar change, or shift of emphasis, can be seen in recent Western studies of modernity. See Wagner 1994; but this tendency toward a revisionist understanding of modernity can be seen in several essays in the collection "Multiple Modernities," in *Daedalus*, February 2000, which is not confined to the West.

2. In the Bengali tradition of religious thought the most famous enunciation of the practice of humility comes from Caitanya in his famous *sloka*: *trnadapi sunicena taroriva sahisnunal amanina manadena kirtaniya sada harihl*. But there is a highly conventionalized form of moral abjection which makes the saint-devotee describe himself as a sinner ineligible even for God's redemptive grace.

3. One can compare Sibnath Sastri's unwillingness to talk about the sexual side of his conjugality with a similar kind of reticence in the poet Mahadevi

Varma: see Francesca Orsini's essay in this volume, and compare Jawaharlal Nehru's silence about his private life in his celebrated *Autobiography* (1936).

4. Though it would be wrong to believe that the relationship between the great figure, such as Rama or Krishna, and the great narrator, such as Valmiki or Vyasa, is a straightforward one of recording, it is a far more complex relationship.

5. There are some well-known autobiographical narratives from medieval India: the best known of these, precisely because it tells the life of an ordinary individual, is *Ardhakathanaka* ("Half a Tale") by the merchant Banarasi Das, written in Hindi during the reign of Jahangir in the seventeenth century.

6. Compare how, in Jonathan Parry's essay in this volume, a man who had led a fairly adventurous sexual life regarded the double bed in his daughter's house as an almost pornographic object.

CHAPTER 5

The Past in the Present

Instruction, Pleasure, and Blessing in Maulana Muhammad Zakariyya's
Aap Biitii

Barbara D. Metcalf

Between 1970 and 1981, near the end of his long life, the scion of a family of pre-eminent Islamic scholars and holy men wrote and published, ultimately in some seven volumes of well over 2,000 pages, a work he simply entitled *Aap Biitii*, an ordinary Hindi term for one's own life story, whether written or oral.[1] The book is a rich source for the history of the reformist, quietist Islam that has been so pervasive in Muslim religious life in colonial and post-colonial India.[2] Above all, it is an intimate and detailed record of what one influential religious scholar himself wanted to be remembered for and the teachings he wanted others to remember. The work at the same time illuminates long-standing traditions of modeling morally exemplary lives and telling stories about them, even while it yields glimpses of one particular iron-willed, passionate scholar whose active life spanned half a dozen decades before and after Partition.

Maulana Muhammad Zakariyya Kandhalawi (1897–1982) chose to call his work an *aap biitii*, preferring this word over more elevated terms commonly used for a biography or autobiography—although one edition at least added in parenthesis a Persianate translation of his title as *khud-nawisht sawaanih* (Muhammad Zakariyya n.d.b, vol. 7, title page). The original title is, however, particularly apt. Muhammad Zakariyya was, in fact, as the English idiom has it, simply "having his own say," and much of the work was an actual transcript of his speech. He himself was clear that this was a modest, incomplete, sometimes repetitive document. The work was produced piecemeal, responding to specific stimuli or occasions. Indeed, the power of the work in part derives from its production in painful and challenging circumstance, to which the author responded by exuberantly marshaling what, in the end, seemed nothing less than the totality of his life's experiences.

Despite its episodic and disjointed production, the work continues in print, and several volumes have even been translated into English, primarily for the benefit of those beyond India and Pakistan who do not know Urdu (Muhammad Zakariyya 1993, 1996). The appearance of the book belies its casual production. It is typically published to look like a holy and special book. My own two-volume edition, recently printed in Karachi, is covered in padded, marbled green plastic, embossed in gold, with the title in a sunburst of arabesques (Muhammad Zakariyya n.d. a and b). A ribbon bound in the spine serves as bookmark. The author is celebrated on the cover as the "Shaikh of Hadith," the title by which he is best known. It was bestowed on him by his own Sufi master to acknowledge his role as the chief teacher of prophetic tradition (*hadith*) at an eminent theological seminary. The cover also describes him as "The Blessing of the Age," "The Pillar of the World," and "The Sojourner in Medina." The book is special, and its subject is clearly special. The titles taken together identify him as a scholar; as a devotee of the Prophet Muhammad (and, in his last days, resident of the Prophet's city of Medina); and as a Sufi of the highest rank.

Muhammad Zakariyya may have written the book at the end of his life, but in some ways he had been preparing for it his whole life long. He, and his father before him, were great storytellers and lived in a milieu where stories of the elders were a focus of scholarly work, instruction, and everyday conversation. By the time he was a young man, there had been several decades of printed Urdu biographies, and he himself was an avid reader of these biographies, many of which he cites in his own life story. He was, in fact, inspired at one point in his account to recall his long-term love for biographies going back to childhood. Always a night owl, he explained that he would read biographies after the night prayer, staying awake the whole night on occasions—for example, when he waited up for his elder, Maulana Husain Ahmad Madani (1879–1957), who often arrived on a night train. The subjects of biographies he remembered enjoying were those of his elders in the reformist Deobandi tradition, and the names that flowed from his pen, all well known in those circles. The biographies he noted as his favorites—of Hazrat Rashid Ahmad Gangohi, Hazrat Khalil Ahmad

Saharanpuri, Hazrat Mahmudu'l-Hasan Shaikhu'l-hind, Hazrat Ashraf Ali Thanawi, Hazrat Husain Ahmad Madani, Chacha Sahib Marhum (Maulana Muhammad Ilyas)—are all of figures who lived into or in the twentieth century and who were central to the Deoband movement of "scripturalist" reform centered around a theological academy founded some ninety miles north-east of Delhi in 1867.[3] "All my life," Muhammad Zakariyya wrote, "I have loved reading the lives of the elders" (Muhammad Zakariyya 1969: 25). These stories had shaped the way he lived his life and now shaped the way he retold his own. In writing his own life story, moreover, he included anecdotes about many of those he knew or knew of. His explicit goal in writing was to influence the lives of those who read, just as he himself had been influenced.

It rapidly became, as well, a way to have a good time. Early on in his account, at the point when he was about to launch into his stories of childhood chastening (no less), he invited the reader "to listen to a few incidents." "Whether you enjoy them or not," he continued, "I will enjoy writing them!" (Muhammad Zakariyya 1969: 35).

This text was intended for the specific audience of participants in the reformist tradition, the intimacy of its audience suggested, for example, by the shorthand way of referring to those discussed. The English translation recently published in South Africa therefore had to include a glossary of names as a key to those otherwise only called "Hazrat Saharanpuri," "the honored one from Saharanpur," or "Chacha Sahib Marhum," "my late Uncle." The emergence of the Deoband *ulama*, with the foundation of their major *madrasa* (college or seminary) in 1867, had coincided precisely with what one scholar has identified as the third of three periods in the early history of print in India, the "post-incunabula." This was the period in the second half of the nineteenth century when the printed book began to penetrate deeply into Indian society.[4] Across Indian society, not only were there more books, but texts continued to serve as a spur to reading aloud and they were used as much that way as for private reading.[5] Muhammad Zakariyya's hesitation to continue writing was put aside, for example, when he learned from letters from other *madrasa* teachers that they were using his *Aap Biitii* in their lessons to the great benefit of their students—the very target he had hoped to reach in the first place (Muhammad Zakariyya n.d.b: vol. 6: 817). The text was also interactive in another way. At one point, for example, Maulana Zakariyya broke his narrative to address readers directly, asking them to make intercessory prayer, and transfer of merit, to those three dozen or so people in his life who were initially opposed to him but then turned their enmity to devotion. It would be, he says, a kind service to him to do so (Muhammad Zakariyya 1971a: 81). An autobiography could thus become an extension of the person himself and, in this case, a tool in creating the kind of relational bonds that defined his life.

Lives as Lessons

It is difficult to exaggerate how important the writing of life histories became for the *ulama* (theologians, or those learned in the law) from the late nineteenth century on. In embracing that genre, they drew on a very old tradition of emphasis on the embodiment of Islamic teachings in the life of the Prophet and subsequently his heirs: the Companions, the Sufis, and the *ulama*. The lives of the holy are meant to be reproduced in written life histories and in the lived patterns of their followers, much as the life of every Muslim is meant to be a reproduction of the "narrations," *hadith*, of the Prophet himself. Indeed, the goal of Muhammad Zakariyya's own popular writings was clearly intended to make it possible for ordinary Muslims to fashion themselves as "living hadith" (Metcalf 1994). For all its resonance with enduring Islamic patterns, however, it is notable that an emphasis on exemplary human models, whether of gods, or prophets, or their past and present holy exemplars, cut across religious traditions in the colonial period. In the Muslim case, this meant in the nineteenth century a centrality from among all the Islamic sciences given to *hadith*.

The privileged place of religious biography is often explicitly discussed in these texts themselves, for example in a preface taken almost at random, the biography of one of Muhammad Zakariyya's elders, Maulana Ashraf AliThanawi (Muhammad Abdu'l-hayy 1972). The preface explains that while the key teachings of faith are to be found laid out in books, it is impossible to understand them without a long-term practical example before one's eyes. For this reason, a living pro-phet, whether Moses and the Torah, Jesus and the Gospels, or Muhammad and the Qur'an, conveyed every divine book in order to make its teachings visible. Now, in the era after prophethood, one must seek a guide who exemplifies prophetic behavior, or seek out the reports of such a guide. The author of the preface was a disciple of the author, Dr Abdu'l-hayy, whose *shaikh*, in turn, was the subject of the biography. He called Dr Abdu'l-hayy "a *mujassam tazkirah*, i.e. "a memory rendered corporeal," of his *shaikh* (Muhammad Abdu'l-hayy 1972: *daal*). "*Tazkirah*," whose root meaning is memory or aid to memory, is the common term for a biographical memoir. Thus the person and the biography are, at some level, the same, since both are triggers to recollection. These texts were explicitly didactic. For example, one recent collection of five biographies, each a *tazkirah* of a holy man, is entitled *Dars-i hayaat*, "Lessons from life." The title page explained that it was "a complete curriculum of an enlightened lesson in dying for Allah and in living for Allah" (Muhammad Fakhru'd-din 1972). For Muhammad Zakariyya the pedagogic potential of life stories was central.

In telling stories about himself and others, Muhammad Zakariyya deployed the conventional rhetorical strategies of the Persianate tradition for this genre, a rhetoric whose contours can perhaps most easily be seen by contrasting it to persistent themes in Anglo-American biographical writing (Lewis 1991; Hermansen 1988). In the latter, put simply, accounts focus on some singular figure, proceed chronologically, with the life presented as an unfolding, linear story, the fruit of "development" and "influences," in which the protagonist independently takes action and where the subject is distinguished by what makes him or her distinctive (Metcalf 1993b, 1995).

Muhammad Zakariyya presents *his* story with an approach that contrasts with this meta-narrative in at least three striking ways, in each drawing on a long heritage of Indo-Persian life story. First, his material is presented with no concern for chronological development, and, hence, for the presumed notion that a life makes sense in terms of the development that sequentially creates a particular personality and character. Rather, the focus is on a person whose essential character is a given and whose life story is best told by recounting episodes—anecdotes—which yield lessons for moral understanding. Second, the episodes do not show an actor identifying goals, making plans, overcoming obstacles, and progressively moving toward some kind of success—the cluster of activities that might be summed up as his demonstrating his "agency." Indeed, the rhetoric of the text suggests the opposite: a life fundamentally shaped by forces larger than one's self, above all by divine power evident in the charisma of elders to whom one owes allegiance, both living and dead.

Finally, and related to this, the material is not presented as Muhammad Zakariyya's exclusive story at all, but, throughout, as the story of his relations with other people. He counts, as part of *his* life, stories of the elders he has interacted with or whom he, in turn, knows from stories recounted by others. Indeed, one might say that the "autobiography" is not much about Muhammad Zakariyya at all. Muhammad Zakariyya's own life gains significance not by individuality but by devotion to a particular pattern exemplified in specific anecdotal evidence about model figures both living and dead.

The strength of such a genre for didactic ends is clear. No specific set of circumstances, no crucial stages in development, no particular sociological or historical conjuncture is deemed necessary to live as one should. In Indo-Muslim culture, or perhaps Islamic or Indic cultures generally, a particularly pervasive way of thinking about the person is an assumption of the given-ness of personal qualities. In this model, which resonates with old Eurasian humoral theories, a person is endowed with certain qualities that persist throughout life. Since character does not develop over time, there is no need for chronology or for dwelling particularly on childhood—as autobiographers informed by Romantic individualism and subjectivism unfailingly do. Each person has a temperament but, whatever it is, in the logic espoused by Muhammad Zakariyya, it can be used constructively to seek out and respect those who follow Prophetic examples, both to receive their blessing and to aspire to live as they do. Disrespectful and undisciplined students, whose actions spurred Muhammad Zakariyya to write in the first place, had no excuse.

Aap Biitii yaa Yaad-i Ayyaam

These characteristics of life stories—the goal of instruction, the passivity of the subject, the inclusion of stories of other people—all made Zakariyya's autobiographical venture less an act of hubris than, arguably, one of humility. The *Aap Biitii*, moreover, was initiated under duress. In 1963, Muhammad Zakariyya had been denounced in print when his seminary was torn by student unrest. The first volume includes a reply from the principal, Muhammad Zakariyya's own reply, and a section he subsequently compiled of anecdotes about the dedication and abstemiousness of the elders of the school. In 1968, Muhammad Zakariyya added to these three documents yet another response to work written about him, this time, surprisingly, by one of his admirers. Neither of the "offending" documents was included in the volume.

Then, in 1970, while recovering from eye surgery in Aligarh and unable to undertake his scholarly work, Muhammad Zakariyya, by now a man in his eighth decade, in a compressed period of only eighteen days began dictating stories about his life which would ultimately comprise Volumes Two through Five of his *Aap Biitii*. When he came to publish these writings in response to many requests, he began the compendium with the original *Aap Biitii*, now labeled "Volume One," and called the first of the new volumes, *Yaad-i Ayyaam*, "Memories of Days [Past], Volume One; *yaa* [or] *Aap Biitii* Volume Two." The work is typically known, however, as the *Aap Biitii*, and it is that title and numbering that is used here.

He began Volume Two with a discussion of the centrality of right intention, an abiding theme in Sufi guidance. This triggered the memory of a conversation he had had on this subject with a political leader who ultimately became his disciple. This in turn stimulated a section on the restrictions he had placed on student involvement in political activities, which he saw as part of what had undermined student behavior in his day. He then wrote at length on his own studies, his daily routines, his teaching practices, and a list of his eighty-three writings with notes on the context of their production. Implicitly, he offered a testimonial to a life of extraordinary discipline and devotion. In Volume Three, he retold stories of his "bad habits," followed by accounts of his "sorrows and joy," an organizing strategy that recalls the oral genre of women's life stories as reported in ethnographic accounts of this geographic area (Grima 1992; Narayan this volume).

In Volume Four Muhammad Zakariyya returned to stories of the elders he was privileged to know over four eras, presented successively in terms of the "favors of Allah" directed toward the author through them. He also included a collection of letters these elders had written to him and a travel account of five of his own visits to the holy places of Mecca and Medina. In Volume Five Muhammad Zakariyya wrote of his own heart-rending experience of Partition, primarily in Delhi, followed by exemplary stories, once again, of elders he had known and of others known through the Islamic tradition.

Volume Six, well over a thousand pages, represents the longest volume of the work. Muhammad Zakariyya explained that he thought that he had ended the *Aap Biitii*, but that between the imploring of his friends and the stories reverberating in his head, he had decided to continue with more stories about the elders beyond those he personally knew. He organized these stories not by individuals, as he had done earlier, but by moral qualities illustrative of the ideals of a holy life.

Finally, in Volume Seven, completed the year before he died, he provided virtually a journal of his final years set in India, Pakistan, and the Holy Places. Overall, the *Aap Biitii* is an overflowing and heterogeneous approach to talking about one's "own life" and could hardly be more different from the linear, developmentally organized, representation of individual lives in conventional biographies and autobiographies written in the modern West.

Maulana Abu'l Hasan Ali Nadwi ("Ali Miyan," 1914–2000), his biographer, identified three subjects that Muhammad Zakariyya had sought to report: "the episodes of his life that offered instruction; the perfections, and conduct of life of his teachers and shaikhs; and, finally, episodes of 'sincerity and sacrifice.'" Ali Miyan continued that the end product was "a speaking picture, and living, breathing image" of an age now past (Abu'l Hasan Ali 1982: 106). This last comment reminds us why a reformist like Muhammad Zakariyya, for whom it was so problematic to have texts or representations focused on their own person or lives, wrote at all. He wrote about the past in order to shore up the present, writing about "days gone by" not with nostalgia but with ramrod conviction to transform the present.

Muhammad Zakariyya lived in a dense network of learned and holy men, dead and alive, whose teachings, charisma, and interactions formed the texture of his world. He was closely related to leading political figures of the day, among them Maulana Husain Ahmad Madani, the leader of the Jamiyyat Ulama-i Hind, which had allied with the Indian National Congress, and Sayyid Atau'llah Shah Bukhari, leader of the Ahrar. But their political world was on the margins of what was important to him, and he focused on what he took to be eternal models of behavior that looked primarily within. He wrote about his life not to talk about himself but because he thought the kind of life he represented was at risk, not least from the new generation of students who, he believed, should have been its guardians but who, instead, gave way to worldly tastes and political distractions.

The "Strike" and the Defense of Proper Relationships

The beginnings of the *Aap Biitii* merit careful attention because they are profoundly revealing about what Muhammad Zakariyya took to be central to his life. As Ali Miyan concluded, what was central to him was the seminary itself. It was the site of his own "education and training,

his intellectual and ethical development, and his acquisition of knowledge and excellence." It was, moreover, the only means, in his opinion,
"for preservation of religious knowledge, true guidance for Muslims,
and prevention of corruption of belief and action." The *madrasa* was
"the focus of his thought and attention, the site of his imaginings and
hopes, and the refuge of his soul." And from the seminary stemmed the
relationships that "were dearer than his own life and family" (Abu'l
Hasan Ali 1982: 226). Nothing made Muhammad Zakariyya angrier
than a student "strike" (the English word was always used) which risk-
ed what to him held value over any worldly or political institution or
gain. Muhammad Zakariyya's overriding goal in the *Aap Biitii* was to
recall students to a time when students obeyed their teachers with
fidelity and love.

The seminary mattered because of the kind of people who were
there and the kind of people who had gone before. Both the strikers
and their opponents focused on personal behavior. The strikers' polemical attacks singled out Muhammad Zakariyya himself. The then
principal, Maulana Muhammad Asadu'llah, had been reluctant to
dignify the attack with a response, in part because he had assumed the
author to be using a pseudonym and claiming a non-existent organization. "When the attack was first published," Asadu'llah wrote, "I
ignored it because of its frivolity and shallowness, and I assumed that
all those who knew the school and the Shaikh would too. Indeed, I assumed that such an attack would, if anything, increase people's bonds
[to the Shaikh]" (Muhammad Zakariyya 1969: 4). But then when the
report came to be widely circulated, Asadu'llah felt he had to make a
public statement, although he knew "it would be a burden to the
Shaikh," whose forgiveness for writing he therefore sought.

The strikers apparently made four devastating accusations against
Muhammad Zakariyya: imperiousness; (greed for) wealth; (quest for)
absolute power; and favoring his own people. The strikers in short denied him the qualities that defined model religious leadership: humility, self-denial in worldly goods, withdrawal from worldly power, and
openness toward all without discrimination. Maulana Asadu'llah cut
to the heart of the matter in his answer. Muhammad Zakariyya, he
flatly stated, reproduced in his life the pattern of the great figures of
old: Asadu'llah called him *baqiyu's-salaf,* a "reminder" or "remnant" of
the ancestors. Far from materialist in his goals, he listed his disciplined and sacrificial services to the *sharia*: his scholarly works on *hadith*
known throughout the world, and his teaching at the Mazahir coupled

with his dedication as "spiritual patron" to the members of the biggest and most far-reaching religious movement among Muslims in the world, "known as Tabligh," whose leading figures, because of him, support and bring their blessed presence to the Mazahir.[6] He provided explicit details of Muhammad Zakariyya's financial arrangements with the school and his gifts to it. He described how Muhammad Zakariyya interrupted his scholarly work for no one. He invoked his very "personality" and "nature" to refute the accusations that he was a person who sought power.

Asadu'llah turned the final charge on its head. The attack claimed that Muhammad Zakariyya favored his own people. In fact, it was a blessing that all the trustees of the school had been in a relation of "belief" in him and "love" for him. As it happened, Asadu'llah continued, they had chosen him, not he, them. As for the teachers and employees, they shared in his circle and he was nothing less than "the entry way to the very grace of Allah himself." The strikers had missed the point. Muhammad Zakariyya was a link in great chains of spiritual blessing of his elders and teachers, a recipient of their blessing and a channel of blessing to those who in turn looked to them. His disciplined labor and his relation to material wealth was, moreover, not motivated by acquisition. Whatever he happened to have flowed through him to others. This is a recurrent image of the Sufi *pir*, who is a font of material largesse with no obvious source of income of his own.

When Muhammad Zakariyya replied, he limited himself to two incidental statements in the pamphlet, points Asadu'llah had not even taken into account, one of fact and one of interpretation, which clearly troubled Muhammad Zakariyya greatly. The first was the charge that he had forbidden the *madrasa* to provide the striking students with food. The second was that he had severed the bond of Sufi initiation with supporters of the strike. As for the first, he made an absolute denial that he had intervened to deny the students food, and, to show how far that accusation was from the truth, he pointed out that he himself had fed the strikers at his own table. As for the second complaint of severing Sufi initiation, he embraced the charge with enthusiasm as "completely true" (Muhammad Zakariyya 1969: 73).

Muhammad Zakariyya justified his response by invoking the reaction of two great elders, Maulana Husain Ahmad Madani and Maulana Ashraf Ali Thanawi (1864–1943), who had recommended expulsion of striking students in earlier strikes at the "mother" *madrasa* of Deoband going back four decades. To explain further, however, he reports Hazrat Madani's emotional reaction, during one of the earlier strikes, to seeing Muhammad Zakariyya with one of the strikers from Deoband (whom he did not in fact know to have been involved). Just as Madani was upset then, Muhammad Zakariyya describes himself as filled with hatred now when he sees the very faces of the strikers (Muhammad Zakariyya 1969: 73–5). Under these circumstances, what benefit could there be to initiation and why should these people stop their own spiritual progress? Muhammad Zakariyya cites *hadith* that describe the Prophet's great love for his wife Aisha, on the one hand, and his hatred for Hazrat Wahshi, on the other: hate and love are beyond control, he points out, even for the Prophet, and dependent on one's temperament which, in this tradition, as noted above, is a given and not a product of experience or environment (Muhammad Zakariyya 1969: 105–7). To use such capacity for hatred, or any other innate personality characteristic, to a legitimate end is to live as one ought—and here, from Muhammad Zakariyya's own perspective, his rage was being used to the good.

The students, "guests of the Prophet" as he ironically calls them, were the ones, Muhammad Zakariyya implies, who were motivated by a quest for materialism and worldly power. They wanted, he writes, fancier diplomas, a different kind of light in the courtyard, better food, courses in literature so they could sprinkle their discourses with fancy allusions, a "degree" so they could get employment! *This* is a student (*taalib-i ilm* or "seeker of knowledge"), he asks? He could not believe that his students, those whom he himself had taught from the *hadith* "the position, dignity, religious standing, and responsibility attendant on their position," could abandon their studies for such purposes (Muhammad Zakariyya 1969: 78). Muhammad Zakariyya had told the students under his influence that it was not legitimate for them to read newspapers; he had also opposed the formation of voluntary organizations in the *madrasa*. Such distractions, he felt, had cost students focus in their work. In a publication on an earlier strike quoted by Muhammad Zakariyya, Ashraf Ali had written that religious education itself was worship.

At the end of his statement, Muhammad Zakariyya summed up his argument, implicitly fitting himself into the Sufi model of openness and tolerance on the one hand, disciplined relations of submission and obedience on the other. His *table,* like the bountiful *langar* of the Sufi shrine, was open, even to non-Muslims (Muhammad Zakariyya 1969:

104–5).[7] *Baiat* was not. On this he quoted one of the student strikers who reportedly had said in words unthinkable for a disciple: "There's no shortage of *pirs* in the world," and, lest that seem bitter, he modestly added that he was not worthy of such rank in any case, despite the opinion and kindness of the elders. But, then, in a chilling finale, he categorized sin as being of two kinds, *shaitaanii* and *haiwanii*. The latter are sins of instinct and he had always, he said, for his forty years at the school, insisted that students who committed such sins be forgiven and reinstated. But the former sins, the sins of Iblis—par excellence those of pride, rebellion, and exaltation of the self—merited complete separation from the perpetrators. Maulana Thanawi, writing about an earlier strike, had identified its essence as "a breaking of relationships" (*qat-i taaluqaat*). Maulana Muhammad Zakariyya was ratifying what had already happened. Nothing in Muhammad Zakariyya's life mattered more to him than *taaluqaat*—to humans, to the Prophet, and to Allah—and for him these relationships were mediated through the Arabic *madrasa*. The striking students, in his view, were guilty not of rudeness to him, but of sundering their relation to the Prophet and Allah himself.

The Guidance of the Elders and the Temptations of Materialism and Pride

When Maulana Muhammad Zakariyya again wrote about himself, it was in response to someone widely regarded as the pre-eminent Muslim religious figure in India of the late twentieth century, Maulana Abu'l Hasan Ali Nadwi ("Ali Miyan") who, ironically, after Muhammad Zakariyya's death, would write his "official" biography (Abu'l Hasan Ali 1982). Ali Miyan, "ghost wrote" (Muhammad Zakariyya 1969: 24) an introductory chapter dealing with Muhammad Zakariyya at the request of the biographer of the second amir of the Tablighi Jamaat (who had died in 1965), Maulana Muhammad Yusuf Kandhalawi, Muhammad Zakariyya's beloved cousin and colleague (Muhammad Saani 1967). Such a chapter was (Muhammad Zakariyya 1969: 24) part of the conventional introduction to a biography in the Arabo-Persian tradition, which typically situates the subject in the context of his genealogy and family members.

In large part, Ali Miyan's account resonates with the broad themes sketched above as characteristic of Indo-Persian biography, in terms of seeing Muhammad Zakariyya's character as innately given, the key moments of his life as the product of divine intervention, and his life as a whole the model and memorial of the great figures of the past. Ali Miyan emphasizes not only his evident services to religious learning, but he also reports many marks of Allah's favor through divine signs. Muhammad Zakariyya was born in the holy month of Ramadan at the very time of the night prayer and thus received the blessings of the family and villagers gathered at an auspicious moment. His paternal grandfather, a great *aalim* (theologian) and saint, proclaimed that the new baby was his "replacement," and indeed he was to die that very month. He writes that Muhammad Zakariyya was the recipient of divine dreams and visions, and even underwent physical transformations when absorbed in teaching the *hadith* of the Prophet and when hearing of him or being in Medina. Something like a bolt of lightning would come on all present, especially when he finished teaching a book and prayed (Muhammad Saani 1967: 115). Maulana Muhammad Zakariyya himself, in his hundreds and hundreds of pages, described almost none of this.

Yet Ali Miyan, the cosmopolitan intellectual, also drew on Western theories of development and psychology. His presentation was largely chronological, and, as he would do more extensively in the full biography, he tried to analyze his subject's personality over his life course. Albeit only in footnotes, he raised the issue of upbringing, crediting Muhammad Zakariyya's father "with methods which would drive today's psychologists and educationists, who indulge a child's every whim and preach complete license, to distraction" (Muhammad Saani 1967: 78). Ali Miyan stressed the importance of the influence of environment on a child, in Muhammad Zakariyya's case the opportunity to live amidst holy and learned men in childhood. He identified Muhammad Zakariyya's "power of observation," evident in his stories of those days, with shaping his own life story, *aap biitii*, and his tastes. Indeed, Ali Miyan described Maulana Muhammad Zakariyya with several characteristics that were not the conventional paradigmatic virtues of a holy and learned person: among them, "courage," "capacity," and "breadth," by which he meant an ability to deal with multiple and conflicting demands on his energy and time. But he also characterized him by the trait which was that of the Sufi par excellence, namely, passion in his devotion to the Prophet.

What was there not to like? Muhammad Zakariyya did not mince words: the chapter about him was like a drop of urine in a bottle of rose-water that pollutes the rest. First of all, if anyone was going to tell his story, he was the one who would do it, and he invoked an Urdu couplet to say he would speak "his own reproach"—there is no need to listen to anyone else. "In the end, they will say: 'What more is there to say?'" And indeed in this section and throughout he emphasizes his flaws of temper, stubbornness, and unsociability as if to show the students, and others, that anyone could aspire to model behavior. Second, although more obscurely, he insisted that Ali Miyan had written "those matters which ought not to have been written about and left out those which should have been included" (Muhammad Zakariyya 1969: 24). Presumably by the reference to what should have been excluded he meant the marks of divine favor, since the reformists generally saw such signs either as a distraction from moral behavior for oneself or a motive for undue veneration of someone else. Perhaps he also disliked the very idea of his life presented in such an appreciative, chronologically un-folding, form. All he said, however, was that Ali Miyan "[had] written about Iran, Turan, and other foolish things which will not benefit anyone, whereas [what he now would include] were the things that were to be written about" (Muhammad Zakariyya 1969: 35).

As in his response to the striking students, Muhammad Zakariyya ignored most of the offending document and chose only two seem-ingly random points to respond to, in this case a four-page section oc-curring early in the chapter entitled "two delicate tests and divine grace," and, second, two footnotes on the subject of his father's "nur-ture" (Muhammad Saani 1967: 95–9; footnotes 78, 83). Muhammad Zakariyya expressed dismay that Ali Miyan, despite being informed about other trials and episodes of his upbringing, did not include them. Muhammad Zakariyya's response consisted of a retelling of five "tests," from his period of maturity, and their resolution, as well as eleven stories of his childhood upbringing. In short, he shifts the focus and the framework of his life by focusing on his own weaknesses and the importance of the love and blessing of Allah, his father and other elders in shaping his life.

Muhammad Zakariyya followed convention in making chrono-logical movement or development irrelevant. The episodes were not organized from the earliest to the latest. Muhammad Zakariyya, as in the narratives of "sorrows" noted above, identified the first set of episodes, in fact, explicitly as "trials" or "afflictions." Moreover, Muhammad Zakariyya did not suggest that he ever improved (Muhammad Zakariyya 1969: 31). Throughout, he displayed his flawed character, the instinctual reactions he had that he could not control. Only through Allah's grace, and the love and blessing of his father and other elders, were temptations resisted. Thanks to them he had "begun to be counted among humans, " but nothing had changed his character—any more, he says, than putting a dog's tail in a pipe makes it straight (Muhammad Zakariyya 1969: 33, 50, 52). This is not a story of Muhammad Zakariyya's own agency or development.

Muhammad Zakariyya first recounted an episode which occurred three days after his father's death when he declined an opportunity presented to him by his father's great shaikh and mentor, Maulana Abdu'r Rahim Raipuri (d. 1919–20), who transmitted to him an offer to move his father's bookshop to a situation where he would have had had expert advice and help. His father had died leaving a substantial debt, and now Muhammad Zakariyya had not only that burden to deal with, but also the responsibility of maintenance for his mother and sister. Hearing this proposal, Muhammad Zakariyya said, he felt the very earth sink beneath him. He rejected the proposal on the grounds that he could not move to a place distant from his own spiritual guide. In fact, Hazrat Raipuri was pleased with this answer and blessed him, explaining that he had spoken only because of the insistence of yet another elder who had made that offer, someone who could indeed help, but who also wished Muhammad Zakariyya close by. At this, Muhammad Zakariyya was enraged, and this reaction he saw as his fault, repaying kindness with anger.

Three other episodes involved his turning down generous offers of employment. To an offer from Hyderabad that would have given him perhaps thirty-fold his salary at the Mazahir, he wrote only one line, "It is not for me to be dependent on favors" (Muhammad Zakariyya 1969: 30). To an offer from Bengal, shortly before Partition, he again wrote back a curt one line. He regretted his emotional make-up that produced such responses but attributed his refusals as an escape from temptation owed only to Allah, who, like his elders, showed him kindness.

In turning to trials earlier in his life, he reported his response to an offer of marriage into a rich family when he was still a child:

The name of Mirza Surya Jaah is often mentioned in the life stories of Muhammad Ilyas and Muhammad Yusuf. He had great affection for my grandfather, Maulana Muhammad Ismail, and he wanted his daughter, Qaisar Jahan Begum, to marry my father. My grandfather, in fact, did not want this marriage, and my father concurred. Nonetheless, my father and uncle kept up very close relations with Qaisar Jahan Begum and visited her house often. When I went there as a child, she would wrap me up carefully and put me to sleep with her. She would say to my father, " You turned me down, but he is my child and he should marry my daughter." My father retorted, "How can I choose for him what I turned down for myself?" She still persisted. As a test, my father asked me my opinion. I blurted out that it would be beyond me to walk around serving a *paandaan*!

The story behind this was that Qaisar Jahan's husband loved her devotedly, and he did, indeed, prepare and offer her *paan* (betel). This was a shocking sight to Muhammad Zakariyya, as he explained, since in his family the women did the serving. His father was not pleased with the answer and said it had a whiff of arrogance about it. When he himself had been asked about marrying into the family, he had answered more appropriately, "If I marry that princess, I will not be able to sleep on a rough mat," that is, he wanted a humble life. Muhammad Zakariyya concluded that his father was right (Muhammad Zakariyya 1969: 31–3).

Muhammad Zakariyya continued with the stories of his upbringing, stories that presumably sprang readily to his pen since, he explained, he loved telling them and would recount them while teaching. These were, moreover, only a selection: he could, he declared, in a reference that evoked his pleasure in storytelling, write an entire "Arabian Nights" of such stories! These stories, like the earlier episode, invariably showed Muhammad Zakariyya in the context of relationships of protection and blessing, and, like them, they parade his flaws of anger, distractions in pleasure, and pride. Again, however, thanks to Allah and his elders, he claims to have escaped temptation, which, again, like employment and the wrong kind of marriage, for the most part revolved around material lures.

In the stories, Muhammad Yahya, Muhammad Zakariyya's father, slapped a toddler who offered him his cherished embroidered pillow but called it "mine." He mercilessly beat an eight-year-old who caused a disruption to prayer by resisting help. He beat him again for praying when he should have been studying. He prohibited him from keeping money, or accepting any food or drink. He investigated all matters involving money or potential lying. He withdrew the promise of an excursion because the boy was too excited at the prospect. Muhammad Zakariyya learned to "re-gift" any beautiful clothes that came his way after his father's fury at his being dressed extravagantly by the family's womenfolk.

The whole account was permeated with court-like rhetoric, with behavior referred to as "crimes," the matter that led to a beating being staged as a "trial" until the truth came out, the father's rules for behavior termed "*qaanuun.*" The judicial rhetoric was mutual. When Muhammad Yahya accepted an invitation to visit a friend, he wrote—with Muhammad Zakariyya's own pen, the latter adds—that now the leg irons of Muhammad Zakariyya, a chain that had held him in place, had finally been lifted. By this, he later explained to Muhammad Zakariyya—who had written of how he missed him and feared harm to himself in his absence—his presence was no longer necessary since now Muhammad Zakariyya had established his own close communication with Allah. He humbly prayed in response that Allah make this opinion true (Muhammad Zakariyya 1969: 53).

In the final section of this volume Muhammad Zakariyya provided a document written for the teachers and leaders of the school, consisting of fifteen episodes, given as examples, relating to the elders of the Mazaahiru'l-Uluum (Muhammad Zakariyya 1969: 54–71). These were stories, he said, that he feared would no longer be remembered as the older generation passed away. It was his *aap biitii* in the sense that it included "whatever [he] had seen or heard about the elders during [his] sixty years at the school, from the time he was a student at the age of thirteen to the present" (Muhammad Zakariyya 1969: 54). It was meant to offer lessons in the "strictness" and "punctiliousness" of the elders: above all, their extraordinary scrupulousness in the use of the *madrasa*'s resources, their punctuality, high standards of teaching, and penury. The document surely served to strengthen the side of the current leadership as they associated themselves with such worthy exemplars of the school's elders. Indeed, Muhammad Zakariyya himself, though he could never counter his attackers directly by citing his own virtues, by writing about the virtues of those he personally knew, could indirectly identify himself with their distinctions. As for the image he presented of himself, he succeeded in both showing how even he, flawed as he was, escaped the damning lures of materialism and world-ly ambitions thanks to accepting the blessing and guidance of Allah and his elders.

A Sufi in the Modern World

In the classic categorization of Muslim religious leadership as either Sufi or scholar/*aalim*, Muhammad Zakariyya would likely be assigned the status of an *aalim*. He was, after all, a formidably learned scholar of Prophetic tradition and an eminent teacher in a major seminary for most of the twentieth century. But, as I have argued elsewhere, if this dichotomy of types of leadership holds in some contexts, it does not for many schools of *ulama* in modern India, where a "composite" type of leadership, albeit tilting in one direction or the other, is common (Metcalf 1982; also Sanyal 1996). The face that Muhammad Zakariyya explicitly and implicitly presents of himself in this extraordinary work, so lengthy and presumably so unstudied, is, perhaps surprisingly, in fact one that resonates deeply with paradigmatic models of the world-renouncing Sufi that are familiar across Muslim societies, but not necessarily associated, as they were in the India of this period, with *ulama*.[8]

Muhammad Zakariyya in fact was well known for his opposition to students' becoming Sufi disciples and engaging in the time-consum-ing disciplines of *zikr* and *shugl* because he feared that would interfere with their studies. Moreover, like other Deobandis, he did not parti-cipate in the customary *urs* celebrations or encourage pilgrimage to the graves of holy men. He was not well known as a channel of miracles or healing. He claimed to have no liking for amulets (Muhammad Zakariyya 1996: vol. 5: 315). Yet, for all that, in other ways his life seems to have had Sufi experiences and teachings at its heart. The long pages of his autobiography are filled, line upon line, with references to his relationships to elders whose light and blessing he sought and lived in. Those associated with the *madrasa* at Saharanpur, among countless others, were particularly devoted to two great Sufis, Hazrat Maulana Abdu'r Rahim Raipuri, and his son, Hazrat Maulana Abdu'l Qadir Raipuri (d. 1955), with whom both Zakariyya and his father had pro-found and enduring bonds. Muhammad Zakariyya's own shaikh and guide was Hazrat Maulana Khalil Ahmad Saharanpuri. At several points in the *Aap Biitii* he wrote at length on technical issues in the relationships of saints and their disciples, providing dramatic examples he himself had seen, or heard of, among great saints of the past on the transfer of *nisbat* (Muhammad Zakariyya 1993: vol. 4: 156; 1996: 419–36). His response to the strikers engaged issues, par excellence, of the Sufi: the open table and the initiatory bond.

Of the many stories he included of what he always called his own shaikh's "favors" to him, one in particular gives a sense of the depth of the relationship coupled with the wit and affection that fills so many of the stories. Muhammad Zakariyya notes that he tells this particular story only because friends pressed him to. Once, during a discussion of the elders and paradise, Zakariyya describes himself as unduly bold in asserting to Hazrat Saharanpuri what he had to take with him when he entered paradise, to which his shaikh immediately agreed. Some time later, Hazrat Saharanpuri arrived at the *madrasa* while Zakariyya was teaching and went off with someone else for refreshments at a nearby house. Zakariyya protested that the person should have waited for him, whereby Hazrat Saharanpuri said, "I did not promise to take you everywhere; the place where I promised to take you, there I will take you." Since that episode, Zakariyya writes, hope for mercy had driven out fear (Muhammad Zakariyya n.d.a: vol. 4: 92). To accept the blessing of the shaikh meant acceptance of his authority as well, an acceptance Zakariyya embraced, and the current generation of students did not.

The rhetoric of the entire account fosters an interpretation of events characteristic of Sufism that suggests a kind of passivity to events. The very term *aap biitii* has at root the meaning of "what has happened to one" and particularly "an account of one's sorrows," that is, a focus on events like deaths that are indeed beyond one's shaping or control (Ahmad 1974 [1896]; Fallon 1986 [1879]). Muhammad Zakariyya reacts to attacks, responds to readers' demands, and, most importantly, claims to shape his life and activities at the direction of the elders. He explicitly worried about predestination and concluded that indeed the end is beyond one's control but the route open. To illustrate this, he provided several examples, including a pedestrian one along the lines of being a person fated to eat chicken, a food of the rich. This could be the result of becoming rich oneself; becoming a "*hazratji*" and given such gifts—like himself in fact; or simply be someone else's cook. He did "fieldwork" to reach this conclusion, questioning people who came to him for amulets: they spoke freely about their lives, assuming he needed the answers to help him (Muhammad Zakariyya 1971a: 150–1).

Although the Deobandis were circumspect about visits to graves, Zakariyya, who relished time spent in *zikr*, especially loved recitation at the grave of Hazrat Hafiz Zamin, a nineteenth-century saint. He also tells of a time when traveling in Punjab when he found himself at the grave of the great reformist saint Shaikh Ahmad Sirhindi (1564–1624). He was traveling with relatives to a wedding. "After reaching Sirhind Shariif, I remembered nothing. I do not know how I got off the train and how the ticket inspector let me off the platform without a ticket. Soon I found myself at the grave of Hazrat Mujaddid Sahib . . . The whole day I remained there at the latticed screen behind the grave . . ." When he got home all he could do was explain that he himself did not know how he got there or returned.

Intrinsic to the charisma of the Sufi is belief that he lives a life of discipline and self-denial. Muhammad Zakariyya's discipline focused around his teaching and writing, which no worldly goal could disrupt and which was so intense that mealtimes or sleep could be missed unaware; all his elders, he noted, had great bodily control over waking and sleep (Muhammad Zakariyya 1996: 89). During Ramadan his devotional practices were unrelenting. Once a person who came to see him simply gave up. "Through Allah's grace the month of Ramadan occurs where we live too," he said, "but for us it doesn't take the form of a fever!"(Muhammad Zakariyya 1993: 86) He lived simply, his one-room house of mud-baked brick explicitly compared to the house of the Prophet Muhammad (Muhammad Zakariyya 1996: 52). He rejoiced in a student so dedicated that he forsook his curry to eat dry bread so that he could continue studying (Muhammad Zakariyya 1996: 131).

A contemporary Sufi might boast that he differed from the *ulama* who were salaried employees, receivers, not givers (Werbner 2001: 153). But as the episodes of his youth show, Muhammad Zakariyya similarly resisted salaries and financial dependence.

Although constrained to accept a salary from the *madrasa*, he ultimately (through the blessing of the second Hazrat Raipuri, he explains) was able to decline the salary for teaching (Muhammad Zakariyya 1996: 29) and in due course rejoiced that he was able to repay whatever had come from the *madrasa* entirely. Many of his anecdotes showed how scrupulous the elders were in relation to the resources of the school. Muhammad Zakariyya's economy seems to have had as its principle trust in Allah coupled with acceptance of unsolicited gifts and loans, repaid by rolling over more loans (Muhammad Zakariyya 1996: 106). That his father died indebted hardly seems surprising. Muhammad Zakariyya explained how, as a mark of God's great blessing, when he and his party were penniless in the Hijaz, a fellow Indian, worried about the Bedouins, asked him to keep his considerable wealth until they returned to India. With this money, Muhammad Zakariyya could meet his party's urgent needs, confident that resources would appear to repay the trust when he got home (Muhammad Zakariyya 1996: 205). Muhammad Zakariyya's scrupulousness in relation to finances was premised on a belief that any dishonesty would reap instant punishment: he claims to have observed in his lifetime, for example, the illnesses, law suits, and thefts experienced by those who had misused the resources of the *madrasa*.

Zakariyya's approach to finance was not without controversy. He was berated by younger relatives in Kandhla for living off charity when he could have had a salary. Muhammad Zakariyya confessed to having shown some undue pride when, later, that same relative saw him solve a property issue for the family by his mere presence (Muhammad Zakariyya 1993: 137–40). He was also the despair of his bookshop manager since he refused to deal with colonial courts and copyright on the one hand, and continued to ruin his budget by feeding all comers on the other (Muhammad Zakariyya 1993: 339). Like the classic Sufi, whatever he had was meant to be given away. He had resources, he was able to feed others, he provided gifts for weddings, and he ate well himself—his self-denial did not always extend to food (Muhammad Zakariyya 1996: 62). Little wonder that the strikers were confused into thinking he was misusing school resources.

More like a Sufi than like the stereotype of the *aalim* were, as well, his relations to competing schools of *ulama* and politics. The *ulama* are thought to be strident defenders of minute points of difference, engaging in "fatwa wars" of mutual denunciation (Werbner 2001: 330). Muhammad Zakariyya, in contrast, said that he looked upon differences among the *ulama* as a mercy (Muhammad Zakariyya 1996: 119) and he wrote at length about his good relations to the rival reformist school, the Ahl-i Hadith (Muhammad Zakariyya 1996: 323–7). He approvingly told an apparently well-known story urging those "in a high position of academic activity or in Sufism or in any other religious service" to look down on no one, even warning against those who out of pride looked down on non-Muslims (Muhammad Zakariyya 1996: 444). As for politics, he strove to be open to all sides and speaks of his motivations as being shaped more by his connections and love than by ideology. He explains wearing the homespun of the nationalist movement in terms of his devotion to Hazrat Madani (Muhammad Zakariyya 1993: 363 and 1996: 77). The quietist *ulama*, like the Sufis, have seen their interests best served by the pluralist, liberal state, with whom they cooperate pragmatically. Indeed, Muhammad Zakariyya wrote a critique of the foremost Islamist of the subcontinent, Maulana Maududi (Muhammad Zakariyya 1971a: 159–60).

Quietism does not mean being apolitical. Although Muhammad Zakariyya discouraged students from being involved in political activities, he pointed out in one case that students at the *madrasa* could learn all they needed very quickly once their studies were over since politics had the place of a maidservant "in our house!" (Muhammad Zakariyya 1993: 73). In Zakariyya's account of his relations with the leader of the Ahrar movement there are hints of the classic Sufi fable of the political leader who always comes to see the superior power of the holy man, a further suggestion that political connections are inevitable yet meant to be kept in their place (Muhammad Zakariyya 1993: 59–63).

The anthropologist Pnina Werbner, in her study of a late-twentieth-century Sufi, identified her subject's key characteristics as being "entertaining, authoritative, capable of fearful anger, and mischievous" (Werbner 2001: 336). All these characteristics readily apply to Muhammad Zakariyya, including a quite remarkable streak of "holy foolishness," shared by his companions, that one might not expect. To take only one account, he describes a visit to the household of the daughter of Hazrat Maulana Rashid Ahmad Gangohi (d. 1905), the great Deobandi elder. In the company of Maulana Ilyas, the founder of Tablighi Jamaat, and Maulana Madani, the three turned the household upside down. Welcomed into the ladies' section of the house, they playfully ate all the fine dishes brought to them so that each time a family member went to fetch the bread, he would return to find all the food meant to be eaten with it already gone. Finally Hazrat Rashid Ahmad's daughter, whom they all cherished, appeared herself to tease them that for three worthies addressed by others as "hazrat" they actually were all still children (Muhammad Zakariyya 1993: 24–6).

What did it mean that Muhammad Zakariyya, in presenting himself in all these many dimensions, embraced the Indo-Persian rhetoric with its dominant characteristic of passivity? In a recent study Jill Ker Conway identified the Western autobiographical tradition of individualism, achievement and overcoming obstacles as a primarily male story, with roots in Greek myth. The female story, she points out, rooted in women's medieval spiritual autobiographies, emphasizes passivity, reliance on the will of God, and the importance of enabling relationships with both God and elders. Indeed this "relational," rather than "positional" or "linear," writing is often taken as key to women's self-narratives (Peterson 1993: 82). In these stories there is no place for claims to leadership or agency, and the writer is likely to engage in self-deprecation. Conway speculates that the stories may be one thing and "real" events another, the stories just strategically deployed to make the actions and the life of the narrator acceptable, particularly if the subject is undertaking novel or controversial activities (Conway 1998; see also Margadant 2000).

It is tempting to explore this perspective in the case of Maulana Zakariyya, particularly since others regard Maulana Zakariyya's life story as one of leadership and success. Maulana Asadu'llah describes, for example, his role in shaping the affairs of the Tabligh movement and expanding the *madrasa*. Zakariyya himself recounts situations where he is clearly responsible for the outcome, though he presents himself as wholly passive. He attributes the majority of his books to the request of some elder: but the fact remains that he wrote dozens of books. He defies family conventions, for example in arranging marriage partners. In what sense is all this "passivity?"

Rather than see rhetoric as one thing, however, and reality as the other, rhetoric may be the reality. The strong modern European assumption that individuals seek freedom from submission and constraint, for example, as imposed by the traditions of religion, colors the assumption that the rhetoric is a cover. In fact, there are other traditions, including the one represented by Zakariyya and by the Islamic tradition he espoused. In this tradition, we encounter strong individuals—though not individual*ism*—yet an energetic commitment to, and pleasure, even passion, for disciplined submission (to Allah and to elders) that entails disciplined action. This, too, is "agency." And there is pleasure in the life, and the stories of the lives, that result.

This pleasure, even passion, becomes the driving force for the disciplined behavior and focus that link the believer to his elders, to the Prophet, and to Allah. "Passion," not "passivity," may be seen as the key to the disciplined submission that is Zakariyya's goal and his source of purpose in his world.

The substance of his life, as Maulana Zakariyya writes it, is the study of *hadith*, which ties him to the Prophet and thence to Allah, and the sustaining, remembering, performing, and cherishing of "enabling relations," to use Conway's term, with his elders both living and dead. He cherishes their kindnesses; and he longs to be with them during the holy month of Ramadan, on *hajj*, in scholarly service to them, or at any time of illness or need. He assigns the Id sacrifice to their benefit; he seeks their intercessory prayer; he rejoices at their visits; he hopes to be present at the all-important moment of their death; and then he welcomes their posthumous visitation in dreams. His is a life dense with scholarship and dense with (male) relationships. As in Western male biographies, there is little space given to private life except for a few touching accounts of the deaths of his womenfolk intended for the moral lessons they yield as examples of a blessed and auspicious death that confirms *their* relations to Allah and his Prophet. An aunt, for example, dies joyous as she sees the Prophet approach (Muhammad Zakariyya 1971b: 304).

What emerges from the account is the life of a person of extraordinary discipline and dedication, for whom every moment was a precious opportunity for worship, service to learning, and devotion to his elders. His life moved between intense concentration on his scholarly work and life in the midst of networks of the holy and learned. He insisted on his many flaws, a way of counterbalancing what might otherwise seem undue pride at writing at all, and, of course, he said nothing of the signs of divine favor or a pattern of God-given excellences that made him a "reminder of the ancestors." Nor did he give anything like the picture, so evocatively drawn by Ali Miyan, of his role in the lives of thousands of disciples, devotees, and participants in the pietist movement of "internal conversion," Tablighi Jamaat, for which he served as a pivotal figure, a source of guidance and blessing.

Not only Maulana Zakariyya, but his autobiography, like other life histories of the holy, was considered by his followers to be a source of blessing, *baraka,* the very words on the page a source of charisma. In this logocentric tradition, words always have power. The texts are interactive, most obviously when read aloud. Not only, however, does *baraka* flow to the reader; the reader in return may be stimulated to good actions that redound to the credit of the author or are explicitly requested by the author. At one point in this text, for example, Maulana Zakariyya breaks his narrative to address readers directly, asking them to make intercessory prayer, and transfer of merit, to those three dozen or so people in his life who were initially opposed to him but then turned their enmity to devotion. It would be, he says, a kind service to him to do so (Muhammad Zakariyya 1969: 2: 83–4).

The autobiography is an invitation to its readers to confirm, or make an empowering choice to voluntarily accept, rules more stringent than those of any bureaucracy or state they may be embedded in. This kind of life is sanctioned by the precedent of the great elders of the past, and holds out the promise of relationships with them and with those who continue their tradition. Readers—whether in India or beyond—are enjoined to find transcendent meaning in the routines of everyday life, the presence of a moral community, and the promise of future rewards, their own lives shaped by, and shaping, the kind of relationships whose stories Maulana Zakariyya loved to tell.

References

Abu'l-Hasan Ali Nadwi. 1982 [1944]. *Hazrat maulaana muhammad ilyaas aur un kii diinii dawat.* Lucknow: Al Furqaan.

———. 1982. *Hazrat shaikhu'l- hadiis maulaana muhammad zakariyya* Lucknow.

Ahmad Dihlawi, Sayyid. 1974 [1896]. *Farhang-i asafiiya.* 4 vols. Delhi: National Academy.

Asghar Husain, Sayyid. 1920–1. *Hayaat-i shaikhu'l hind.* 2nd edn. Deoband.

Conway, Jill Ker. 1998. *When Memory Speaks: Reflections on Autobiography.* New York: Knopf.

Darnton, Robert. 2001. "Literary Surveillance in the British Raj: The Contradictions of Liberal Imperialism." *Book History* 4: 133–76.

Fallon, S. W. 1986 [1879]. *A New Hindustani-English Dictionary.* Lucknow: Uttar Pradesh Urdu Academy.

Faruqi, Ziya-ul-Hasan. 1963. *The Deoband School and the Demand for Pakistan.* Bombay: Asia Publishing House.

Grima, Benedicte. 1992. *The Performance of Emotion among Paxtun Women: "The Misfortunes which have Befallen Me."* Austin: University of Texas Press.

Haq, M. Anwarul. 1972. *The Faith Movement of Maulana Muhammad Ilyas.* London: Allen and Unwin.

Hermansen, Marcia K. 1988. "Interdisciplinary Approaches to Islamic Biographical Materials." *Religion* 18: 163–82.

Husain Ahmad Madani. 1953. *Naqsh-i hayaat.* 2 vols. Deoband: Maktaba-i diiniyya.

Lewis, Bernard. 1991. "First-person Narrative in the Middle East." In M. Kramer (ed.), *Middle Eastern Lives: The Practice of Biography and Self-Narrative,* pp. 20–34. Syracuse: Syracuse University Press.

Margadant, Jo Burr (ed.). 2000. *The New Biography: Performing Femininity in Nineteenth-Century France.* Berkeley: University of California Press.

Manaazir Ahsan Giilaani. 1955–6. *Sawaanih-i qaasimii.* 3 vols. Deoband: Daftar-i daaru'l ulum.

Masud, Muhammad Khalid (ed.). 1999. *Travellers in Faith: Studies of Tablighi Jamaat as a Transnational Movement.* Leiden: Brill.

Mayaram, Shail. 1997. *Resisting Regimes: Myth, Memory and the Shaping of Muslim Identity.* Delhi: Oxford University Press.

Metcalf, Barbara D. 1982. *Islamic Revival in British India: Deoband, 1860–1900.* Princeton: Princeton University Press.

———. 1990. *Perfecting Women: Maulana Ashraf 'Ali Thanawi's "Bihishti Zewar."* Berkeley: University of California Press.

———. 1993a. "Living Hadith in the Tablighi Jamaat." *Journal of Asian Studies* 52: 584–608.

———. 1993b. "Remembering Mecca: Mumtaz Mufti's *Labbaik.*" In Robert Folkenflik (ed.), *Autobiography and Self-Representation,* pp. 149–67. Stanford: Stanford University Press.

———. 1994. " 'Remaking Ourselves': Islamic Self-fashioning in a Global Movement of Spiritual Renewal." In Martin E. Marty and R. Scott Appleby (eds), *Accounting for Fundamentalism.* Chicago: University of Chicago Press.

———. 1995. "Narrating Lives: A Mughal Empress, a French Nabob, a Nationalist Muslim Intellectual." *Journal of Asian Studies* 54: 474–80.

Muhammad Abdu'l-hayy. 1972. *Maasir-i hakiimu'l-ummat.* Gaya: Daaru'l-kutab imdaadiyya.

Muhammad Aashiq Ilaahi Miirathii. n.d. a. *Tazkiratu'l khaliil.* Saharanpur: Ishhaatu'l ulum muhammad muftii.

———. n.d. b. *Tazkiratu'r rashiid.* 2 vols. Meerut: Maktaba-i aashiqiyya.

Muhammad Fakhru'd-diin. 1972. *Dars-i hayaat.* Gaya: Madani kutub khaana.

Muhammad Saani Hasani. 1967. *Sawaanih-i hazrat maulaana muhammad yuusuf kandhlawii.* Lucknow: Nadwatu'l-ulama.

Muhammad Zakariyya Kandhalawi. 1969. *Hazrat shaikh aur un kii aap biitii.* New Delhi: Idaara-yi ishhat-i diinyaat.

————. 1971a. *Aap biitii nambar 2 yaa yaad-i ayaam nambar 1.* Saharanpur: Kutbkhaana Yahyawii.

————. 1971b. *Aap biitii nambar 3 yaa yaad-i ayaam nambar 2.* Saharanpur: Kutbkhaana Yahyawii.

————. 1971c. *Aap biitii nambar 4 yaa yaad-i ayaam nambar 3.* Saharanpur: Kutbkhaana Yahyawii.

————. 1971d. *Aap biitii nambar 5 yaa yaad-i ayaam nambar 6.* Saharanpur: Kutbkhaana Yahyawii.

————. 1974. *Aap biitii nambar 6 yaa yaad-i ayaam nambar 5.* Saharanpur: Kutbkhaana Yahyawii.

————. n.d.a *Aap biitii (Yaad-i ayyam)* [Volume 1 *(Aap biitii* 1-5)]. Karachi: Mahadu'l khaliilu'l islaamii.

————. n.d.b *Aap biitii (Yaad-i ayyam)* [Volume 2 *(Aap biitii* 6–7)]. Karachi: Mahadu'l khaliilu'l islaamii.

Muhammad Zakariyya. 1993. *Aap Beti.* Volumes 1, 2, and 3 [English translation]. New Delhi: Idara Ishaat-e-Diniyat.

————. 1996. *Aap Beti.* Volumes 4 and 5 [English translation]. New Delhi: Idara Ishaat-e-Diniyat.

Peterson, Linda H. 1993. "Institutionalizing Women's Autobiography: Nineteenth Century Editors and the Shaping of an Autobiographical Tradition." In Robert Folkenflik (ed.), *Autobiography and Self-Representation,* pp. 80-103. Stanford: Stanford University Press.

Sanyal, Usha. 1996. *Devotional Islam and Politics in British India: Ahmad Riza Khan Barelwi and His Movement, 1870–1920.* Delhi: Oxford University Press.

Sikand, Yoginder. 2002. *The Origins and Development of the Tablighi-Jamaat (1920–2000): A Cross-country Comparative Study.* New Delhi: Orient Longman.

Werbner, Pnina. 2001. "Charisma and Living Sainthood: The Anthropology of a Global Sufi Cult." Typescript. Now published as *Pilgrims of Love: The Anthropology of a Global Sufi Cult.* Bloomington: Indiana University Press, 2003.

Notes

1. A version of this essay has also appeared in Barbara D. Metcalf, *Islamic Contestations: Essays on Muslims in India and Pakistan,* Delhi, Oxford University Press, 2003.
2. For background on Deoband, see Metcalf 1982 and Faruqi 1963.
3. These may have included Muhammad Aashiq Ilaahi Miiratii (n.d. a) and (b); Manaazir Ahsan Giilaanii (1955–6); Husain Ahmad Madani (1953); Abu'l-hasan Ali Nadwii (1944); and Asghar Husain (1920–1).

4. A.K. Priolkar, "Indian Incunabula," in D.N. Marshall and N.N. Gidwani, *Comparative Librarianship: Essays in Honour of Professor D.N. Marshall* (New Delhi, 1973), pp. 129–35, cited in Robert Darnton, "Books in the British Raj: The Contradictions of Liberal Imperialism," in *Printing History*. Priolkar dates this period of expansion in the use of print from 1868 to 1900.

5. William Lawler described popular readings in his "Report on the Bengal Library for the Year 1878": "Frequently in this very town of Calcutta an observant passer-by sees a large crowd of natives collected round a tailor or native grocer's shop to hear a man . . . reading a tale in Musulmani-Bengali, in which the auditors appear to take the most lively interest. . . ." Quoted in Darnton 2001: 171, n. 20. The popular Deobandi text for women, *Bihishti Zewar*, included instructions in the text itself for readers to gather other women to whom it should be read out aloud (Metcalf 1990).

6. For background on Tablighi Jama'at, see Abu'l Hasan 1982 [1944]; Haq 1972; Metcalf 1993a and 1994; Masud 2000; Mayaram 1997; and Sikand 2002.

7. See Werbner 2001 for a convincing argument that scholars haves missed the implications of the *langar* for understanding the paradigmatic pattern of the "world-renouncing" Sufi.

8. Werbner's study (2001) of a contemporary Sufi saint, Zindapir (d. 1999) sets up significant contrasts—above all in his focus on disciples and not scholarship—but also some striking similarities in personal discipline, economic dealings, and political attitudes to a scholar like Zakariyya.

CHAPTER 6

Hamara Daur-i Hayat

An Indian Muslim Woman Writes Her Life

SYLVIA VATUK

Introduction

I n the 1950s an Indian Muslim woman wrote, in a series of instalments, a reflective and richly detailed account of her childhood, her memories of growing up in Hyderabad in the 1920s
and early 1930s in a close-knit religious and scholarly family of illustrious ancestry but very moderate means.[1] She titled her narrative
Hamara Daur-i Hayat ("My Life"). The author of this memoir,
Dr Zakira Ghouse (hereafter ZG), had been living in Chennai (Madras) for more than forty-five years when she died in 2003 at the age of
eighty-two. When ZG was in her seventies she completed a doctoral
dissertation for her PhD in Urdu from the University of Madras—
certainly one of the oldest persons, in the one-and-a-half centuries of
that institution's history, to have achieved such a distinction!

Having found her early hopes for a medical career thwarted by family and personal circumstances that I will elaborate below, ZG spent
almost her entire life (except for a ten-year period of employment as
a lecturer of Urdu in a Madras women's college) as a housewife and
mother, albeit one who could never completely reconcile herself to devoting her time and energies exclusively to those roles. Nowadays her
sons and daughters, all of them highly educated, live abroad, as do all
but one of her grandchildren. Her elder daughter's son, an engineering
student, lived with her in their small Madras home. There she occupied one room, surrounded by the books, papers, and writing materials that for the better part of her life had filled all of the waking hours
she could spare from other responsibilities.

I first met ZG in early 1984, when she came to Hyderabad to visit her mother and younger sister, whom I had come to know earlier that year. I was in the early stages of an anthropological field study of Muslim family, marriage and kinship organization. Influenced by other members of ZG's large extended family (*khandan*), I had already begun to reorient my inquiries in a much more historical direction than I had originally planned. The family seemed to have an unusually strong sense of collective identity, built largely around the past that they shared (Vatuk 1990). They told countless anecdotes about the lives and accomplishments of their ancestors, and I had learned that they were drawing for knowledge and inspiration not only on a rich store of orally transmitted lore but also on a diverse body of written records, some of them dating back several centuries.

True to my professional training, I considered recording the *khandan*'s genealogy to be one of my first tasks. ZG welcomed my interest in her family's history and offered her assistance. With the help of a century-old *shajra* compiled by the son of one of her ancestors (Madini 1871–2), other family documents (notably an extensive biographical register of the *khandan* compiled by her mother [Majid 1984]), and her own and her mother's prodigious memories for names and past events, ZG spent countless hours detailing the genealogical connections among more than a thousand descendants, collaterals and relatives-by-marriage of the *khandan*'s founding couple. Later we moved on to examine other family records, notably a collection of biographical essays written for family "magazines" by various men and women of the family in the first half of the twentieth century.

ZG's account of her childhood was written in sixteen instalments[2] for one such magazine, *Mushir-un Niswan* ("The Woman's Advisor"), founded in 1935 by ZG and a girl cousin.[3] In this venture they were following the example of a group of older male relatives who, for more than a decade, had been putting out a monthly journal, called *Bazm-i Adab* ("The Literary Society"), for circulation among the various households of the *khandan*. Like that journal, *Mushir-un Niswan* was handwritten in only one copy in ordinary school notebooks that, by the time I saw them, were yellowed and brittle with age. It was issued on a more-or-less monthly basis until 1956 and again for a few years in the late 1970s. The contributors were mostly girls and young women, but boys and men of the family also wrote for it from time to time and it was read by family members of both sexes and all ages.[4]

When I first began trying to read *My Life*, I found that I could not easily decipher ZG's handwriting. My Urdu vocabulary was also rather limited. Furthermore, there was much in these essays that an outsider, unfamiliar with the people, the setting, and the events described could not readily comprehend. So ZG and I worked out a system whereby she would read her story aloud into my tape-recorder, explaining and elaborating upon what she had written and answering any questions I might have as she went along. In 1989 I was able to have *My Life* and her comments on the text translated into English.[5] The text I am dealing with here thus represents three different periods in ZG's life: the first, from 1921 to 1934, when ZG was growing up in Hyderabad; the second, 1953–4, when she was writing about what she remembered from the first; and the third, the month I spent with her in the winter of 1989. At that time she recalled other incidents and told me of feelings that had not made their way into the written text when she was composing it in the 1950s. She also corrected "errors" in the original that she attributed to its having been entirely a work of memory. Although she once refers therein to "my habit of writing a daily diary," there is no indication that she used this or any other document to help recollect the past. It is possible that she did not actually develop this "habit" until later in life.

In both the written text and her later commentary, ZG not only relates events and describes the emotions they evoked, but engages in conscious reflection about the past. Writing in 1953 she repeatedly remarks upon the extent to which her society has changed since she was a child, particularly with respect to women's roles and ways of life.[6] Here, and again thirty-six years later, she marvels at how different things were "in those days" from what they are "today." Furthermore, throughout her account, and in her later commentary on it, she tries to place the things that happened to her in the 1920s and 1930s within a larger life narrative, that of a very sensitive young girl, who from an early age felt seriously deprived, both materially and emotionally. Her response was to determine to make a different life for herself, one for which there was no real precedent in her extended family. She decided she would go to school, continue on for higher education and become a doctor, thereby gaining the respect and admiration of those who were inclined to regard her as a person of little importance. For various reasons, she was unable to realize this ambition and for years suffered great emotional distress on that account. But later she was able to achieve other academic goals that brought her considerable satisfaction and enabled her to come to terms with having had to abandon her earlier dreams.

Women's Narratives and Woman's Voice

Feminist scholarship in the fields of history, anthropology, and literary studies has in recent years regarded as one of its major challenges the "recovery of women's voice," buried as it often is in the unrecorded past or in the unwritten lives of contemporary non-literate and often oppressed and marginalized peoples. The "silencing" or "muting" of women's voices, especially in societies that are strongly male-dominated, has often been noted in this connection (e.g. Personal Narratives Group 1989). It is not surprising that among scholars of South Asia—a region of the world in which men's right to exert authority over and constrain the mobility and freedom of expression of the women in their lives is rarely openly challenged—the question of whether and how the real "voice" of women can be heard (and, if heard, deciphered) has become an issue of lively discussion. Some have gone so far as to suggest that the South Asian woman *has* no "voice" in the true sense of the term (Spivak 1985). Even when she is heard to speak, it is in a language that is by definition not her own: the form of her discourse originates in male modes of thought and expression, its content constrained by cultural prescriptions about "appropriate" feminine ways of thinking, feeling, and behaving.

One of the only ways to hear woman's true voice, some anthropologists of South Asia have suggested, is to listen to her folktales, her poetry and her songs, and try to decipher the indirectly expressed, often subversive messages that they contain (Raheja and Gold 1994; cf. Abu-Lughod 1986). Others have tried to meet the same challenge by eliciting women's oral life stories (Jacobson 1978; Khare 1996; Viramma, Racine and Racine 1997). This method has a long history within anthropology, during which there has also been lively discussion about how such materials ought best to be elicited, utilized, and interpreted. In recent discussions one of the issues most often raised is the reflexive one: that this kind of life history is *elicited* by a socially positioned researcher, rather than spontaneously produced by its subject. Also questioned by critics is our usual practice of mining these texts for generalizations about the *culture* to which the narrator belongs and

ignoring his or her unique subjectivity and way of being-in-the-world
(cf. Watson and Watson-Franke 1985: 161–84). Feminist ethnogra-
phers have also been faulted for downplaying individual variation in
their reading of the life histories they have elicited, although many have
explicitly tried to use them "to establish the simultaneous uniqueness
and typicality of the women being written about" (Visveswaran 1997:
602), while redressing some of the gender imbalance in a literature that
has long described "other" cultures chiefly from a male perspective.

Historians, trying to recover South Asian women's voices from
written autobiographical narratives (whether in published or manuscript form), do not have to deal with the first of the above-mentioned
issues, but may be equally vulnerable with respect to the second.[7]
South Asian women's autobiographies are far from plentiful and those
that do exist provide a window into the lives of only a select sample of
the region's female population: mainly, women of the upper socio-economic strata who enjoy some public prominence (in politics, the professions, social reform, literature, or the theatre) or are closely related
to notable men in the same fields of endeavor (Ghosh 1986; Mukherjee
1988; Papanek 1988; Karlekar 1991; Sarkar 1993, 1999; Flemming
1994; Bhattacharya 1998). They have been used by historians mainly
as primary documents for answering questions about such matters as
the development of women's education or their political participation
during the independence struggle (Borthwick 1984; Basu 1988). But
more interesting to a feminist anthropologist is what they reveal about
the gender ideologies and dynamics current at the time they were written. How was feminine identity culturally constructed, inculcated in,
and experienced by the writers and by other women of the writers'
class, religious community or region who did not have the opportunities, abilities or inclinations to write in an autobiographical vein?

Of particular concern is the question of to what extent the female
autograph, directly or indirectly, expresses a willing conformity to
existing cultural norms of gender relations and role definition. Is there
evidence of her having evaded or even challenged received gender ideologies? The notion that women in societies with marked gender asym-
metry develop ways of "negotiating" the conditions of their lives
within the constraints imposed by cultural definitions of femininity
has been particularly useful to me in examining ZG's account of her
childhood (Kandiyoti 1988).

Given the fact that ZG grew up in a period of great ferment over issues of "women's place," it would be surprising indeed if her account contained no evidence that she was aware of gender inequities and even contested certain aspects of her society's prescriptive definitions of the female role. One would expect her to have experienced some tension and conflict as she tried to reconcile in her personal life the contradictory models of ideal womanhood to which she was being exposed within her family and kin group, on the one hand, and from the wider quasi-colonial milieu of the Nizam's Hyderabad, on the other. And indeed one finds this to be the case. If anything, ZG appears to be more conscious of such gender issues than most women of her generation who grew up in a similar milieu. This is evident not only in her 1989 commentary, but in the 1953 text itself.

In terms of my method, the cautions of some post-modernist literary critics of the biographical genre are of considerable value. Skeptical of the very notion of "reliability," insofar as it entails a commitment to the positivist search for absolute "truth," they stress that, like any other text, autobiographies are both historically situated and personally, culturally, and socially motivated, "embodiments of one or more points of view rather than objective, omniscient accounts" (Ochs and Capps 1996: 21). Not "immediately referential of lives," but "works of artifice and fabrication," one should not expect to find in them neutral information about the past they purport to represent. In examining an autobiography one must attend to the specific personal, social, and historical contexts within which the author was motivated to create it, discover its intended audience, and determine the nature of the relationships among audience, author and subject at the time it was produced (British Sociological Association 1993: 2). One must also analyze the author's "use of genre conventions, temporal and other structuring, rhetoric, and authorial 'voice,'" and be attentive to silences, to the things that the author deliberately chooses not, or is simply not allowed, to say. One must read between—or even "against"—the narrative lines in order to find clues to the author's larger "project" or what is often, pejoratively, referred to as his or her "hidden agenda" (Middlebrook 1990: 155).

ZG's Autobiographical Models and Audience

Unpublished biographies and autobiographical accounts written by older male relatives provided one model for ZG's life story. Especially influential were the writings of a paternal uncle, Muhammad Mazhar, to whose support of her educational and literary endeavors in later years she often referred in her oral commentary (Mazhar 1949, 1951; Vatuk 1999). All her life ZG had been a voracious reader and, although she does not include the titles of any published biographies or autobiographies in her account of the books she read in childhood, there is little doubt that in her young adult years she had ample opportunity to develop a familiarity with these genres. She doubtless read Urdu translations of English biographies,[8] and was exposed to older Arabic and Persian traditions of biographical writing (Lambton 1962; Gibbs 1968; Eickelman 1991; Roded 1994) that had found their way into Urdu, as that language developed its own literary traditions.[9] The influence of these can be seen in at least two features of ZG's account.

First, she begins her account by placing herself at the end of a long line of praiseworthy ancestors. Only after recalling for her readers how and why their forbears first came to India and what their descendants accomplished does she turn to her own life story. The topical, rather than chronological, organization of her account also follows indigenous biographical traditions. Rather than relate events in order of their occurrence, she does so by subject: "socialization," "education," "surroundings," "hobbies," "amusements," and so on.

My Life was not written for publication. Its intended audience was ZG's extended family, men, women and young people who were the usual readers of *Mushir-un Niswan* and were familiar with the broad outlines of her life story. Many had been present when the events she describes took place or had heard about them from other eyewitnesses. Some had been on very intimate terms with her, notably her mother, about whom ZG naturally has a good deal to say in her childhood reminiscences.

Having such a limited audience gave ZG a sympathetic space in which to freely express herself about things that she might not have wanted to reveal to strangers. It spared her the necessity of going into detail about painful events and situations in her life. She could allude to them elliptically, knowing that her readers, sharing with her a common body of historical knowledge and understanding, would fill in, as they saw fit, whatever she left out. But the nature of her audience also made her engage in a certain amount of self-censorship. She had to be sensitive to the possibility of violating her readers' privacy or causing them offense. So she rarely relates incidents that reflect poorly upon the individuals involved. If she must do so, she tries to balance what she says by praising the person's positive qualities and explaining what extenuating circumstances compelled him or her to behave in such a way.

ZG also seems to have felt obliged to avoid or treat gingerly certain controversial religious or social issues (including those related to the changing roles of women) about which some members of the family held strong views. When she does offer an opinion on such a topic, she makes a blanket apology to all who might disagree. Her account, indeed, begins with a passage anticipating the possibility "that some of my words may cause offense" and disclaiming any such intent. This introductory section is altogether apologetic in tone, as if to justify the temerity implied in proposing to write an autobiography. (Indented sections are direct quotations from *My Life*. ZG's oral comments are inserted in italics.)

> In an earlier issue of *Mushir* the late MM Uncle wrote about the lives of certain deceased ladies of the *khandan*, in alphabetical order. And [readers were] asked to write articles on the same topic. I didn't do that. But then the thought occurred to me that, although my own life is not so important, it is, nevertheless, something that should be written about or people invited to read about . . . So I have put on paper some rambling and confused thoughts. I can't ask you to read it but I know that most of you will definitely do so. I'm not saying this out of egoism but it is a fact that personal life is a subject that people are eager to read about . . . [So] my personal life is my chosen topic and on that topic my pen runs swiftly! I know that self-praise is a defect, but allow me to say that:
>
> My purpose is simply to relate what actually happened.
> I don't consider it a credit to my character to talk about myself.[10]

Throughout her account ZG also uses a number of rhetorical devices to display deference to her readers.[11] She is self-critical, claiming poor writing skills along with various character faults. She asks her readers' forgiveness immediately after any passage that could possibly be interpreted as self-congratulatory, self-aggrandizing, or boastful. In presenting herself with exaggerated humility she follows a long and respected tradition of the Persian and Urdu prose style in which she was trained. However, her self-effacement is not simply formulaic. It clearly serves a vital purpose: to deflect potential criticism of the literary activity in which she engaged from those with whom she has—and wishes to maintain—the closest possible of intimate ties.[12]

ZG's strenuous efforts to avoid giving offense were not always successful. The relationship between the writers of *Mushir-un Niswan* and its readers was always a dialogic one. Feedback, whether critical or adulatory, from the audience was a regular feature of every issue of the magazine. Sometimes it was written right in the margins of the offending article or in some other blank space on the page. ZG pointed out one such entry, made by an uncle in the margins of *My Life,* where she had written:

> It is possible that this series, like so many others, will remain incomplete, because, living in the countryside,[13] I seldom [have the time] to write articles. However, I am pleased that this series has been so well read and has also had an impact on a number of readers. [*Here MM Uncle has commented: "Silence is the best form of praise. Instead of praising you [out loud], the best way is to remain quiet"* . . . *Then below that he has written that he wishes to respond to what I* . . . *had written about school education. We blamed our elders for not educating us. He writes, "These were our reasons, this is why we did not send you to school."*]

Sometimes a reader would even confront the writer in person. At one point in ZG's narrative she recalls an amusing incident in which a cousin, twelve years old, was traveling by train from Hyderabad to Madras, accompanied by an older male relative.

> At one of the stations . . . the train stopped. Thinking that the train would remain there for some time, that gentleman got down onto the platform and began offering his prayers. He was still busy praying when the train started to move! [The boy] was frantic, but kept a cool head . . . After finishing his prayers, the gentleman realized what had happened. He sent a telegram to the stationmaster at the next stop . . . The guard came [to the compartment] and reassured [the boy] and he reached Madras safely. [*This article was written long after the fact and when that gentleman read it he was very annoyed. One of my aunts told me, "Look, he has read this article and is going to question you about it." After that I didn't see him for a while, but once I was on the stairs of the* madrasa (seminary or college) *and* . . . *he met me* . . . *and asked why I had written such a thing. I don't recall what I responded.*]

ZG's Family

ZG was born in 1921 into a Sunni Muslim family (of the Shaf'i *maz-hab*) whose ancestors had come to the south-western coast of India by sea from Arabia at least five centuries earlier.[14] The men had been religious scholars (*ulama*), dependent for employment and patronage on successive Muslim rulers of the Deccan, most recently the Adil Shahi sultans of Bijapur and the nawabs of the Carnatic. ZG's three great-grandfathers (two brothers and their sister's son—ZG's parents were first cousins and so had one of their grandfathers in common) were senior officials in the court of the last nawab. After his death without male heirs in 1855, the British abolished the nawabi, leaving these men and their sons with no source of livelihood. They had never accepted the legitimacy of British rule over the Carnatic, and the dire situation in which they now found themselves did not soften their hostility to the colonial power. Unwilling to study English and allow themselves to be co-opted by qualifying for employment in the colonial administration, many of the younger men left for Hyderabad, to use their Urdu and Persian language skills in the service of a Muslim ruler.

ZG's paternal grandfather was one of these. He got a job in the Nizam's administration and gradually rose to a mid-level clerical position. In 1910, while assigned to instruct the heir-apparent, Osman Ali Khan, about the work of his government department, he found himself accused, together with a number of prominent officials, of participating in an alleged conspiracy against the Nizam and his British Minister of Finance. He was exiled from the state and returned with his wife and children to Madras and thence to Mecca, where, due to the outbreak of World War I, the family remained for the next five years. By this time the old Nizam had died and the new incumbent pardoned ZG's grandfather and allowed him to return to Hyderabad in a new post in the Department of Religious Affairs.

The usual practice in the *khandan* was to educate children of both sexes at home. Older boys sometimes pursued advanced studies with scholars outside of the family, but always in a personalized, tutorial setting. ZG's father had been among the first young men in his extended family to be school-educated. He was still in high school when the order came for his father's exile. His marriage, to a cousin selected by his father, had recently been celebrated. He and his wife accompanied his parents to Mecca and there she gave birth to two daughters, but both died within a few days. Given their fate, everyone in the family was concerned about the outcome when, back in Hyderabad, she became pregnant with ZG.

> I came as a result of prayers and desires, since I had devoured the two who preceded me [*Instead of saying "she was born after the two earlier ones died," they use the idiomatic phrase "she was born having eaten the first two."*] Therefore, Mother used to tell me, care and precautions were strongly emphasized. For instance, I have heard that in Ramadan, before my birth, Mother was forbidden to fast. [Maternal] Grandfather used to get annoyed, but she insisted on fasting anyway . . . On the 17th Rabi-ul Awwal, 1340 (18 November 1921), on a Friday at four-fifteen in Haji Manzil,[15] . . . in the room where Brother MA is now residing, I came into being from oblivion. Consider it good fortune or bad that after my birth I did not join my earlier two dead sisters. Instead, I am still carrying on in this world . . . Such a long life! I sometimes think, "how useless my life is! If I did not exist, what would have happened? Of what value is a life like mine, so useless and without purpose?"

ZG's father enrolled in the Urdu-medium Osmania University to study for a BA degree, but he never passed the final examination and for many years was unable to find regular employment. His resulting financial difficulties were compounded by his taking a second wife, an outsider to the *khandan*, for whom he set up a separate residence.[16] He fathered several children by each wife; in all, five daughters and one son survived to adulthood.

Until ZG was in her teens, she and her parents lived in the large extended family household headed by her paternal grandparents. Since her father had no regular job, they were financially dependent on the earnings of her grandfather and later of her uncle. This situation caused ZG's mother great discomfort. As a result, she constantly tried to instill in them the importance of self-effacement and consideration for others. She impressed upon them that they were beholden to others for shelter and support and must therefore not cause trouble, be demanding or call attention to themselves by unseemly behavior.

> [W]hen one lives in a joint household, one has to be attentive to the needs of others . . . particularly [if one's] economic position is lower than [their's] . . . Mother was extremely sensitive about any mistakes [we might make] . . . Let me mention just one such incident. Once,

meatballs had been cooked . . . I had arrived early [from school] and because I had a good appetite and there was lots of food in the pot, I and the other children who were with me took more than our share. So there was not enough left for those who came later. The woman in charge [of the kitchen] obviously felt annoyed. Nothing was said to me but, by chance, Mother came to know about it. Then she told me severely that in the joint family system nothing should ever be done without thinking of others. [*I was quite old at the time but, even then, she told me that I should be careful when I eat.*] And this fact, this thought, is still well preserved in my mind. I still try my best to see that no-one's interests are hurt because of me. Often I fail and then my conscience pinches me severely.

Thus, from an early age, ZG was made to rein in her spontaneous childish impulses. This contributed to her feelings of material and emotional deprivation, relative to the other children in her extended household and in her *khandan* at large.

By the grace of God, I grew up in a house full of people . . . I had a number of companions, many elders, a host of younger ones. Wealth and well being raises a person's status a lot . . . I should not write [this], but I am writing, that because . . . Father was unable to get any particular employment and did not achieve anything of note, our status within this well-off *khandan* was very low. Probably I will never be able to forget the wounds [I incurred] during that period. I used to see that for most of my peers there was ample love and pampering, well being, money and carefreeness. But I used to feel that for myself and for my sisters and brother these things did not exist. I used to think, "Why isn't there any love and affection for us in this world?" According to my childlike understanding, I used to wonder what was lacking in us. "What is the defect? What is wrong? Why are we not considered deserving of equal love?" Anyhow, that bitter time has passed. Thank God that He enabled us to become [people] of some worth. Worthy enough that now, at least, we have begun to be looked upon with some respect.

ZG was somewhat uncertain even about her parents' love for her. Her relationship with her father was fairly distant. He was not at home very much and, when he was, "We were always afraid . . ., we were always shaking and could never speak to him directly." As the first of her mother's children to survive infancy, ZG was the object of a good deal

of maternal attention in her early years. In raising her, ZG's mother
followed a carefully worked-out schedule, something quite unusual
for the time. When ZG was older her mother prepared written time-
tables and encouraged her daughter to follow them:

> . . . for a few days I would follow the timetable but then my early en-
> thusiasm would wear off . . . Then, after a few days I would start again
> with new zeal. I made separate programs of my own, set up a new
> timetable, resolved to lead my life with order and regularity. But again,
> the same topsy-turvy pace resumed!

Unlike some of the other women in the household, ZG's mother
was not in the habit of displaying affection for her children. ZG visibly
struggles in her autobiography to come to terms with this aspect of her
mother's personality. She says that she is convinced that, despite an
apparent inability or intentional unwillingness to show it, "Mother
used to love me a lot; she still does. She has a special regard for me.
However, . . . for her, the place for feelings is in the heart. They should
not come out of it." She goes on to suggest that perhaps her mother's
kind of love is of a higher order than love that is more openly expressed.
But, she adds, now that she is grown, she has also come to realize that,
in the days of which she writes, her mother "had no sense that she herself was loved and therefore had no place [in her heart] for such sentiments [in relation to others]." Recall that when ZG wrote these lines
her mother was still living and was certainly meant to read these
musings of her daughter on mother-love.

The Women's World of Home

In ZG's childhood the women of "respectable" (*sharif*) families did
not often have reason or opportunity to leave their homes. Shopping
was done by servants or by men. There were few visits even to close
neighbors, other than those belonging to their immediate kinship
circle. Whereas the men of the family in those days were themselves
moving in a relatively wide extra-familial social circle, they still preferred that their womenfolk keep aloof from outsiders. Women of the
older generation also helped enforce the family's long-standing practices of female seclusion (*goshah*) and social exclusivity. The younger
women of the family were already beginning to chafe somewhat at
their domestic confinement, however:

[*Members of my khandan wished to socialize. The male members probably didn't like it, but as far as the women were concerned, they wanted to expand their circle of friends. My cousins had been introduced to the two Hindu girls, sisters, who owned the carriage that took HB to school.*] Often [when HB was being picked up or dropped off from school] they would go up to the carriage and the two young women would converse with them . . . At that time I had not yet begun to attend school. Involuntarily the desire was born in me: "Oh, would that those people knew me too and talked to me like that!" In those childhood days, living in such a limited and enclosed environment, every outsider seemed a great personality!

There were periodic opportunities for women to travel outside of the city, however. There was much visiting back and forth between Hyderabad and Madras for weddings, childbirth, and other life-cycle events. Several men, including ZG's maternal grandfather, held government jobs in which they were posted to district towns. Their families often accompanied them. Occasionally women had the opportunity to travel further afield, to visit Muslim shrines in other parts of India or even sail to Mecca for *hajj*.

Wherever they went, of course, women were strictly secluded. They were invariably accompanied on their travels by one or more male relatives and there were special arrangements to shield them from public view while in transit.[17] Upon leaving home, long sheets of fabric, held up by servants, were stretched between the house door and the curtained carriage that would take them to their destination. Upon arrival the same procedure was repeated. In trains or ships they always occupied separate "ladies" compartments.

In ZG's account, the home appears almost as a closed world, in which women were a constant presence while men came and went. Her early education, like that of other girls in her family, was acquired at the hands of women, mainly her mother and two grandmothers. She also learned a great deal informally from some other young female relatives, whom she greatly admired, not because of their domestic skills (for which ZG admits having little interest or talent) but because of their intelligence and wide-ranging interests.

Men held ultimate authority over women and their activities. However, women had their own ideas, opinions, interests, and desires and were even able to prevail, on occasion, when these ran counter to those of their male kin. Thus, for example, several mothers insisted that their sons and daughters be sent to school, despite indifference or opposition from male relatives. Thus it was that in 1931, entirely on the initiative of her mother, a younger girl cousin of ZG, was enrolled in school:

> The courage of my respected Aunt [father's brother's wife] deserves a thousand praises! Tolerating all the harsh words, she saw to it that Sister H reached her educational destination . . . [*That is, people criticized her* . . . *Probably H's father didn't have any strong opinion on the matter, but it was not the custom of the*khandan, *so he didn't want to say anything (in favor) of it. But he also didn't want to interfere with his wife's wishes.*]

There is a strong undercurrent in ZG's account of a contrast between the female experience and view of the world and that of men and boys. There is some evidence in the text, and more in ZG's commentary on it, that girls and women had agendas for their current lives, for their futures and the futures of their daughters that were somewhat ahead of those of their mildly reformist fathers and husbands. Young women assumed, as their elders did, that their primary roles in the future would be those of wife and mother. But they still wanted to learn what the modern world had to offer, and not simply because it would make them better wives and mothers. They and their mothers had also clearly begun to think about the possibility of women combining other roles with the accepted domestic ones. They had more confidence than did the men of the family in their own ability to resist any potentially harmful influences that might emanate from books or contacts with unrelated women. Thus, without rejecting them totally or in any way radically, they can be said to have resisted some of the implications of their culture's definition of the female as a person in need of comprehensive male protection. In the largely female space of the home they found ways to expand their horizons by their own efforts, following men's example when available and accepting men's help when offered. When necessary they tried to arrange things so that their activities did not come to the attention of men who might wish to exert their authority to constrain them.

Although ZG does not say so, subsequent events indicate that even the accepted notion that every woman must marry and depend for her livelihood upon a man's earnings was beginning to be questioned during this period. Through their exposure to contemporary literature and to the example of individual professional women whom they saw (for example, the visiting nurse and teachers at their school) or read about in women's magazines, girls had became aware that there were alternatives to marriage and motherhood.[18] A woman could remain single and support herself, and even her parents, by taking a job, as long as it was in a setting where her modesty could be preserved. And if she did marry, an educated woman could work and contribute to the family's expenses, as could a widow left with an inadequate pension. In a *khandan* that had suffered and was continuing to suffer downward occupational mobility, the knowledge that the earnings of their sons and sons-in-law might well be insufficient to maintain a family provided a further motive to rethink the traditional assignment to women of an exclusively domestic role.

For ZG and her sisters, the troubled relationship between their parents provided a further reason for seriously considering the possibility of remaining single and preparing for careers by which to support themselves and their mother in the future. When her husband died relatively young and left her to share a small pension with her husband's other widow, their mother herself began to think that it would be better if her daughters did not marry: "[*She thought*], '*after the pain I have suffered, why should my daughters suffer it too?*'" Ultimately, of the three sisters, ZG was the only one to marry. The others obtained postgraduate degrees and have only recently retired from government employ as a teacher and a university librarian, respectively.

A Religious and Scholarly Milieu

ZG attributes many aspects of the kind of person she became to the religious and scholarly atmosphere of her childhood home:

[*Compared to other houses of the* khandan, *ours was more religious.*] There were special activities: prayers, fasting, recitation of the Qur'an [*All day long, somebody was reading something*], performance of group prayers in the early morning . . . [*At dawn was the call for prayer. Almost the whole household woke up: children, men, women . . . (I remember) MM Uncle . . . leading the prayers. Everyone would join in.*] . . . [Paternal] Grandmother and Father's Sister used to sit and discuss religious issues. [All of] the minor things forbidden in Islamic law were strictly avoided. [*Photographs for example. Now they have been proven to be permissible. But in those days my grandmother and aunt were so particular that they never got their photograph taken.*] . . . Getting photographed was bad, but even keeping a photograph was considered a sin. Listening to the gramophone was bad [*People wouldn't even listen to music*]. Going to the cinema and non-observance of purdah were probably the biggest crimes in that period.

The men of her family, deeply devout and observant Muslims, were also very socially and politically aware. They read newspapers,[19] attended public meetings, and discussed current events in informal gatherings of male friends and work associates. Some wrote articles for local Urdu newspapers. One had taught himself to read English—over his father's objections—and translated English newspaper articles into Urdu for the local press. They participated in, and some were involved in the running of, voluntary organizations dedicated to issues of Muslim education and welfare.[20]

Bringing these models home, they established a family men's club and held meetings in which speeches were delivered on current events and social issues. They organized a children's club, in which they provided instruction in essay composition and oratory, teaching the youngsters first to copy essays that their elders had written and then to compose original pieces along similar lines. They set essay topics—such as "Proper Clothing for Women," "Should Girls Go to School?" or "My Favorite Pastime"—for family magazines and sponsored oratorical contests for youngsters of both sexes.

> . . . the literary, nationalistic and scholarly atmosphere [of our home] also influenced my character. There were several family societies . . . that were actively working for reform of and service to the *khandan* . . . At dinnertime, when all of the members of the family gathered, discussions took place and comments were made about literary, scholarly, political and national issues.

In this period elite Hyderabadi women had begun to form voluntary associations of their own: once or twice some young women of the *khandan* had the opportunity to attend their meetings:

> A Ladies Club had become very popular [in the city] . . . There was a separate fee for joining and a fixed monthly or annual membership fee. The ladies of the royal family and other respected guests were invited. Meetings and plays, etc. took place . . . Besides that, daily or once or twice a week, one could go there to spend the evening and pass the time

with different interesting activities. Once or twice ZB and JB went there. When I saw them leaving I felt a great desire to accompany them: "Oh, if only I could go too, if only I could join the club too!" But in those days, to have such a desire fulfilled was unusual.

So the young women replicated such activities in their own family women's clubs, holding regular meetings at which speeches were delivered and articles read aloud from newspapers and magazines. When ZG was six or seven years old she and her peers sat in on these gatherings, marveling at their elders' courage in standing up to speak before an audience! Later, in their early teens, they organized a club of their own, along the same lines.

A Passion for Reading

ZG was, like her mother, an avid reader, devouring the works of all of the prominent Urdu writers of her time (and earlier): Nazir Ahmad, Rashid-ul Khairi, Abdul Halim Sharar, and the women writers Muhammadi Begum, Nazr-i Sajjad Haidar, Walida Afzal Ali and others:

I had a strange obsession with reading. I didn't care about the time or the place. In those days there was no electricity [in our house] . . . There was a lantern in my room: when Mother got annoyed with my incessant reading she would turn it off. [On moonlit nights] I would lie there for a little while, holding my breath. After a while, when she fell off to sleep, I would take my book into the moonlight and continue reading, going to bed only after I had finished it. [*Father used to sleep in the adjoining room, so there was also the fear that, if he should find me reading in the dark, he would be angry. So I had to take precautions. Sometimes the door of his room was ajar; if I heard him getting up I would hide the book.*]

Long sections of her account are devoted to the difficulties she had getting access to books and to the stratagems she employed to overcome them. Generally speaking, it was older women and girls of her own age who were most cooperative in this respect, whereas many of the men of the family, ambivalent at best about the girls' desire to expand their knowledge of the world through reading, tried to prevent their obtaining what they considered "unsuitable" fare. As members of a scholarly family with a proud tradition of female literacy, they expected their daughters to learn to read and even to write.[21] They were concerned, however, about possible exposure to corrupting influences, whether from direct contact with outsiders of inferior breeding or from reading literature (such as novels) that might lead them to abandon their domestic roles, come out of seclusion or deviate from accepted standards of feminine modesty. Such fears, of course, echoed those of most Muslim reformers of the period (Devji 1991).

After leaving his studies, ZG's father had set up a small lending library in rented quarters. The girls of the family were not allowed to go there, however, nor could they persuade her father to bring books home for them to read. They were tantalized by the knowledge of this rich store of books lying always just beyond their reach. Sometimes he would bring books home at night for his own and his brother's enjoyment. ZG did not share the men's literary tastes—they were fond of detective stories—but she was so desperate she would read anything she could get her hands on.

[*My father—rather, men in general—thought that women shouldn't read such books . . . When he left in the morning he would hide the book under a window. As soon as he left, HB and I would go and get it . . . We knew that he would be back at four, but sometimes he would come early. We would stand in the window and read, so that when we saw him coming we could immediately put it back!*]

Once, hoping that he would leave without them, she hid some books that she had started reading and badly wanted to finish. Her plan backfired, however, when he reported to her mother that the books were missing (and perhaps also his suspicions as to who had caused them to disappear) and instituted a successful search.

An older married cousin whom ZG greatly admired was also a voracious reader—it was said that she enjoyed reading so much that she would keep her nose in a book even on her way to take a bath! She owned many books, but her husband insisted that they be kept in a locked cabinet, lest they fall into the wrong hands. Such male authority was reproduced in the next generation in the person of this couple's son, slightly younger than ZG, who shared her passion for books. Although he had fairly ready access to his mother's library,

God knows for what reason, but Brother H . . . considered scholarly generosity to be illegal! [*He wouldn't share his books with others . . . Whenever WB got hold of a book, she would give it to me. I would give books to her. He would snatch books from us and read them. But he would not give his books to us!*] Even now, when I remember it, how frustrated I feel! Brother H would bring a book from his mother's cabinet and read it in front of me. Sitting still, I would keep praying in my heart, "Please God, may H have pity on me and give me the book after he finishes reading it." But that gentleman would just look at me victoriously, take the book, and disappear from sight!

He evidently considered it his prerogative to retain a monopoly over an activity that he knew his girl cousins enjoyed as much as he did. Such behavior, if displayed by one of them, would certainly have earned a scolding.

Much of the literature that ZG read in her childhood was specifically meant for women and was didactic and reformist in intent, encouraging women's education (so as to make them better housewives and mothers) and attacking "wasteful" and "non-Islamic" rituals and customs (cf. Metcalf 1991). The ideal woman in the stories she read was knowledgeable and enlightened, capable of running a modern household and raising modern sons while retaining the traditional feminine virtues of modesty, patience, self-abnegation, gentility, and religiosity. Negative female characters were either ignorant, petty, and intriguing, or highly Westernized and alienated from their own religion and culture. ZG identified, as she was meant to do, with the virtuous female heroines. In the novel *Jauhar-i Qadamat* Rashid-ul Khairi (1971) contrasts two sisters:[22]

> Zahida was the product of orthodox culture, and Shahida . . . was a typical daughter of modern society. [. . . *she was a fashionable girl. Her father had sent her to an English-medium school. The other was brought up in a totally Eastern way. (The author) compares the two and obviously, because he preferred Eastern ways, he shows that the Westernized girl's life ends in hardship, whereas the Eastern girl has a happy ending.*] One felt dislike and repulsion for the character of Shahida, while the character of Zahida appeared to shine like a star . . . I read that book over and over again and each and every word is still as if engraved in my mind.

In other novels the same author attacked customs that, in his view, caused hardship to women: polygyny, child-marriage, arranged marriages in which the spouses were ill-matched in terms of social background or educational level, and the legal double-standard in matters of divorce:

He favored the oppressed class of women and . . . in our time, in the environment by which we were surrounded, it was easy to see how oppressed women were [*He was on the side of women. He used to write . . . that (they) should be treated well, be given their rights . . . In our day it was obvious that men dominated women. (He) wrote what I felt strongly about, so I liked him.*][23]

Understandably, one of the things that ZG felt strongly about was polygyny. She enjoyed novels about polygynous marriages, especially those in which the two wives lived together harmoniously, as in *Gudar ka Lal*, a three-volume epic about the varying fortunes of three inter-related families, first serialized in a women's magazine in 1911–12.[24] One of the heroines is a second wife who manages to repair the previously hostile relationship between her husband and his first wife, thus bringing about domestic happiness for all: "[*S*]*he tolerated every insult and hurt . . . and was so nice to [her co-wife] that in the end she too became a good wife.*" Again, in *Raushnak Begum*,[25] a first wife magnanimously ensures the happiness of her husband's second marriage (to an Englishwoman) by allowing the latter to believe, to the end of her life, that she is his only wife. ZG writes: "The job of analyzing why, in my childhood, I especially liked this [part of the story] is one for a psychologist, not for me!"

I Shall Study Medicine!

The idea that she should become a doctor seized ZG's imagination quite early in life. There were no Western-style doctors, male or female, in her *khandan*. But some of her ancestors had been *hakims* and she had often heard the story of the ancestress who had learned the rudiments of Unani medicine from her father and thereafter was often called upon by family members to treat common illnesses.

A midwife named Josephine, an Indian Christian, was regularly called in to assist whenever a baby was about to be born in the household. She provided the only real-life medical role model for ZG:

Because I was the youngest girl in the house, or for whatever reason, she paid particular attention to me and talked to me very affectionately. Obviously, in those days my world was very small, very limited. I had not seen any big doctors or executives. So Josephine's arrival seemed to be an event of special importance. She was respected [by everyone] . . . Some gentleman of the house would always walk behind her, carrying her bag. She would arrive with great pomp, in an open carriage, dressed in clean clothes; obviously, by contrast with my confined world, her free world seemed very worthy of admiration. . . . [*That is, she did not wear a veil. The way she dressed, her style, and so on, all were very attractive to me.*] I got it into my head that, if I became a doctor, then I too would gain respect, love and a high position in life.

ZG also had at least one literary role model, another character in the above-mentioned book, *Gudar ka Lal*:

I was very impressed by . . . this fictional Surayya [who], after overcoming innumerable difficulties . . . became a doctor . . . [Her] character was an ideal one . . . I wished that I might acquire all of the skills, arts, and knowledge that Surayya had and adopt all of her good qualities . . . So, from that time on, I began to think about becoming a doctor.

Finally, an incident from her early childhood lent strength to her ambitions:

I don't recall when, nor do I have any real memory of it . . . but I have heard so much about it . . . that I feel as if it were a recent event . . . Father got a notebook made for me, with a gold-colored cover. In it was written the alphabet and also, in bold letters, the sentence, "I shall study medicine." Right below that, a respected elder [*my paternal uncle*] had written "Should not study that!!"

ZG is unsure about her father's motive for writing this sentence, especially given the fact that, until she was eleven years old, he took no real steps to see that she got an education.

This is from a time when it was considered wrong in our *khandan* to send girls to school, let alone give them the idea of pursuing higher studies . . . But my late father, compared to some other individuals in the *khandan*, was forward-looking . . . It is possible that those words [reflected] his real desires . . . Perhaps he really wished me to pursue higher education, to attain high goals . . . But when I was a child he was not in the position to pay any particular attention to my education. A net of anxiety encircled him from every side; he was exhausted by worries about his [lack of] employment.

By the time ZG was ten years old, two of her girl cousins had begun attending the Nampalli English-medium school, established by the

Nizam's government in 1887–8 for "respectable" girls of all religions, and ZG desperately wanted to join them:

> Until then, . . . except for Urdu (of which I had learned a lot, thanks to Mother) and my Qur'anic education (under the guidance of my paternal grandmother), I had hardly learned anything. I used to get very upset when I saw the school carriage coming to the house. [*I had such a compelling desire to board it!*]

The following year, upon her return home one day from a visit to her maternal grandparents, she was greeted with the news that her father had been buying books and other supplies to prepare her for admission to school. A bachelor maternal uncle had apparently provided the catalyst for his decision. The two men started giving ZG lessons in English and mathematics. When the new term began she began her formal education at Nampalli School. Though extremely self-conscious about having to sit in grade two at the advanced age of twelve years, she was thrilled to have finally been given this long-awaited opportunity.

Later Life

In her concluding installment, ZG tells the reader something about her later life. After marriage she lived with her husband in various district towns of Hyderabad State, where he was posted in connection with his government job. Conditions in many of these places were relatively primitive by comparison to those in the houses her family occupied in Hyderabad and Madras. She mentions the unavailability of servants, the strict seclusion that she had to maintain as the wife of a government officer, and her isolation from family and other social contacts. In one of these postings, there was no well inside the house: because of the need to maintain seclusion, she had to wait each day until dark before going out to fetch water for cooking and washing.

Four children were born; while raising them and keeping house she read as often as she could. She began to study "privately" for her BA in Urdu, periodically going to Hyderabad so that her mother and sisters could help her with childcare while she prepared for exams. She eventually passed and then began working toward an MA. She was still consumed by the desire to do something meaningful with her life. In her narrative she repeatedly uses the metaphors of a volcano about to burst in her head, of her mind "burning," as she struggled to attain the goal—now somewhat down-scaled from what it had been in her childhood—of becoming a college teacher. Finally she obtained her Master's degree and—with the help of an influential family acquaintance—was offered a job at a girls' college in Madras. Although her husband had initially been very reluctant to allow her to study for her MA, because it would give her educational qualifications superior to his own, he had eventually assented. He also acquiesced at her determination to accept this job, even though it meant living apart from her and the children for several years until his retirement enabled them to be together again.

At the time she wrote *Hamara Daur-i Hayat,* ZG was about to take up this new job. She had reached a point in her life where she had at last achieved something that she considered meaningful and significant, despite the fact that her original goal of becoming a medical doctor still eluded her grasp. It may well be that it was because she had finally overcome the feelings of inadequacy that had so dominated her earlier years that she was inspired to write about her life at this time and was able to do so with such insight and self-reflectiveness. By the time ZG read her life story to me, looking back upon her childhood and also recalling her state of mind at the time she wrote the narrative, she was finally in a position to assess her entire life, one in which she has at last found satisfaction and contentment:

[*Now I feel that whatever happened was for the best. It was better for me to study Arts. I started reading and writing to hide my mental anxieties and worries. I had made it a cover, but it ended up being my destination . . . I think that I might never have been able to attain my present position, had I become a doctor.*]

Conclusion

I have presented here only some of the highlights from this story of the life of one woman, as she first experienced, then wrote, and finally commented upon it, looking into the past and describing what she saw there through the veil of many intervening years. Like everyone's life, this one is unique: one might suppose that ZG, both as an individual and in terms of her family situation, is so unusual that her story has little broader relevance for scholars. I have tried to show, however, that it provides an important kind of lens for examining patterns of female socialization and gender dynamics in Muslim culture, not only during the period about which she writes but over the subsequent seven decades of Indian history. On the basis of this one woman's experience, it is possible to say something of more general significance about the process by which women generally in her culture at that period of time acquired a gendered self-identity and transmitted it, though not without alteration, to the next generation.

In spite of the idiosyncrasies of ZG's voice, we can learn much from it beyond details of her individual subjectivity. Most importantly, we see how a young girl can work within the framework of her culture's definition of "woman" to develop a strong sense of self and personal identity and to construct a kind of future for herself that no one could have imagined when her story began. There are many such stories that could be told; I feel most fortunate that I have been given the privilege of hearing this one.

REFERENCES

Abu-Lughod, Lila. 1986. *Veiled Sentiments: Honor and Poetry in a Bedouin Society.* Berkeley: University of California Press.

Basu, Aparna. 1988. "A Century's Journey: Women's Education in Western India 1820–1920." In Karuna Chanana (ed.), *Socialisation, Education and Women*, pp. 65–95. New Delhi: Orient Longman.

Bhattacharya, Rimli (ed. & transl.). 1998. *Binodini Dasi: My Story and My Life as an Actress.* New Delhi: Kali for Women.

Borthwick, Meredith. 1984. *The Changing Role of Women in Bengal 1849–1905.* Princeton: Princeton University Press.

British Sociological Association. 1993. "Editorial Introduction. Special Issue: Biography and Autobiography in Sociology." *Sociology* 27: 1–4.

Devji, Faisal Fatehali. 1991. "Gender and the Politics of Space: The Movement for Women's Reform in Muslim India, 1857–1900." *South Asia* 14: 141–53.

Eickelman, Dale F. 1991. "Traditional Islamic Learning and Ideas of the Person in the Twentieth Century." In Martin Kramer (ed.), *Middle Eastern Lives: The Practice of Biography and Self-Narrative*, pp. 35–59. Syracuse: Syracuse University Press.

Flemming, Leslie. 1994. "Between Two Worlds: Self-construction and Self-identity in the Writings of Three Nineteenth-century Indian Christian Women." In N. Kumar (ed.), *Women as Subjects: South Asian Histories*, pp. 81–107. Calcutta: Stree.

Forbes, Geraldine (ed.). 1994. *Manmohini Zutshi Sahgal, An Indian Freedom Fighter Recalls her Life.* Armonk, NY: M.E. Sharpe.

Forbes, Geraldine, and Tapan Raychaudhuri (eds). 2000. *The Memoirs of*

Dr. Haimbati Sen: From Child Widow to Lady Doctor. T. Raychaudhuri (transl.). New Delhi: Roli Books.

Ghosh, Srabashi. 1986. " 'Birds in a Cage:' Changes in Bengali Social Life as Recorded in Autobiographies by Women." *Economic and Political Weekly* 21: WS88–WS96.

Gibbs, Hamilton A. R. 1968. "Islamic Biographical Literature." In B. Lewis and P. M. Holt (eds), *Historians of the Middle East*, pp. 54–8. London: Oxford University Press.

Hermansen, Marcia K. 1988. "Interdisciplinary Approaches to Islamic Biographical Materials." *Religion* 18: 163–82.

Jacobson, Doranne. 1978. "The Chaste Wife: Cultural Norm and Individual Experience." In Sylvia Vatuk (ed.), *American Studies in the Anthropology of India*, pp. 95–138. New Delhi: Manohar.

Kandiyoti, Deniz. 1988. "Bargaining with Patriarchy." *Gender and Society* 2: 274–98.

Karlekar, Malavika. 1991. *Voices from Within: Early Personal Narratives of Bengali Women*. Delhi: Oxford University Press.

Khairi, Rashid-ul. 1971. *Jauhar-i Qadamat*. Karachi: 'Allamah Rashid-ul Khairi Akedami.

Khare, Ravindra S. 1996. "A Paradoxical Gift of Memory: The Pain, Pride, and History of an Untouchable 'Kitchen Poetess.' " *Anthropology and Humanism* 21: 19–30.

Lambton, Ann K. 1962. "Persian Biographical Literature." In B. Lewis and P. Holt (eds), *Historians of the Middle East*, pp. 141–51. London: Oxford University Press.

Leonard, Karen. 1978. *Social History of an Indian Caste: The Kayasths of Hyderabad*. Berkeley: University of California Press.

Madini, Maulawi Ahmad-ul. 1871–2. *Tarikh-i Ahmadi* [Persian]. Unpublished manuscript.

Majid, Amat-ul. 1984. [*Biographical Register*]. [Urdu]. Unpublished manuscript.

Mazhar, Muhammad. 1949. [Maulana Muhammad Murtuza ki Halat]. *Ruh-i Taraqqi* 8–9 [Special Issue]. Hyderabad.

———. 1951. "Meri Zindagi." *Bazm-i Adab* 25/5. Unpublished manuscript.

Mazumdar, Shudha. 1989. *Memoirs of an Indian Woman*. G. Forbes (ed.), 2nd ed. Armonk, NY: M.E. Sharpe.

Metcalf, Barbara D. 1991. *Perfecting Women: Maulana Ashraf 'Ali Thanawi's "Bihishti Zewar."* Berkeley: University of California Press.

Middlebrook, Diane Wood. 1990. "Postmodernism and the Biographer." In Susan Groag Bell and Marilyn Yalom (eds), *Revealing Lives: Autobiography, Biography, and Gender*, pp. 155–66. Albany: State University of New York Press.

Minault, Gail. 1989. "*Ismat*: Rashid ul Khairi's Novels and Urdu Literary Journalism for Women." In C. Shackle (ed.), *Urdu and Muslim South Asia*, pp. 129–38. London: School of Oriental and African Studies.

———. 1998. "Women's Magazines in Urdu as Sources for Muslim Social History." *Indian Journal of Gender Studies* 5: 201–13.

Mukherjee, Meenakshi. 1988. "The Unperceived Self: A Study of Nineteenth Century Biographies." In K. Chanana (ed.), *Socialisation, Education and Women: Explorations in Gender Identity*, pp. 249–72. Delhi: Orient Longman.

Naim, C.M. 1987. "How Bibi Ashraf Learned to Read and Write." *Annual of Urdu Studies* 6: 99–115.

Ochs, Elinor and Lisa Capps. 1996. "Narrating the Self." *Annual Review of Anthropology* 25: 19–43.

Papanek, Hanna. 1988. "Afterword: Caging the Lion, a Fable for Our Time." In Rokeya Sakhawat Hossain, *Sultana's Dream*, pp. 58–85. New York: Feminist Press of the City University of New York.

Personal Narratives Group (ed.). 1989. *Interpreting Women's Lives: Feminist Theory and Personal Narratives*. Bloomington: Indiana University Press.

Raheja, Gloria, and Ann Gold. 1994. *Listen to the Heron's Words: Reimagining Gender and Kinship in North India*. Berkeley: University of California Press.

Roded, Ruth. 1994. *Women in Islamic Biographical Collections: From Ibn Sa'd to Who's Who*. Boulder, CO: Lynne Reiner Publishers.

Sarkar, Tanika. 1993. "A Book of Her Own. A Life of Her Own: Autobiography of a Nineteenth-century Woman." *History Workshop Journal* 36: 35–65.

———. 1999. *Words to Win: The Making of "Amar Jiban": A Modern Autobiography*. New Delhi: Kali for Women.

Spivak, Gayatri. 1985. "Subaltern Studies: Deconstructing Historiography." In Ranajit Guha (ed.), *Subaltern Studies: Writings on South Asian History and Society, IV*, pp. 330–63. New Delhi: Oxford University Press.

Suhrawardy, Shaista Akhtar Banu. 1945. *A Critical Survey of the Development of the Urdu Novel and Short Story*. London: Longmans.

Vatuk, Sylvia. 1990. "The Cultural Construction of Shared Identity: A South Indian Muslim Family History." In P. Werbner (ed.), *Person, Myth and Society in South Asian Islam*. Special Issue, *Social Analysis* 28: 114–31.

———. 1999. "Family Biographies as Sources for an Historical Anthropology of Muslim Women's Lives in Nineteenth-century South India." In J. Assayag (ed.), *The Resources of History: Tradition, Narration and Nation in South Asia*, pp. 153–72. Paris and Pondicherry: École française d'Extrême Orient and Institut français de Pondichéry.

Viramma, Josiane Racine, and Jean-Luc Racine. 1997. *Viramma: Life of an Untouchable*. London: Verso.

Visveswaran, Kamala. 1997. "Histories of Feminist Ethnographies." *Annual Review of Anthropology* 26: 591–621.

Watson, Lawrence and Maria-Barbara Watson-Franke. 1985. *Interpreting Life Histories.* New Brunswick: Rutgers University Press.

NOTES

1. A much earlier version of this essay was presented at a conference on "Language, Gender, and the Subaltern Voice: Framing Identities in South Asia," at the University of Minnesota, Minneapolis, in 1991. I thank the participants in that conference—and especially its organizer, Gloria Raheja—for their useful comments and suggestions for revision, which I have, regrettably, taken a very long time to heed.

2. In addition to this text, ZG has written numerous other autobiographical sketches and essays, some of them published, that allow me to place this account of her childhood within the broader context of a life that now spans more than eight decades.

3. On the first page of the first issue ZG, as editor, states the objectives of the magazine: "(1) to raise woman from her low position to the highest and (2) by saving [her] from oppression and cruelty, to make her the companion and intimate friend of her life's partner, in the true sense." Shortly after this passage was written, the second line was crossed out—apparently in response to reader criticism—and the words "to get men and women the rights that Islam has established for them" were written underneath.

4. Altogether approximately 170 different girls and women and 30–40 boys and men contributed to *The Women's Advisor* over the years; some wrote only one or two pieces, while others, including ZG, wrote more than a hundred.

5. The English translation fills approximately 400 double-spaced pages, about a third of which is ZG's running commentary on the original manuscript. I am grateful to Dr Yasmin Zaim for the initial translation and to Professor C. M. Naim for generously participating in what is still an ongoing project of polishing, editing, and annotating it for eventual publication.

6. The 1948 annexation of the Nizam's dominions into the newly independent Indian Union had only recently occurred. It and the events leading up to it had been accompanied by dramatic social change for the Muslim population of Hyderabad, one aspect of which was that the strict observance of female seclusion (*goshah*) diminished in many families as levels of female education and women's entry into the workforce rose.

7. Geraldine Forbes was one of the first historians of modern India to realize the importance of such autobiographical texts for writing South Asian

women's history: see Mazumdar 1989; Forbes (ed.) 1994; Forbes and Raychaudhuri (eds) 2000.

8. ZG had a limited reading knowledge of English, having studied almost entirely in Urdu-medium schools in her early years and later having studied privately for her BA, MA, and PhD.

9. The genre closest to that of Western biography is the *tazkira* ("memorial"). Strictly speaking a collection of the lives of a *set* of men, selected on the basis of their sharing in common a particular occupation, religious orientation, place of origin, or the like, the term may also be used for a biography of a single individual, or for a collection of essays by several different people about one particular individual's life and accomplishments. The subjects of a *tazkira* are typically male, usually men who have had a public life of some note, but accounts of women's lives are by no means unknown in the Islamic biographical tradition. As Roded notes, they are fairly numerous in Arabic, especially in early collections, though their prevalence declined significantly "immediately prior to the advent of Western influence on the . . . genre" (Roded 1994: 136). By the late nineteenth century, Western models of biographical writing had also made a substantial mark upon Urdu writers' approach to biography (see Hermansen 1988).

10. This is my own very free translation of the first verse of a poem (*qita'*) entitled *Bayan-i Musannif* ("About the Author") by the famous Urdu poet Ghalib. Like the lines from other Urdu poems with which her account is liberally sprinkled, these were probably familiar to most of her adult readers. I am very grateful to Frances Pritchett for identifying them for me.

11. For one of these, note the wording of her title, wherein she refers to herself in the first person plural (*hamara*), instead of the singular (*mera*). While this usage is quite characteristic of idiomatic spoken Deccani Urdu, I am tempted to see a particular significance in the way it is used here. Whereas in English a speaker, in choosing the plural pronoun, assumes either a "royal" or an "editorial" voice that encompasses others imperiously and/ or authoritatively, in Urdu the superficially similar usage seems rather to deflect attention *away* from the speaker, from the "I"-ness of her voice, in order to dilute the negative connotations of her daring to assertively call attention to herself as an autobiographical subject.

12. Sarkar makes a similar observation with reference to Rashsundari's *Amar Jiban*, written almost a century earlier in Bengal. As if to justify the "transgressive act" of writing an autobiography, the author employs a "novel mix of rhetorical modes . . . to mask a public unveiling of her life and recast it as an expression of Vaishnavite self-abnegation and humility as well as of proper womanly modesty and obedience" (Sarkar 1993: 36, 45).

13. In a small town where her husband, an excise officer, was posted.

14. Some of the background information about ZG and her family is to be found in the autobiographical account I am discussing here, but most comes from interviews and other published and unpublished sources, including essays written by ZG herself.

15. "Haji's Residence." Each *khandan* house bore a distinctive name, often some variant of the given name, title or nickname of the male household head or his wife. "Haji" refers to ZG's paternal grandfather, who had made the pilgrimage (*hajj*) to Mecca.

16. Polygyny, while not unknown in the *khandan*, was quite rare and generally disapproved of. Unlike arranged first marriages, second marriages were unions of personal choice, typically to women of inferior social origins. *Khandan* women almost never interacted socially with these women and they usually lived in separate establishments, the *khandan* effectively closing its collective eyes to their existence. Only rarely were their children considered eligible for marriage to the offspring of *khandani* women. As long as a man was financially able to maintain two households and give his first wife a reasonable share of his attention, the situation might be tolerable. But if she and their children experienced neglect or impoverishment, no one would fault her for feeling misused.

17. The *burqa* had not yet been adopted in families of their social stratum. It did not become popular until after 1948, when women of the *khandan* first began to move about on foot. Initially they did so only at night; later they went out in the daytime as well.

18. These changing ideas probably had an influence on marriage practices, though they were not the sole cause of the observed rise in age at marriage and increase in the numbers of lifelong spinsters after 1940. Prior to this it was very rare for a woman to remain single; those who did not marry lived as dependents in their parents' or brothers' households. But in the birth cohort to which ZG belonged (1920–9) and in the two that followed, roughly 15 per cent of the females who reached thirty failed to marry. The percentage is slightly higher among school-educated than among home-educated women.

19. ZG mentions reading popular Urdu women's magazines: most of these are mentioned by Minault 1998. She does not mention reading newspapers herself, however. Doubtless the men read them mainly in libraries or in reading rooms and at the homes of friends. There was no radio in the house, this being one of the modern Western inventions to which her paternal grandfather and others had strong objections.

20. As Leonard notes, in Hyderabad, as elsewhere in India, "the development of voluntary associations accompanied the expansion of education and marked the changing social boundaries." A diverse array of voluntary

organizations developed in the city in the years between 1879 and 1920. The British Resident and military officers and some "modern" officials and members of the nobility took the lead in this (Leonard 1978: 149). It was toward the end of this period that the men of ZG's family and others who, like them, were positioned only on the fringes of this elite stratum of society, began to take part in such activities.

21. In many Indian Muslim families of their class, women were taught to read but not to write, lest they misuse this skill for writing love letters and the like (cf. Naim 1987).

22. For a synopsis, see Suhrawardy 1945: 110–12.

23. Minault observes that Rashid-ul Khairi, although at one level a champion of women's rights, did not advocate women's challenging male authority or asserting their right to better treatment by society. He aimed instead to bring about a change of heart among those who oppressed women (Minault 1989: 134–5). This aspect of his thinking, if indeed she was aware of it, did not temper ZG's enthusiasm for him.

24. The author wrote under the name of Walida ("Mother of") Afzal Ali. I have not been able to locate a copy of the novel. For a synopsis and critique, see Suhrawardy 1945: 141–6.

25. The author is Mahmuda Begum. This novel is also unavailable, but see Suhrawardy 1945: 148–50.

CHAPTER 7

Cowherd or King?

The Sanskrit Biography of Ananda Ranga Pillai

DAVID SHULMAN

The Problem

In the middle of the eighteenth century, a highly successful Tamil politician (statesman? portfolio capitalist?) of middle-range caste, deeply enmeshed in the confused intrigues of the French, British, Mughal–Hyderabadi, Maratha, and various other, local contestants for control over pieces of the Coromandel coast, commissions a biography in Sanskrit—the story of himself as told to, or by, his humble Brahmin amanuensis. Why Sanskrit? And if Sanskrit, why the somewhat forbidding register of arcane prose mixed with often opaque, no less forbidding verses? And why a biography in any case? Such questions are, in this instance, particularly pressing because this biography hides in the penumbra of a much larger and better-known work, supposedly the first true "diary" ever composed in South India (or at least the first to have attracted eyes other than its author's). Did the consciousness that inspired Ananda Ranga Pillai, *dubashi* (translator and commercial factotum) of the French governor Joseph Dupleix in Pondicherry, to record, year after year, the events and musings of his days—"whatsoever wonderful or novel takes place" (Ananda Ranga Pillai 1984–5: 1:1)—also impel him to see to the composition of a suitably flattering biography? Can we, on the basis of these two texts and others generated by the circle of Tamil, Telugu, and Sanskrit poets that orbited around this powerful figure, characterize his imagination, his sense of self, the perhaps unconscious vision of the temporal and social space that he inhabited?

Such a space, like all cultural spaces, has a specificity that can be ana-
lytically defined. The present case calls our attention precisely because
its hero seems poised on the brink of that transformation we conventionally name "modern." He lived in the ambience of French Pondicherry and was clearly molded, at least in part, by profound exposure
to European ways. At the same time, his perceptions, both as recorded
in the diary and as we find them mediated by his Sanskrit biographer,
seem deeply rooted in the family and caste milieu from which he emerged, a milieu that is simultaneously celebrated and reimagined in the
literary works centering on Ananda Ranga and his circle. He speaks to
us, both directly and indirectly, with a distinctive, individualized voice
not unrelated to seventeenth-century antecedents, but also echoing
some of his contemporaries among the poets of the Tamil South. I will
tentatively refer to the sensibility emerging from these sources mentioned as "proto-modern," in a sense to be demonstrated empirically
in what follows. Note that this term suggests that we may have to move
"modernity," in at least several critical components, *backward* in South
India by many decades, at the least. Moreover, we may well want to
posit, as a hypothesis, the likelihood that these components evolved
largely through processes internal to the late-medieval culture and not
primarily through external causes. Continuities may turn out to be no
less striking than radical innovations in the crystallization of a modern
sense of time, causal relations, and the imagination of self.

The diary, let it be said at once, is, as many have observed, rather disappointing if we are looking for introspection, penetrating self-under-
standing, or any of the usual components of what we think of, perhaps
too readily, as the "subjective." Even as a record of political events it
often makes dull reading. Flashes of feeling are all too rare, and in any
case usually limited to recurrent grumbling against Ananda Ranga's
rivals, including his dark nemesis, Madame Dupleix. Not for this
author the candid self-disclosure of his seventeenth-century predecessor in autobiographical narrative, Banarasi of the *Ardha-kathanaka*,
who tells us, "I will narrate my story in the common language of middle India, freely revealing all that lies concealed. And though I speak
to you of my virtues, I will also disclose my sins and follies" (Banarasi 1981: 2). Anyone tempted to derive Ananda Ranga's literary
habit—if we can dignify the diary with this name—from an indi-
rect acquaintance with Rousseau, Saint-Simon, or Lenglet,[1] however
watered down or mediated by the French expatriate-adventurers of

mid-eighteenth-century Pondicherry, should think again. The sources for this diary come from elsewhere,[2] almost certainly from within the indigenous Deccani tradition of individualistic self-expression that slowly intensified and ramified in this region through the centuries we refer to as "Nayaka."[3] Somewhat paradoxically, it is the Sanskrit biography, the *Ananda-ranga-campu* of Srinivasakavi, that reveals, even more than the diary, something of a "proto-modern" awareness, and that speaks to the complexities of character and impulse in its protagonist. Notice, too, the choice implicit in this form—not autobiography per se but biography as driven by an autobiographical impulse;[4] biography, that is, as a stage, and a relatively early one at that, in the actor's filling up with a self that can be communicated, on this highly individual level but still in the third person, with other, potentially receptive selves.

The biography, we may note in passing, had a happier fate than that of contemporaneous Tamil works such as Tiyakaraya Tecikar's *Ananta-rankan-kovai*, which was not, it seems, actively commissioned by its hero, and which required considerable efforts through a middleman close to Ananda Ranga before the latter would allow for its first public performance (*arankerram*) and for suitable gifts to be made to the author.[5] Ananda Ranga was a generous, if at times capricious, patron of poets and musicians. But Srinivasakavi, his Sanskrit biographer, may have enjoyed a special status. He tells us he has composed a book about Ananda Ranga—a worthy, wealthy subject—that, like "another kind of garland," should find favor in the eyes of "all who *have* eyes" (8.39). "Another kind" of garland suggests that the author has a sense of having created something unprecedented. He gives a date for the composition—Kali 4854 (AD 1752) (8.41).

Other than this date, his name, and the names of his parents (Gangadharadhvari and Parvati, of the Srivatsa family), we know nothing about the poet-biographer. It is nonetheless clear that he completed his work in the glow of his hero's good fortune—for the years 1749 to 1752 were the acme of French imperial policies in South India. For a brief period Dupleix, Ananda Ranga's patron, seemed to be sweeping aside all opposition; his protégé in the Carnatic Wars, Canda Sahib, had been named Nawab of the Carnatic, while Dupleix was able to mastermind the appointment of the Nizam in Hyderabad;[6] the English and their allies were in general retreat following a series of humiliating military defeats. Ananda Ranga played a significant diplomatic role in consolidating the French position; his successes constitute the subject matter of the final cantos of his biography. Less than two years later, Canda Sahib was dead; the English, under Robert Clive, were on the ascendant all over the Carnatic (beginning with the capture of Arcot in September 1751); and Dupleix was recalled to France under a cloud. The relatively brief heyday of French ambition, centered in Pondicherry, was apparently the appropriate time to compose and publicly recite a Sanskrit biography of the Tamil *dubashi* who had proved indispensable to the French commanders. This context also explains, in part, the structure of the biography, which moves from the heavily genealogical opening (cantos 1 through 4.15) through a relatively brief central section focused on Ananda Ranga's personal history (marriage, the birth of his children, his first appointment in Pondicherry: cantos 4.16 through 6.14) to a patterned "heroic" conclusion describing the political and military campaigns of 1749–50 (cantos 6.15–8.36). The account conveniently breaks off *before* the assassination of Muzaffar Jang, the main French ally, on his triumphant march back toward Hyderabad in early 1751. This means that the military narrative (marked off with the title heading *atha yuddha-sangati* at 6.15 in one of the two surviving manuscripts) can follow the wholly triumphant progression through danger and trial to final victory that the heroic template demands.[7]

Kala-jnana, *Wisdom of Time*

In many ways, the early cantos of this work are the more original and intriguing in terms of the issues I have outlined. We have heroes aplenty in eighteenth-century South India, victorious in life or, preferably, in death,[8] whose stories follow a culturally determined logic; but how does one begin an official biography of a still-living subject who is primarily an interpreter-turned-merchant-diplomat, born in the caste of cowherds (Itaiyar), son to an enterprising father of obscure background and rather moderate attainments?[9]

By inventing a lineage. A royal one, reaching deep into the past, would no doubt be best. Cowherds, it seems, have real advantages in this respect. Here is what our Sanskrit poet has to say about the origins of Ananda Ranga's line. It all began with a promise made by Krishna to his foster-father, the cowherd Nanda, who begged the god to come down (*avatar*) again, from time to time, in *his* (cowherd) clan, in some part (*amsa*) of himself, to burn away the enemies that keep popping up in the world. Krishna agreed: he would do this to punish the evil Yava-nas—that is, Muslims—and to protect the good (1.38–40). By the time we get to Ananda Ranga's birth, the baby, the biographer's subject, is indeed an *amsa* of Vishnu, and the purpose of his birth is precisely that promised generations before to Nanda (3.6). So now we know why the future *dubashi* was an Itaiyan by birth. Nonetheless, it is im-portant to recognize the extreme attenuation in this biography of what we might call the "mythic identity-model" which is integral to earlier, Nayaka-period Sanskrit biographies such as Ramabhadramba's *Raghu-nathabhyudaya*. In these earlier works, the mythic identity of the hero is a matter of central concern; this hero mostly re-enacts, sometimes ironically, sometimes in a mode of extreme intensification and literal-ization, his inherited divine paradigm (Narayana Rao, Shulman and Subrahmanyam 1992: 191–202). Not so Ananda Ranga, whose iden-tification with Krishna is almost perfunctory, lacking affective texture. At no point does the biography attempt to work out the potential parallels or linkages with this particular mythic past.

Instead, it takes "prehistory" in a new and rather unexpected direc-tion, very rich in consequence. Nearly half of the narrative will go into unfolding this prehistory, beginning with a distant ancestor of Ananda Ranga who is called Vijayanandana—the son of one Govinda, a cow-herd descendant of the mythic Nanda, who was living in Ayanapuram (Ayanavaram) near Madras. Our poet tells the story in a prose passage which could be said to be the true beginning of his text:

> Once this Vijayanandana, no longer a mere boy, was playing, like the young Krishna, with his companions, the adolescent cowherds, when he arrived at a certain wilderness area, replete with water and grass for his herd. Now there was a great scholar, famous all over the earth, a master of the entire corpus of classical texts and the author of commen-taries on all the Vedas, who was also a classmate of the "Lion of Logic," Vedanta Desika. In his extreme poverty, he had worshiped in his heart the highest goddess (*para-sakti*), hoping to obtain wealth through her; but she had rejected him repeatedly, telling him that because of the heavy burden of evil deeds he was carrying he was simply not worthy of attaining riches without undergoing a new birth. This so disgusted him that he turned away from the world and took on the life of a wand-ering renouncer. With it came his name, Vidyaranya—Wilderness of Wisdom—and knowledge of ultimate truth (*brahma-vidya*), rooted in profound reflection.

No sooner was this achieved than the great goddess (*bhavani*), concluding that he was as good as reborn, sent the Goddess of Wealth, Sri, with all her jewels and ornaments, to him; and though he was indifferent to her by now and refused again and again to allow her to approach him, she kept following him like his shadow, smiling. He looked at her with aversion. He wanted only to station her somewhere or other, to attach her to some worthy man, if he could only find one. Searching, he arrived at that same wilderness spot and noticed Vijayanandana—especially his dignified appearance. Leading him on with gentle words, he brought him to the banks of the Tungabhadra River. There he collected a large army for him, put down all rival kings in that region, and constructed a great, expansive city for him, the City of Victory, with walls of gold, a city blessed with godly words, circled by the roaring waters of the Tungabhadra. It was like the den of a kingly lion who was easily capable of subduing the arrogant elephants who were his enemies. It was a good place, and Vidaranya was pleased when he anointed Vijayanandana king over it. Vijayanandana ruled wisely for a long time; all the kings of the earth bowed at his feet (1.46).

This is a cowherd's version, extended, gently twisted and transformed, of a well-known tale of origins, which makes the great fourteenth-century scholar Vidyaranya the real founder of the imperial capital Vijayanagara. Telugu sources in particular are fond of asserting the primordial link between the City of Victory and Vidyaranya, who is to be identified, at least on one level, with the historical figure of Madhavacarya-Vidyaranya, *mahant* of the Srngeri *math* from 1374–5 to his death in 1386 and brother of the Vedic commentator Sayana. Hermann Kulke has brilliantly illuminated the historic role of this Madhavacarya, at the same time distinguishing him from a Madhava-mantrin who served the family of the early Vijayanagara rulers in the mid-fourteenth century (Kulke 1993: 208–39). Vidyaranya-Madhava-carya and his brother Sayana, perhaps acting in concert with King Harihara II, were responsible for the creation of a neo-Vedic tone, almost an ideology, that the newly fledged and expanding Vijayanagara state adopted for its own purposes (Kulke 1993: 237–8). But some two centuries later—only *after* the fall of the Vijayanagara capital to the Muslim armies in 1565—the prestigious figure of Vidyaranya crystallized anew in the hands of Telugu chroniclers and in popular and oral accounts of the Vijayanagara state, as the founder-prophet who both selected the site for the capital city and, because of his superhuman knowledge of past, present, and future, was able to foretell the precise moment of its eventual destruction. These traditions, known by the genre-category of *kala-jnana*, "TimeWisdom," and embodied in texts such as theTelugu *Raya-vacakamu* and a series of Sanskrit works named after Vidyaranya,[10] have been discussed at length by Phillip Wagoner from several rich perspectives (Wagoner 1993: 33–50).

We will return to the *kala-jnana* in a moment, for it figures as naturally in the Ananda Ranga biography as it does in the Vijayanagara native historiography. Note first, however, the displaced and secondary character of this dynastic origin: Ananda Ranga is a scion of the earlyVijayanagara kings, but his first royal ancestor became king mostly by a kind of mistake. The Goddess of Wealth relentlessly pursues only a man who does not want her—who wants, in fact, only to get rid of her and, for this purpose, fastens on the first available candidate, the innocent Vijayanandana. This cowherd clan is regal by default. Irony is braided into its vision of the birth of a great kingdom. Popular tradition in South India establishes a tenuous connection between Vidyaranya and Vedanta Desika—the latter is said to have composed his *Vairagya-pancaka* in negative response to an invitation by the former to receive royal honors in the new city[11] —but here this linkage serves mostly to enhance Vidyaranya's own somewhat reluctant role in founding a city where he can, at last, leave the importunate goddess to her own devices, in the loving care of his cowherd surrogate as husband or king.

It is not, all in all, a very flattering portrait of the founding father of this family, who wanders into kingship more or less by chance, as in so many South Indian folktales of the innocent or simpleton turned king. Still, the episode seems designed primarily to serve as background to another one of Vidyaranya's backdated prophecies, where "chance" gives way to a more determinate pattern:

> Once the worthy guru [Vidyaranya], who knew all three times (*tri-kala-jna*), discovering in himself certain well-defined and diversified blessings (*vihita-vividhasir*), spoke joyfully to [Vijayanandana], who was by nature deeply devoted and pleasing in all his ways. "Son of Govinda," he said, "there will arise in your family five handsome kings, living embodiments of Desire, praised by all other kings. A certain son of a servant-girl, named Krsnaraya, will then take over this rich kingdom by force, driving away the five elder brothers. The five, Rama and the rest, heroic sons of Vira Nrsimha, will live long on earth as his

subordinates. The eleventh from you, called Ramaraya, will establish the lineage." When he heard these words from Vidyaranya, Vijaya-nandana obeyed him happily (1.46–50).

This laconic passage is, one feels, the real point of the entire story of origins and, as such, a suitable entry into the emerging biography. There is an important linkage with Krsnadevaraya, identified, as in other popular accounts, as the son of a maidservant. But the five broth-ers are mysterious; the Vira Nrsimha closest to Krsnadevaraya was his half-brother and immediate predecessor on the throne. Something has become jumbled, it seems, in this postleptic projection, and the names of the supposed kings between Vijayanandana and the more substan-tial foundational figure, Ramaraya—given at the start of Canto 2—are an incoherent mixture of well-known Vijayanagara rulers, some of the sixteenth and seventeenth centuries, and obscure or unknown names.[12] There may be an authentic historical connection here with the so-called Yadavas of Candragiri—for this Ramadevaraya's son, Kaladhara, is said to have left Candragiri for Ayanapura—and thus an attempt on the part of the poet-genealogist to preserve a memory of Itaiyan origins in the Tirupati–Candragiri area from the period when the remnants of the Vijayanagara state came to rest there before finally disappearing.

Leaving aside the problem of correlating this list[13] with some grounded historical context, we can observe something of the unusual mode of its presentation. The *Ananda-ranga-campu* emerges in part from a rich context of historiographical works composed in South India from the sixteenth century on; within these works, retrojected predictions of the *kala-jnana* type are one recognized mode of struc-turing perceptions of the past. I call such prophecies "retrojected" since they are always embedded, as in the present case, in texts composed long after the supposedly foreseen events; that is, they always offer what is, in effect, a historical sequence which is, however, couched in a *prospective* idiom. We might ask ourselves what is to be gained from this strangely skewed method of narrating past events—why, that is, the historian or biographer insists on telling the story as projected forward, so to speak, as if the sequence were still unfolding in a more or less determinate present-future. There is, as we will see, a relation here to the biographical or autobiographical uses of astrology—another prospective template embedded by the subject in a largely retrospective frame. The question is particularly striking because the pattern we are observing stands in so marked a contrast to contemporaneous developments in European historiography and biography/autobiography: Gabriel Motzkin has shown how, in eighteenth-century Western Europe, a newly fixed, surprisingly rigid vantage point of retrospection begins to generate what we think of as modern "history," that is, "the experience of the present as past, the experience in which the past appears as a whole in its evanescence" (Motzkin 1992: 36). The individual's understanding of his or her own past is a critical element in this newly crystallizing paradigm: "Retrospection is first of all an attitude applied to one's own life. As such, it requires that one take one's own life both as one's own and as ineluctably gone from one" (Motzkin 1992: 37).

Kala-jnana texts effectively reverse this orientation. They view past events, sometimes very remote from the author and his presumed audience, as non-contingent future. This is one way to tell a coherent life-narrative—as forward-looking and foreseen emergence out of a pre-existing, structured template.[14] The past thus appears as a visionary but definite future and is narrated in the future tense. This choice is meaningful on many levels. Think of our present example in the Ananda Ranga biography in terms of framing. There is the actual *kala-jnana* prophecy uttered by Vidyaranya, the omniscient author who must be postulated for all such statements: "X will happen" (five kings will be born, plus the real ruler, the son of the maidservant, etc.). This prediction, the epistemic core of the text, is, however, narrated retrospectively, as a past event in its own right: "A said that X will happen." The listener or reader, however, operates within a still wider, split frame in which knowledge of the "events" seems to zigzag both forward and backward while privileging the latter direction: B (the author of the text) tells us that A said that X will happen; but we must regard X as having already occurred (unless, as in the astrological model, certain parts of the process remain incomplete). Moreover, this complex pattern seems to be critical to the entire biographical enterprise, appearing as it does at the point of departure for the story that is waiting to be told.

Our example is, in fact, simpler than most. In the *kala-jnana* sequence in the *Rayavacakamu*, for instance, Vidyaranya's prophecy is narrated by Mullandra-dindima Pumbhava Sarasvati, a "soothsayer/prognosticator" at the court of Vira Nrsimha Raya,[15] in response to the king's question: "Before the city of Vidyanagara (Vijayanagara) was built, where was Vidyaranya Sripada?" (Wagoner 1993: 79). The question seems to be searching for that fixed point in the past—located in the eponymous seer who commands all temporal knowledge—on which to balance the uncertain and ambiguous present-future. In fact, the king's soothsayers have just finished a lecture to his military commanders on "what was fated and what was not, on what had happened, what was going to happen, and what was happening now" (Wagoner 1993: 79). The real thrust of all this, however, is toward identifying Krsnadevaraya, the next ruler, as the thirtieth king in an envisioned or known series of thirty kings, and as situated at a point 300 years into an envisioned sequence of 360 years—after which the great city and state will be destroyed. So *within* the text, the royal listener knows exactly where he stands. But again, the listener situated at the outer frame knows perfectly well that all this is long past: Z, hearing B (the soothsayer) say to C (the king) that A said that X will happen, is fully aware that X has already happened. Actually, I have simplified this frame considerably by cutting out another level that is structured into it—for the whole of the *Rayavacakamu* is presented to us as a report by a *sthanapati*-emissary to his royal master and patron, Kasi Visvanatha Nayanayya of Madurai, this identification being, in itself, certainly "fictive" (so that we thus have, in effect, yet another frame-level to deal with). That is: Z (the listener/reader) is hearing the report of W to Y (whom Z probably recognizes as a fictional persona) of what B (the soothsayer) reported to C (the king) as to A's prediction that X would happen, and that, as Z knows, *has* already happened long ago.

I wish to resist the temptation to think of this sequence as deliberately anachronistic—projecting a seventeenth-century reality backward onto the early-sixteenth-century setting of the royal court of Vira Nrsimha and Krsnadevaraya. In my view, it is far more likely that we are dealing here with a structure of many-layered and differential temporalities, very rich in depth or volume, in which a historical character of, say, the seventeenth century can truly loop into a historical moment which we, all too easily, insist must have been "prior." Moreover, it is not without meaning that such loops take the form of retrospective, forward-looking predictions. The deeper one goes in a series of such intricately interwoven frames,[16] the more space becomes available for contact with the inner process of an event, temporally and causally conceived and defined—or, if you prefer, of a narrative of personal origins in relation to the trajectory of an ongoing life. In such a model, "pastness" is not given, certainly not as a fixed point or points in a linear chain, but is rather capable of varying degrees of realization and reality, of moving forward or backward in relation to the interlocking sequences of which it must necessarily be part. The same understanding, incidentally, may well apply to the "futureness" of the future.

Still, we have the pressing question formulated above: why go to such lengths? What is being said? Why embed the past as future? Why the insistence on this form? In Ananda Ranga's case, the prophecy itself is even somewhat lame and elliptical, seemingly remote from the concerns of biography focused on his military and political career—very remote, that is, from the cowherds of Candragiri with their mythic memories of Vijayanagara. And yet nearly half of this biography is, in fact, taken up with genealogical materials, as I have said; the biographer reaches far back into prehistory in an attempt to create a vital context out of which his hero can take shape. This movement itself diverges from a classical pattern. If the *Ramayana*, for example, tells the story of Rama in terms of his future descendants, his *ayana*—as the very name of the text tells us—in the present case we have biography as the retrojected narrative of the hero's forefathers. The cowherd lineage has to be fleshed out or, indeed, retroactively invented if the Itaiyan hero at the end of the line is to come alive. More to the point, such a life narrative seems to unfold in a temporal mode in which some events, at least, pre-exist as structured potential that pre-dates their enactment and that, without fully determining the form of that eventual enactment, lays down lines of force within which the active subject can enter into play. In this sense, the latent temporal template is very much like the linguistic template that moves any speaking subject from the primary, *potential* word, alive in awareness, via its externalization (*padartha*) to the fully contoured object. Incidentally, the historian's role now achieves a further urgency, since by *knowing* the predictive template one creates space for action. The point is critical to our analysis, for in the second, truly "biographical" half of this biography we will find Ananda Ranga acting with tremendous initiative, constantly making creative choices and fashioning a reality out of what his biographer calls his "sheer intelligence." He is certainly not a passive object of determinate predictive processes, although the knowledge of past prediction seems to provide a legitimating power to his rise from cowherd to *dubashi*—in effect, to the role of a quasi-king.

The exfoliation of an embedded seed is not a mechanical business. The template has its own inherent, interactively operative dynamism: history, in works such as the *Rayavacakamu*, is all about this dynamic, including the unexpected configurations that arise as it begins to blossom and bear fruit. Knowledge has a part in the process. As Velcheru Narayana Rao tells us, "It is a certain willingness to see things realized that brings the event to happen" (Narayana Rao 1996: 204). To some extent, this is also the measure of the subject's freedom. If we follow through on the contrast with retrospection in the eighteenth-century European mode, it turns out, to our surprise, that retrospection-as-future, unrolling forward even as the outer frames point us backward, offers a significant degree of autonomy to the subject fashioning the forms of his own emergence into time. Once again, the astrological model of structured potentiality, potentially knowable in advance, is germane. Recall that in our small *kala-jnana* segment of the biography, the indispensable Vidyaranya, the man who commands time by knowing it, searches in himself and discovers there "certain well-defined and diversified blessings." Both definition and its potential diversity in emergence lend themselves to this kind of temporal scheme.

Garbhadharaka/Karuventiya Pillai, Patron of Poets

It is not enough, however, to posit a tale of origins, with its *kala-jnana* aspect, such as that we have just studied. Between the distant ancestor Vijayanandana and Ananda Ranga, our text counts eighteen generations—nine leading up to the *vamsa-karta* we have already encountered, Ramadevaraya, and eight between the latter and Ananda Ranga himself. Not all of these worthy progenitors merit the biographer's attention. There is one, however—a certain Garbhadharaka, Ramadevaraya's grandson—who enjoys a brief narrative flourish, for Garbhadharaka, like our hero Ananda Ranga, was a generous patron of poets. Yet he had his own, rather idiosyncratic methods:

> Once eight refined poets—Kumuda and others—together with thousands of their disciples came from Golconda (Golakunda) to Ayananagaram, their tongues alight with language. They had heard about the virtues of gracious Garbhadharaka—about his openness to scholars and the good fortune he brought to poets—so it was almost like seeking out God himself, who could also be called a poet. When they arrived at the village, someone pointed out to them the man they were looking for—at the threshing floor. He was entirely absorbed in

searching for grains of rice left over from the threshing. "How can someone like that give anything to people like us?" they thought. Still, since his fame had spread through the earth, they approached him and spoke graciously; and he, at once intuiting their intention, broke into a radiant smile and led them to his splendid home. He seated the poets on seats fashioned from gold and at once gave them vast riches and golden vessels.

In their astonishment they placed their fingers on their nose. Observing this, dissembling, he said to them:

> When I was picking up, one by one,
> grains of rice that had fallen
> in the fields as my servants
> were threshing grain,
> in your hearts, great poets,
> you despised me.

> But I was following the rule
> that what the wise say
> must be true: that rice,
> that is, is wealth
> or pearls.

He loaded them down with cows, elephants, swift horses, and this opened their hearts as the moon opens the night lily with its rays. So one by one the poets blessed him (2.3–10).

N. Palarama Aiyar, the author of a Tamil commentary on the *Anantarankan-kovai*, reports another version of this story, whose hero is now known by his Tamil name, Karuventiya Pillai.[17] He brings the skeptical poets home, spreads the banana leaves, and covers them with gold coins, which he asks his guests to eat. When they protest that only rice will appease their hunger, he asks them: "So you put aside these coins? And I—should I put aside the grains of rice, that are worth more than gold?"

The story provides another fixed point in the production of a proper pedigree for our cowherd diplomat. His distant ancestors now include a lavish donor, connoisseur, and oral poet, whose frugality would have done credit to a Puritan. Indeed, the vignette seems designed partly to convey something of this latter quality—perhaps a touch of the thrifty merchant attaches early on to the cowherd clan. We could also derive the story from the *catu* world of oral poetics, which unquestionably enveloped Ananda Ranga in Pondicherry; many stories and surviving verses speak of his relations with poets such as Patikkacuppulavar and Namaccivayappulavar, great eighteenth-century talents, and of his largesse toward dancers and other artists (see Narayana Rao and Shulman 1998). Garbhadharaka's verses, seen as improvised on the spot, belong naturally in this milieu. The trajectory that leads from Deccan pastoralism to the company of Huna princes and merchant-buccaneers thus proceeds via the Time-Wizard Vidyaranya and the witty *catu* patron and poet, father of merchants, who is not above scouring the fields for a few grains of unthreshed rice.

Father and Cousin: Tiruvenkata sends
Guruvap Pillai to France

Further down the genealogical line of descent we encounter, at last, Ananda Ranga's father, Tiruvenkata, and his mother, Laksmi. A pilgrimage to Tirupati bears fruit: Krishna "descends" to earth once more, in the form of the child Ananda Ranga. The third canto of the biography tells of his birth, the mother's death, and Tiruvenkata's decision to establish himself in trade first in Cennapattanam, then in Nutanarajadhani, i.e. Pondicherry. The same logic of biography-as-genealogy applies to the poet's lengthy narrative about Tiruvenkata—in some ways, a more vivid portrait than that of Ananda Ranga himself. Here, for the first time in this text, we find the textures and implicit notions of agency and causality that deserve an attribute such as "realistic" or even "proto-modern." To illustrate, I cite one short example.

This passage has to do with the celebrated case of Guruvap Pillai, Ananda Ranga's cousin, mentioned above.[18] Guruvap Pillai's father, Nayaniyap Pillai, brother-in-law to Ananda Ranga's father Tiruvenkata, had risen to prominence as chief *dubashi* in Pondicherry during the time of Hebert (from 1709). It was, in fact, Nayaniyap Pillai who was responsible for Tiruvenkata's moving with his family to Pondicherry, when ARP was a young boy. Eventually, however, Hebert turned against his Tamil *dubashi* and had him imprisoned, unjustly; he died in prison in 1717. Tiruvenkata and Guruvap Pillai fled Pondicherry for Madras; the latter—another early diarist!—then proceeded to France to seek redress from the hands of the Duke of Orleans. Our biographer tells the story in the following condensed prose passage:

After that he (Tiruvenkata), aspiring to Himalayan heights of forti-
tude, his good name celebrated without exception by all officials because of the attitude of patient responsibility he embodied (like the
great snake who bears the whole burden of the earth on his head),
wished to see his two sons in Cennakesavapura [Madras]; he also wanted to pursue the weighty matter of Guru[vap Pillai] and Nayana
[Pillai].[19] With the permission of his master [at Pondicherry], he went
to Madras and boldly planned his moves. He sent his own account of
the affair with his relative [Guruvap Pillai], who went by sea, in a ship
piloted by a highly professional captain, to see the French king of the
Western Huns [the Duke of Orleans] and to inform him orally of the
matter. Hearing his report, the King was delighted and sent an order
back to the dutiful new head of the city [Pondicherry],[20] who was in
any case well aware of Tiruvenkata's professional competence. This
Governor [de la Prevostière] sent an emissary respectfully to invite
Tiruvenkata to return to New Town [Nutana Putabhedanam = Puduc-
ceri/Pondicherry], and he did so, together with his sons and followers.
Upon arrival, the Governor said to him, "You are highly intelligent.
Please take upon yourself complete authority over our affairs." With
his own hands he bestowed upon him the royal seal, and for a long time
Tiruvenkata made all the subjects happy by his just rule (4.1).

This is one long sentence in Sanskrit, most of it, in fact, a single *tat-
purusa* compound. Unraveling the entire utterance backwards, as the
grammarians demand, we expose the following literal structure, omit-
ting all adventitious modifiers:

> Tiruvenkata . . . /wanting to see his sons, /after taking leave and going
> to Madras,/ was invited back by the new Governor intent on seeing to
> the orders sent by the Huna king delighting in the report heard from
> [Tiruvenkata's] relative, who carried his [Tiruvenkata's] secret message
> by sea in a boat . . ./

It looks simpler like this, much simpler than it sounds when read
forward and certainly no longer or more complex than much medieval
Sanskrit prose. Yet the surface appearance is misleading. Something
rather new is evident in this dense and polished style. We might think
of it as more factual and event-oriented than rhetorical, despite the inevitable stock tropes. It also has to be read differently from its classical
models. The single long compound strings out the whole sequence of
events beginning with Guruvap Pillai's voyage to France and including

his meeting with the Duke of Orleans, the latter's response to his oral message, the consequent directive to the new governor, and de la Prevostière's embassy to Tiruvenkata in Madras. On first hearing, this series is bunched together in near simultaneity, each segment flowing seamlessly, almost timelessly, into the next; Tiruvenkata, waiting in Madras, has not moved, though he has set in motion the strangely compacted chain; the events eddy around him, the single subject and witness, the grammatical center and actor, the modified amidst cascading modifiers. In itself, this structure is capable of suggesting a strong notion of personal activity, really a causal argument: Ananda Ranga's father is the prime force shaping events, carefully calculating and projecting their direction, foreseeing consequence and advantage.

But if we want to understand a sentence like this as it emerges naturally into audible sequence, we have to segment it in such a way that the internal relations between "events" become transparent—and this means, among other things, breaking up the integrity of the compound, pausing for breath and clarification at invisible resting points *within* it, thus stretching it in unexpected ways, creating space for ourselves as listeners. The result is a new kind of sequence, with its own temporal rhythm and highly evocative emphases. Reading like this, we can begin to experience something of the long and no doubt terrifying sea voyage that Guruvap Pillai must undergo; we see him meet the duke and note the impact of the face-to-face encounter and the force of the orally delivered message (about French injustice and a father's death); we stop for a moment to let the duke compose his orders to the governor in Pondicherry, and we wait the long months necessary for them to be delivered; we may even detect a hint of the new governor's annoyance at being told what to do by someone so far away, in Paris, someone removed from the local realities of dependence on less-than-straightforward *dubashis*, for example. All of this—a rather complicated series of causally connected movements by autonomous agents, all of them still linked to the primary subject-agent, Tiruvenkata—comes through in the subtle tones of the telling, which manages both to idealize the image of Ananda Ranga's late father and to evoke the gentle disjunctions of life as experienced in a realistic, almost modern manner. This Sanskrit is a living language, clearly capable of surprisingly novel tones, a language still evolving under the impact of swiftly expanding sensibilities—a far cry from the artificial pandit's language that so often claims continuity with the classical tradition today, two and a half centuries after our Pondicherry biographer.

A Diplomat and His Son

Halfway into our text, we at last begin to learn something about its primary subject. After the death of Ananda Ranga's father, Tiruvenkata, in 1726, Ananda Ranga was, we are told, invited by the (French) Huna-raja to assume his father's post (4.16).[21] He built himself a splendid new house—still to be seen in Pondicherry—and in it he installed a curiosity recently imported from Europe:

> It stands by itself inside the house—
> no great apparatus—and tells the hours
> without pause, to the utter amazement
> of astrologers, absorbed in calculations,
> and the delight of Brahmins who now know
> when, precisely, to report, each day
> to King Sriranga for their dole. (*Ananda-ranga-campu*, 4.22)

Did the local astrologers come to terms with this outlandish device that could tell time "without pause" and without calculation? We may be skeptical as to the extent that Newtonian time penetrated into the everyday reality of eighteenth-century Pondicherry; but the diary, at least, consistently reports time in both European and Indian hours (see Alalasundaram 1998: 83). Notice also the highly realistic tone of the verse just cited: if we are still in the domain of *kavya*, this poem nonetheless occasionally focuses sharp observation on real objects seen in themselves and not as components of a figurative and usually inflated reality. To a certain extent, this statement could apply to the biographer's stance *vis-à-vis* his hero and subject as well.

Clocks and astrologers may not belong to quite the same functional domain, but they do coexist in Ananda Ranga's universe. In some ways the central segment of this most "personal" piece of the biography is the detailed and precise description of the *jataka* chart of Ananda Ranga's son, Annasvami/Muddu Vijayananda-ranga, born after four daughters, in 1748. As our poet says, the birth of this male child was an event the father had long yearned for—clearly a major element in the happy period of Ananda Ranga's ascendance, the years from late 1746 until 1751–2 that form the true focus of this biography. The two decades preceding his son's birth are collapsed in the biography into a relatively compact account of Ananda Ranga's marriage and house-building activities, interspersed with an official mission to Hunakheta (Parangipettai, Porto Novo, 5.27).[22] With the son's arrival, however, there is a sudden shift into a triumphant and heroic mode—the astrological considerations issuing immediately into the complex political and military maneuvers in which Ananda Ranga excels and which promise (however briefly, as we, unlike the Sanskrit biographer, know well) a French empire centered on the southern Coromandel coast.

The astrologer, Subrahmanya of Nyasa-grama,[23] makes his own promises. The newborn child will live for seventy-three years and will become a famous king, like Rama, destroying all enemies (6.5–6). The reasoning behind this prediction is set out in great technical detail, on the basis of the chart, in a learned *gadya* passage that is in its own way a *tour de force*. Astral configurations merge with hyperbolic and paranomastic descriptions of the baby's beauty, features, dress, and so on. This is also a good moment to remind listeners that this male child comes from the line of Garbhadharaka, the hero of the earlier *catu* vignette (6.10). Continuity, it seems, is now assured. The astrologer is richly honored and rewarded, in cash (*dinaraih*) and kind (6.8). Our modern editor, Raghavan, allows himself a skeptical note: "A brilliant career for the boy as is here predicted is not apparent from the horoscope."[24] There are, after all, advantages to retrospection. More to the point, this elaborate passage, marking the acme of the biographer's portrait of Ananda Ranga in his personal and family milieu, at roughly the center of the entire work and the point of departure for the heroic events to come, reactivates the prophetic *kala-jnana* mode discussed above. This time, however, the prophecy is individualized and truly oriented toward the future, though not that of the actual, slightly shadowy subject of our text—but rather that of his son. Here, perhaps, is where the minimal subjectivity we might expect in biography is somehow to be found.

War follows. Step by step, Ananda Ranga leads the French to victory, cleverly outwitting the uncomprehending English and their unsavory Hyderabadi and Arcot allies in a series of brilliant moves. The former—ultimately, one might think, the more serious threat—are derided as "corpulent as whales;" the French king has brought them under his control through the "sheer intelligence" of Ananda-ranga (6.29). We learn this in a speech by Canda Sahib to his ally Hira (Muzaffar Jang), who has been sent south by the Delhi padshah to subdue the Hyderabadi pretender Nasir Jang (son of the famous Nizam Asaf Jah).[25] This speech has much to recommend it as a fairly realistic account of the political realities in Pondicherry. The French ruler "sits quietly and without fear" only because his minister (*amatya*), Ananda Ranga, is constantly alert, and strong enough to protect the French interests (6.28). Canda's plan is to send gifts and letters to Ananda Ranga, who has anyway cared for Canda's family during the years of Canda's imprisonment by the Marathas, and to ask for military assistance in the campaign against Nasir—for Ananda Ranga can sway the French into sending soldiers, armed with rifles, and artillery. It works: Ananda Ranga consults with Dupleix, and the two agree to equip Canda's son, Saraja (Raza Sahib), with over a hundred artillery pieces and a terrifying force of musket-bearing foreign soldiers. This force joins Hira and Canda at Amur/Ambur in August 1749, where the hostile ruler of Arcot, Anwar al-Din Khan (Anavarddhi-nrpa, 6.24), is killed. This is the beginning of the French wave of military victories, and the first sign that Ananda Ranga's strategic plan may work.

We need not work our way through each subsequent stage of this process. There are surprisingly realistic and human touches at many points. After Ambur, for example, when Canda and Hira come to thank Ananda Ranga at Pondicherry, he courteously and modestly disclaims any credit (deliberately echoing Kalidasa's polite hero, Pururavas): "It is not I who am the active cause (*hetu*) in a matter such as this. The main thing is the king's conspicuous power. The echo of a lion's roar, from a cave deep in the mountain, still shatters arrogant foes" (6.59).[26]

The power of Dupleix must be conspicuous to be effective; by implication, Ananda Ranga's role is to make this possible while remaining largely invisible himself. He speaks to the man whose position he has salvaged, and who is now wholly in his debt, in language that rings true for this setting—elevated, suggestive, self-effacing in a subtly self-glorifying way.

As in many of the *kavya*-style histories composed in the seventeenth and eighteenth centuries in South India, a factual and object-oriented focus mingles with the more familiar, heavily figurative and hyperbolic style inherited from earlier poets—although in the present case, the former, relatively restrained tone could be said to predominate. Throughout, Ananda Ranga is seen as prescient, energetic, and entirely competent, "able to achieve the unachievable" (7.45), steadily moving the French and their allies toward a clear-cut victory over their confused and eminently corruptible foes. One should, perhaps, bear in mind Raghavan's understated characterization of this Carnatic campaign: "There was more intrigue and conspiracy than fighting, and it is the former which finally settled the affairs."[27] Srinivasa-kavi methodically documents this process—both its few full-fledged military engagements and the deeper and more insidious business of demoralizing Nasir's supporters, who, thanks to Ananda Ranga's amazing skill in such matters, become increasingly reluctant to fight the French. The course of events is well known from other sources, and the biography has little new to add in the way of hard facts: we watch the French forces as, together with Canda Sahib and Muzaffar Jang, they turn first against Maratha Tanjavur, exacting vengeance for Canda Sahib's long and humiliating captivity in the hands of the Marathas; this strategic success is followed by a temporary setback in the bungled battle of Villiyanur—shockingly close to Pondicherry itself—in April 1750, in the course of which Muzaffar Jang is captured by the enemy forces. The denouement comes in October 1750, in a series of typically disorganized, almost whimsical clashes near Senji; as we know from other sources, and as Srinivasakavi tells us in graphic, concrete detail, the French victory is won largely through the devastating effect of bad weather—a long and violent rainstorm—on the already internally divided and far-from-enthusiastic enemy forces. Nasir, frustrated and enraged, harangues his own generals in insulting terms; one of them, Himmad Bahadara (Himmat Bahadur), the Pathan ruler of Kurnool, whose penchant for violent fits of rage is also well documented, and who has anyway been secretly won over by Ananda Ranga, takes this opportunity to behead Nasir. This happy outcome, which fully vindicates Ananda Ranga's tactics, is achieved only moments before Muzaffar Jang was to have been executed at Nasir's command, although Srinivasakavi surprisingly fails to mention this melodramatic background to Nasir's demise.

He does, however, tell the story with poignant economy in a prose passage very representative of his simultaneously sober and colorful style:

> He [Nasir] could see that his army, attacked from all sides, was utterly demoralized—as if terrified whenever someone merely clapped his hands—and that, although in the past they had been victorious thousands of times, they could hardly use their weapons, like a herd of monkeys; they also seemed to have no sense of how the battle-plan was

going. He also considered his own strength, and the coming to fruition of all the inauspicious omens: "Oh the power of destiny (*niyati*)! How fierce is this battle! How vast the Huna army! Alas, look who is running away, and who is winning. And what use are these counselors and relatives who just sit there while a man like myself is reduced to these straits?" He was consumed inside by rage and began to scream harshly at his generals, even those worthy of respect. As he was moving through the field on the back of a mountainous elephant, a certain monstrous Yavana named Himmad Bahadara, who had been insulted once too often and was now very angry, and who had, moreover, been secretly corrupted by Vijaya Ananda Ranga, came close to him and severed his head with a sharp weapon. Thus Nasara [Nasir] joined the vanguard of Death's own forces (7.47).

Perhaps it was, after all, a close call. Victory was almost in Nasir's grasp—if only his soldiers had understood their situation, if he had controlled himself at this moment of despair, if the rain would only have let up . . . and if only Ananda Ranga, the brains behind the French campaign, had not been so good at what our poet delicately refers to as "the third means" (*trtiyam upayam*—in the *Arthasastra* map of politics, 7.44), that is, *bheda*—sowing dissent in the enemy's ranks.

Triumph on the battlefield is followed by celebration: the biography concludes with an account of the festivities in Pondicherry, beginning with a long description of Ananda Ranga's daily routine, from the moment he awakes, dresses, ritually studies himself in the mirror, and so on—a passage lifted from the Nayaka-period *abhyudaya* literature that we have elsewhere referred to as "A Day in the Life of [X]" (Narayana Rao, Shulman and Subrahmanyam 1992: 58–66). As noted earlier, this entire sequence, beginning with Hira's appearance on the scene as a potential ally of the French and concluding with the Senji battle in 1750, is patterned to allow Ananda Ranga's achievement to appear untarnished. The biographer, writing in Pondicherry in 1752, thoroughly conversant with the political reality in which his subject operated, must surely have known of Muzaffar Jang's assassination in January 1751, on his way to Hyderabad (by the same Himmat Bahadur who had killed Nasir) and of the English takeover of Arcot. The exigencies of patronage and dependence and the requirements of the *kavya* frame have joined in producing an artificial closure to the biographical venture.

Conclusion: The Person in the Text

Let us say at once: we are very far from Boswell, far even from Xenophon or Plutarch,[28] far from Banarasi of Rajasthan. If we focus on the diary, which needs to be read together with the *campu*, we can say much the same thing: we are a long way from Rousseau, Lenglet, or Solomon Maimon (to remain with eighteenth-century exemplars). One could go on for quite some time saying what the surviving records of Ananda Ranga's unusual life are not. Above all, the sense of an atomistic individual scanning the obscure landscape of his innerness, or that of his subject, is surely missing from these two texts.

For all that, I want to argue that the *Ananda-ranga-campu* is a proto-modern biography, using both terms with some care; and I will try to say what I mean by this characterization. Closely related to this attempt at a tentative analytic definition is the question of Srinivasakavi's sources and possible models. The above discussion has disclosed something of the range: a mythic genealogy built around a *kala-jnana* prediction, an oral *catu*-borne vignette, segments of "pure" *kavya* lyrical description à la Dandin (springtime, monsoon, autumn), simple self-serving panegyric, an *abhyudaya* segment on the hero's daily ritual routine (the culminating component in this series)—and, let us not forget, something not quite new, the relatively tough and realistic narrative of non-fictionalized events, taken here to a level beyond that of the earlier Nayaka-period historical *kavyas*. The mere fact that the poet has combined in non-mechanical ways these rather diverse paradigms, all of which he commands, thereby producing a new literary form centered on an individual whom he certainly knew and wished to describe from various perspectives—as a many-faceted yet singular subject—this fact alone sets the *campu* apart and probably warrants our naming it with this foreign name.

We still need to situate this text in its true milieu and to formulate the primary features brought together within the compass of its portrait. Srinivasakavi did not invent the major vectors of a historical "life." He had at his disposal plentiful sources of an indigenous historiographical corpus in Sanskrit and, in particular, Telugu; to some extent also in Tamil. Perhaps the Sanskrit models were closest to the surface: from Nayaka times, the *Sahitya-ratnakara* of Yajnanarayana Diksita and Ramabhadramba's *Ramabhyudaya*, to name only two;

from Maratha Tanjavur, Sridhara Venkatesa's *Sahendra-vilasa* (on Shahaji); from further back in time, the Hoysala dynastic prose-history *Gadyakarnamrta*, by Sakala-vidya-cakravarttin, or the *Pandya-kulodaya* of Mandala-kavi, or a long series of similar texts; or, still deeper in the past, Bana's classic *Harsa-carita*. For the record, let me say that the latter, a unique biographical *kavya*, for all its pronounced literary features and fantasy-driven tones, includes moments of re-markably personal, convincingly realistic and grounded first-person reporting (especially in Canto 2, where Bana tells us his own story).[29] And so on. Medieval Sanskrit historiography is far more extensive, in range and depth, than is sometimes recognized; and the continued vitality, inventive curiosity, and linguistic creativity of Sanskrit lite-rary production, at least in South India, is clearly evident in the late-medieval works just noted. All the above texts show us an internalized aware-ness of the distinction between fact and fiction, clearly visible in textural features, the necessary precondition for composing either "history" or "biography."

Similarly for the Telugu and Tamil historical and biographical materials, which emerged with striking consistency from the middle-range village contexts we have been calling "the *karnam* culture" and which achieved a particular sophistication by the time of Srinivasakavi (Narayana Rao, Shulman and Subrahmanyam 2002). The *Raya-vacakamu*, with its *kala-jnana* segment, was mentioned above. Similar texts have survived, each with its distinctive vision of the past, its im-plicit theory of cause and sequence; the tradition reaches its finest flowering in an unparalleled historiographical masterpiece from the late eighteenth century, Ditta-kavi Narayana-kavi's *Ranga-raya-caritramu* (on the Bobbili War of 1757, in Ananda Ranga's lifetime; various figures mentioned in our Pondicherry biography also turn up in the latter work). In Tamil, compositions such as Patikkacuppulavar's *Tontai-mantala-catakam* and its analogues, by poets directly linked with Ananda Ranga himself, reveal something of the same historical-biographical fascination characteristic of this period. If Srinivasakavi nonetheless chose to write in Sanskrit, in a period of normative poly-glossia—Sanskrit being, in effect, simply another, elevated speech register available to the educated elite—his choice may have some-thing to do with the ramified and subtle forms of expressivity *in prose* that the Sanskrit historiographical tradition had already worked out.

The choice of prose for a biography is itself significant, a statement rich in implication for a subject that is at least in part conceived as down-to-earth, visibly matter-of-fact, and not entirely complete. As several of the examples cited earlier should make clear, Srinivasakavi's primary originality lies in the prose passages that fill the text, as *campu*, of course, requires. In the middle of the eighteenth century, Tamil, at least, had yet to elaborate prose styles of an expressive power equal to those easily accessible in Sanskrit; some have claimed, in fact, that Ananda Ranga himself was the first to write a modern, colloquial Tamil prose, in the informal form of his diary entries (see Zvelebil 1973: 272–5). He was not, however, imitated—the diary was not meant for public consumption—and his biographer looked elsewhere, to more prestigious models.

A consciousness playing at new forms, composing in innovative prose style (mixed with poetry in the lyrical meters) an image of an individual of many parts and aspects, who is nonetheless whole and singular, strikingly separate from other individuals: can we call such a consciousness "proto-modern?" Here are some of the features we have isolated. The biographical subject emerges out of a strongly articulated genealogy; he lives out an ancestral logic. A biography is in some ways a mythic account of this logic, which is rooted in a temporal substratum we have called "astrological," a Time-Wisdom that speaks the past as future, or that, more generally, sees events as unfolding within a space of structured or defined potentiality, proleptically knowable and, in fact, already known. Retrospection, in this temporal mode, tends to move forward rather than backward and to highlight the subject's freedom to act in accordance with what he knows. The agent's acts have causal effect within the field of their operation—a pre-existing future template of many possible configurations—and can be narrated, that is, organized into an intelligible sequence, as such. Reality—as a domain of visible objects, realia—is interesting. Factuality exists, distinct from fiction. Motivations are often complex. Inner monologues take place and can be recorded—recall Nasir's last moments—but they tend to be relatively rare. The individual subject is nonetheless *not* a type (in Ananda Ranga's case, for example, that of an *amatya*-minister). Similarly, the available mythic prototypes—Krishna for our hero—are attenuated to the point of near irrelevance. But at the same time, the great modern myth of decentering—the painful insistence on a split awareness that is subject to alienation, uprooting, a loss of organic connectivity and wholeness—has yet to appear. Neither Ananda Ranga nor Srinivasakavi could possibly have dreamt of it, despite Raghavan's apt definition of the "mist-like pathos" that informed our hero's sensibility.[30] Neither mist nor pathos is proto-modern. Another century or more would go by before South Indian voices would begin to articulate this ironic modern mythos, and before plaintive biographies and autobiographies could be recorded in a voice we so readily recognize as our own.

REFERENCES

Alalasundaram, R. 1998a. "Ananda Ranga Pillai as a Diarist." *Journal of the Institute of Asian Studies* 15: 75–92.

———. 1998a. *The Colonial World of Ananda Ranga Pillai, 1736–61.* Pondicherry: Published by the author.

Ananda Ranga Pillai. 1984–5. *Diary.* New Delhi: Asian Educational Service.

Banarasi. 1981. *Ardhakathanaka, Half a Tale.* Transl. Mukund Lath. Jaipur: Rajasthan Prakrit Bharati Sansthan.

Berkson, Carmel. 2000. *The Life of Form in Indian Sculpture.* New Delhi: Abhinav.

Handelman, Don. in press. "Toward a Braiding of Frame." In David Shulman and Deborah Thiagarajan (eds), *Behind the Mask: Possession, Dance and Healing in South India.* Ann Arbor: Center for South and Southeast Asian Studies, University of Michigan.

Kulke, Hermann. 1993. *Kings and Cults: State Formation and Legitimation in India and Southeast Asia.* Delhi: Manohar.

Momigliano, Arnaldo. 1993. *The Development of Greek Biography.* Cambridge, Mass.: Harvard University Press.

Motzkin, Gabriel. 1992. *Time and Transcendence: Secular History, the Catholic Reaction, and the Rediscovery of the Future.* Dordrecht: Luwer.

Narayana Rao, Velcheru. 1996. "Texture and Authority: Telugu Riddles and Enigmas." In G. Hasan-Rokem and D. Shulman (eds), *Untying the Knot: On Riddles and Other Enigmatic Modes*, pp. 191–207. New York: Oxford University Press.

——— and David Shulman. 1998. *A Poem at the Right Moment: Remembered Verses from Premodern South India.* Berkeley: University of California Press.

———. 2002. *Classical Telugu Poetry: An Anthology.* Delhi: Oxford University Press.

———— and Sanjay Subrahmanyam.1992. *Symbols of Substance: Court and State in Nayaka-Period Tamil Nadu.* Delhi: Oxford University Press.

————. 2002. *Textures of Time: Writing History in South India, 1600–1800.* Delhi: Permanent Black.

Raghavan, V. See Srinivasakavi.

Srinivasachari, C.S. 1991 [1940]. *Ananda Ranga Pillai: The Pepys of French India.* Delhi: Asian Educational Service.

Srinivasakavi. 1948.*Ananda-ranga-campu.* Edited with critical introduction, notes, and Sanskrit commentary by V. Raghavan. Tirucchirappalli: Palaniappa Bros.

Subrahmanian, N. See Tiyakaraya Tecikar.

Tiyakaraya Tecikar. 1955.*Ananta-rankan kovai.* Critically edited with introduction and notes by N. Subrahmanian. Madras: Government Oriental Manuscripts Library.

Venkata Raghotam.1992. "Merchant, Courtier, Shipper, Prince: The Social and Intellectual World of an Eighteenth-century Tamil Merchant." *Journal of the Institute of Asian Studies* 9: 9–20.

Wagoner, Phillip. 1993. *Tidings of the King: A Translation and Ethnohistorical Analysis of the Rayavacakamu.* Honolulu: University of Hawaii Press.

Zvelebil, K.V. 1973.*The Smile of Murugan: On Tamil Literature of South India.* Leiden: E.J. Brill.

NOTES

1. On the "fureur des memoires" that interested Lenglet, at the turn of the eighteenth century, see Motzkin 1992: 64.
2. Note that there was an earlier diary kept by the intriguing figure of (Chevalier) Guruvap Pillai, Ananda Ranga's cousin, who was in France, where he converted to Christianity, from 1719 to 1722. (See Ananda Ranga Pillai 1984–5: 8: 404.) On Ananda Ranga and his diary, see the fine essay by Alalasundaram 1998a, and this same author's book, 1998b. See also the outdated monograph by C.S. Srinivasachari 1991 [1940]; also Venkata Raghotam 1992.
3. See discussion in Narayana Rao and Shulman 2002.
4. I thank Sudipta Kaviraj for remarks underlying this formulation.
5. See the editor's introduction: Subrahmanian 1955: xxvi.
6. First Muzaffar Jang, in 1750; following the murder of the latter, Salabat Jang (July 1751).
7. Note that the ARP diary covers the years 1736 to 1761 (the diarist's death). The final entries are attributed to Ananda Ranga's nephew, Appavu (Tiruvenkatam III), who also is said to have kept a diary of his own in subsequent years.
8. See discussion in Narayana Rao, Shulman, and Subrahmanyam 2002.

9. This father, Tiruvenkata Pillai, is extolled at length in 2.41 where, among other gifts, he has learned the languages of all countries. Other sources confirm that Ananda Ranga's father knew French, English, and Dutch; see Raghavan 1948: 34, n. 2.

10. *Vidyaranya-krti, Vidyaranya-kala-jnana*, etc.: see Wagoner 1993: 184.

11. See Raghavan's note, 1948: 23 of text.

12. The list goes: Ramacandra, Ambadeva, Rajasekhara, Cola Nrsimha, Ramacandra, Langala Gajapati, Acyutadeva, Vira Nrsimha, Ramadeva, Tirumala, Sriranga, Venkatapati, Hemanta, Krsnaraya: 2.1.

13. Partly recapitulated in the Telugu *Ananda-ranga-rat chandamu*: see Raghavan 1948: 32, n. 2. There thus seems to be a well-developed family genealogical tradition behind this series.

14. "Template" may be too constricting a term unless we allow it to include the potentially shaping impact of the individuals operating, with considerable autonomy, within the *kala-jnana* field. Cf. Berkson 2000: 284 for a useful analogy from iconography, and further discussion below.

15. That is, Krsnadevaraya's immediate predecessor, perhaps to be identified with the Vira Nrsimha mentioned in the *Ananda-ranga-campu*.

16. I acknowledge my indebtedness to Don Handelman's remarkable essay, in press.

17. Introduction to the edition cited in n. 5, xiv.

18. See n. 2. For further details, see Alalasundaram 1998: 75; Raghavan 1948: 38, n.1 and sources cited there.

19. Marginal note to ms. P: "to take vengeance for the death of his [Guruvap Pillai's] father."

20. de la Prevostière (d. 1721).

21. In fact, twenty-three years were to pass before Ananda Ranga would be officially appointed to the post of *dubashi*. Tiruvenkata Pillai *never* enjoyed such an appointment, although, like his son, he managed to make himself indispensable to the French administrators at Pondicherry.

22. Following the success of the first such mission, the Hunapati at Pondicherry asks Ananda Ranga and his brother to continue looking after French affairs (5.36–8). Canto 5 is, however, mostly taken up with an account of Ananda Ranga's marriage, the marriage of his younger brother Tiruvenkatam, the birth of the brothers' first children, and *kavya*-style description of the monsoons and autumn (including Ananda Ranga's philanthropic activity during the rainy period, providing shelter for those without homes).

23. Identified by Raghavan with Vaippur.

24. Raghavan 1948: 47, n. 1.

25. See the full annotation by Raghavan 1948: 48ff., for the political background to this stage of the Carnatic Wars.

26. Cf. *Vikramorvasiya* 1.15. We should also note the beautifully colloquial verses of Canda Sahib's that precede Ananda Ranga's statement.
27. Raghavan 1948: 66, n. 1.
28. See the masterful analysis by Momigliano 1993.
29. An adequate analysis of this text in its relation to later Sanskrit historiography is still very much lacking.
30. Raghavan 1948: 17.

CHAPTER 8

Life Histories
as Narrative Strategy

Prophecy, Song, and Truth-Telling in
Tamil Tales and Legends

STUART BLACKBURN

Introduction

L ife histories in South Asia possess not only extraordinary historical
depth but also a bewildering variety of forms, as the essays in
this book make clear. And in these respects the subcontinent
is little different from other regions across the world, in which the felt
need to tell a person's story is among the most powerful of cultural impulses. As outlined in the Introduction to this volume, scholars from
various specializations are increasingly turning to these life histories,
and three primary assumptions underlie this recent research. First
is the idea that stories about personal lives are imbued with an extra
dose of truthfulness, that autobiographies speak directly to us and that
biographies are based on "true-life" experience; for this reason, it is
thought that these life-historical forms, including diaries, journals,
and so on, are somehow imbued with the veracity of the spoken word.
A second, and related, assumption motivating some research on life
histories is that they often chronicle the experiences of marginalized,
disadvantaged or silenced people, and that these otherwise unrecorded
lives provide us with new insights into human history.[1] Third, there
is a widespread belief that life histories (from published autobiography
to handwritten diaries) are expressions of newly emerging definitions
of the "individual" or "self."[2] Indeed, this is one of the goals of the present book: to examine life histories in order to question the shibboleth

that Indian society is composed of collectivities of caste and religion, and to explore the history of selfhood and individualism in India.

In the Introduction to this book, we have already raised doubts that life histories are necessarily evidence of individualism, and in this essay I want to raise further questions. My starting point is that although most life-historical texts discussed in the published literature are singly authored (from autobiographies to oral personal histories), many in India are not. Rather, like most traditional Indian literature, life histories contained in oral literature are told by many people, over a long period of time, and sometimes a wide geography; in other words, although these life histories are individual in their subject, they are nonetheless collective in their social practice. Specifically, I will look at two kinds of oral stories: legends and folktales; we would not at first think of either genre as life histories, but many examples in both do use the life of individuals as the central plot. I will also approach these texts not as expressions of selfhood or personal lives, but as statements about the significance of the story of a life as a cultural category and a narrative strategy. I will suggest, more generally, that the existence of life histories, indeed their pervasiveness in India, does not so much indicate a sense of individualism as the fact that life history is a readily understood template suitable for storytelling.

These traditional, collectively authored texts serve as a counterweight to the widespread "myth of the solitary genius," which underlies some life-historical research. An "individualized nature," the focus on a single life and a specific setting, is precisely what Hatch and Wisniewski identify as the element that distinguishes life histories from other narratives.[3] The authors also highlight what one of their contributors calls the "focus on the sense-making systems of individuals . . . [not] communities or societies" (Hatch and Wisniewski 1995: 116). Life histories may indeed be "sense-making systems" utilized by individuals in storytelling, but I would emphasize the cultural constraints and generic logic that shape those "systems" into narratives. Authors and tellers may use these interpretive schema but they certainly do not create them; the very fact that a life history is defined by its specific setting means that it is governed by local social practices and literary conventions, which are generated not by individuals but by groups. To assume, on the contrary, that life histories are wholly, or even largely, the products of the individuals who write and speak them is appealing, even flattering, but also tautological since individualism is what those histories are assumed to represent in the first place. Finally, an assumption of individual control over life-historical narratives conveys upon them the aura of authenticity: once the distortions of tradition, with its conformities and pressures, are removed, the now unfettered author is free to tell his or her own story, the real story.

Truth-telling is indeed a salient feature of Tamil oral texts; but they are considered true not because they are told by an individual about an individual—straight from the horse's mouth—but rather because they have been told by many people, over time, and carry a collective moral weight. As Hayden White has argued, narratives only become "histories" when they attempt to set the record straight by advancing one perspective over against others, either implied or explicitly cited.[4] However, we can extend White's point by suggesting that one culturally favored mode of setting the record straight is the telling of a person's life, and this is true in the legends discussed below. In fact, the discussion goes beyond histories and into the fictive genres of the folktale, where truth-telling is also a popular narrative device. I found that even in this most fictitious narrative form, the life of an individual is a vehicle for revealing wrongdoing and naming the guilty. Both folktales and legends, as I hope to show, use life histories, sometimes as full texts and sometimes in abbreviated form, such as a prophecy or song, to reveal "what really happened."

Below I will first discuss the legends or histories known in Tamil as *carita*, and then the folktales, or *kathai*. Although all the texts discussed come from Tamil, I assume that their features are not unique to that language. These two categories of *carita* (*caritra, carita, caritai, carittiram*) and *kathai* (*katha*) have local variants all over India, and their narrative scope is more or less consistent; moreover, some of the legends and all of the tales have versions in other Indian languages.[5]

Varieties of *Carita* in Tamil

When first thinking about this topic, I was struck by the fact that so many traditional Indian texts employ life history as a narrative frame and use some form of *carita* in their title: from the early Sanskrit *Buddhacarita,* to the late medieval Marathi *Lilacaritra* and Malayalam *Ramacaritam,* to a large number of later (AD 1600–1800) South Indian texts, both oral and written in Persian, Telugu, Kannada and Tamil, including legends of places and of dynasties collected by Colin Mackenzie and his assistants. Some of these later texts have come under the collective scrutiny of Narayana Rao, Subrahmanyam and Shulman, who have demonstrated, among other things, that the historiographical impulse was not borrowed from the West.[6] Despite this new scholarship, the number and variety, and sometimes length, of these precolonial histories is considerable, so that we have not yet arrived at a satisfactory classification of them nor found an appropriate language for their analysis. A brief survey of *carita* texts in Tamil is given here because they are essentially life histories: with the exception of some historical chronicles, they narrate events, or those believed to have happened, in the lives of poets, mythological characters, gods or cultural heroes.

As a genre in Tamil, *carita* covers a broad range of texts, in both verse and prose, including hagiography, literary biography, biography of cultural heroes and historical chronicle.[7] In this wide generic reach, *carita* resembles *purana*, except that *carita* texts are usually shorter, less grandiose and contain (what is believed to be) more factual content; the lives of the Saiva poet-saints, for instance, appeared in the framework of a sectarian *purana*, whereas the lives of popular poets (Valluvar and Kampan), told as entertaining, nearly secular stories, circulated as *carita*. *Carita* crosses over from historical fact into fiction, too, since the first three novels in Tamil at the end of the nineteenth century are identified as *carita* (*Piratapa Mutaliyar Carittiram, Kamalampal Carittiram, Patmavati Carittiram*). Using *carita*, and not *katha*, in the title conferred a degree of truthfulness on these novels, which as literary experiments were subject to criticism as fabulations and impediments to literary modernism.

Perhaps the earliest life-historical text in Tamil is a compendium of the lives of Saiva poet-saints, the twelfth-century *Periyapuranam*, which is attributed to Cekkilar but draws on earlier sources.[8] A great deal has been written about the theology of this text, but what is striking for us is its biographical impulse in recording, sometimes in fine detail, episodes in a poet's life.[9] Although a hagiographical halo hangs over the *Periyapuranam*, it also tells stories of individual lives, which continue to be orally transmitted, published, included in schoolbooks and filmed.

A later and more obscure anthology of life histories is *Flos Sanctorum* ("The Lives of the Saints"), written by the Jesuit missionary Henri Henriques; issued from Cochin in 1586, this is a massive work of nearly seven hundred pages covering the history and ceremonial calendar of Christian saints.[10] The stories of Tamil Muslim saints are also numerous yet little studied; we await a full-scale study of Tamil hagiography, Hindu, Islamic and Christian.[11]

The first self-identified *carita* text comes fairly late in Tamil (*Tamil Navalar Caritai*), presumably because the term is Sanskrit-derived and was kept out of literary discourse until the late medieval period, although it was undoubtedly used for oral texts much earlier. This is an interesting but unstudied anthology of about 250 verses, which has been assigned to the late seventeenth century but not published until the early twentieth century.[12] Perhaps inspired by Henriques' Christian anthology, it is an early attempt at modern literary biography in Tamil, with the more fantastic mythic material sidelined in favor of popular legend. It contains brief notices of the most popular of Tamil poets, including the grammarian Agastya, the poet Valluvar (author of the famous *Tirukkural*), his sister, Auvaiyar, his brother Kapilar, and many other ancient poets, as well as the medieval Kampan. The lives of some of these same poets, plus other Telugu and Marathi poets, were published in *Biographical Sketches of Dekhan Poets* (1829, Calcutta) and again in *The Tamil Plutarch* (1859, Jaffna), while more extended narratives were collected in *Vinotaracamancari* (1871, Madras). The biographical impulse in Tamil, however, is older even than the seventeenth-century text cited above, since many of these stories of poets' lives circulated in oral tradition, where many still exist today, before they were set down in printed prose.[13] Given the role of literature and language in the formation of Tamil identity, it is not surprising that the traditional historiography of Tamil literature, as understood until, say, the early twentieth century, was largely a series of these literary biographies, linked by a thin thread of chronology. Until recently, in other words, Tamil literary history was narrated as a series of life histories of poets.

What we might call "modern" literary biography in Tamil, written under the influence of Western models, probably dates from 1822. In that year Muttusami Pillai, the manager of the College at Fort St George in Madras, wrote an account of the life and work of Constantius J. Beschi (1680–1747?), the Italian Jesuit missionary who was an influential figure in Tamil literature in the early modern period.[14] Muttusami Pillai's text outlines Beschi's life in a few pages, followed by a list and brief description of his twenty-one books (in Tamil and Latin), culminating with an extract from "Tempavani" (Beschi's epic poem on the life of Joseph) in both the original Tamil and English translation. By the time commercial publishing was fully established, by the mid nineteenth century, biography was becoming an important literary genre in Tamil, boasting famous books on the life of Queen Victoria

and of Lord Clive. Excepting the famous eighteenth-century diary of
Ananda Ranga Pillai (for which see Shulman's essay in this volume),
autobiographies appeared in Tamil only in the first half of the twentieth century.

If literary biography is one dominant form of *carita* in Tamil, the
other is the historical chronicle, in which the hero is neither poet nor
prose writer but a raja whose reputation is based on military and political exploits. Most, but not all, of these historical chronicles in Tamil
are composed in verse, usually to be sung, sometimes in a ritual context, with or without musical accompaniment, as indicated by a variety
of words in their titles (*cintu, ammanai, kummi, patal*), which are song
genres. These sung biographies of historical heroes I call "ballads" because that is the closest term in English, and when we compare them
with Scottish or Border ballads, the term is not misleading. We can list
about two dozen major historical ballad texts in Tamil, while dozens
more are known from field research, with others still undoubtedly
unreported.[15]

Although our knowledge of these ballads is limited, we can think of
them along a continuum of more or less biographical content and intent. At the most biographical end of the spectrum, we have texts in
which the life of the hero or heroine dominates over historical events;
many of these texts are known by their eponymous hero: Madurai
Viran, Desingu Rajan, Kattabomman, the Maradu brothers, Puli
Tevan, Tampimar ("The Brothers") and Aivar Racakkal ("Five Rajas").
Other texts focus somewhat less on a person and more on a specific
event (*The Battle of* [Yusuf] *Kan Cakipu, The Battle of Iravikutti Pillai*),
or on a dynasty (*Tanjavuri Andhra Rajula Caritra, Karnataka Rajakkal
Cavistara Carittiram*), again as reflected in their titles.[16] These event-
and dynasty-centered texts tend to emphasize place rather than person,
but they do share life-historical features with other *carita* texts in
Tamil.

Two *Carita* Texts

In what follows, I discuss two legends, or *carita* texts, as illustrations
of how life histories are used as a narrative strategy for truth-telling.
The first is the *Aivar Racakkal Katai* ("The Five Rajas"), a long ballad
describing events in the southern Pandyan country set (mostly) in the
first half of the sixteenth century, although the date of its composition

is uncertain. The second historical text is the *Tampimar Katai* ("The Brothers"), a shorter ballad about political intrigue and death in Travancore in the early eighteenth century. Both texts were composed to be sung as a *vil pattu* ("bow song"); and while "The Five Rajas" is no longer sung, "The Brothers" is still performed in villages on the Tamil Nadu–Kerala border in local temple festivals dedicated to the deified brothers.[17]

1. The Five Rajas

Running to more than five thousand lines, the *Aivar Racakkal Katai* (known in various forms as *Panca Pantiyar Katai, Kannatiya Patai Por, Ulakutaiyar Perumal Katai,* and *Vetum Perumal Katai*) is a rambling account covering almost four hundred years of political history in a small corner of the southern Tamil country. The only published text of this ballad was printed by Madurai University in 1974, due solely to the persistence of the editor. Like the famous Tamil scholars who a hundred years before had rediscovered "lost" Tamil classics, Na. Vanamamalai spent a decade of intense searching before finally finding a palm-leaf manuscript of "The Five Rajas;" but the eighty leaves of that manuscript were crumbling, half-eaten by ants and worms. Then, unexpectedly, a friend sent him a complete version of the ballad, handwritten on paper in 1828, and this version led to another, still incomplete copy. Assembled from these three sources, his 1974 scholarly text is a composite, a linking together of several independently circulating episodes. While it is certain that these story-episodes were sung in the bow song tradition in southern Tamil Nadu, we have no reports of those performances, nor do we know that the ballad was ever performed as printed. The history of its composition is uncertain, perhaps late seventeenth century, probably in Tirunelveli District, and most probably over a generation or two.

"The Five Rajas" begins, after invocations to Murukan and Vishnu, by creating a past for the hero, Raja Kulacekaran; a genealogy links Kulacekaran's line of the southern Pandyans with the great dynasty of Pandyans who ruled at Madurai, some 200 hundred miles to the north, and who, with the blessing of Siva and Parvati in the famous temple there, conquered the "Kongu country [to the west], Kosalya and the northern Ganga, the Telugus and the Cheras." Kulacekaran's line became known as the "southern Pandyans" because as a result of

Muslim rule in the fourteenth century they were forced to move their court out of Madurai to the south, to Tenkasi ("southern Kasi") and to Valliyur, an even smaller town on the present border between Tirunelveli and Kanya Kumari districts. With the consolidation of Vijayanagara rule over the Tamil country, toward the end of the fifteenth century, the southern Pandyans fell and Valliyur was captured.[18] The text tells us that the Valliyur fort was built in the thirteenth century, but this is very likely an attempt to establish a pedigree for a less-than-ancient line of rulers. Reading any sort of historical record from this ballad would be brave; what we can say is that, as is true of so many epic histories across the world, the text looks back to a time of lost glory.

Rambling and disjointed, the text does cohere around the life of Kulacekaran Pandyan, who, with his four brothers, ruled the southern Tamil country and fought a war with an unnamed Kannada raja. The story itself begins, like many traditional Indian narratives, with childlessness, the worrying lack of an heir to the throne, which forces the existing Pandyan raja and his wife, Malaiyammal (about whom a separate story exists), to undertake pilgrimages, make temple offerings and perform charitable acts. All fails, however, until an astrologer (*cociyan*) appears and tells them that the queen must perform a special *tapas* (or renunciatory act) in the Bhagavati (Minaksi) temple at Madurai.

The appearance of the astrologer is an important event, which we will return to more than once; his words, in both legends and tales, shift the narrative tone from the mythic to the life-historical by introducing a degree of specificity, which then leads to a series of events demarcating the life of the hero. In our text, the astrologer declares that the raja's wife, soon to be the mother of Kulacekaran, must perform her *tapas* in a certain temple, with particular results. And when she becomes pregnant, the text describes one of the common life-historical patterns in *carita* texts: the month-by-month changes to the mother's body. In "The Five Rajas," only three months are listed—the fifth, the seventh and the tenth, when she gives birth—but we are given more details of the rituals which are performed at specific times during the pregnancy. Especially elaborate are the descriptions of the *cimantam*, which occurs during the seventh month, and of the delivery-hut built in the final month.

The astrologer appears again at the birth of Kulacekaran, which is narrated with proper planetary details, and he again predicts good fortune. Then follows a long lullaby, a second life-historical feature in historical and folktale texts, and one closely related to the first; in fact, the lullaby may be seen as a female counterpart of the male astrologer's prediction in that the song also provides an outline of the hero's life. Most of the song lines are formulaic, but the lullaby includes specific details as well, for example, the horse on which Kulacekaran will fly (a common motif in Tamil *carita* texts). As part of a traditional life history, and not a modern biography, however, the lullaby also contains hagiographical elements and likens the hero to two earlier Pandyan kings.[19] Following his birth, the narrative of the hero's life is centered on a series of special events at specific times: he is fed his first solid food in the eighth month; at five years he is taught the alphabet and horsemanship; then he learns, as do most heroes in traditional Tamil histories, a catalogue of martial arts. This catalog functions as "the education of the hero," and its major events, including the viewing of a drama in performance, are described in considerable detail.

Then comes the wedding of the hero. In his sixteenth year, Kulacekaran is married and goes to visit his mother, at the ancient capital of the Pandyans at Madurai, where he is installed as the new raja. From this point in the story to the dramatic battles with the invading Kannada raja, we watch Kulacekaran travel to Kancipuram, with a full retinue of soldiers, officials, tributary rajas, musicians, instruments, singers and dancers, and return along a route marked by ritual baths at famous pilgrimage sites. This journey is written in the manner of an *ula*, a Tamil poetic genre describing a royal procession and the reactions by various groups of women to the raja's resplendent figure. Finally, with a brief diversion to narrate a local temple legend (at Muppantal) , Kulacekaran sets up camp at Kottaru near Nagercoil.

At this point, and for the next thousand lines, we hear about the events leading up to the building of Kulacekaran's fort at Valliyur; these events constitute a place legend, one of several independent stories incorporated into "The Five Rajas." But this place legend is also central to the plot since the fort at Valliyur is the nexus which brings the rivals into conflict. Before the hostilities begin, however, Kulacekaran is allowed some pleasure; settled in his camp, he falls in love with an itinerant singer, offers her gifts and invites her to live with him. When the raja goes hunting one day and sees a strange event—his dogs are driven away by a hare—he summons the astrologer once again. The soothsayer tells him that Kali, goddess of victory, resides on that spot and that he should build a fort there, which "will stand for 58 years before falling as the result of a woman." The fort is built and duly destroyed, not by a woman but by a flood, which forces the raja to order red bricks from Kancipuram to rebuild the fort. Finally, the text narrates the completion of the Pandya raja's fort at Valliyur in the Kollam year of 442 (= AD 1226), on Friday, the eleventh day of Avani.[20]

Now, with the youthful (sixteen-year-old) Kulacekaran safe in his fort at Valliyur, the drama builds. A band of itinerant singers and artists draw the raja's portrait, which they display to onlookers while they travel the country singing his story (that is, the very text in which they appear). Reaching the Kannada country, they sing for the daughter of the raja, who falls in love with Kulacekaran's portrait. When she informs her father, he sends a messenger to Valliyur to arrange a marriage with Kulacekaran, but the proud Pandyan refuses. Invoking the glorious past of his displaced predecessors, and scorning the upstart Kannada raja, Kulacekaran insults the messenger; the Kannada raja promptly responds by invading with a huge army. In the end, his four brothers are killed and Kulacekaran is taken captive, but on the way back to the Kannada country, where he is to marry the princess, he commits suicide by swallowing a crushed diamond. The Kannada princess commits sati and dies.

Before this somewhat predictable conclusion, however, two semi-independent stories are narrated, and these are important because they highlight the moral slant of *carita* texts. The hero is defeated and dies, but this would not have been possible and the enemy would not have succeeded without treachery and deceit. The first of these episodes involves another astrologer, this time in the guise of a messenger from the invading raja; gaining an audience with Kulacekaran, he is able to convince the young raja that he must destroy the southern wall of his fort: it is too weak to withstand the enemy's onslaught and must be rebuilt, he claims. When, against all advice of his own ministers, Kulacekaran believes this "northerner" and orders the wall to be razed, the Kannada army seizes the opportunity and advances. The second episode introduces the more innocent character of a woman who sells curds in the Valliyur fort. One day she accidentally drops her pot in a stream but later finds that it has surfaced inside the fort. Unwittingly she has discovered the secret water supply, an underground channel, for the besieged fort, and naïvely she tells everyone who will listen, including the spies of the Kannada raja. The invader then has this secret water supply blocked up, forcing Kulacekaran and his brothers to flee, and eventually to be killed or captured and then to commit suicide.

"The Five Rajas" may not at first fit our idea of a life history, but it does narrate the history of the life of an individual. The life of the ill-fated Kulacekaran is the narrative strategy chosen to present a diffuse history that stretches over four hundred years, collapses several dynasties into one and extends from the southern Tamil country to the Kannada country. But the life of the hero is not simply a device to create a semblance of coherence; it also attempts to persuade us of what really happened when the valiant southern Pandyans were wiped out: it was the result of deceit (plus a gullible raja and some bad luck). Finally, as noted, the most succinct articulation of the life history comes from the astrologer, the one who knows and speaks the truth.

2. The Brothers

In historical and geographical reach, as well as plot, this second *carita* text is quite different from the first. Unlike the loose temporal and spatial structure of "The Five Rajas," with its many independent episodes, the ballad of "The Brothers" is compact. The action (narrated in 1,900 lines as opposed to the more than 5,000 in "The Five Rajas") takes place between 1721 and 1729 in Travancore (or Tiruvitamkotu), when rival claimants to the throne faced each other in intrigue and war. The plot moves directly from event to event, with little elaboration of detail and few tangential episodes. Here, in this ballad which is still sung in southern Tamil Nadu to induce intense spirit possession and dancing, we have no magic horses or romantic interludes. This is not the life history of a founder or a reviver of a dynasty: there are no place legends, no forts built on the spot where hunting dogs are chased by hares. It is instead the life history of two brothers who never became rajas. The ballad's eponymous heroes are Valiya Tampi and his younger brother, Kunju Tampi, who are the sons of Raja Rama Varma; the two brothers fought with the raja's nephew, Marttanda Varma, but lost their claim to rule Travancore. The ballad champions the cause of the brothers; history is not always told by the victors.

Despite numerous differences, as a life history in the *carita* genre, "The Brothers" bears a strong resemblance to "The Five Rajas." Both · stories are situated in known places and both narrate the life history of named historical figures. Even more striking are the narrative similarities that underlie these (and other *carita*) texts: the dramatic tension in both stories stems from a refusal of a marriage offer: the spurned party plots revenge and only achieves victory over the smaller but proud enemy by trickery.[21] In "The Five Rajas," as we have seen, the Pandyan Kulacekaran refuses to marry the daughter of the Kannada raja, while in "The Brothers" the heroes refuse to marry their sister to Marttanda Varma. Deceit in "The Five Rajas" occurs when the Kannada raja sends an astrologer as a Trojan horse into the Pandyan camp and again when the Kannada raja dams up the fort's secret water supply. Trickery in "The Brothers" is verbal and more subtle. During negotiations with Valiya and Kunju Tampi, Marttanda Varma swears to an intermediary that he "will not harm the Tampis as long as this life [= my life] continues." The "life" to which he refers, however, turns out to be a fly held in his hand behind his back (in Tamil *îyuyir* can mean either "this life" or "fly's life"). When he crushes the insect and is no longer bound by his pledge, Marttanda Varma deceitfully invites the brothers to his palace where he kills them both.

In other respects, too, this eighteenth-century text resembles not only "The Five Rajas" but many other *carita* texts in Tamil: the battles are described in detail; the catalog of towns and villages through which the armies march is long; the hero travels in procession to a sacred site; the hero dies in defeat; and the women commit sati. More than this, the astrologer's prophecy and the chronological narration of the heroes' education clearly reveals the life-historical pattern of this ballad.

The story begins when Kittinattal and her brother leave famine-stricken Ayodhya in North India and come South (passing the now minor town of Valliyur, incidentally), and reach Suchindram, an important temple-town five miles from Kanya Kumari. At the festival there, Raja Varma sees her, takes her into his court and marries her; soon his new wife gives birth to a son, Valiya Tampi. The astrologer is summoned, and as in "The Five Rajas," he supplies a summary of the hero's life. The *cociyan* draws a diagram with eight sacred emblems, rolls his stones over them, consults his palm-leaves and says,

> Listen, good king, while I tell the horoscope;
> There is good fortune for this boy; the planets
>   and stars are faultless.
> And there is more to say, good king,
> After this son, your queen will have another,
>   and finally a girl.

But then the brothers will die,
    and this is how:
Another raja born to rule this world
    will see their sister;
He will make gifts of silk and soft beds
    and ask for her hand.
He will demand, the brothers will refuse
    and then he will murder them,
He will cruelly murder them both!

The astrologer's prediction comes true: Valiya Tampi is born, Kunju Tampi arrives two years later, and then their sister Koccu Matammai is born. What is unusual is that the astrologer enters again, after the sister's birth, and delivers another, longer prophecy, which is virtually a synopsis of the whole ballad. He foretells that Rama Varma will go in procession to take a ritual bath at Kanya Kumari, that he will die from smallpox and that Marttanda Varma will rule, with the brothers as allies. Then, the astrologer continues, Marttanda Varma will desire their sister, the brothers will oppose him, and the young raja will deprive them of the tax rights to villages (given by the dying Rama Varma); they will quarrel and become bitter enemies, forcing the brothers to raise an army. In the end, although the brothers initially defeat Marttanda Varma and seize his forts, the raja will bring a large army and trick the brothers into coming to the palace at Nagercoil, where he will lie to them and murder them with his sword.

After this summary of the plot in the form of the astrologer's prophecy, we have a description of the education of the heroes. As in "The Five Rajas," but even more elaborately, the narrative is told as a series of events in the heroes' lives: for example we read: "When Valiya Tampi was five, Kunju Tampi three and Koccu Matammai was two, the boys learned all the languages, including English." The ages of the siblings are repeated again and again, when they learn to ride horses and elephants, to use swords and spears, to hunt and to read and write. Because the Tampis remain unmarried (unlike Kulacekaran), these rites of passage in their youth represent the central events in their life. As we noted in "The Five Rajas," the astrologer's prophecies and the education of the hero convey a degree of chronological specificity.

And here again local history is narrated as life history, and the biographies of the brothers provide a narrative strategy for telling the truth about what happened in early-eighteenth-century Travancore. These events are controversial enough to be the subject of other Tamil ballads, no longer sung, which narrate them from a perspective more sympathetic to Marttanda Varma. "The Brothers" ballad, on the other hand, still lives in the cultural memory of certain groups, whose ancestors were allied with the brothers' cause, as an accurate account of the lives of the sons of Rama Varma.[22] Performances, at temples where the murdered Tampis are deified and worshiped, are scripted from a palm-leaf manuscript: a man, sitting next to the singer on the platform, reads the manuscript line by line and the singer immediately sings those same lines, one by one. This scripted performance style, which is very unpopular with singers because it effectively removes the scope for improvisation, is thought to ensure veracity.

During a performance I recorded in 1978, the "reader" occasionally had trouble reading the now unfamiliar shorthand used on palm-leaves, and the singer sometimes could not hear what he said over the musical accompaniment. More than once, the fast-paced performance had to pause; but when it did, someone in the audience shouted out the correct line and it swung back into routine. Though reduced to performances in a handful of minor temples in a small corner of Kanya Kumari District, the ballad narrates events that had considerable impact on the later history of South India: Marttanda Varma's victory over the Tampis led directly to the military expansion of Travancore during the first half of the eighteenth century, with consequences for the later history of South India as a whole. In presenting a locally perceived true account of these crucial events, the ballad also takes a moral stance toward them; sung in villages beyond the Travancore court and palace, the song champions the brothers, who are shown to have been deprived of their birthright to rule. As with "The Five Rajas," and even more forcefully, this local ballad demonstrates that a life history, as an extended prophecy by an astrologer, is believed to tell a true account of the past.

Folktales

In respect of truth-telling, folktales appear to bear little resemblance to these life histories in India or anywhere else. Folktales, and especially the fairytales discussed below, are fictions, which, unlike *carita* texts, are told and heard as stories without historical intent or content.

Although I collected these tales in 1995–6, like oral tales across the world, they have no date either for their contents or their composition; they may not be ancient but they present themselves as timeless. And this is what separates them from historical texts: folktales (with very few exceptions) are set in no place, and therefore everywhere, with no named historical figures, and therefore everyone.[23] In sum, folktales are fictitious stories about generic characters, not historical accounts of individuals. Nevertheless, they do contain life histories.

Many readers will be familiar with Vladimir Propp's 1928 structural description of the folktale (the fairytale, in fact), which demonstrates that this genre also contains a biographical pattern;[24] but that life pattern is truncated. The folktale pattern begins with the birth of the hero, moves through various adventures and concludes with the marriage of the hero, unlike *carita* texts, which usually continue to the death of the hero. Since Propp's pattern focuses on a male protagonist, other folklorists have identified a pattern for the "innocent persecuted heroine," but these female tales also typically end with a marriage;[25] Tamil and Indian heroine tales do sometimes extend beyond marriage, but most do not. Although the biographical pattern is truncated in this way, a striking feature of these tales (especially the female-centered ones) is the narration of a character's life *within* the story; closely resembling the historical texts discussed above, the heroine's life history is retold or summarized as part of the plot itself, and often by song, usually a lullaby. What finally persuaded me that these fictive tales are life histories is that this retelling of the heroine's life is employed as a vehicle for telling the truth. Not the truth of external, historical events—tales are fictive—but the truthfulness of the narrative events.

Let me illustrate these points with reference to two or three tales, which I collected and translated from oral tradition in Tamil (though most have parallels in other Indian languages).[26] In one extremely popular Tamil tale, known to folklorists, as "The Singing Bone," and to others as the Scots ballad "Barbara Allen," a bush growing over the grave of the murder victim reveals the identity of the murderer through a song. In many Tamil versions of this story the tell-tale song is short, sometimes only a few lines, but it nevertheless contains the kernel of the entire tale. In one version, told to me by a sixty-year-old woman, a brother is falsely accused by his sister of mistreating her, an accusation that leads the family to kill him. Later, when the sister is to be married, the family cannot find the flowers needed for the wedding, until they come to a rose bush growing over the brother's grave. His older brother approaches and sings:

> Flowers, flowers! Brother,
>   We need flowers for sister's wedding,
> Flowers for her wedding.

And the rose bush answers:

> My flowers will wilt
>   in the hair of a murderess
>   who said her brother beat her;
> My flowers will fade
>   on the head of a she-devil
> My flowers will die
>   in her hands.

One by one the family members approach the bush, and one by one the rose speaks to them and reveals what really happened in the past. In some tellings of this tale, the rose bush addresses each of the family members by their kin relation ("Don't pluck me, mother/father/brother"), so that the identity of the murderer is only divulged when the bush sings: "Don't pluck me, murderess! Don't touch me!"

In other Tamil tales, especially those of the persecuted innocent heroine, the song or speech that reveals the truth is much longer, and sometimes retells the heroine's entire life history. She is born, abandoned, married, disfigured (typically blinded), and finally reunited with her husband; but before that restoration, her story, or that of her children, is sung or told. An example of this longer, revelatory song is found in a tale called "The Wooden Doll." A brother and sister are driven away by their stepmother; when the sister dies in childbirth, the brother raises the baby girl until she is buried alive by a jealous woman, who then deceives the brother into marrying her. Finally, when a goldsmith finds the child and asks for her story, she says, "Make me a wooden doll and I'll tell you." Then, holding the doll in her arms, the girl sings this lullaby (notice that in the third and fourth stanzas she sings in the persona of her dead mother):

> 1. Isn't it true, little doll,
>   that grandfather married grandmother
>   and that mother and uncle were born.

2. Isn't it true that
      grandmother died
      and grandfather married again?

3. Isn't it true, little doll, that
      stepmother tried to kill us
      and father left us in the forest
      instead of killing us?

4. Isn't it true that
      we were left all alone
      and ran to this village?

5. Isn't it true, little doll, that
      mother and uncle got some rice
      and when she was cooking
      a *sannyasi* gave her a lemon?

6. Isn't it true that
      she ate it and got pregnant
      that uncle earned money
      and they lived together?

7. Isn't it true, little doll, that
      mother died and uncle raised me
      that a woman tricked and married him?

8. Isn't it true that
      she buried me in a goldsmith's yard,
      that he found and raised me?

9. Isn't it true that
      he gave you to me,
      My little wooden doll?

Spanning three generations, the song retells the whole tale, which narrates the life of the grandchild, that is, the little girl who is buried, found and then sings this lullaby to her wooden doll. As with the astrologer's prophecy in the *carita* texts, the song (which recalls the lullaby in the "The Five Rajas") is a concise narration of the life of the main character in the folktale.

Although the prophecy (and lullaby) in the *carita* texts predicts what will happen and the song in the tales recapitulates what has happened, both prophecy and song are used to tell a life history and to establish an accurate version of events. The events in the folktale are not historical, not understood by tellers or listeners to have taken place outside the tale, yet within the tale, in the eyes of the characters, they are contentious events, and are debated as true or false. What we see, time and time again, is that establishing a true account of these ima-gined events is the crux of the story. The bush above the victim's grave names the guilty party, just as the lullaby in "The Wooden Doll" proves the identity of the child, who is then rescued by her uncle (the brother), who in turn punishes those responsible for her suffering.

Another Tamil folktale that uses the retelling motif to reclaim an identity is called "The Three Golden Sons;" in this popular story the heroine and her children make their revelation in the quasi-legal context of a *panchayat* or tribunal. A raja's wives conspire to abandon his youngest wife's newborns and replace them with cockroaches; seeing the insects, the angry raja blindfolds the young mother and locks her in a pen, while the seven children are abandoned and then raised by a series of foster-mothers. In the end, the eldest child, a girl, summons a *panchayat* where she is asked to explain what is at issue be-tween her and the powerful raja. Standing before the assembly of fifty-six rajas, she speaks:

> Kind sirs, our father married three women but had no children. His fourth wife was our mother. When she got pregnant, he said to her, "You'll give birth soon; when you need me, ring the bell." She rang the bell, but the other wives blindfolded her, threw us away and put seven cockroaches in our place. We were raised by a rat and then went home, but the other wives saw we were still alive and had the rat killed. The rat gave us to Kali, who raised us until the wives saw we were alive and planned to kill Kali. So Kali handed us over to Nagamma, who raised us for a while and sent us home because we were old enough to eat rice. We went home, and soon it came time for Nagamma to be killed, so she gave us to Ganesa, who told us to find our parents and live with them. At home, we saw that our mother was blindfolded and fed food fit for a dog. Now, tell me, how could the raja, how could our father, do this?

As with the song over the grave and the lullaby to the doll, this speech retells the tale, establishes the truth (including here the identity of the speaker) and leads to a moral judgment. In this tale, the children are restored to their father and the deceitful wives are punished.

Lastly, we can look at the Tamil version of Cinderella, which, like all versions of this folktale (AT 510), is called after the girl herself; in our Tamil example she is known as "Sattitalaicci," or "The Pot-Head Girl." This tender tale tells the life history of the heroine in a straight-forward manner, with few deviations and digressions. Sattitalaicci is born and goes to school, where a teacher desires her and tricks her parents into abandoning her. Assuming the guise of an astrologer (that key figure in the ballads), the lecherous teacher convinces them that if left alive she will bring ruin to the family: she must be placed in a box, with all her (future) wedding clothes and jewelry, and floated in a river. This is done and the teacher tries to capture the box, but he dies in the attempt and the box is found by a washerwoman, who helps Sattitalaicci find work in a rich man's house. Putting her clothes and jewels in a small clay pot, which she places over her head, Sattitalaicci works as a servant, sweeping, cooking and making cowdung cakes. When she takes the cows to graze in the fields, however, she climbs down a deep well, takes off her rags, combs her hair, puts on make-up (a *pottu*),[27] and wraps herself in her wedding clothes; then she climbs out again, smears her face with dirt and returns home as an ugly servant girl. Finally, of course, her beauty is discovered by a young man, and despite initial opposition, they are happily married in the end.

This final tale differs from the others considered in that the heroine's life history is not retold in a song or speech; closer to plots of the *carita* texts, here the tale itself narrates the life history of the heroine. However, as with both the folktales and historical texts, the story of Sattitalaicci's life is narrated as a series of revelations—of her future, of her identity and finally of her past. Once more the ubiquitous astrologer articulates her future, although in this case the soothsayer is a liar. He is a charlatan, who only plays the role of an astrologer in order to get hold of the girl whom he desires but cannot marry; prophecy, even when false, is used to reveal a life history. Again, as we have seen in other texts, the key question is the heroine's true identity, which is revealed only when her eponymous pot is smashed and she can marry. Lastly, her past, especially the cruel, false prophecy of the schoolteacher, is revealed on her wedding day when she identifies herself to her astonished parents. The marriage is not just closure; it is also a revelation of the girl's identity and restoration of her rightful place in society.

Conclusions

In this essay I have attempted to throw some new light on life histories by approaching them not as expressions of the self or individualism but as cultural texts produced by many people over time and space. Analyzing two very different genres in Tamil—historical ballads (*carita*) and folktales (*katha*)—I found that texts in both categories are life histories in that they tell the life of a person, whether legendary king, local hero or imaginary heroine. More important than pattern, however, is the use of life histories as a narrative strategy to reveal the truth, the truth of what is believed to have happened either in the historical past or within the story. The issue here is not the old debate over fictional versus historical truths, but the desire to establish, through narrative, one's identity by a correct version of past events in one's life.

This truth-telling can assume the form of either an entire text, like the ballad of "The Brothers," or a shorter account, such as the astrologer's prophecy, a song or ordinary speech, which retells a character's life within the story. Although the folktale typically does not tell a full life history, its concise recapitulation of a biography in song or speech sharpens our understanding of the truth-telling function of more fully developed life histories. As we have seen, the cameo narration in the tales is a vehicle for establishing a true account of the character's past life, just as the longer *carita* text is an attempt to present (from one perspective) a true account of past events. In this respect, the short lullaby sung to the wooden doll functions very much like an entire ballad. In brief, life history is not only a narrative form; it is also a narrative strategy.

Still, in the end, we are left with the question: Why do these texts use life history as a vehicle for storytelling? One answer, following the psychologist Jerome Bruner, might be that it is natural to choose life histories to narrate stories because they closely resemble our personal experiences.[28] From this perspective, narrative plots and other time-keepers, such as calendars and curriculum vitae, are primarily means of organizing otherwise random experience. But there is more to explain, since life histories do not merely organize events; they also take a moral stance toward them. However clichéd White's comments on history and narrative have become, I believe that he hit on something important when he pointed out that stories become histories when they are told from a perspective, albeit self-serving, that accuses and condemns, or champions and celebrates. So, in the betrayal of Kulacekaran and the murder of the brothers, as well as in the song above the grave and the speech in the *panchayat*, life history, as both whole narrative and internal summary, makes an ethical judgment. This is perhaps the enduring significance of life histories—that right and wrong are expressed in the form of human lives.

REFERENCES

Arunachalam, M. 1976. *Peeps into Tamil Literature: Ballad Poetry.* Gandhi Vidyalayam: Tiruchitrambalam.

Bayly, Susan. 1989. *Saints, Goddesses and Kings: Muslims and Christians in South Indian Society, 1700–1900.* Cambridge: Cambridge University Press.

Blackburn, Stuart. 1988. *Singing of Birth and Death: Texts in Performance.* Philadelphia: University of Pennsylvania Press.

————. 2000. "Corruption and Redemption: The Legend of Valluvar and Tamil Literary History." *Modern Asian Studies* 34: 449–82.

————. 2001. *Moral Fictions: Tamil Folktales in Oral Tradition.* FF Communications 278. Helsinki: Academia Scientiarum Fennica.

————. 2003. *Print, Folklore and Nationalism in Colonial South India.* New Delhi: Permanent Black.

Bruner, Jerome. 1986. *Actual Minds, Possible Worlds.* Cambridge: Harvard University Press.

Dundes, Alan. 1978. "The Hero Pattern and the Life of Jesus." In Alan Dundes, *Essays in Folkloristics,* pp. 223–70. Meerut: The Folklore Institute. (Also in Alan Dundes, *The Interpretation of Folklore,* Bloomington, 1980.)

Filipsky, Jan. 1990. "History Motivated: Historical Ballads in Tamil." In Mariola Offredi (ed.), *Language versus Dialect: Linguistic Essays on Hindi, Tamil and Sarnami,* pp. 113–26. Delhi: Manohar.

Freeman, James. 1979. *Untouchable: An Indian Life History.* Stanford: Stanford University Press.

Hardy, Friedhelm. 1992. "The Sri Vaisnava Hagiography of Parakala." In Christopher Shackle and Rupert Snell (eds), *The Indian Narrative: Perspectives and Patterns,* pp. 81–116. Wiesbaden: Harrassowitz.

Hatch, J. Amos and Richard Wisniewski. 1995. "Life History and Narrative: Questions, Issues and Exemplary Works." In Amos and Wisniewski (eds), *Life History and Narrative,* pp. 113–35. Washington DC: Falmer Press.

Jones, Steven Swann. 1993. "The Innocent Persecuted Heroine Genre: An Analysis of its Structure and Themes." *Western Folklore* 52: 13–42.

Kanakacuntaram Pillai, T. (ed.). 1921 [1916, 1st edn]. *Tamil Navalar Caritai.* C. Kumaracami Naydu Sons: Chennai.

Mines, Mattison. 1994. *Public Faces, Private Voices: Community and Individuality in South India.* Berkeley: University of California Press.

Muttusami Pillai, 1840. "A Brief Sketch of the Life and Writings of Father C.J. Beschi, or Varamamunivar." *Madras Journal of Literature and Science* 11: 250–300. (Original Tamil version written in 1822 and reissued in 1933 as *Varamamunivar Carittiram*, ed. Rev. K.M. Gnaninather. Tiruccinapalli: Christian Diocese.)

Narayana Rao, Velcheru, David Shulman and Sanjay Subrahmanyam. 1992. *Symbols of Substance: Court and State in Nayaka Period Tamilnadu.* Delhi: Oxford University Press.

———. 2002. *Textures of Time: Writing History in South India, 1600–1800.* New Delhi: Permanent Black.

Peterson, Indira. 1994. "Tamil Saiva Hagiography." In Winand Callewaert and Rupert Snell (eds), *According to Tradition: Hagiographical Writing in India,* pp. 191–228. Wiesbaden: Harrassowitz.

Ramaswamy, Sumathi. 1994. "The Nation, the Region, and the Adventures of a Tamil 'Hero.' " *Contributions to Indian Sociology* 28: 295–322.

Skaria, Ajay. 1999. *Hybrid Histories: Forests, Frontiers and Wildness in Western India.* Delhi: Oxford University Press.

Subrahmanyam, Sanjay. 1999a. "Recovering Babel: Polyglot Histories from the Eighteenth-Century Tamil Country." In D. Ali (ed.), *Invoking the Past,* pp. 280–321. Delhi: Oxford University Press.

———. 1999b. "Friday's Child: Or how Tej Singh became Tecinkurajan." *Indian Economic and Social History Review* 36: 69–113.

Vanamamalai, Na. 1969. "A Study of Historical Ballads in Tamil." In Vanamamalai, *Studies in Tamil Folk Literature,* pp. 49–98. Madras: New Century Book House.

———. 1974. *Aivar Racakkal Katai.* Madurai: Madurai University.

Viramma, Racine, Josiane Racine and Jean-Luc Racine. 1997. *Viramma: Life of an Untouchable.* London: Verso [transl. Will Hobson; original French edition, *Une Vie Paria. Le Rire des Asservis, Inde du Sud,* 1995].

White, Hayden. 1980. "The Value of Narrativity in the Representation of Reality." In W.J.T. Mitchell (ed.), *On Narrative,* pp. 1–24. Chicago: University of Chicago Press.

NOTES

1. A good example for Tamil is Viramma, Racine and Racine 1997; see also the Racines' essay in this volume.
2. See Mines 1994.
3. Hatch and Wisniewski 1995.
4. White 1980.

5. Skaria 1999 discusses a different set of historical genres among a tribal society in Western India.

6. Narayana Rao *et al.* 1992, 2002; Subrahmanyam 1999b.

7. Here I would agree with Subrahmanyam (1999a) that the Tamil *talapurana* is a separate genre altogether.

8. A more complete consideration of life-historical texts in Tamil would begin with the ancient panegyrics, or *puram* poems, and trace a line through to early medieval texts, such as the *Pantikkovai* and the *Nantikalambakam*.

9. See, for example, Peterson 1994. On Tamil Vaishnava hagiography, see Hardy 1992.

10. Henriques also translated a catechism and confessionary into Tamil and printed them in the 1570s, the first books printed in any Indian script.

11. See Bayly 1989, especially pp. 115–23.

12. *Tamil Navalar Carita* may be the first Tamil text to use *carittiram* (or its variants) in its title; "*carittiram*," according to the Tamil lexicon, is dated to a work by Oppilamani Tecikar (of the late seventeenth or early eighteenth century). "*Caritai*" first occurs in a Tevaram poem (eighth century?).

13. The most famous of these legendary poets, Valluvar, Auvaiyar and Kampan, are memorialized in a series of large statues that stand on the seafront in Madras.

14. Muttusami Pillai 1840 (English translation); Muttusami Pillai 1933 (reissue of 1822 Tamil original). See Blackburn 2003 for a discussion of this biography.

15. See Vanamamalai 1974; Filipsky 1990; Arunachalam 1976; Ramaswamy 1994.

16. Similar texts were also produced, on request, for Colonel Mackenzie and his team in the early nineteenth century.

17. For a commentary and a translation of one performance of "The Brothers," see Blackburn 1988.

18. Vanamamalai 1974: 26.

19. Vanamamalai 1974: 46. Vanamamalai notes that this line is also found in the *meykirtti* (preface) of inscriptions of two Vijayanagara rajas (Kulacekaran and Sundara Pandyan I).

20. This episode of the hare chasing off hunting dogs is widespread in place legends in South India (e.g., the stories of Kattabomman).

21. The *Tanjavuri Andhra Rajula Caritra* also contains a spurned marriage alliance at the heart of its drama (Narayana Rao *et al.* 1992: 305–9); and in the *Kan cakipu cantai*, the eponymous hero is defeated when one of his own (a French commander) betrays him (see a summary in Bayly 1989: 207–13).

22. The Nadars, the most numerous caste in the area, supported the Brothers because they felt that Marttanda Varma's tax regime was excessive and because they are patrilineal, which is the basis of the Brothers' claim to the throne.
23. The opening formula for a Tamil folktale is "in some place" (*oru ûrile*).
24. On this point, see Dundes 1978.
25. Jones 1993.
26. Full texts in translation for the folktales discussed here are found in Blackburn 2001.
27. A *pottu* is made with ash and/or vermilion in the middle of the forehead, for beauty or piety. Cf. *tilak*.
28. Bruner 1986.

CHAPTER 9

"Honor is Honor, After All"

Silence and Speech in the Life Stories of Women in Kangra, North-West India

KIRIN NARAYAN

When I first announced my intention to record women's life stories in Kangra in 1991, I was cautioned by Vidhya Sharma that not everyone would have a story. A bemused woman in her early thirties, Vidhya announced that she, for example, did not have a life story. "Look, it's only when something different has happened that a woman has a story to tell," Vidhya said, speaking Hindi. "If everything just goes on the way it's supposed to, all you can think of is that you ate, drank, slept, served your husband and brought up your children. What's the story in that?"

As Vidhya made clear, stories could be silenced on account of their sheer mundane predictability. As I began to elicit women's life stories, I also became aware of the presence of other kinds of silences constraining narrative forms. On the occasions that women spoke out, breaking silences, the sorts of issues that might have remained unspoken in other stories were thrown into sharp relief. In this essay, I draw on a body of Kangra women's life stories to address the methodological and theoretical issues surrounding silences in life stories more generally. I use the term "life story" rather than "life history" in order to draw attention to the fragmentary and constructed nature of personal narratives (cf. Peacock and Holland 1993).

Since the 1920s, anthropologists have acknowledged life stories as powerful and riveting data for personalizing cultural, historical, and social forces. However, it is rarer that anthropologists have reflected on the unspoken aspects of such stories. In his authoritative 1945 statement "The Use of Personal Documents in Anthropology," Clyde Kluckhohn counseled: "interpretations must go beyond the manifest content of the interviews. What the informant does *not* say, when and how he says what he does, may have for the subtleties of both cultural and psychological analysis an importance equal to that of the explicit content" (Kluckhohn 1945: 146).

How does an anthropologist move beyond manifest and explicit content to comprehend the unsaid? Can this be done without violating other people's integrity and dignity? In this essay, I argue that silences within life stories may best be understood in the context of other life stories, through the interpersonal negotiation of the life-story form, and with reference to other arenas for self-representation. I will share with readers a puzzling contrast between the kinds of stories I recorded from fourteen upper-caste Kangra women who were all over forty, and two young low-caste women in their early twenties. I then set these stories and silences within their cultural context. Finally, I return to the larger analytic issue of how scholars might conceptualize silences in life stories so that we may better appreciate the contours of what is actually spoken.

Background

Kangra is a valley in the foothills of north-west India: a lush region of fields, plumed bamboo groves, fir-covered hills, and to the north, a view of the Dhauladhar or "White Bearing" mountain range of the Himalayas. Though most families in this administrative district of Himachal Pradesh are associated with agriculture in one capacity or another, the economy really hinges on remittances sent in from men working beyond the region. As Jonathan Parry's excellent overview *Caste and Kinship in Kangra* (1979) demonstrates, Rajputs are the dominant caste, and their ethic of honor—called *izzat* or *laj*—pervades regional culture. The honor of a household is tied partly to the comportment of its women, whether daughters or in-marrying brides. Marriages are mostly arranged along the principles of village exogamy and caste endogamy or hypergamy. For women, moving with marriage from their parent's home (*mape/piyokhi*) to the home of their in-laws' (*saure*) is a central life event. Since property is transmitted patrilineally, and young married couples are expected to live patrilocally in the extended joint family of the groom, women are often disempowered in their rights to inheritance or the control of land (Sharma 1980). The control of land in Kangra, as in most of North India, has historically been in the hands of the "high" (*oonchi*) caste men, with the lower or "small" (*choti*) castes offering services of various sorts to the upper castes, including as poor field laborers. Post-Independence land reforms and reservations in favor of "scheduled" and "backward" castes have meant that many members of lower castes now have access to small landholdings, are educated, and hold jobs in government. Nonetheless, on the whole, comparing lower-caste and higher-caste households, I witnessed more poverty among the lower castes, differences in the folklore drawn on by women, and also—based on a limited sample—a difference in the form and content of life stories.

I first visited Kangra in 1975, as a teenager; in 1978, my American mother moved to a village there. I have visited her practically every year since then. Between 1990 and 1991, and again in spring 2002, I made her home a base for fieldwork on women's oral traditions in the region, researching women in her village and in a handful of different village settlements across the valley. Following customary norms of informal gender segregation in household spaces, my interactions in the different households I visited were largely confined to women, whether in the inner spaces of kitchens or enclosed courtyards.

The concept of life story, as we know, is culturally contingent. When an anthropologist attempts to record life stories, what he or she hears may be shaped partly by the repertoire of available narrative forms within a particular cultural setting (cf. Brumble 1988: 21–47; Crapanzano 1984). At the same time, the account elicited by an anthropologist is likely to bear the imprint of the anthropologist's own questions and relationship with a subject (cf. Dwyer 1982; Rosaldo 1976).

In the course of researching the songs that Kangra women sing when they gather together, I discovered that, on occasions when women of roughly equivalent castes and ages assembled, they sometimes also exchanged confidences about what had recently been happening in their lives. They called this practice *lathrota* or *dukh-sukh karna*—that is, "performing sorrows and joys." Notice how "sorrow" comes before "joys." In a manner reminiscent of the Pakistani Paxtun women written about by Grima (1991), sorrowful matters were the most readily narrativized, and recurred as a leitmotif through women's self-narrations.

While *lathrota* was common, the practice of recounting an entire life from start to finish seemed to have no place in everyday life. I tried to elicit life stories with invitations like, "Tell me when you were born, what happened in your childhood, where you got married, what has happened since then." Not a single woman followed this exhaustive sequence, though: rather, they tended to elaborate on particular dramatic episodes, whether from their own lives or the lives of female relatives. Since our sessions were tied into the informality of household visits, sometimes a teller would break off simply because someone new had arrived, a child needed attention, or it was time to cook, apparently feeling no need to bring the story to the present moment.

I first used the term "life story" (*jeevan ki kahani*) using Hindi in my enquiries. I soon found, though, that most women preferred the English term "story," referring to their life stories as *apni stori* or "one's own story." They also sometimes described in the regional dialect (Pahari) what was performed before my recorder as "confidences" (*lathrota*), "talk" (*gallan*), "talk of the past" (*pichleya diye gallan*), or "yarns" (*gappa*). In a more playful vein, a woman of the Barber caste referred to her animated reminiscences of returning from Lahore during Partition, and of being widowed in her twenties in terms of the most widely used ritual tale at village functions, the Satyanarayan *katha*. "You're taking my Satyanarayan *katha* back to America!" she exclaimed giddily, evoking a laugh from everyone present in the room.

Just as the Satyanarayan *katha* depicts a series of suffering individuals who find redemption by performance of the appropriate ritual, the narrative form of women's own stories emphasized suffering and how it eventually passed. Statements like "I never had a peaceful moment," "I've really lived through difficult times," "There's no happiness in my fate," or "Now that a time of happiness has come, even then there's no happiness," recurred in many of the fourteen truncated life stories I heard from upper-caste women. Further, like the Satyanarayan *katha*, which was performed before an audience who already knew all or part of the story's content, so too women were often telling their own stories in the company of other women who had heard these tales of tribulation before. Listeners of all ages would nod, cluck, correct, insert questions, or commentary. I too treated this as a conversation, freely interjecting my own questions.

Life Stories from Upper-caste Women

If the folksongs I was researching mostly described possible scenarios and conflicts with a joint family at different moments in a woman's life, the life stories I elicited focused on the unusual twists and turns of fate. Such unusual circumstances were associated with assorted factors: kinship arrangements (such as being raised by a widowed aunt or being a co-wife), historical interventions (like leaving Lahore at Partition, or a husband's miraculous return after twelve years of being lost in action in Burma), tragedy (like early widowhood), or atypical accomplishment (like being the first female matriculate of a village). Women often spoke of the suffering of their female ancestors (mothers, grandmothers, aunts), as though these matrilineally related women stood on a continuum of selfhood. Just as *pariyaan* or fairies were passed along from high-caste mother to daughter, protecting a woman's fate, so too suffering seemed to be matrilineally transmitted through narrative.

Rather than present many of these upper-caste narratives in partial form, I will focus here on Meena Rana, a Rajput woman. Meena began her narrative by telling me about her maternal aunt (or *Masi*), whose mother-in-law had died, and then began to appear "like a shade from a dream," beckoning for her son. Sure enough, Masi's husband died. Masi was just sixteen, a childless young widow in the home of her elder brother-in-law who refused her space, land, and support. The elder brother-in-law's wife gave Masi tea boiled with previously used leaves, adding salt rather than sugar, and served her just one round bread (*baturu*) a day. Masi returned to her parents' home describing her misfortunes, but, as Meena said, "In those times, people considered it a matter of shame to stay in one's mother's home after marriage." Instead, Masi's father arranged for her to claim a portion of her husband's family house and a small area of land, instructing, "Daughter, live with modesty and honor. Don't get involved in any dirty misconduct (*gandhi harkat*). If you urgently require something, then come to me and I'll give it to you." Masi replied, "I'll work with my own hands. I'll earn for myself, and I'll eat for myself." She farmed her land and raised cows and buffaloes, selling their milk, and sheep, selling their wool. Feeling lonely amid this hard toil, she approached her elder sister, Meena's mother, who had four daughters and one son, asking if she might have a daughter. Meena's mother replied, "Take her! I already have three daughters." Masi asked the three youngest girls; two refused, but Meena agreed. Looking back, she said, "These things are matters of fate (*kismat*)."

Meena, then, had gone off with her Masi as a young child and did not see her own parents until a visit ten years later. Masi raised her in a way that Meena never felt financial hardships, teaching Meena women's work of tending the livestock and tending the home. Then, when Meena had finished school and was eighteen, Masi asked her own father (Meena's maternal grandfather) to look for a groom. Many Kangra Rajputs serve in the Indian army, and the groom that Meena's grandfather located was a young soldier.

At the time of recounting this story, Meena was a handsome woman of about forty with strong white teeth and a ready laugh. Like several other women I knew who had been "extra" daughters and were adopted by a childless relative who gave them their full attention, she had tremendous self-confidence. At weddings, she was known for her brilliant and outrageous performances of bawdy skits. My recording was made one afternoon in the company of Tayi, an elderly aunt-in-law, and Simmu, Meena's youngest daughter, who was then six years old. To present a sense of the conversational strands woven into the performance of life stories in the company of female relatives, I include the comments of Tayi and Simmu.

> *Meena*: Now, when there were just two months left for the wedding—my wedding took place in 1972—then, my wedding was to happen on February 9. And on January 1, there was a big war—with Pakistan. Her father [*indicating Simmu*] was in Firozpur at that time. He too fought in the war, with the other soldiers in the army. Then her father was wounded.
>
> *Tayi*: Nine bullets hit him! Bullets here [*in the foot*] bullets here [*on the chest*]. This was on the border of Firozpur and Pakistan. Then, Kirin, I suffered a lot. We received a telegram saying "He's been wounded and is 'serious'—in a critical condition. We have no idea what will happen now."
>
> *Simmu*: Tayi, why was he shot?
>
> *Tayi*: They were trying to kill him.
>
> *Simmu*: Why?

Tayi: To kill him. That's what soldiers do—try to kill people.
Meena: Then my Masi felt enormous pain too: "I've raised another person's child. She's not even of my own womb. And even then, I don't have any happiness." She felt enormous pain: "If I hadn't raised her, maybe that would have been better. Now I've raised her, and I've even promised her in marriage, but who knows whether he will live or die? And then too, suspicions fall on a girl—who knows what kind of girl she is. You know how awful people here are. They say, "This girl is no good. Who knows what her stars are like? Her influence fell on him and he died." People say those kinds of things.

As rumors came in each day that the potential groom had died, or had had his leg amputated, Masi was in turmoil. She went to her own father, asking, "Bapu, what should I do? How can I marry her to a cripple?" Her father replied, "No, with a man, it's a question of just one. However he is, whether he is a cripple, or he's blind, she must marry him. This is her fate. Even if one were to marry her to a healthy man, he'd become just like this."

Masi was so worried that she ran a high fever, but Meena stated, "Whatever happens, that's my fate." The groom-to-be was brought home fifteen days before the marriage. Beaming broadly, Meena reported that a huge crowd gathered to view him as he stood in the courtyard, almost as though Rajiv Gandhi was to visit. "Her Daddy [*indicating Simmu*], he was very 'smart.' In those days, he used to be so handsome! Now he has grown dark. At that time, he had such a fair complexion. Then when he stood in the courtyard, everyone was happy looking at him."

The wedding took place while some bullets were still lodged in his body. Subsequently, he underwent an operation to extract them, and specifically asked his mother to bring his new wife to the hospital. Meena's glow when she spoke of her husband seemed to indicate an ongoing happiness in their marriage. Yet having recounted these dramatic and difficult times, Meena did not have much to add about her subsequent years of raising children beyond her regrets that she did not have a chance to live "outside" with her husband more often before he retired from the army: as she stated, almost formulaically, "There's no happiness (*sukh*) in my fate."

Life stories like Meena's snugly contain implicit cultural assumptions of commonsensical causation (cf. Linde 1993). The appearance of a beckoning ghost may cause a close surviving relative to die.

Upper-caste widows seeking to uphold family honor must never re-marry or engage in "dirty" (sexual) misconduct, regardless of their age; indeed Tayi, listening in, had herself been a fourteen year-old widow who lived celibate and childless with her husband's brother's family. Sons are prized, but daughters are disposable, and can be loaned out in adoption. Turning points in lives are scripted by fate, and mental agitation may lead to bodily illness. The influence of a man's or wo-man's stars affects a mate, even before marriage. (While Meena's ac-count points to suspicions that her fate caused her husband to be crippled, an older Brahmin woman, Asha Devi, told of how her hus-band's powerful stars, so terrible for his womenfolk that his first wife was bedridden, also caused Asha Devi, his younger co-wife, to develop a high fever and lose all her hair after their engagement.)

Meena Rana did not speak her husband's name; rather, she referred to him as the father of her daughter who was listening in. Indeed, in all the life stories I heard, husbands and older kin were never named. Husbands were usually just called "he" (*sai*), and other kin were re-ferred to by their kinship terms. This prohibition on speaking the names of elders undoubtedly also suffused the linguistic texture of these stories. Since codes of modesty (*sharm*) tied to respect rendered it inappropriate for any portion of an elder's name to surface in speech, Kangra women drew on an elaborate system of substititions in their conversations, stories and songs. For example, if a father-in-law's name was "Roshan Lal," one could never say the word *lal* for "red," but have to use a term like *rongli* instead. Though Meena was mostly speaking Hindi in this narration, the presence of her elderly aunt-in-law would have certainly made such substitutions necessary, even if I was not aware of it.

In stories like Meena's, then, dramatic events were highlighted. Suf-fering was described in the lives of female relatives with open reference to the wicked persons responsible . Suffering in a woman's own life, though, was referred to in terms of her own fate, God's will, or the in-fluence of planets. Told in the company of female relatives in homes controlled by men (whether husbands or brothers), these accounts all struck me as curiously devoid of suffering associated with the actions of anyone in the joint family who was presently alive.

On account of my mother's residence in Kangra and my own re-current visits through time, I was often aware of conflicts within fami-lies that never surfaced in women's narrations. It gradually became clear that to maintain family honor, ellipses and omissions were a necessary part of upper-caste women's narrations of their lives in joint families. This insight was highlighted when Urmilaji, a woman I had been working closely with on folktales, finally confided her life story when we once found ourselves entirely alone in the household. It was a painful story that seemed to mirror some themes in her repertoire of folktales. Yet when I asked if I could include her story in the book (Narayan 1997), she demurred. "My life? Why write about it? No, no." Urmilaji vehemently shook her head and asked: "Why should we put others' failings into this book? Each person has their own karma. Who am I to pass judgment?" Lives, then, clearly implicated other lives in a network of relations. The linguistic norms stemming from modesty and honor that prevented the explicit naming of elders also appeared to block direct mention of family conflicts.

Life Stories from Women of a "Small Caste"

Although most of the women I worked with on songs and stories were upper caste, during a return visit I also came to know two young women in their early twenties who stood lower in the caste hierarchy. These women, Anita and Rita, referred to the caste from which they came simply as a "little caste" (*choti jati*), but members of other castes tended to contemptuously refer to this caste as "Chamar." Chamar literally indicates the profession of leatherworking, though no one of the caste currently did that work. Nonetheless, Chamars were regarded as Untouchable by the upper castes in the area, and in most villages, they lived in a set-apart area.

Anita was a smart, animated and outstandingly pretty unmarried woman of twenty-two. She had learned of my interests in women's songs, stories and lives from a city immigrant to Kangra whom I sometimes visited and for whom Anita did menial work. Anita took me aside, out of her employer's earshot, to ask more about my research and to listen to recordings of songs. Within a few meetings she excitedly offered to donate what she called "*apni* (my) '*stori*'" for my research. "My story would make a great novel!" she declared. "Not just a novel, it would make a film!" I gladly agreed to tape her, but first, Anita said, she needed to arrange for her friend Rita to come meet me so they could give me their stories together.

The next time I visited that village settlement, Anita introduced me to her friend. Rita was a pale, reserved young woman who made Anita, who was also small, look positively robust. While Anita giggled and joked Rita regarded me with a piercing stare. Gradually, she warmed up. I learned that she was twenty-four and married, with a son and daughter. Sitting in the protected space of my host's guestroom, the two young women started filling my tapes with their stories. They spoke animatedly in Hindi, listening attentively to each other. They both interspersed their narratives with dramatic and emphatic phrases like "all of a sudden" (*achanak hi*) or "absolutely" (*ekdam*) in a manner that reminded me of Hindi film or television serial dialog. As my cassettes wound on, it became clear that these life stories were of a different order from what I'd been hearing so far.

Anita spoke first, and I reproduce some dominant events in her story here simply to show how these interwove with her friend's tale. Anita was the eldest of three daughters, and when she was ten, her "Mummy" died of tuberculosis. Within a year, their father remarried, and as Anita said, laughing, "And my 'story' became a different one (*apni stori dusri ban gai*)." When their father left to work in a factory near Ludhiana, the "new Mummy" fought all the time with her stepdaughters. Eventually she gave birth to two prized sons. Anita and her sisters were often not given enough food to eat, not allowed to attend school, and were sometimes beaten. Though Anita had asked her employer and a village health worker to intervene with the stepmother after fierce fights, she said that she didn't want to tell her father of some of the struggles as he would get angry during his infrequent visits home. Yet, as though emboldened in the course of recounting her difficulties, she resolved to speak out to her father: "Even if conflict comes out of it, I must tell my full story (*apni stori puri batai deni*)," she declared.

Rita spoke second, beginning her narrative with the declaration: "My 'story' is just like hers." She went on to mention how shared experiences had brought them close:

> Anita has no mother. And I too have no mother. I know what it's like to live like that. We became girlfriends. She's as dear to me as my own child . . . Even if I have to suffer beatings because of this, or have to suffer anything else because of this, I still can't live without talking to her. And her story is just like mine. It's only when you've heard another person's pain that you understand them. Those that don't understand another person's heartaches: what do they know?

Like Anita, Rita's mother had died when Rita was a child. Like Anita, who was battling the harsh, self-centered stepmother, Rita was struggling against her callous mother-in-law. The two young women were also bonded by the opposition their families showed to their friendship.

Rita's father was a farm laborer. She had grown up desperately poor. As she said, "We didn't receive proper clothes to wear, we didn't eat many vegetables. We'd eat a lot of salt, but we managed to eat." An upper-caste schoolteacher noticed that Rita was not attending school and personally contributed clothes and fees for Rita to enroll. Pretty and quick, Rita excelled in her studies and in school performances, once even being given the honored role of Indira Gandhi for a school play. But by the fifth standard, when she was about ten or eleven, Rita's father had decided that studies were an unnecessary extravagance for a family so close to the edge of survival, and she was pulled out of school to tend the younger children and help out in the fields.

A central part of Rita's life story was the dramatic account of how she had met her husband-to-be at a wedding where he was a member of the groom's party and she was a relative of the bride. They exchanged some glances at the wedding, and later, this tall, moustached young man sent messages through a go-between, escalating into a dramatic declaration of love. Rita quoted him as saying, "If you don't say anything, and if you go and marry someone else, then I'll carry you away from there." Smiling a little as unmarried Anita giggled with romantic delight, Rita told us of her response.

> Then I got scared, and my love for him grew. I said, "If you have forcefulness (*himmat*) of this sort, just you try and touch me! I may remain single, but I haven't let anyone near my honor. I won't let you near either." Then I thought, "If he has such a strong will to marry, then it's my wish too. We'll get married. What is there to that?"

All this sounded like such high drama to me that I cut in to ask if Rita had seen any Hindi films at the time, which she denied. (Films, shown in town, were a province of men; television had brought films into homes and women's lives mostly by the mid to late 1980s.) She returned to her story. Her husband-to-be prevailed upon his parents to arrange his marriage to Rita, who was after all of an appropriate caste and background. Although the marriage was eventually arranged, Rita saw its root in love with the drama as well as stigma of dishonor that a "love marriage" (*prem vivah*) could locally evoke.

It was after this marriage that some of Rita's most serious hardships began. Her parents-in-law were constantly squabbling, and Rita was used as a tool in their war. Her husband also gave up his job at a tea factory. "He left that job. Who knows why? I thought, "I'm new around here and how can I scold my husband?" Then too, that's not a wife's duty, her *dharma*. I watched and I watched. He worked in the fields. He worked in the house. He worked in the jungle. This is how the time went passing by. About one or one and a half years passed."

Rita found herself pregnant within a few months. She waited for some sign from her in-laws that she was to be given medical care and special food. But this never came, and she had stillborn twins: "a big blow" (*dhakka*), Rita said. To make matters worse, after the babies died, she was chastised and beaten by her in-laws. Although it was bitter winter, they did not feed her well.

I asked where Rita's husband was at the time. She said: "He was at home. But he was not earning. So what could he do? And I thought, "I knew him before I married, so now how can I scold him?" That's why I didn't say anything to him. I endured everything." When Rita learned that she was pregnant again, she began to take initiative for herself. "I began to have self respect," she stated. She went to the local health workers of her own accord and procured the care she needed, giving birth to a healthy boy. Before the boy was a year old, she also gave birth to a daughter. By the following year, her third child, another son, was born, and she went to the hospital fifteen days after birth to have her tubes tied. "I did this all by myself. I didn't ask anyone. I didn't even ask my husband. I signed the form all by myself for that operation."

As Rita's father-in-law had more mouths to feed, there was rising tension in the household. Rita became the butt of her in-laws' discontent, and was beaten several times. Finally, Rita spoke out to her husband: "All that's happening is because of you. If you were earning properly and giving them money, then none of this would be happening. When we can pay our own expenses, then none of this will happen."

Yet when her husband left for work in the plains, Rita had other problems. A neighbor attempted to molest her, and she complained to the village *panchayat*. Later, her mother-in-law spread the word that she was having sex with the father-in-law. The father-in-law beat Rita for speaking out in what he called "insolent talk," saying "You have sons, but if you had only daughters, it would have been easy to throw you out of the house." During one violent family quarrel, her husband's younger brother struck his parents, who were beating Rita, and then hit her too. Later he apologized to her. Telling of this episode, Rita said, 'I'm not lying about this. I have never hidden a single thing from anyone to this day."

Worse yet, when other members of the family were absent, her father-in-law did indeed make sexual advances. Rita thought that his behavior was perhaps due to her having known her husband before marriage: "He might have thought 'She fell in love with my son and married him, and now he's been gone for three or four months. Maybe she'll have those desires again.' " Perhaps Rita's sterilization made the father-in-law more confident in his advances, not fearing reproductive consequences. Rita suspected that her mother-in-law had conspired to bring this situation to crisis by going off and leaving them alone in the house for extended periods of time, even though Rita had tried to tell her what was happening. Rita was outraged by her father-in-law's behavior:

> Why would I do this? I am a mother of children. And then too I am not going to do these hellish deeds. I have a husband. I wouldn't do a thing like this. If one did things like this, if we Hindustani women began to do things, then what would happen? Honor is honor after all. And if you want to go to hell, then go to hell for a reason! Why go to hell for no reason? That's not a good thing to do, is it? If one starts to do things like this with a mother and father then how will we live, who will carry on the world? I felt tremendous fear.

One night, when her father-in-law came menacingly toward her, Rita didn't scream, for fear of alerting neighbors to the improprieties in the house. Instead, she calmly told him that if he could convince his own daughter to sleep with him first, only then would she herself comply. This enraged her father-in-law.

> Then he got really irritated and began to come toward me to hit me. I was sitting near the hearth. I picked up a burning log from the flame and said to him in anger, "Come, lay a hand on me, and I'll burn you up." The children were asleep. How could children understand? At that time if I'd screamed or called for someone, then too I'd be dishonored. So I marshaled all my strength to pick up that log from the hearth. I stubbornly faced him: "If you come touch me then I'll brand you. All your life you'll have this scar where I burn you." After all I was to be dishonored. But I refused to do this wicked deed (*galt kam*).

More recently, Rita confided she had also been fending off her brother-in-law, who had returned from looking for work in the city, educated, unemployed, unmarried and simmering with hormones and frustration. Her husband was still off trying to generate an income from the plains. The house had no doors within it, and Rita said she was currently fearful of going to sleep and would often sit upright, surrounded by her small children, singing to herself and knitting or embroidering.

Anita and Rita had together enrolled in an NGO-sponsored project for training poor local women in pickle-making. For both, preparing ingredients for pickles brought in some income, and they helped each other with accounts. Yet both families colluded in keeping them apart. Rita's brother-in-law slapped Anita for setting foot in their courtyard. He accused Anita of being a loose unmarried woman, and claimed that for household honor, he had to "control" his sister-in-law from associating with her. Simultaneously, Anita's stepmother claimed that the two girls' friendship made them talk against their families.

In presenting me with their stories, both young women were defying familial authority. "Our stories will be told!" Anita asserted giddily, asking for a copy of her own tape so she could replay it on her stepmother's cassette player. (I should add that this was one case where I did not comply, fearing the consequences.) Both women requested that I not share what they had disclosed to me with others in the Kangra area—not in their village, my mother's village, or any of the villages I visited. "You can reveal this to anyone outside," said Rita, "just not anyone in this area." With tranquil self-confidence, she added, "The truth, after all, is the truth" (*sacch to sacch hi hai*).

Before they went home, the two young women informed me of the twinned names, Anita and Rita, that they wanted appended to their stories as these went out into the wider world. A few days later, they returned in costume to commemorate their friendship for my camera: Rita dressed as a dignified bride in red, and Anita, standing tall beside her and bursting with mischief, wore a man's trousers, shirt, and Kulu cap. They were clearly representing themselves as a *jori*, the ideal of a twinned pair that is often linked with the conjugal bond as a "single two-person entity" (Kakar 1989: 84) and yet may also be a powerful ideal for girlfriends' intense, twinned bonding (Narayan 1983).

Family Honor and Personal Honor

"Honor is the beloved thing (*izzat sabse pyari hai*)" I often heard upper-caste Kangra people say. "If you lose your honor, you lose everything."

Since women's chaste, demure, and circumspect behavior was so central to family honor, it is no wonder that the stories of upper-caste women bore silences. Indeed, Partition narratives from Punjab have horrifyingly revealed how ideals of family honor sometimes resulted in the ultimate silencing of women, forced suicide in the face of dishonor by strange men (Butalia 1998: 133–84; Menon and Bhasin 1998: 32–64). In Kangra, the necessity of such silences was also expressed through various folklore forms. In one widely sung song, an argumentative wife who goes storming off to her own parents is indignantly told, "If you eat his earnings, you have to listen to his words." Sent back to her husband, he takes her indoors and counsels that in the future she should not broadcast their disagreements, "Matters of the heart should be kept in the heart," he says. "Don't bring a [dishonorable] blot to your life." As a singer commenting on this song said, "If you speak about fights in the house to others, it only makes the fights grow; it's best to keep them in your heart." Despite such counsel against speaking out about conflict in the family, the very existence of such folksongs, as well as folktales, provided women with other, more acceptable avenues for expression of conflicts.

Family honor, then, appeared to shape the stories shared by upper-caste women in the company of female relatives. I sensed these silences through displaced references to suffering in the lives of female relatives, occasional oblique references to suffering in the present, and tendrils of village gossip that the teller implicated chose not to address. In rare, intimate contexts where there was trust, it seemed potentially compromising or humiliating personal tales could be told, yet a listener might be asked to conceal these from public view. Judging from women's songs, a husband's home and his village were usually places for women to remain on guard. One wedding song lamented a bride's departure for her in-laws' home, asking, "Without a mother of one's own, without one's own father, to whom will we confide our sorrows?"

Standing in contrast to these upper-caste silences, the stories of Anita and Rita bitterly express suffering and conflict within their families. No doubt there were silences in Anita and Rita's stories too, yet both women continually asserted that they would not hide anything, that they felt an urgency to tell their complete stories. Any upper-caste woman hearing such stories, I suspect, would dismissively say that "small castes" had no honor. Yet Rita and Anita had both mentioned honor, or *izzat*, much as the older upper-caste women did; if anything, they emphasized honor more. The main difference was that for them, family honor (*ghar ki izzat*) was at odds with a sense of personal honor (*apni izzat*). Family honor led Rita to stifle a scream that neighbors might overhear when her father-in-law lunged toward her. Yet personal honor allowed her to defy expectations of a submissive daughter-in-law to turn against him with a burning log. Personal honor gave Anita the sense of urgency in telling her own version of family conflict, even if it might make for further conflict. Their tales might sacrifice family honor, but their telling vindicated the teller's personal honor.

In articulating unspeakable family matters like unrestrained child abuse, ongoing violence and unwanted sexual advances, Rita and Anita were aware of the transgressive nature of their stories: this was why I was asked not to reveal these events within Kangra. At the same time, these young women seemed compelled to tell their stories rather than to participate in silence, and I was positioned as a witness who would bear these testimonies into the wider world. In this sense, the stories of Rita and Anita would appear to be modeled on a figure of the *virangana* or warrior woman, who fiercely surfaces in Indian folklore, as "a model of female heroism based not on self-sacrifice and subservience to the male, but a direct assumption of power combined with righteousness and adherence to truth (*sat*)" (Hansen 1992: 30).

Unfortunately, I have not yet had a chance to tape much of Rita's repertoire of songs and stories to know the extent to which she has internalized this model of the *virangana*, and how folk traditions among lower castes might possibly sustain it. But a folktale that Rita had learned from her father and retold one afternoon pointed to divergences in women's roles from versions known more widely among upper castes. A king wanting a spring to flow was advised to sacrifice someone from his family. In the version known to upper-caste women through songs, the king's daughter-in-law was tricked into arriving at the spring, and ended up being bricked up alive as she tearfully pleaded with the masons. (In the adjoining state of Chamba, this becomes the legend of Queen Sunayana, who offered herself in sacrifice and is now worshiped as the beautiful brass-headed Suhi Mata.) In Rita's version, though, the daughter-in-law overheard the plans and at first attempted to remain silent. But her husband discerned her sadness and forced her to tell him what was on her mind. Instead of her being sacrificed alive for the well being of the king's domain, the two of them stole out of the castle, and went galloping off into the wider world for a new set of adventures. Here, then, was a caste-based recasting of an available folk narrative form that offered a model for a woman to speak out against her in-laws and affirm the conjugal bond. Similarly, while folksongs sung by upper-caste women tended to point to conflicts and suffering within the joint family, the few songs I taped from Anita and Rita emphasized how women's marital bond was under threat from powerful men outside the family—a king, a *thekedar* (contractor), or even a stationmaster—who might make lower-caste women their prey.

Why, in the cases of Rita and Anita, was personal honor so marked, sacrificing family honor? Can it be related to these women's caste status: after all, why should they have a stake in a patriarchal social structure and ideology that oppresses them? Stigmatized within larger society as well as in their respective families, what was left for them to hold proudly to but their personal honor? Further, might these young women's defiance be related to the changing political status of members of various Scheduled Caste groups, who since Independence had been increasingly speaking out against injustice? Again and again in their narratives, the young women turned to powerful figures outside the family for intervention against mistreatment in the family (employers, *panchayat* officials, medical officials), much as members of Scheduled Caste groups might turn to representatives of the state for intervention against local, caste-based harassment.

Yet caste and its changing political horizons, I believe, is not sufficient explanation for the differences in these accounts. Anita and Rita's speaking out also appeared to be linked to their age, literacy, and exposure to mass media. In their early twenties, Anita and Rita were a good sixteen to sixty years younger than the upper-caste women whose stories I had previously heard. However truncated their schooling, literacy coupled with enterprise had enabled these young women to take on an increasingly bureaucratized world and to make use of government resources like healthcare or NGO programs. Reading bureaucratic forms and signing her own name was vital to Rita's ability to make personal decisions like sterilization, separating herself as an individual with volition apart from her husband and his family. The chance to participate in the cultural activities promoted in a government school also allowed Rita the memorable experience of acting the role of Indira Gandhi and seeing herself not just as a village girl of a small caste, but as a powerful leader of the nation.

Exposure to films and programs on television appeared to have extended new narrative forms to these young women. Indeed, Anita's style of narration began each new twist in the tale with the melodramatic "all of a sudden" and Rita's reiteration of the dialog between her and her husband-to-be smacked of Hindi film dialog. The influence of film and television appears to have coaxed these women to strengthen their identity as nationalist women—Hindustani *aurat* and icons of honor (cf. Mankekar 1999). As Rita said, "If we Hindustani women began to do [immoral] things, then what would happen? Honor is honor after all."

In breaking the silences associated with family honor through asserting feisty personal honor, Rita and Anita were bypassing patriarchal authority within their families to turn, as citizens, to the authority of the state. They were also addressing themselves to the wider horizons beyond the village that they were continually exposed to on television and which appeared in their midst in the less glamorous form of an anthropologist carrying a tape-recorder that could spread their tales.

Conclusions

What wider points about the relation between speech and silence might these Kangra women's lives illuminate? How might we find ways to conceptualize silences in the spoken form of life stories so that we are neither suspiciously belittling a narrator's accountability nor subjecting a narrator to bludgeoning inquisitions? Is it possible for scholars to undertake an exploration of silences without distressing, offending, bullying or betraying the people with whom they work?

Woven through life stories are silences both conventional, on which speakers would probably not directly reflect, and intentional, where speakers are actively involved in concealment. Further, there are unconscious silences, silences of forgetting, and even silences associated with a breakdown of language through the experience of unspeakable horror (Das and Nandy 1986). So that any particular individual telling a life story is not compromised by her own silences being set to scrutiny, I envision at least three general ways of comprehending silence and the conditions under which silences become speech.

1. Examine a Body of Life Stories

While anthropologists have typically addressed the self-revelatory content of one life story at a time, moving beyond one life story to compare several brings expected narrative forms and their transgressions into clearer focus. This method of juxtaposing life stories was pioneered by Oscar Lewis (1960) in his work with a poor Mexican family, where each family member recounts his or her own stories, revealing multifaceted, cross-cutting and even diverging perspectives on the same episodes. In the Indian context, the life history of Viramma has a small section at the end, where Viramma's husband, Manikkam, speaks out, making politics and inequality his focus, whereas Viramma has mostly talked about her moral worth as a fertile woman, a mother, and a pious, knowledgeable believer in various spirits and deities (Viramma, Racine and Racine 1997). This glimpse into Manikkam's account reminds us of how gendered interests and conventions pervade the said and the unsaid in narrative form. Similarly, in Jonathan Parry's essay in this volume, the juxtaposition of Somvaru's life story with that of his daughter reveals hidden parts in both.

Ideally, I should have also approached Kangra men for their life stories. To have done so would have put me in a better position to argue that the narrativization of suffering was tied to gender (I suspect that it is). Instead, working with a range of women, I became aware of the differences in social location between women.

Juxtaposing the differences between the life stories of women like Meena with the stories of Rita and Anita throws light on how even within one region and within one gender, different selves are created by factors such as age, caste, literacy and access to benefits from institutions outside the extended family. What is spoken by Rita and Anita reminds us of all the conflicts that may possibly remain unspoken in upper-caste women's stories that seek to maintain family honor over personal truth.

The stories of older and younger women convey a sense of generational shifts. Ideally, one would also collect life stories in a society through time, as Roger Keesing has done, so shedding light on how changing social conditions may precipitate silent subjects into speaking ones. Among the Kwaio of the Solomon Islands, Keesing at first found men ready to talk about their lives, while women "were fragmented and brief, distancing themselves from serious autobiography with reciprocal jests" (Keesing 1985: 29). On return visits, he found that men's efforts to codify cultural rules and conventions or *kastom* as a form of postcolonial resistance to outside influences had also inspired women to think of culture as an objectifiable "thing" and to lay claim to their own accounts of *kastom* in which women's importance was given its due. When Kwaio women finally spoke out, they were doing so in counterpoint to the men who had previously been working with Keesing to codify *kastom*; also senior women recounted their lives "*as moral texts*, as exemplifications of the trials, responsibilities, virtues and tragedies of A Woman's Life" (1985: 33, emphasis in original). Speaking out, for Kwaio women, was a bid to power. Similarly, in India, one can point to changing perceptions of women's agency associated with women's movements as giving momentum to the oral history documentation of women's experiences during Partition (Butalia 1988; Menon and Bhasin 1998), breaking the silence on widespread violence against women not just from men of other communities, but also from women's own kin concerned with family honor.

BUTALIA

2. Acknowledge the Interpersonal Process

Life stories, orally told, are performances and, as performances, they emerge in the interaction between storytellers and particular audiences, which include the anthropologist (Narayan and George 2001). While I did not re-elicit life stories from the same women in different contexts through time, the work of anthropologists like Vincent Crapanzano (1980) and Laurel Kendall (1989) makes clear that what is told and what remains silent may change even for the same person. What Roger Keesing (1985: 37) called "the politics of the elicitation situation" is crucial: the age, gender, accepted status, pre-existing projects, and research collaborators of an anthropologist all factor into what he or she is likely to be told, in addition to the larger social and political context. As Keesing acknowledges, his recording of Kwaio women's life stories was partly on account of shifting circumstances in Kwaio society, and partly because he had returned with a woman anthropologist who participated in the collection of women's life stories. Anthropologists, then, are also implicated in the production of speech and silence within life stories.

Most women I had recorded were speaking to me from joint-family settings, whether as daughters-in-law or as an unmarried sister. It was appropriate, then, that they told of pain in the lives of their female ancestors, or with relatives with whom ties had snapped: people with whom there were ongoing bonds and dependencies could not be spoken of in these semi-public accounts lest the honor and solidarity of the joint family be threatened. I can only wonder whether, if I had met any of these women alone or traveled with them to their natal homes and asked for their stories again, the silences around family honor would remain as marked. Further, from the vantage of these older women, the fact that I was myself part-Indian and a younger woman perhaps made them emphasize respectable tales for my own moral instruction.

Rita and Anita, though, spoke out outside their own homes, and with the desire that I broadcast their stories elsewhere. They spoke at a time of extreme personal uncertainty for themselves, when both were dealing with daily familial harassment. That I was older than them was perhaps key to their choice of me for their confidant. Just as they had turned for personal vindication toward other figures perceived as powerful in the past, so they now turned to me. The audience provided by an anthropologist representing an outside world, then, shifts the balance of speech and silence, sometimes inspiring retellings that might locally be kept under wraps.

In paying heed to the desires for the fates of their stories that subjects of life histories may express, scholars may also become enmeshed in local systems of speech and of silence. Like Esperanza, the Mexican peddler woman written about by Ruth Behar (1993), subjects may ask that their stories be kept hidden from nearby neighbors or relatives, while acknowledging that it is fine to refer to this obliquely in general terms, or to spread it as testimony to distant audiences. Or, like Rigoberta Menchu, they may defiantly affirm the presence of unspoken secrets within their texts as a form of resistance to scrutiny by outsiders (Sommers 1999).

3. Look at Other Narrative Forms Available for Self-representation

When life stories are considered within a range of available discourses for self-representation, what is not spoken of within the conventional form of life stories becomes clearer. As a schoolteacher once said to me, about songs that she did not herself sing, "The person who becomes a singer or a storyteller is one with a lot of pain. She wants a way to express this pain. There are some things you can't say directly, but you can say them in this form. Songs and folktales become a form of solace."

While I had been seeking personal revelations through life stories, this statement took me full circle back to songs and folktales I had also been collecting. I was reminded of the Yukon elders who collaborated with the Canadian anthropologist Julie Cruikshank (1990) insisting that their myths were *part* of their lives. Urmilaji, my mentor, used these symbolic forms to give her life meaning—as she said, they now "sat inside" her heart. Other women whose life stories and songs I had taped echoed this use of collective symbolic forms to make sense of their personal experience. Shakuntala Devi, for example, said, "Anyone can sing, but it's only when you've experienced pain that you really understand the song." Or Meena Rana's Tayi once said, "Singing a song like this, you weep. You sing about the pain in your heart. Then you get some solace in your heart that there have been times like this for others in the past." For these women singers, collectively shared oral traditions could be seen as a complementary discourse to personal life stories, with the anonymity extended by oral traditions in fact allowing greater disclosure of emotion. This a situation akin to that of the Bedouin women described by Lila Abu-Lughod (1986) who, bound by the code of honor and modesty, did not express strong emotions in their everyday speech, but instead drew on short poetic songs. In Kangra, as elsewhere in India, women's growing access to other narrative forms—novels, films, or television serials—potentially also provides new modes of discourse and points of reference for conceiving and narrating their own life experience (Das 1990; Mankekar 1999).

Letters are an unsatisfactory medium for presenting life stories in their complexity, but they are useful for updates. Through the years of correspondence with friends in Kangra, I have observed that while narrators often stress suffering while speaking about their lives, the conventions of letter writing tend to emphasize that all is well, with flowery wishes for the good health and happiness of the receiver. A letter from Rita that arrived on June 1, 2001, written in colloquial Hindi, points to happy endings all around. Here is a quote from the aerogramme: "You asked about my situation so listen, sister (*didiji*). My husband has got a job and I am living happily along with my children and him in Shimla. And Anita has been married. . . . Everyone is happy."

To summarize, the patterns of silence behind speech give substance to what is actually said. While we may never be able to pin down exactly what these silences might be, awareness of the lurking presence of such silences draws attention to the artful, interpersonally negotiated, and politicized construction of life stories. As scholars, we may be tantalized by silences in personal narrative, wishing to uncover and disclose them. Yet we too are morally implicated in the collection and presentation of other lives. If the people we work with choose silences in the domain of personal narrative, it may perhaps be less profitable to ferret out the specifics of the unsaid than to search for general patterns across stories, take heed of how our own presence shapes texts, and be alert to other cultural domains where the insights or emotions suppressed in personal testimony may break into articulation. Marking the boundary between the sayable and the unsayable, the writable and the unwritable, silences in life stories point us toward constructions of morality and personhood in the context of the cultures we study and, by extension, in the culture of academe.

REFERENCES

Abu-Lughod, Lila. 1986. *Veiled Sentiments: Honor and Poetry in a Bedouin Society.* Berkeley: University of California Press.

Anderson, Kathryn, and Dana C. Jack. 1991. "Learning to Listen." In S.B. Gluck and D. Patai (eds). *Women's Words,* pp. 11–26. New York: Routledge.

Behar, Ruth. 1993. *Translated Woman.* Boston: Beacon.

Brumble, H. David. 1988. *American Indian Autobiography.* Berkeley: University of California Press.

Butalia, Urvashi. 1998. *The Other Side of Silence: Voices from the Partition of India.* New Delhi: Viking Penguin.

Crapanzano, Vincent. 1980. *Tuhami: Portrait of a Moroccan.* Chicago: University of Chicago Press.

———. 1984. "Note on Life Histories." *American Anthropologist* 86: 953–60.

Cruikshank, Julie. (In collaboration with Angela Sidney, Kitty Smith and Annie Ned). 1990. *Life Lived Like a Story.* Lincoln and London: University of Nebraska Press.

Das, Veena. 1994. "Biography: Women's Lives in Contemporary India." *Thesis Eleven* 39: 52–62.

———, and Ashis Nandy. 1986. "Violence, Victimhood and the Language of Silence." *Contributions to Indian Sociology* (n.s.) 19: 177–95.

Dwyer, Kevin. 1982. *Moroccan Dialogues: Anthropology in Question.* Baltimore: Johns Hopkins University Press.

Grima, Benedict. 1991. "Suffering in Women's Performance of *Paxto.*" In Arjun Appadurai, Frank Korom and Margaret Mills (eds), *Gender, Genre and Power in South Asian Expressive Traditions,* pp. 78–101. Philadelphia: University of Pennsylvania Press.

Hansen, Katherine. 1992. *Grounds for Play: The Nautanki Theater of North India.* Berkeley: University of California Press.

Kakar, Sudhir. 1989. *Intimate Relations: Exploring Indian Sexuality.* Chicago: University of Chicago Press.

Keesing, Roger. 1985. "Kwaio Women Speak." *American Anthropologist* 87: 27–39.

Kendall, Laurel. 1989. *The Life and Hard Times of a Korean Shaman Woman.* Honolulu: University of Hawaii Press.

Kluckhohn, Clyde. 1945. "The Use of Personal Documents in Anthropological Science." In L. Gottschalk, C. Kluckhohn and R. Angell, *The Use of Personal Documents on History, Anthropology and Sociology,* pp. 79–173. New York: Social Science Research Council Bulletin 53.

Langness, L. L. and Gelya Frank, 1981. *Lives: An Anthropological Approach to Biography.* Novato, Ca: Chandler and Sharp.

Lewis, Oscar. 1961. *The Children of Sanchez.* New York: Pantheon.

Linde, Charlotte. 1993. *Life Stories: The Creation of Coherence.* New York: Oxford University Press.

Mankekar, Purnima. 1999. *Screening Culture, Viewing Politics: An Ethnography of Television, Womanhood, and Nation in Postcolonial India.* Durham: Duke University Press.

Menon, Ritu and Kamla Bhasin. 1998. *Borders and Boundaries: Women in India's Partition.* New Brunswick: Rutgers University Press.

Narayan, Kirin. 1983. "Birds on a Branch: Girlfriends and Wedding Songs in Kangra." *Ethos* 14: 47–75.

———. 1995. "Songs Lodged in the Heart: Public Culture and the Displacement of Regional Women's Culture." In Smadar Lavie and Ted Swedenburg (eds), *Displacement, Diaspora, and Geographies of Identity,* pp. 181–213. Durham, N.C.: Duke University Press.

———, in collaboration with Urmila Devi Sood. 1997. *Mondays on the Dark Night of the Moon: Himalayan Foothill Folktales.* New York: Oxford University Press.

———, and Kenneth M. George. 2001. "Interviewing for Folk and Personal Narrative." In Jay Gubrium and James Holstein (eds), *The Handbook of Interviewing,* pp. 815–83. New York: Sage.

Parry, Jonathan. 1979. *Caste and Kinship in Kangra.* London: Routledge and Kegan Paul.

Peacock, James L. and Dorothy C. Holland. 1993. "The Narrated Self: Life Stories in Process." *Ethos* 21: 367–83.

Personal Narratives Group, ed. 1989. *Interpreting Women's Lives: Feminist Theory and Personal Narratives.* Bloomington: Indiana University Press.

Rosaldo, Renato. 1976. " 'The Story of Tukbaw:' They Listen as He Orates." In F. Reynolds and D. Capps (eds), *The Biographical Process,* pp. 121–51. The Hague: Mouton.

Sharma, Ursula. 1980. *Women, Work and Property in North West India*. London: Tavistock.

Sommers, Doris. 1999. "Sacred Secrets: A Strategy for Survival." In Sidonie Smith and Julia Watson (eds), *Women, Autobiography, Theory: A Reader*, pp. 197–207. Madison: University of Wisconsin Press.

Viramma, Josiane Racine and Jean-Luc Racine. 1997. *Viramma: Life of an Untouchable*. London: Verso.

CHAPTER 10

Beyond Silence
A Dalit Life History in South India

JOSIANE RACINE AND JEAN-LUC RACINE

The silence we are referring to in our title is not, as one may believe, the silence of the so-called Untouchables: they define themselves, as Viramma (whose life history is the center of this essay) would say, as noisy and talkative. But whom are they speaking for? Who is listening to them? The deepest silence is not theirs. It is mostly the silence born out of the higher castes' contempt and deliberate ignorance. It is also, up to a point, the silence which persists after attention has been paid to a certain type of Dalit voice, to a certain model of subalterns, for Viramma and her type do not belong to these groups, which are known for voicing their anger or for their public struggle.

In this essay, we comment on the life history of Viramma, a Tamil illiterate agricultural laborer and midwife from a Pondicherry village who died in 2002. She was a Dalit (Untouchable), whose life history we collected, edited and published fifteen years after one of us, Josiane, started to listen to her. This is an Indian history, which develops itself in one of the most specific and gloomy spheres of Indianness: Untouchability. But we shall not confine ourselves to this Indian context alone, nor to the tragedy that Untouchability is. In assessing Viramma's life history, much broader issues need to be addressed, some of them directly related to history, others of interest to non-historians. The status of orality, the analyses of autobiographies, the question of language and social hierarchies, the vision of what is "scientific" and what is "popular" have long been debated by scholars of literature, cognitive sciences, sociology, philosophy of language, etc. We are certainly not

equipped to offer a comprehensive synthesis of these diverse procedures of knowledge, but we feel free to consider what some of them
have to offer us.

The Question of Testimony

We begin with a brief discussion of four suspicions involved in collecting and textualizing life histories. The first of these is the historian's
suspicion of contemporaneity. In a recent book, *The Ocular Witness*,
sociologist Renaud Dulong begins: "Today we have only dubious testimonies. The authority of the most credible witnesses is submitted to
a quasi transcendental preliminary suspicion, and contested on the
basis of the cognitive and memory processes which back it" (Dulong
1998: 9). This is true in court for judicial enquiries. This is also true
for historians. Reinhart Koselleck (1990), as well as Paul Veyne (1971),
have called for an epistemology of distance that alone may offer the
guarantees professional historians request, for history can be constructed only through a specific perspective which rejects the so-called
collective memory and the testimony of the actors (Dulong 1998:
217).

A second suspicion is against the notion of the self. In his classic
study on autobiography, Philippe Lejeune defines it very strictly: an
autobiography is "a retrospective narrative in prose, made by a real
person about her own existence, when she gives emphasis to her individual life, particularly the history of her personality." Thus, the form
of language (narrative in prose), the topic (individual life, history of a
personality), the author's position (the author as narrator), the narrator's status (the narrator is the leading character, the narrative is
retrospective) are all necessary ingredients. If one of these qualities is
missing, the text is not an autobiography: it could be a journal, a biography, an essay, memoirs, etc. (Lejeune 1975: 14) The genre implies
what Lejeune calls "the autobiographical pact" linking the author to
the reader through the affirmation of a single identity unifying the
author (whose name stands on the cover), the narrator and the main
character.

Writing about himself, the author can never be really trusted, even
when he proclaims, as did Rousseau in his *Confessions*, that he will "say
everything." If he is a writer or an artist, the sensitivity of his mind will
be seen as a dubious warrant of truth. To write about oneself beyond

what is required within the genre of memoirs is seen as suspect, almost unnatural: the distance from self-analysis to exhibition may be short. If the author is a political figure, the suspicion is still greater: the auto-biography will be seen as an exercise in self-justification. In both cases, the narrator, choosing himself as character, is suspected of adorning the past in order to build his image for posterity. A third case is illus-trated by authors who have lived through tragic circumstances, either as criminals or as victims. The problem here is different: will they be heard? Foucault notes how the terrible narrative of Pierre Rivière, who killed his mother, his brother, and his sister in 1835 met with silence, immediately and totally (Foucault ed. 1973: 11). This silence is also met sometimes in the narratives of the victims of the holocaust: for long, some of them doubted if it would be possible to relate their ex-perience, and those who did relate it were often received with doubt and embarrassment.

In his study of autobiography and the subjective impulse since 1800, Jerome Buckley recalls how Emerson considered subjecti-vity the central attribute of the age, "the key of the period" (Buckley 1984: 4). Analyzing a much older and larger Western tradition from St Augustine to Goethe, K. J. Weintraub has underlined how "the value of the individual" has been recognized and how the "idea of the indivi-dualized person is a part of the modern form of historical conscious-ness" (Weintraub 1978: xi). Would this be true in India as well? The traditional Indian historian, as in Europe, worked for the king, the sultan, the emperor. Even Abul Fazl, while proposing a new concept of historical time in his *Akbar-nama*, has not written a personal bio-graphy of the emperor.

The third issue is the intellectual's suspicion of popular orality. In the Indian context, we note not just a weaker perception of individu-ality but also an assessment of the relevance of orality. Which orality, however? In the ancient Indian tradition, argues Charles Malamoud, the "prejudice against writing" was strong: "What is connected with writing is suspect, feared, and despised." "Knowledge is first of all the deep-toned spoken word, *vac*," and the Brahmin reciting Vedas is miles above the scribe (Malamoud 1997: 86–9). Writing is at best the shadow of speech, at worse the accounts kept, including the files pre-pared for judgments by Yama, the god of the dead (Malamoud: 96).

But beyond the sacred ritual utterances, is popular orality better acknowledged in India than in the Western tradition? On the one hand, the contempt for the lower classes, especially for illiterate Untouchables, does not need to be underlined. In India, as in Europe, the popular classes have long been perceived by the upper classes—and by most intellectuals—as being devoid of culture. It was striking to find in Viramma's high-caste landlord almost the same words that La Bruyère used in the seventeenth century when traveling across the French countryside. For both, poor illiterate peasants working in the field were like "beasts in the forest." For Viramma's landlord (whose mother-tongue is Telugu), what Paraiyars speak is not *pontamil*, the "golden Tamil" of old, nor even the standard Tamil used at school and in the media: it is "degraded" speech, defined with paternalist contempt by the high-caste landlord as a "half-language."

On the other hand, India is still a vibrant oral culture. Far from the monopolies of the twice-born and from Vedic recitations, oral narratives have a relevance that European culture, privileging the written medium, has forgotten. Sudhir Kakar has underlined their decisive significance as follows:

> The spell of the story has always exercised a special potency in the oral-based Indian tradition, and Indians have characteristically sought expression of central and collective meanings through narrative design. While the twentieth-century West has wrenched philosophy, history, and other human concerns out of integrated narrative structures to form the discourse of isolated social sciences, the preferred medium of instruction and transmission of psychological, metaphysical, and social thought in India continue to be the story. Narrative has thus been prominently used as a way of thinking, as a way of reasoning about complex situations, as an enquiry into the nature of reality (Kakar 1989: 1).

This is certainly true at the level of the day-to-day existence of millions of Indians. But looking at the intellectual history of India, and particularly at the way culture, education, science, communication, and law have been professionalized since the late nineteenth century, it appears that the pre-eminence of oral knowledge is now confined to ritual use. At the same time, however, the authority of the written word has been dramatically enhanced by the development of modernity— the Brahmins, as a caste, were in fact the first to understand it, and to adjust to the process.[1] As a result, the status of orality and the value of oral narratives as a tool for knowledge have been downgraded.

Lastly, we have suspicions against "the third party," or the intermediary between the narrator and the reader. The third party is often an academic in collected life histories, or a professional ghostwriter in celebrity biographies. One position, articulated by Geneviève Bollème in *Le Peuple par Écrit*, addresses the relation of members of popular classes with writing. According to her, "[t]he people write and talk only when they have been invited to do so: members of a specific social category are treated as simple informants; writers present them, offering their guarantee, and these people move to a scene where they appear as living documents" (Bollème, 1986: 237).

> Their words . . . we shall collect them, we shall listen to them, we shall channel them, we shall keep them, bound by power on all sides. We shall consider them as a result of our well wishing, of our good and generous willingness. These are not the words that people speak. This discourse is not important, having lost its strength, being lassoed, trapped with an infinite art, with the very patience. This bound discourse is not theirs (Bollème 1986: 257).

A second type of argument is based not on opinion but on scrupulous research work. Collected life histories, such as Viramma's, have become a genre by themselves, largely through the efforts of anthropologists. Some of these narrators could write, others merely read. Some were illiterate. David Brumble's analysis of hundreds of "autobiographies" of American Indians is probably the most systematic attempt to theorize the genre, and to bring forward its possible limitations. The important point here is not really the pertinence of the concept of autobiography. True, these biographies are not always "auto," where the narrators were illiterate, and the writing of their narrative are not even their own "graphy." The concept of life history is broader and more convenient, for it leaves open the question of the third party. Since the 1960s, comments Brumble, some American authors involved in life histories have called for a "total unveiling" of the procedures of writing such narratives. Others, such as Vincent Crapanzano, author of a Navajo biography, have lamented the subterranean role of the Western cultural background of the third parties in their rendering of life histories of American Indians. More important to us was the subterfuge Brumble denounces under the term "absentee writer," which erases the third party from the narrative, as if the narrator was alone in telling the story of his/her life (Brumble 1993).

The Need for Witnesses: From Oral Tradition
to Life History

What Henri Moniot has called "the history of peoples without history" has destroyed the traditional prejudices against orality, and it is worthwhile here to record the similarity between mainstream perceptions which, in the colonial vision of the world, have for long excluded so many peoples from history, with upper-caste Indian perceptions, which have excluded Dalits from history. Both rely on the false observation that "they have not done anything noticeable, they have not produced anything of lasting value," the implicit criterion of value being either material (preferably monumental) or written culture, the two often going together. Peoples without writing and illiterate groups were thus treated with the same contempt. We are not so interested here with the use of "oral traditions" for reconstructing the past of some African societies, as with what Moniot has to say about orality: "One cannot judge orality and memory on the basis of what they are in societies which put on writing all that is important" (Moniot 1974: 109). Oral traditions, as tools of knowledge, have therefore to be validated through a threefold critique. The textual critique calls for "observing the conditions and the circumstances of the collection, and how the testimony has been received." The sociological critique is that an oral tradition survives because of its functionality, which has to be identified, for it could be ideological, political, practical, aesthetic, apologetic, entertaining, etc. The third (cultural) critique addresses the references recognized in the considered group, be they formal, conceptual or value-marked (Moniot 1974: 110–12).

Heir and Witness: A Typology and Viramma's
Life History

These recommendations for making use of oral traditions are formulated for historians trying to reconstruct the past. They rely upon interlocutors who are the depositories of these traditions; and these narrators are seen as heirs preserving, but also enriching, a cultural legacy. Most of these methodological points appear valid as well for another type of orality, involving not so much an old legacy as a recent past. In these circumstances, we have to listen to witnesses more than to heirs. This is particularly true when testimonies—dramatic fragments of life histories which have suddenly changed their course for the worse—are a recollection of something which is the antithesis of oral tradition, of a cultural legacy: something hardly expressible, so unutterable that sometimes it was not believed. A number of French historians have worked on Nazi concentration camps, and this type of research has added much to the debate on the relevance of personal testimony. As Dulong emphasizes, the veteran from the trenches of the World War I, or the survivor from the camps of World War II, are offering through their testimonies "an essential item to the vigilance apparatus." What they say, and sometimes what they write, does not have to satisfy the criterion of impartiality. Such a witness enters a public space, and in a way turns into a public prosecutor: his or her message is not just informative, it stands as well as a political questioning of society as a whole (Dulong 1998: 16).

When a member of a group with primarily an oral tradition tells his or her life story, he or she is the bearer of a cultural legacy: Viramma, as a storyteller and singer, is thus heir to Tamil Dalit culture. But she is also a witness of her times. Her testimony is not just the egotistical exercise of autobiographer and her "I" is not expression of a "bourgeois individualism." Talking about herself, she talks as well of her family, of her community, of life in the Dalit ward (the *ceri*), of the system of relations and unequal power governing the village. As a subaltern telling her life history, she sheds light on those who are outside her community. Moreover, because unlimited time was given to Viramma, she was able to recollect her life not only in its historical continuity, but also in its totality—covering joys and sorrows, material dimensions and beliefs, legacies of the past and dynamics of change. We have to recognize the specificity of the life histories of common people. On a certain level, they offer less than the life histories of people who have been personally involved in decisive historical events. But, on the other hand, the apparent banality of their life, the lack of distance which characterizes those who have not looked for or accepted alternatives, offers perceptions of a different nature: their recollections are less tense but also more comprehensive than testimonies that give deliberate emphasis to dramatic episodes. Life histories such as Viramma's are representative of at least a part of the so-called "silent majority."

From Orality to Textuality

Our published account of Viramma's life was an unexpected outgrowth of a research project in ethnomusicology focused on oral culture in Tamilnadu.[2] The emphasis was on music and song as expressions of culture and society. In a strongly hierarchical society, it was important not to be perceived as too personally associated with one of the castes or one of the families of the village. I (Josiane) belong to a Christian family which converted centuries ago. Although at present my family owns no property, our caste is one of traditional landowners, so it would have been easy to get an introduction to a village: through relatives who have land or through servants working for them. A third way would have been to rely upon groups involved in social, political, or development activities, but this would have stuck on me a specific ideological label.

I chose a fourth way. In 1972 Jean-Luc, then teaching at the French College, Pondicherry, met a Tamil teacher wishing to learn French. He came from a village some forty kilometers outside Pondicherry, settled amongst paddy and sugarcane fields. He was from a small peasant family, but, with his brother working on the land with his father, he had chosen scholarship. He was very much appreciated in Karani, where he was an excellent schoolteacher. Later, he got a college degree in Tamil. He was at that time teaching in a government high school; he was fond of music and played the flute, and devoted his attention to Tamil grammar and lexicography. Years later he got a doctorate in this field and became known in Pondicherry for his active involvement in the Tamil cultural movement. Thanks to him, Karani became Jean-Luc's first field research site. When I visited Karani a few years later, it appeared to be an ideal place for research: a standard village, with a handful of Brahmins attached to the main temples; well-off families of landowners (Reddiars), a mix of small peasants, most of them Vanniyar, and, off the *ur* (the main settlement of the village), a large *ceri*, where the Paraiyars (Untouchables) lived. In Karani I was an outsider, but also someone socially and geographically localized. Later, people were not surprised to see me alone (they knew that I was married to Jean-Luc), and the personality of our friend provided a perfect introduction. He was respected by all as a dedicated and compassionate man of learning; he had family links with the village but no longer lived there, and thus was not associated with any internal strife.

My topic of research helped also to cross caste barriers: orality and music define a cultural universe present in all castes. I had planned at the start to cover the entire musical life of the village. I began my enquiries and collected my first recordings amongst the few Brahmin families (religious repertoire, life-cycle songs). Amongst non-Brahmins families the repertoire also encompassed hymns dedicated to village deities and lineage gods, and historical ballads: too broad a scope, obviously. I decided to restrict my collection to the secular repertoire. Very soon, the village families who sang secular songs, as they say "for passing time," suggested that I call singers from the *ceri*, the Dalit quarter. Five or six names were suggested, but the women expected to sing were reluctant to come for a "large audience."They were told that no one would make fun of them, and that they would get some money for singing. A first attempt, in the street, failed: the *ceri* singers were not at ease there, on a public space in the *ur*. It was better when only women were invited to go to the garden. In the enclosure, one singer was asked to sing an *oppari*, a funeral lament. Her song was so moving, some people started to weep. She suggested that I go to the *ceri* temple, where the *ceri* singers would be more at ease. The *ur* families, however, were reluctant: the *ceri* was said to be dirty, unclean, unsafe. I would meet drunkards there. But two days later I went there with Jean-Luc and our teacher friend (on his first visit to the *ceri*), and we were offered a selection of the musical genres in the *ceri*. When we left, a group of women came and said, "Why don't you come again? We have so many songs to sing." And pointing to the *oppari* singer, they said, "She knows hundreds of them, more than anyone else."

The *oppari* singer was Viramma. She quickly appeared to be the best singer, with the largest repertoire—not just *oppari*, but also ballads, lullabies, and field songs. She had a moving attachment to oral culture: she loved oral stories, the traditional street theatre (*teru kuttu*), the performance of the *naiyandi* instrumental ensemble, which indulges in romances, humorous songs and dance, while the ritual orchestra, the *paraimelam*, serves the village community when needed, both in auspicious circumstances, when the *ur* deities were out in processions, and in inauspicious ones, during funerals. Viramma and her husband Manikkam were Vettiyar, a sub-caste of Paraiyars from which players of the *parai*, the funeral drum, are chosen by rotation each year.

My attention was focused not just on the repertoire, but also on the social experience conveyed by oral culture. I needed to know about the musicians and the singers. Short biographies were therefore collected. Hearing Viramma opened the way to an unexpected development: what was supposed to be a short background note of a few pages transformed itself in a long and rich experience whose result, *Une vie paria*, was published some fifteen years later. All through the 1980s, wherever we were living (Pondicherry, France or Calcutta), I went to Karani to carry on the collection of Viramma's life history.

Collecting the Life History

Initially, Viramma could not understand that her life could interest me, used as she was to disrespect and contempt, even inside her own community, simply because she was a woman. To collect songs, yes. But her history? She first tried to make dignified statements, in a mix of colloquial and standard spoken Tamil. I made it a rule to always listen to them with interest, without interrupting her, never asking her to cut a long story short. Her dignified style was, of course, a protection she was building for herself in this phase of mutual discovery. Little by little her style became more relaxed, but her discourse remained rather glorified. A second phase started after she became confident enough to question me about my life. I obliged. A personal relationship was building up between Viramma and myself. Whatever the differences of age, background and socio-economic status, we had something to share. Tamil is my mother tongue, and there was no need of a translator, even if Viramma's colloquial Tamil was not exactly the one I speak. I am non-vegetarian and do not respect food restrictions, which also pleased Viramma and made her at ease. We were women, and a little later I had my first child. Motherhood was very important for Viramma, and my new status, as the married young mother of a boy, brought me closer to local gender models.

Viramma understood quickly enough that I had a genuine interest in her life history, but did not clearly understand why. She always thought that her life offered no event worthy of a book. On the other hand, she hoped her songs would be broadcast by the local radio and in "foreign lands." That no such thing happened was for her a real disappointment, and a source of complaint against me. At least Viramma appreciated being listened to carefully, without being praised or condemned, not merely because I had developed an active sympathy for her but because I was genuinely interested in her life history. She knew also that, on any subject of her choice, I would give her my opinion when asked.

At the beginning I tried to follow a chronological line and to address what seemed to be key issues to me (domination, development, conflicts). Our conversations were not uncontrolled chats or quick question-and answer dialogs. Soon I learned to let her talk with her own rhythm, on whatever was really significant for her. Time was not a constraint. When I was out of the field for weeks, it helped me to assimilate her sayings and enter more deeply into her world. It helped also to come back to her with requests for precision or for clarifications when differences occurred between two conversations on the same topic. For Viramma could come back as much as she wished to issues or events she had already talked about. Time helped her as well to re-collect her own past. The rhythm we adopted allowed us to avoid ready-made discourses or complacent statements that were supposed to please me. Everything was taped. Listening to the tapes was a great enjoyment for Viramma and others. Her relatives and the *ceri* dwellers never refrained from commenting on her narrative, sometimes deri-sively, sometimes adding details and sometimes approving fully her statements. Hearing the tapes, collectively or not, helped very often to recollect more precise memories from the past. The tapes were not immediately utilized. We talked either in the *ceri*, on the small *tinnai* (veranda) bordering her house, with a lot of people rambling, listen-ing, and eventually commenting, or when walking across the field, when Viramma had something or someone to show me. We talked also at my parents' house, in Pondicherry, where Viramma sometimes came for the day.

As our relationship developed it became obvious that the time of recording was not to be limited. We had, consequently, to reach agree-ment about a fair payment. My main concern was to disturb as little as possible, Viramma's life pattern. She remained an *adimai* ("bonded laborer") of the village headman, an agricultural laborer attached to the family of the Reddiar. Still, it would have been offensive to meet her with empty hands, without any gift for her or her family. When visiting us, she would always bring a chicken, or some seasonal products such as peanuts, cookies, jackfruits, and red rice cakes. I was eager to settle the financial problem at the earliest because I could guess the expect-ations in Viramma's family on this front. Being married to a foreigner, I was considered a well-off woman from whom money could be easily obtained.

The economic relationship between us was easily settled. Our conversation did not normally disturb her work, either as an agricul-tural laborer or at the cowshed of her master (as an *adimai*, she had work almost round the year, besides her personal tasks of collecting firewood, cutting grass for her own cow, etc.). In practice, the days spent together were remunerated as if Viramma were working for me: I paid her a daily wage; if she came home with me, I added money for the bus ticket, food, and coffee. Of course, I gave the ritual gifts in cash or in kind offered at festivals. The money she collected from me was in a way additional income, but an irregular one, for I was not always there. However, if money was welcome, it was certainly not Viramma's ultimate motive for speaking at length. The reward was not viewed as the payment of a service. It was seen as a dharmic practice: high-caste people, endowed with money, are expected to be benevolent, and the relationship we developed did not alter this basic duty.

Our relationship was an addition to her normal life, not a substitute for her standard relationships, even if some relatives openly commenting adversely upon her visits to Pondicherry. The collection took years because of my life, not because of Viramma, who was not in any event banking on it for increasing her income significantly: she never realized, during these years, that she would later receive a share of the copyright, directly from the publisher: books were outside her scope. She simply asked why the book I was talking about was not yet finished (a good question!) and why no TV or cinema team came to record her songs: she knew that some semi-professional Paraiyar orchestras had been recorded by the local All India Radio station and that some of them also had contacts with the cinema industry in Chennai.

The result of the collection would have been different if Viramma had not enjoyed telling her life. Her pleasure was manifold. That we succeeded in building a relationship of reciprocal trust was decisive but not the only reason. Besides the affective dimension of our relationship, beyond her fondness for narration, Viramma found in our long conversations what everyone may easily imagine: introspection, the interest that many enjoy in having the opportunity to reappropriate one's past and remember the dead. It was not just an exercise of nostalgia, but also a rare opportunity—not offered to all of us—to reassess one's own life.

From Tapes to Book

Very different books could have been written with such rich taped material. The rigorous way we chose our own owes a lot to the advice given by Jean Malaurie, the founder-editor of "Terre Humaine," the series in which *Une vie paria* has been published. Before our book,

Terre Humaine had published a number of life histories collected by
a third party, some written directly in French, a few translated from
English, particularly life histories of American Indians.[3] Drawing
from his long experience, Malaurie discussed with us the process of
conversion from tapes to books. We decided to be as faithful as we
could to Viramma's perceptions and ideas, and to her language. In
form and in substance, her own words were the guidelines. We were
witnesses and collectors, and as such we had to stick to what Viramma
said and to dissociate our comments from her narrative.

A life-history collector has to edit the oral material accumulated:
firstly, to order the story; second, to delete insignificant repetitions. As
far as ordering the life history was concerned, we chose a compromise
between chronology (particularly valid during the formative years,
from childhood to the maturation of the mother of "a bunch of children") and the topicality of later chapters. In most cases, Viramma's
stories were topical enough for a whole chapter (reflections on children, sacrifices to the lineage god, the work of an agricultural laborer,
etc.).

As noted earlier, people in the *ceri* constantly commented on
Viramma's narrative. We have kept the most significant side comments: those of Viramma's son Anban, who had his own strong views
on the fate of Paraiyars; and those of Manikkam, Viramma's husband,
who gave very precious information on his relationships with the landlord, especially on a topic he knew much better than his wife: politics.
But once we had opened a door in that direction, we exerted no pressure to elicit comments on what kind of action might be required in
the face of atrocities against Dalits. For a full decade, Viramma expressed her feelings about subordination and oppression, but she never
elaborated an analysis about atrocities which were commented upon
in the media. Her silence was itself more representative of her perceptions than what an artificial questions-and-answers session on this
crucial issue would have produced.

The transition from orality to textuality left open the question of
another conversion: that of Viramma's Tamil into French. The problem was threefold: how to render Tamil expressions when their French
equivalent was differently connoted; how to render Viramma's level of
language; and how to transmit cultural parameters unknown to
Europe. We selected the way which seemed to us the most respectful
to her own words, and the most respectful to Tamilness. We preferred

to translate, as closely as possible, Tamil expressions rather than use a standard French but "un-Indian" equivalent. When needed, we chose to retain a Tamil word (and hence to enlarge the glossary) rather than substitute for it a French word which would miss its specificity. We decided also not to have recourse to the type of popular French, used for instance by Celine, rich in contractions and slang: it would have been artificial, and we chose rather to translate Viramma's Tamil as simply as we could, but without diluting its sexually-oriented swear words and insults, which may also, as Viramma herself underlined, express fondness in a specific context. One can hardly guess the demanding task that such a translation is if one has never done it.[4]

A final methodological point might be addressed here. We have mentioned earlier how, in his study of a number of life histories of American Indians collected by anthropologists, David Brumble exposed the subterfuge of what he called the "absentee writer." In many life histories collected by academics, there is no clear information about how the story has been collected, and how orality has been converted into text. The writer does not appear clearly dissociated from the narrator, and the reader may sometimes wonder whose words, or even whose ideas, he/she is faced with. The absentee writer hides himself behind his text, except perhaps on the title page, where quite often his/her name is the only one to appear.

We rejected this ambiguous procedure and chose to present our book in two parts. Viramma's narrative is the core of it and stands by itself. These are her words, her ideas: ordered, edited, translated as best we could, but her own. No hidden intermediary: I am constantly referred to by Viramma herself, who addresses me as "Sinnamma" ("younger sister/aunt," which expresses well our respective positions, as seen by her, for it connotes both respect and junior status for me (even when Viramma, after some years, occasionally addressed me with the intimat e *ni* instead of *ninge,* normally used by village Dalits speaking to people of higher castes, she carried on using "Sinnamma"). Jean-Luc is mentioned a few times as well, as are my children and my father. The second part of the book offers our comments and a critical apparatus. In the French edition, this second part is almost as long a the narrative itself, for Plon accepts for Terre Humaine what very few general publishers are ready to accept: a load of information, analyses and methodological notes that would not be out of place in a doctoral dissertation.

The Contents of Viramma's Life

What should one remember from the narrative of an old woman recollecting not jut her personal past, but also what were the lives, the beliefs, the values of a generation of Dalits that is now disappearing? First of all, her personality—a mix of strength and weakness, a deep humanity moved by an indomitable taste for life. Her acceptance of what she saw as her caste dharma is certainly striking, but she was not blind or naïve. At the crossroads of personal recollection and collective memory, we may identify a few important points. First, a sense of belonging is what best characterized Viramma and her world. The word "Paraiyar," or "Pariah," depending on how it is used, can be either a deliberate insult, a condescending mark of scorn or an inescapable fate. But unlike her husband and her son, who were more politically conscious, Viramma has always used it just as a mark of her own identity, her caste name. This is why, respecting her vocabulary, we have kept it, even if it is no longer used publicly. We have kept it, above all, because Viramma has always seen herself as such, accepted herself as such, and stayed faithful to the words used in her everyday life: *paratchi*, a Paraiyar woman; *paraceri*, the settlement of the Paraiyars, and the *paraimelam*, the Paraiyar orchestra, whose flat drum, the *parai*, is said to have given the caste its name, even if it is more precisely the attribute of the Paraiyar subcaste, the Vettiyar, to which Viramma belongs. Bearing witness to her words and her vision of the world, we have not wanted to put the term "Dalit" artificially in her mouth. She was unaware of the word throughout the ten years of our conversation, and she still didn't know its meaning in the late 1990s. Neither have we toned down her forthright language, considered by more puritan or more hypocritical local opinion to set her caste apart.

For her, as for so many, meaning and identity were found in a place, a community, a framework of life and thought, and an established order of things, even if that framework and that order can only be defined as oppression, obstructing emancipation. Viramma bears testimony to an ideological system representative of the old order of the world, as her son Anban would say. In narrating her life, and expressing her views, Viramma did not formulate a critique of that system: she simply relates, in her own words, how it functions in the village space, in the heads of "those from the high castes"—and in the heads of the so-called "Other Backward Classes" in today's parlance. From the portrait she draws of all of them, in Karani or in the surrounding villages, we are able to understand how the system held for so long and why it is cracking apart today.

Domination, Consensus and New Expectations

Violence has been very much a part of Viramma's experience: the physical violence of a master, the brute force of thugs beating up Dalits on behalf of powerful men with political ambitions, or the violence encountered in police stations. But on the whole, what Viramma's life depicts is less the excruciating violence of killings, which draws the attention of the media and which sustains political debates and strategies, than the silent violence of a system of oppression which has worked so intensely and for so long that Viramma herself testifies how it can be internalized by those who have been submitted to its rule. This is the violence of hunger, which Viramma has known in difficult times, and which pushes her to conclude "today, I live well . . . I live without starving," as if this basic entitlement were by itself a victory over the shadows of the past. This is the violence of sickness, which killed nine of her twelve children in their prime. This is the violence of words or of gestures, expressed in all possible shades of contempt, when upper-caste landlords, government officers or simple peasants talk to Dalits, or talk about them; the violence of bondage, debt, economic dependence; the violence of a fate of uncertainty; the violence of sex, sometimes proposed and sometimes imposed upon poor women, who are expected to lie down for a little money or for medical care at the local hospital. Finally, it is the subdued, general, and permanent violence that sustains the daily practice of Untouchability; the violence of tradition which gives no consideration to "Pariahs."

Observers of Indian village society (a significant number of them having worked in Tamilnadu) have proposed different ways of interpreting the ideological reaction of Dalits to Untouchability. Some, such as Michael Moffat (1979), have stressed the significance of a structural consensus. For Moffat, Dalits accept (or did accept) the "rationale of a system based on purity" which places them at the bottom of the social ladder. This could be largely valid in Viramma's case. Other scholars, such as Joan P. Mencher (1973), have argued that Dalits have neither adhered to nor been taken in by the caste system or by the concepts of karma and dharma. This could be true for only a small minority, and certainly not for Viramma. However, many Dalits have for long questioned the rationale of the social order.

Viramma's husband, Manikkam, a sympathizer of the local Communist Party of India, and her son Anban, more influenced by the Dravida Munnetra Kazhagam (DMK) rhetoric, bear this out. Both have rebelled in their own ways. Manikkam once opposed a master who beat him in violation of the established code of conduct. His resistance was a protest against the disrespect shown by his landlord's son to the notion of the master's dharma as defined by the traditional order. But Manikkam went further, analyzing the social relationships beyond a specific case of brutality. Commenting upon the reluctance of his master to lease him a small plot of land, he saw the age-old rationale of this refusal: to keep the Paraiyars down in full submission in order to compel obedience and obeisance from them and to ensure the safety and security of the dominant classes.

Viramma's son Anban understands perfectly well how the system works; how economic pressures interact with behavioral rules that have for centuries commanded respect for the powerful and humility in attitude, speech and dress from the dominated. In line with his father, Anban has understood that the powerful do everything to deny his community access to even a scrap of land, and hence access to a little autonomy and a greater sense of dignity. Close to Mencher's type, at least in some of his statements, he rejects the old rationale of internalized submission. He sees himself as a worker getting money for his labor, and no more as the Untouchable son of an *adimai*, attached for generations to the same landlord family which provides food and clothing at festivals, loans, protection and punishment if needed. All is said in a few words which negate the strong but unequal traditional relationship between high-caste landlords and Dalit laborers: "They don't feed me, they don't dress me. I don't owe them a thing. I work and they pay for my work. That's all!" Anban goes further than his father Manikkam, and rejects the supposed divine justification of domination: "Who is this miserable God who made us Pariahs? Why do they become superior and we inferior at birth? Who is this bastard of a God who's done that? If we ever meet him, we'll smash his face in!" (Viramma, Racine and Racine 1997/2000: 191).

All this is too much for his mother, who finds her dignity elsewhere. Viramma was happy to note the improvements brought about to the *ceri* little by little: new house sites, street electricity, a water cistern. She notes that boys and girls are much better dressed than before, copper vessels are much more visible, and some families in the *ceri* now have one member enjoying a "sitting job" in town offices, thanks to the places reserved for Dalits in public employment and education. Happy with improvements, Viramma is afraid of emancipation. The ideological shift which has brought limited material progress to the *ceri* worries her. Viramma is afraid of the spread of new ideas and the politicization of the youth, and nervous about losing the protection of her master, who is more significant to her than the electoral promises of politicians. She fears reprisals and repression from the powerful castes, who are displeased at seeing her community make progress. So she advises her son to remain humble, and she opposes youngsters who—as Anban did once—no longer want to perform their ritual caste duty in the *paraimelam*; she disapproves of the hotheads who argue for only one set of glasses for all castes at the tea stall. Viramma still believes in her caste dharma, which could be easily defined in a few words: acceptance of her social position and respect for the master who feeds his workers. "People want the world to be one, and everybody to be the same, all with the same rights. That is the *kaliyugam*![5] It's good that people want us to be raised up, but it's better if we stay in our place" (Viramma, Racine and Racine 1997/2000: 191). To cool down Anban, she found in herself words which occasionally sound strikingly Gandhian. She still believes that respect would bring more than what revolt will, and she satisfies herself with whatever fringe benefits the landlord allows her by letting her use a corner of his fields.

On the other hand, Viramma's life history would largely endorse the analysis of Kathleen Gough (1981), who argued that the sociocultural world of Dalits offers a worldview distinct from the mainstream ideologies and practices based upon the brahminical model: Dalits, in her view, are less inhibited, have a less authoritarian family structure and a broader sense of solidarity. Not that there are no subtle relationships between the Dalit popular culture and the mainstream model—far from it—but Viramma does embody the liveliness and sociability that Gough emphasized.

The Force of Life: A Woman's Image

Behind Viramma's submissiveness to the dominant social system lies a facet of her personality, a wonderful strength, which to put it simply is the very force of life itself. Her vibrant interest in other human beings, be they itinerant singers, eunuchs, or snake-catcher tribes; her taste for songs, stories and street theater; the abundance of details she was able to provide on rituals and ceremonies, or on the exact types of food being prepared for special occasions, show a lively curiosity about all facets of life. Contrary to popular expectation, the weight of poverty, illiteracy and oppression have not plunged Viramma and her like into a state of hopelessness. The Dalits are not their own masters, they are under the pressure of social domination and systems of beliefs, but they are not dispossessed of their most intimate self. Beyond the social definition of their position, they have something else, which is simply the unflinching, the unfaltering, the unflagging core of humanity. Whatever have been the tragedies and the trials of existence, never has the sap of life dried up under the bark. And here, in the depth of their minds, lies a source of energy waiting to be tapped for their emancipation.

Domination is not the only fact of Viramma's life. Her relationship with the landlord and his family was decisive for her on many accounts: economic, social and emotional. She works not only in the fields of her master, but also cleans his cattleshed in the house compound. Even if she was not allowed to enter his house, she had fed the landlord's son at her breast. Besides, whatever be the need, a funeral, a wedding, an ear-piercing ceremony, a sacrifice to the family god, Viramma and Manikkam turn to the master for a loan, a loan which will never match their full expectation, and which will have to be reimbursed in cash, in grain or in working hours, but which appears to them to be the safest solution, if sometimes a humiliating one. If domination casts its shadow over almost all aspects of Viramma's life, she has a margin of autonomy *vis-à-vis* the higher castes, which she is free to enjoy when it comes to her caste customs, her culture, and her relationships with her kin, which are so important to her.

What Viramma offers us, in this regard, is a vivid portrait of a woman caught between the traditional compulsions of her status and her quest for managing and expanding her margin of autonomy. Each episode of her life, and each aspect of her identity, has been confined within the space delineated by heavy compulsions but also by her frail autonomy. Successively or simultaneously, she has experienced both as a little girl, an innocent child-bride, a teenage wife, a daughter-in-law, a sister-in-law, a mother, and a grandmother. Dalit women are said to be doubly discriminated against: as Dalits, and as women. Viramma, here again, provides a first-person account of what femininity could be. The portrait she offers combines a very traditional perception of a woman—submissive and obedient, but only up to a point, allied with an admirable strength for facing the challenges of daily life and assessing her own rights in the family circle. This balance of strength and weakness is itself a stereotype, but Viramma breathes life into her account of femininity by the mere sincerity of her speech, and by her capacity to analyze in great detail facts, relationships and feelings. She illuminates her truth, the story of her life, which is the memory of her past, her discovery of sex (terrible at the beginning, enjoyed later), her way to bear children, her care for all of them, cherished even when dead, then partly forgotten, her pride and anguish for the surviving ones, her relationship to her lineage god, to the smallpox goddess, to the spirits and to the exorcists.

In many aspects, Viramma simply believes in what was, or what still is, the standard way to look at serious issues. For instance, she thinks that women who are unable to bear children, lose both the "honor and reason for living." Sterility is perceived as a curse, which, however, does not take away a feeling of compassion for those who are afflicted by it. The suffering of the childless is expressed in Viramma's favorite ballad, the "Song of the woman who didn't have a child," often sung when women are bent down, transplanting paddy in the muddy rice fields, along with another favorite and still more tragic ballad, the "Song of Nallatangal," in which the heroine prefers to kill her seven children and herself rather than accept the dishonor of being rejected by her in-laws in time of famine.

Culture, Orality and Memory

The sense of tension and drama, the knowledge that life may always bring pain and suffering, and that the shadow of death is omnipresent, do not, however, crush an inexhaustible vitality like Viramma's. Her taste for laughter, witty comments, jokes, riddles (particularly ribald ones), her love for music and songs, for beauty, and for the security of friendship, remains strong. Music, songs, and street theater have been a part of Viramma's life. Her husband Manikkam played in an amateur local company in his youth, and musicians and dancers "as light as tamarind seeds" were always there to perform during religious festival nights, or for family life-cycle ceremonies, including funerals. "Alas," says Viramma, "these are joys and pleasures of another age, youngsters prefer now to rent a video rather than call for local talents." The slow disintegration of her cultural heritage is not just a source of sorrow for Viramma: whatever some may think about it, neither the commercialization of popular culture through the cinema industry—keen to show "folk orchestras" inspired by the Paraiyar musical genres, particularly the pungent *naiyandi* repertoire—nor the small leaflets and cheap storybooks sold on bazaar pavements and during village fairs, are preserving this legacy. The genuine oral tradition, so vital for illiterates, is not simply transforming itself. It is vanishing, leaving behind only poor and adulterated substitutes, harmonized or re-transcribed for matching what traders of popular culture believe to be the taste of the lower middle classes.

The future of the oral culture with which Viramma is so much endowed defines an additional challenge for the propagators of Dalit emancipation. We shall not enter here into the current debate, but we must perhaps mention what is at stake. The quest for an "alternative culture," or the choice of entering the mainstream culture, involves very different strategies, some preserving more of the community culture than others. Not that the Paraiyar repertoire which Viramma knew so well is uniform or consistent. The legacy of what is called the Great Tradition can be easily identified, as most of the commonly held beliefs and a number of characters are borrowed from mainstream upper-caste traditions. The "Song of the woman who didn't have a child," for instance, is replete with references to characters from the *Mahabharata* and to pan-Indian pilgrimage places. Most of the cultural references of the Dalits in Karani are shared by other peasant castes, some of them also oppressed; but that does not prevent strong differences. Traditionally, these peasant castes were divided between their affiliation to the mainstream ideology (many successful families embarked on the process of "sanskritization" in order to improve their status) and their popular culture. Today, in a context of expanding politicization and increasingly strident caste assertion, both Dalits and peasant castes play their own separate game, promoting their own historical heroes and establishing their own political parties.

Confronted with the mainstream, some Dalit intellectuals face a challenging situation. They reject the mainstream cultural order, but they emulate, in one respect—if in an inverted manner—the high-caste cultural domination that has negated the culture of the "Untouchables." These intellectuals deconstruct their own legacy along with the dominant paradigm, arguing that the oral heritage of the Dalits is simply a mark of internalized subordination. We believe that there is room for this position in the alternative culture that the propagators of Dalit liberation wish to construct. For beyond the "annihilation of caste," to quote the Dalit leader B.R. Ambedkar, still stands the cultural heritage and the denigrated memory, which are key components of dalitness. Whatever her "alienation," in Marxist terms, Viramma appears as a wonderful bearer of this memory. She is also more than the heiress of a faded past. Her lifetime has seen transformation, in the *ceri* and in society at large. Viramma, in her own ambiguous views on such a decisive matter, offers a testimony to the dynamics of change. She is witness to a historical moment.

Dalit Literature and Life History

We would like to assert here the decisive importance of Dalit literature and writings, and also what life histories such as Viramma's, might add to them. The Dalit literary corpus, which began about the 1980s, is more developed in some languages (such as Marathi, Kannada) than in others. From a literary perspective, some commentators have judged it unconvincing, not creative enough: Tamil Dalit writers, according to Kannan and Gros (1996), are still searching for "their" literature. But since the humanity involved in Untouchability is so important, and has been documented for only a few decades by Dalit writers, historians and social scientists might pay more attention to substance than to form, or might relate form to substance without undervaluing the social reality of Dalit community (Pandian 1998a; 1998b).

What might Viramma's life history offer in this context? Perhaps an example of what Jean Malaurie has called *une littérature du réel*, duly recognized by Terre Humaine, which has always given "to oral literature a status equal to written literature" (1993: 13–14). That an academic trained in classical Tamil and textual criticism (Gros 1996: 387) could suspect a deliberate embellishment of Viramma's language is by itself revealing of the difficulty in acknowledging that illiterate agricultural laborers might have an expressive and moving language, deploying strength, beauty and even poetic formulations. But Viramma's testimony offers more, and Kannan and Gros themselves (1996: 149) found in her narrative: "a true sensitivity to beings and things."

Must we be surprised if Viramma's sensibility is not well expressed in the Tamil Dalit literature? In an all-India Dalit community of some 140 million people, whose illiterate members are an overwhelming majority, Dalit writers and essayists, even if they have spent their childhood in villages, have a personal experience somewhat different from those who have spent all their life in the confines of *ceris*. That does not devalue the writers' discourses, of course, and students of history know that emancipation movements have generally germinated in such small "angry" groups more able to denounce the scandal of oppression and articulate the call for change: these writers, along with the activists, have broken the walls of silence behind which their community has been enclosed. The fact remains, however, that besides the voice of rage and the denunciation of the mainstream order, there are also Dalits who remain prisoners of old values, such as Viramma, and people in between, who reject the ideological justification of an unjust order without turning activist, such as Viramma's son Anban.

In a Western context, Geneviève Bollème assumed that writing, for members of "the popular classes" is "a one-way travel." Whatever might have been their intention when they started to write, once they have authored their book and it has been published, they enter a different world. Some Dalit authors who have nourished their writings with their own histories seem to confirm this point. One of the most noted Tamil Dalit authors, Bama, wrote her testimonial narrative, *Karukku*, "suffused with a sense of guilt, a yearning to reunite with the community" since her "very life trajectory is one drifting away from the world of Dalits" (Pandian 1998b: 55). Marathi Dalit literature offers similar examples. Madhau Kondvilker (1985: 11), compelled to return to his village after becoming a teacher, illustrated forcefully in his journal the distressing gap then established between himself and his relatives, his village and his past. Daya Pawar, one of the most noted Marathi Dalit writers, in one of the prefaces of his autobiography, *Balute*, acknowledges it as well: "I am no more the same, even if I am still myself . . . I live no more in the same time nor in the same cultural world" (Pawar 1990: 9). Laxman Mané (1987: 19), whose autobiographical novel *Oupra* received a Sahitya Akademi award, confessed that the success of his book "has transfigured his life." That does not prevent Bama or Mané from struggling for the emancipation of Dalits, and to denounce the domination oppressing them. Their difference with Viramma is, however, obvious, for Viramma does not face the same problem of identity. She was not a Dalit torn between two worlds. She did not have to reject her community or to long for being closer to it: she has always been an intimate part of it.[6]

In other words, Viramma's life history offers an authentic account of a part of dalitness, not the more publicly articulated part, but rather a part representative of a very large section of Dalits. Our book, in English, Tamil and French, received mixed reviews, some very positive, some quite hostile, and we won't summarize them here except to say that they illustrate what is at stake: the understanding of the Other. In his perceptive essay *The Flaming Feet*, D.R. Nagaraj has greatly helped to clarify the issue, when he distinguished, amongst Kannada Dalit literature, the "school of social rage" and the "school of spiritual quest." The first category is clear, and Viramma's narrative does not belong to it. The second category is more ambiguous. For all her constant references to gods, spirits and demons, Viramma was hardly engaged in what we might call a spiritual quest. Read Nagaraj, however (1993: 63): "The second school has been called the School of Spiritual Quest because it tries to understand the world of Untouchability in terms of metaphysical dismay over the nature of human relationship. The ethos of portrayal of life is not informed by anger and agony, but by a celebration of the joys of life and its possibilities, which also includes the will to change." This predicament is much closer to Viramma's vision, even if old Viramma was still afraid of radical change. Conservatives might prefer the second school to the first one. They must, however, be without illusions. Nothing can mask the fact that atrocities against Dalits continue, and that "the Other," the despised ones, are moving on the road to emancipation.

Conclusion

In conclusion, we return to a crucial point of "content" and access to that "content." Let us pose a few questions. Regarding content, is there an acceptable space for grassroots discourses? Some of them might be militant, some of them not. Are the first the only valid ones? Is the non-activist narrative devoid of significance? Is it just an alienated discourse? Or does it unravel unknown dimensions of the mental and material universe of Dalits, not just in moments of tensions, crises or struggles, but also through the slow flow of the daily life, from childhood to old age, taking also a view on gender identity? Do narratives like Viramma's help us to understand better the decisive process of internalization of oppression, the major obstruction on the road to emancipation? Do these life histories enable us to perceive more clearly the dynamics of change, even outside the most visible cases of open struggle for justice? To put it differently, does the much-expected emancipation require neglecting of the memory of the community?

Regarding access to this content, is there a substitute to the type of life history we have collected and published? What is the alternative to listening to the illiterate, if authors and public orators are seen as expressing only a part of the community? We think that what we have done is clear. Viramma was not for us just "material" for a social science study. She was not an informant we have relied upon for writing on Dalits. Unique in a way, but deeply involved in her community and in village society, she was a person we have known for years; we have seen her children grow up, her grandchildren born, and she herself grown older. And she saw, too, our children grow, our relatives die. We have questioned her, for it had to start with questions, but we have above all listened to her, taking care as much as we could to render faithfully her words and her world. We have been a mediation, and mediation is a part of the general process of knowledge and dissemination. At a time of pervasive Dalit struggles, we believe that what Viramma's life history offers is also a necessary testimony, which shows how one adjusts with oppression before the time of revolt, and how this oppression, which has resulted in so many "Broken Lives," to quote the Human Rights Watch Report on Untouchability (1999), has not destroyed the innate strength to which Viramma testifies: a strength that younger generations use now for emancipation.

The debates on subjectivity and authenticity seem to be endless. The question they address in the field of social sciences can be easily formulated: do personal accounts bring something unique and valuable? In his foreword to *Soleil Hopi*, the French translation of Don C. Talayesva's *Sun Chief*, the first life history published in Terre Humaine, Lévi-Strauss answered this question through a metaphor:

Talayesva's narrative reaches immediately, with an unequalled ease and grace, what the anthropologist dreams of all along his life without being able to get it fully: the restitution of a culture "from inside," such as lived by the child and then by the adult. It is as if, archaeologists of the present time, we were unearthing the disjoined pearls of a necklace, and that suddenly we would be able to see them, joined in their original ordering, and set around the young neck they were to adorn (Lévi-Strauss 1959: x).

Procedures of testimony need to be assessed. The significance of a life history must be evaluated. But not at the cost of blindness, not at the cost of deafness. In intellectual quests, as well as in the politics of identity, the urge for absolute purity—and its counterpart, absolute doubt—is dangerous. The work conducted for years by Annette Wieviorka on the representations of the Shoah raises the right recurrent question against the "revisionists": what is a testimony? The goal remains valid as much for the present than for the past, for social sciences as for history: we have "to interrogate endlessly the voices coming to us from the past, and the ways by which they reach us" (Wieviorka *et al.*, 1999). What is true for testimonies on the tragedies of History is valid as well for more "ordinary" life histories.

Dalits are not silent. They are not voiceless. Many have believed they are so only because they themselves were not ready to listen. Dalit writers and essayists are at last read. The inner world of Dalit illiterates can only be heard or read through mediation. As is true for subalterns around the world, they have to be heard. And so much the better if, in oral life histories, the listener and the reader, be they historians or not, happen to find from time to time Lévi-Strauss's necklace . . .

REFERENCES

Bama. 1992. *Karukku*. Samudaya Sintaivu Seyal Aaivu Mayyam: Madurai.

Bollème, Geneviève. 1986. *Le Peuple par Écrit*, Paris: Seuil.

Brumble, David. 1993. *Les Autobiographies d'Indiens d'Amérique*, Paris: PUF (French translation of *American Indian Autobiography*, University of California Press).

Buckley, Jerome Hamilton. 1984. *The Turning Key. Autobiography and the Subjective Impulse since 1800*. Cambridge, Mass.: Harvard University Press.

Cordier, Daniel. 1999. *Jean Moulin: La République des Catacombes*. Paris: Gallimard.

Das, D.P. 1985. *The Untouchable Story*. New Delhi: Allied Publishers.

Dulong, Renaud. 1998. *Le Témoin Oculaire: Les Conditions Sociales de l'attestation Personnelle*. Paris: Editions de l'EHESS.

Foucault, Michel (ed.). 1973. *Moi Pierre Rivière, ayant égorgé ma mère, ma soeur et mon frère . . . Un cas de parricide au XIXè siècle*. Paris: Gallimard/Julliard.

Freeman, James M. 1979. *Untouchable: An Indian Life History*. London: Allen & Unwin.

Gandhi, M.K. 1927. *The Story of My Experiments with Truth*. Ahmedabad: Navjivan Prakashan Mandir.

Gauthaman, Raj. 1994. *Talit Parvaiyil Tamil Panpatu* ("Dalit Perspectives on Tamil Culture"). Pondicherry: Gauri Patippakam.

Gough, Kathleen. 1981. *Rural Society in Southeast India*. Cambridge: Cambridge University Press.

Gros, François. 1996. "Review of Viramma." *Bulletin de l'Ecole Française d'Extrême-Orient* 83: 385–9.

Hazari. 1966. *Untouchable: The Autobiography of an Indian Outcaste*. London: Pall Mall Press.

Kakar, Sudhir. 1989. *Intimate Relations: Exploring Indian Sexuality*. New Delhi: Viking.

Kannan, M., and F. Gros. 1996. "Les dalits tamouls en quête d'une littérature." *Bulletin de l'Ecole Française d'Extrême-Orient* 83: 124–53.

Kondvilker, Madhau. 1985. *Inde: Journal d'un intouchable (1969–1977)*. Paris: L'Harmattan.

Koselleck, Reinhart. 1990. *Le Futur Passé: Contributions à la Sémantique des Tempe Historiques*. Paris: Editions de l'EHESS.

Le Goff, Jacques and Pierre Nora (eds). 1974. *Presentation, in Faire de l'Histoire, vol. 1: Nouveaux Problèmes*, pp. ix–xiii. Paris: Gallimard.

Lejeune, Philippe. 1975. *Le Pacte Autobiographique*. Paris: Seuil.

Lévi-Strauss, Claude. 1959. Preface to Don C. Talayesva: *Soleil Hopi, l'autobiographie d'un Indien Hopi*, Plon (Terre Humaine), pp. i–x (Don C. Talayesva, Leo-W. Simmons, *Sun Chief: Autobiography of a Hopi Indian*, Yale University Press, 1942).

Malamoud, Charles. 1997. Noirceur de l'écriture. Remarques sur un thème littéraire de l'Inde ancienne, in Viviane Alleton (ed.). *Paroles à dire. Paroles à écrire. Inde, Chine, Japon*, Editions de l'EHESS, Paris, 85–114

Malaurie, Jean. 1993. "Une littérature du réel," foreword to *Le livre*, Terre Humaine, pp. 9–28. Paris: Plon.

Mané, Laxman. 1987. *Oupra: L'Inde des intouchables et des Maudits*. Paris: Maren Sell Editions.

Mencher, Joan P. 1973. "Group and Self-identification: The View from the Bottom." *ICSSR Research Abstracts Quarterly* 3: 2–3.

Moffatt, Michael. 1979. *An Untouchable Community in South India: Structure and Consensus*. Princeton: Princeton University Press.

Moniot, Henri. 1974. "L'histoire des peuples sans histoire." In Le Goff and Nora (eds), *Faire de l'Histoire*, 1: 106–23.

Moon, Vasant. 2001. *Growing Up Untouchable in India: A Dalit Autobiogrqaphy*. Lanham (Maryland): Rowman and Littlefield.

Nagaraj, D.R. 1993. *The Flaming Feet: A Study of the Dalit Movement in India*. Bangalore: South Forum Press.

Nora, Pierre (ed.). 1987. *Essais d'ego-histoire*. Paris: Gallimard.

Omvedt, Gail. 1995. *DalitVisions:TheAnti-CasteMovementandtheConstruction of an Indian Identity*. Hyderabad: Orient Longman.

Pandian, M.S.S. 1998a. "Stepping Outside History? New Dalit Writings from Tamil Nadu." In Partha Chatterjee (ed.). *Wages of Freedom: Fifty Years of the Indian Nation State*. New Delhi: Oxford University Press.

———. 1998b. "On a Dalit Woman's Testimony." *Seminar* (471) 53–6.

Parry, Jonathan. 1985. "The BrahminicalTradition and theTechnology of the Intellect." In Joanna Overing (ed.), *Reason and Morality*, pp. 200–25. London: Routledge.

Pawar, Daya. 1990. *Ma Vie d'intouchable*. Paris: La Découverte: Paris (original title in Marathi: *Balute*).

Racine, Jean-Luc. 1998. Introduction to the special issue on "Untouchability and Beyond: French Studies of Indian Dalits." *Comparative Studies of South Asia, Africa and the Middle East* 18: 1–4.

Racine, Josiane. 1996. "Chanter la mort en pays tamoul. L'héritage reçu et le stigmate refusé." *Purushartha* 18: 199–218.

———, and Jean-Luc Racine. 1996. "Viramma's Voice: The Changing Face of Change?" *Indian International Centre Quarterly* 32: 2–3.

———, 1998. "Dalit Identities and the Dialectics of Oppression and Emancipation." *Comparative Studies of South Asia, Africa and the Middle East* 18: 5–20.

Veyne, Paul. 1971. *Comment on écrit l'histoire*. Paris: Seuil.

Viramma, Josiane Racine, and Jean-Luc Racine.1995. *Une Vie Paria. Le Rire desAsservis. Inde du Sud*. Paris: Plon-UNESCO, collectionTerre Humaine.

———. 1997. *Viramma: Life of an Untouchable*. London: Verso-UNESCO (translated from the French by Will Hobson).

———. 2000. *Viramma: Life of a Dalit*. New Delhi: Social Science Press.

Weintraub, Karl Joachim. 1978. *The Value of the Individual: Self and Circumstance in Autobiography*. Chicago: University of Chicago Press.

Wieviorka, Annette and Claude Mouchard. 1999. *La Shoah: Témoignages, savoirs, oeuvres*. Presses Universitaires de Vincennes.

Zelliot, Eleanor. 1996. *From Untouchable to Dalit: Essays on the Ambedkar Movement*. New Delhi: Manohar (2nd edn).

NOTES

1. On this, see Parry 1985.
2. The first English edition of Viramma's life history (Viramma, Racine and Racine 1997) abbreviated the methodological description about the genesis of the book presented in the original French edition. The Afterword written for the Indian edition in English (Viramma, Racine and Racine

2000) provides less information in this regard than the French one, but much more than the English one.

3. E.g., *Soleil Hopi: l'autobiographie d'un Indien Hopi* (Plon, 1959) by Don C. Talayesva and edited by Leo-W. Simmons (*Sun Chief: Autobiography of a Hopi Indian*, Yale University Press, 1962); *De Mémoire Indienne* (Plon, 1977; *Lame Deer Seeker of Visions*, by Tahca Ushte and Richard Erdoes, Simon & Schuster, 1972); *Ishi* (Plon, 1968; *Ishi in Two Worlds*, by Theodora Kroeber, University of California Press, 1961); *Piegan* (Plon, 1970; *Piegan*, by Richard Lancaster, Doubleday, 1966).

4. For those interested in this difficult exercise of converting speech into script, and colloquial caste-marked Tamil into French, we have given in the original French edition diverse examples of our translation choices, including an example of tape-recording to be compared, both in content and in style, with the final translation (Viramma, Racine and Racine 1995: 455–6).

5. In the Hindu cyclic theory of time, *kaliyugam* is the age of disorder, when dharma is no longer respected. It announces the end of a cycle.

6. Viramma's life has not been "transfigured" for she remained in her village and has not changed class. But the book did bring changes. The royalties she received enabled her son to escape from debt, to fulfill his duties as maternal uncle, and to build a new secure house. Viramma's published narrative is seen as having brought fame to the village, to its inhabitants and their way of life. This only confirms the immediate elated reaction in Karani (in the *ur* as well as in the *ceri*) when the copy of the thick French volume, with its photographs and drawings, first circulated. Today, the dead are still living thanks to Viramma's life history, and in his new home, Anban does seem to represent more than a legacy: an everlasting symbol of his now deceased mother.

CHAPTER 11

The Marital History of
"A Thumb-Impression Man"

JONATHAN P. PARRY

Preamble

We were already well into a half-bottle of cheap whisky when I told Somvaru[1] about this volume, and explained that I thought his life story as worthy of inclusion as those of Gandhiji and Nehruji—of whom certain big, big professors would probably write some more. He plainly thought me extravagant. His own children, after all, showed little interest in it. But when he saw I was serious, and even if he continued to doubt my good sense, he agreed that "it should be told." Such is my own rather shaky authority for what follows. I suspect that Somvaru would be even less sure of his ground. Though self-effacement—far less subservience—is no part of his nature, had it not been for me, I do not believe that it would ever have occurred to him that there might be a "public" with the slightest interest in his story. And even if it had, he would have had no way to tell it. Somvaru is illiterate. "Small" people of his sort are silenced both by ideology, and by what Goody (1977) calls "the technology of the intellect."

As to what motivated its telling, I flatter myself that a genuine pleasure in each other's company has played some part. And then there is the strong bond we have developed with Ajay, my intermittent research assistant and close friend, who has been party to many of our discussions and a conduit of news between us when separated by continents. Whenever I thank Somvaru for the hours spent tutoring me on this or that topic, he thanks me for helping him "to pass the time" (*taim pass karna*). Boredom is a constant refrain, not only of the unemployed

SOMVARU'S FAMILY*

Married to
Divorced

Lainu

Suraj

Pushpa

Sushila

SOMVARU

Kavita

Raj Kumar

Sukhit

Dukhit

Janaki

Barle

Rukhmin

Lakhan

* Only relevant details shown

youth of the neighborhoods I am studying, but also of old-timers like him who have retired from industrial jobs. As to his story itself, it has been recorded bit by bit, and out of sequence, over countless conversations which are often largely devoted to other themes—elements of his own biography being introduced to illustrate some general point. Picked up where last we left off, these conversations have continued over the past eight years.

Somvaru's story is only one of several that I have tried to record in detail. Such biographies seem to offer a strategic way of getting a handle on the variable experience of a socially heterogeneous population of workers, most of whom have—in the space of a single generation—lived through an industrial revolution, and many of whom are immigrants from different parts of the country. In this kind of context, generalizations premised on a "likeness of consciences" are more than usually problematic. Life histories are one way of exploring the range.

It is true that a renewed anthropological interest in the genre seems to run with the grain of a shift in disciplinary preoccupations—from "structure" to "agency," from "culture" to "voice," and from the "traditional" world to the putatively "post-modern."[2] My own rationale for collecting such accounts, however, is rather that this is a strategy that is almost forced on me by my informants themselves. Reflecting on my previous fieldwork in a Kangra village (Parry 1979), and amongst "sacred specialists" in the city of Banaras (Parry 1994), I am struck by the contrast. There my informants were generally only too ready to tell me of rules and "customs." But—until I knew them quite well—most tended to be distinctly uncomfortable with direct enquiries about practice, about who had actually done what. That's just as one might expect, and as I did expect when I started the present fieldwork. But it is not what I find. Here people are commonly flummoxed by, uninterested in, or even downright impatient with, questions on rules. But even those I have only just met will volunteer surprisingly detailed information about their own personal biographies, or those of their neighbors. Unlike Kangra Rajputs and Banarasi Brahmins, what they really want to talk about are "events," not "structures." Collecting life histories seems, more importantly, to go with the grain of the (sub-)culture I am studying.

Why should this be? A satisfactory answer would require a paper of its own, but at least a beginning is possible. A "great transformation" has radically transformed the world into which my older informants were born, and this has thrown them together with people from different backgrounds and regions. The old order has been relativized and revealed as ephemeral; and we should not assume that they regret its passing. Many of them came from somewhere near the bottom of the social heap, and their stake in it may not have been strong. They live moreover in the selfconsciously "modernizing" world of one of those giant public sector industrial projects of the Nehruvian era which were specifically designed to blow away the cobwebs of the past—and have, to a greater or lesser extent, internalized its values. But most important is the sheer scale of the changes they have witnessed. In the face of them, the task of subordinating events to timeless structures, and of making individual lives conform to a standardized and de-personalized biographical trajectory, would require some ingenuity—more perhaps than is quite reasonable to expect. Even if Captain Cook might be seamlessly slotted into the ready-made role of the returning Hawaiian fertility deity (Sahlins 1985), history must sometimes get too "hot" to comfortably handle in such a way. The sheer contingency and specificity of momentous novel happenings is liable to insist, making it difficult to interpret them as running in pre-ordained structural grooves. Such events also make it difficult to sustain a belief that what is most fundamental to personhood is an innate and immutable essence on which time and circumstance leave no real mark, that one exists in history "as a rock in the middle of the stream"—even if, according to Bloch (1998a), the Sadah have, despite the vicissitudes of the Yemeni revolution, managed to achieve that remarkable feat. It is not one that my informants seek to emulate. If the "structure" can no longer be taken for granted, the impact that "events" have had on their lives and persons seems beyond all reasonable doubt.

The way in which Somvaru constructs his life story is, I will show, quite different from the "distinctive Indo-Persian cultural and literary tradition" that Barbara Metcalf (1995) has identified. In that tradition, says Metcalf, chronology is irrelevant since the essential personality (the rock in the stream) is present from the start; and what is notable about persons is not their individuality but the way in which their lives can be matched to those of timeless exemplars. Somvaru, by contrast, is a thoroughly "modern" man who sees himself as stamped by history and—in some measure—enlightened by "progress."

His memory is remarkable, perhaps partly because of his illiteracy. Whenever I have been able to crosscheck details he has given me against documentary evidence—for example, his estimates of his earnings at a specific period against his pay-slips, or his land sales against the official records—they have always been accurate. Nor have I ever suspected him of deliberate fibs or fabrication. His body, as he puts it (for he often speaks of emotional states as bodily experiences), cannot endure lies. But reticence—even evasion—is something else, and it is certainly the case that he has occasionally withheld parts of his story that he was not yet ready to divulge. Over the first year of our friendship, I learned—one by one—about four of his marriages. It was not until three years later that I heard of a fifth wife who had never been mentioned before; and it was only in the course of drafting this essay that I finally confirmed my suspicion that he is not in fact the biological father of one of the young women he has raised as a daughter.

But though I believe that he believes in the veracity of what he does choose to tell me, there are some parts of his story which are hard for me to accept as literally true. The most striking example is his often-repeated account of a terrifying encounter with a coven of witches (*tonhis*) when he worked as a bullock-cart driver in his youth. This has a manifestly formulaic quality, and other informants have offered me almost identical descriptions of almost identical encounters of their own. The contradiction—the truthful informant who tells me of (what I regard as) fictional incidents in his life—is perhaps more apparent than real. There is a good deal of evidence that suggests that powerful narratives tend to be internalized as though they were autobiographical memories. Such narratives are stored, that is, in the form of mental models that enable us to imagine that we were actually there (Bloch 1998b). Many of us have vivid "memories" of childhood events when in fact it is very unlikely that what we remember is the event itself, rather than the accounts of it we have had from our parents.

At another level are the much larger number of Somvaru's stories that seem to bear a more direct relationship to really "real" events, and that he has told me on several occasions in more or less exactly the same words. As with most of us, these reminiscences appear to fly on automatic pilot and to reproduce not the memory itself, but the memory of how he has told the story before. And then, of course, there are the "rawer" recollections, previously perhaps completely unprocessed, and often prompted by questions of my own. Given the right stimuli, we "remember"—as the psychologists remind us—much more than we normally "recall" (Bloch 1998b). As it exists in my notebooks, then,

Somvaru's "life history" is a kind of patchwork made up of accounts of incidents which may have been triggered by real experiences but which are now represented in wholly conventionalized and formulaic terms, and which appear to be internalized versions of stories drawn from the larger cultural repertoire; of recollections of previous recollections, and of previously unverbalized memories.

My conversations with Somvaru and members of his family have ranged over many aspects of life, and I have used some of these data elsewhere (Parry 1999a; 2000). Here, with space to address only one theme, I have picked on marriage. The stability of conjugal relations is an issue on which I have recently written in a more general vein, and the present essay is intended as a companion piece to this more analytical account (Parry 2001), and as an illustrative case history of some of the themes it explores. I focus here on the story of Somvaru's marriages by evoking two voices—Somvaru's own and that of his daughter, Janaki. Toward the end of it, I reverse the lens by turning to the story of Janaki's own marriages, which are again told from the same two points of view. Though there are certainly continuities between these marital histories, what interests me more are the *differences* they suggest in how marriage is viewed, and in the emotional tone and content of the conjugal bond. The point of my juxtaposition, then, is to highlight the way in which marriage is changing its meaning—partly as a consequence of the changing spirit of the times and partly as a consequence of class mobility.

In using life-history material to illustrate a general social process, I am obviously making some claim for its representativeness. No question that the details are highly specific; but I believe that they tell us something more general. About whom? Somvaru belongs to the largest "Untouchable" caste in the region, a caste in which marriage is indeed particularly unstable. But in this part of India, and with only minor exceptions, divorce and remarriage are statistically frequent throughout the hierarchy (see Parry 2001 for details). Rather less about Somvaru's marital history is specifically characteristic of people of Untouchable caste than one might perhaps suppose from rhetoric of the higher castes or from the comparative literature on other parts of the country.

But if what follows makes some modest claims to representativeness with regard to the nature of marriage in this region, it makes none in relation to the "typical" experiences and life trajectories of Indian Untouchables. Somvaru certainly does not inhabit the somewhat seedy twilight world of semi-criminal activities evoked in Freeman's (1979) portrait of Muli. By contrast with that of Viramma—"We are Pariahs . . . We have to be humble . . . It's better if we stay in our place"— his attitude to caste would be better characterized as a fairly relaxed contempt for the airs and graces of those who take their superiority for granted (Viramma, Racine and Racine 1997: 164, 191; see also Racine and Racine, this volume). But nor again does Somvaru share much in common with Vasant Moon, a Dalit intellectual from a highly politicized segment of a highly politicized caste, whose recently translated autobiography vividly describes his early involvement in militant Ambedkarite campaigns (Moon 2001). If there is one thing that the published life histories of Indian Untouchables should have taught us, it is that Untouchable lives are no more uniform than those of any other broad strata of the population.

The Place and its People

Somvaru lives in the ex-village-cum-labor colony I call Girvi, which is located on the periphery of the modern Company Township of Bhilai in the newly formed state of Chhattisgarh. The company is the Bhilai Steel Plant (BSP for short), a public sector undertaking, constructed with Soviet collaboration, which began production in 1959. With an area of seventeen square kilometers, and with around 55,000 employees on its direct payroll when I began my research in 1993, it is now one of the largest steel plants in Asia. A little removed from it is the more recent industrial estate with some 200 private sector factories. Immediately fringing the plant's perimeter walls is its spacious and orderly township. Elsewhere the perimeter fence abuts onto what still look like rural villages; while at other points the plant and the township are surrounded by a sea of unregulated urban sprawl which envelops old villages like Girvi, Patripar and Nijigaon in which much of my fieldwork was done. In the mid 1950s, these were small rural settlements in which a bicycle was still a wonder. Since then many migrant workers have moved in, the erstwhile peasants and landless laborers are now better described as proletarians, and the lucky ones have jobs in the steel plant. Lucky because the BSP workforce is the local aristocracy of labor, enjoying pay, perks and benefits that make them the envy of every other working-class family in the area.

Girvi remains the most rural of the neighborhoods studied. Just out of the BSP township you turn down an unmetaled road through a market of new shops, past the Vishnu Talkies and the ice-cream parlor, and on past the new Catholic church until you reach the first house in the village—Narayan Dau's fortress-like new mansion built at the cost of Rs 10 lakhs (a lakh being Rs 100,000), the fruits of a successful career in *panchayat* politics and property-dealing. On this side, the village was by 1993 already almost completely surrounded by new private sector colonies in which—fertilized by soft credit from BSP—the houses seemed to grow out of the ground as fast as the paddy grew in the fields on the far side. But for the narrow-gauge railway line which brings iron-ore to the plant from the Dalli-Rajhara mines, and but for the public sector Bhilai Refractory Plant in one corner, on that side you could have been in real rural Chhattisgarh, as indeed you might have imagined yourself to be in the village itself. Today, most of the remaining fields have been marked out as house-plots (on what was left of Somvaru's land a shopping complex is planned), and many of the old mud-brick village houses have been rebuilt in concrete by recently retired workers on the proceeds of provident fund pay-outs from the plant. A significant number of Girvi men are BSP employees; a significant number (both men and women) work for it as contract laborers, and an equally significant number (exclusively men) do little but booze and play cards. Socially and spatially the village is sharply divided between the so-called "Hindu" castes of the region (that is, more or less every other caste of the old village hierarchy), and the "Untouchable" Satnamis. The latter are converts, believed to be of almost exclusively Chamar origin (though this they bitterly contest), to the sectarian following of a saint called Ghasi Das, who probably died around 1850.[3]

Somvaru's Background

Somvaru is a Satnami. Indeed, he is the *bhandari* of the Girvi Satnami *para* (quarter)—the functionary who presides at Satnami life-cycle rituals and who has the notional role of first amongst equals in its *panchayat*. He was born on a Monday (*Somvar*), as his name suggests, though he does not know the month or the year. His BSP records say it was in July 1935, but they had to write something. Over the past couple of years he has decided that he must be older than that—though you would not suppose so from his vigor and looks.

The only son of an only son, Somvaru had a sister who died some years ago. His father he does not remember at all, though he knows that he had suffered dreadfully from smallpox, as a result of which one eye had "burst." He had contracted the disease from Ganesh's mother, the wife of a neighbor. The couple were lovers. Cholera carried him off a few years later. Shortly after his death, a man from a different village "put bangles" on the wrists of his widow—that is, made a secondary union with her. Somvaru and his sister were left with their father's father's younger brother and his completely blind wife. It was they who got him married, though he was too young at the time to have any recollection of it. But they never sent him to school.

His mother's second husband turned out badly. The couple did not have children, he was violent and she left, returning to Girvi where "she made a new man," a classificatory younger brother of her first husband, Somvaru's father.[4] He had been married before, but his wife had run off. With him she had five sons, but Lainu was the only one of these half-brothers to survive beyond infancy. Though now she was back in Girvi, and living hardly more than a stone's throw from Somvaru, they had little contact until Lainu's father died. He had resented her interest in the children of her first marriage. But after his death she became a regular visitor, and once Lainu was married she often stayed at Somvaru's. With Lainu's wife she could not get on. It was in Somvaru's house that she died in 1976, one year after Somvaru lost his fourth wife and the mother of four of his children.

By Satnami standards, indeed by the standards of the village as a whole, the family was fairly well off. When his father was alive, they had a holding of thirteen acres, though the quality of this land did not allow them to meet their subsistence needs throughout the year. Crop yields were very significantly lower than they are today. Somvaru's father had supplemented their income by working as a coolie in the grain-market at Durg (the district headquarters about eight miles away). After his death, the father's father's brother was forced to sell three of their acres, at the rate of Rs 60 per acre. When he in turn died, Somvaru disposed of four acres to the village's *malguzar* (its principal landlord and revenue collector) for Rs 90 per acre. But when the middle-class housing colonies started sprouting in Girvi's fields in the 1980s, he was able to sell another 2.5 acres for around Rs 3 lakhs. He would have made more had he not been duped by his eldest son, Dukhit, who—on account of Somvaru's illiteracy—had been given charge of the deal, who concealed from his father the real rate per square foot that he had managed to realize, and who pocketed the difference. It was on the proceeds that Dukhit started drinking heavily, eventually becoming a chronic alcoholic, running up large debts, and ultimately committing suicide in December 1995. But to stay with the land, that now left Somvaru with 3.5 acres on the far side of the village which he continued to cultivate until 1996, when he finally sold out for Rs 4.5 lakhs. In 1998, he reinvested (nearly Rs 7 lakhs) in 6.5 acres located in a village about forty kilometers away, sending his youngest son, Raj Kumar, to look after it. But even after this capital outlay, he maintains a healthy deposit account in the bank, which yields enough interest to sustain the household (currently of thirteen members).[5] Smaller sums are deposited in the names of his two surviving sons, his two unmarried daughters and various of the grandchildren.[6]

In his youth, Somvaru had been a leading light of a "*nacha* party" recruited from Girvi's Satnami *para*—a song and dance troupe that performed skits and sketches around the neighboring villages. He specialized in the roles of "joker" and *jhakri* ("old hag"), and in the right mood he will still perform for me the songs they had composed to parody the pretensions of the upper castes and to mock the by now declining power of the *malguzars*. "Weren't they angry?" I ask him. "Yes," he agrees, "but they could not sing as I could."

Apart from the pin-money made by the *nacha* party, Somvaru's first earnings came from a trading trip he made with some friends to Calcutta, where they purchased nine maunds of brass utensils which they sold at a significant profit round the villages back home. But this was a one-off venture, and soon afterward Somvaru got into carting bamboo and teak from the jungle round Dongargarh in collaboration with his first wife's father. It was very hard work, the partnership did not survive the marriage, and there was easier money to be made in the bullock trade, to which he was now introduced by his sister's husband. They bought the better quality beasts reared in Maharashtra, and drove them back on foot for resale in the local markets. Simultaneously, Somvaru worked as a carter for Kodu Sahu, a wealthy co-villager of Oil-presser caste who was a grain trader in Durg—an occupation that afforded (though he does not brag about it) some scope for opportunistic sexual encounters as he traveled the villages. Having narrowly escaped a large loss in a highway robbery on the way back from Maharashtra, Somvaru concluded that the bullock business was too risky.

The construction of BSP had by now made other alternatives easily available, and in 1959 he took a job with a big contractor working on the site, where he helped with the installation of cast-iron pipes. On account of this experience, he was taken on as a regular BSP worker soon after the construction company had made him redundant in 1962. As "helper" to a carpenter, almost his first task was to make a coffin for a Russian engineer who had been killed in an industrial accident. He was then assigned to the Refractory Engineering Department and worked in the Steel Melting Shop, where he was one of a team which was sent into the shut-down furnaces in relays—for ten-minute bursts at a time—to clear out the still red-hot slag. It was terrible work, and the only way to stand it was by strategically timed absenteeism. He would set out by bike for the plant in the morning until he reached a vantage point near Maitri Bagh, where he could see all eleven chimneys of the open-hearth furnaces. If one of the stacks were not smoking, he would know that a furnace was down and that day he would shovel slag. He would take tea by the roadside, and slowly pedal home. That, he claims, is how he managed to survive those early BSP years. His subsequent job was less taxing. He was a forklift-truck driver shifting refractory bricks (with which the furnaces and ladles are lined) around the shop floor. He was still doing that when he took voluntary retirement in September 1987 with a handsome pay-off and a substantial sum in his provident fund account. In the mean time, he had been using a significant proportion of his BSP earnings to operate as a small-scale moneylender, making loans to friends, neighbors and affines.[7]

So much for the material framing of Somvaru's marital history. But before I get to it, I want to highlight one other aspect of his biography that colors his relationship to the world—his illiteracy. He likens it to blindness and represents it as a source of humiliating dependence. When he was sent to fetch refractory bricks in his forklift truck, he was unable to read the identifying numbers, and had to rely on colleagues if he wasn't to be bawled at for bringing the wrong ones. When he tried to visit Lainu in Bengal, he was ignominiously turned off the train without money to get home. The booking clerk had charged him for Kharagpur, but had issued a ticket for the station next up the line. When I sent him a registered letter in the name of "Somvaru Ram," he had to go to sign for it at the main post office, where he was put through the mill by the babus because, though his grandchildren had taught him "Somvaru," he could not manage the "Ram." When we together watched an IPTA[8] street-corner drama, which was part of a government literacy drive, and which consisted of a series of sketches in which buffoon-like bumpkins got themselves into terrible pickles because they could neither read nor write, and though I had been cringing with embarrassment on his behalf, Somvaru was hugely amused. "That's just my story," he told me as we wandered away at the end.

It's a story with some bearing on family politics and power. All but one of the nine children Somvaru has raised are literate, all but two of the rest have got at least as far as the eighth class, and his daughter Janaki has an MA, holds a senior teaching position in a BSP school and is married to the vice-principal of another. Early on in our friendship, I ran into his youngest son, Raj Kumar, late one night in the street. He was drunk. And now he had me alone, he wanted to complain of his father's ignorance and stupidity, of how he had done nothing for his children. Raj Kumar was then in his mid twenties. His only visible occupations were working out a winning formula for making his fortune at *satta* (a numbers racket on which he had already squandered a substantial sum which Somvaru had unwisely settled on him), and avoiding so much as setting foot in what was left of the family fields.[9] I mildly pointed out that his father could compose songs, weld pipes, build bullock carts, castrate bullocks, cultivate fields, and fix motorbikes. But, swaying slightly, Raj Kumar dismissed these accomplishments, describing him as "nothing but a thumb-impression man" (*angutha-chhap admi*). When I briefly visited Bhilai two years back, Kavita, then a ravishing eighteen-year-old and the youngest but one of Somvaru's daughters, had not spoken to him for the past two months— not even, he noted, to ask him for money. He had reprimanded her for sitting out in the street, flirting—I inferred—with the boys. She had called him an "illiterate yokel" (*unparh gavar*) incapable of all understanding. The previous year I had been inveigled into accompanying Janaki's husband on a trip to Bemetra in connection with the divorce proceedings of his elder brother's son. I think they imagined that a foreign professor might impress their lawyer, and as bait I was promised Somvaru's company. But at the very last minute he was told that the trip had been canceled, because—I was told—"an illiterate man like him might say something to spoil the case."

Sometimes this disparagement seemed to threaten a major family rift. Two rival property dealers were pressuring him to sell the last of his land. Emissaries were pestering him daily, and Raj Kumar had taken a fat commission from both to persuade his father in their favor. Eventually one of them succeeded in cajoling him into accepting a small advance, which Somvaru took to be morally binding (as it is in the bullock trade). The problem was that the other had immediately come up with a much better deal. A family council was called in Janaki's house (constructed on a plot carved out of what had once been Somvaru's land), in a middle-class suburb built in Girvi's fields. His children had forcefully argued that he was in no way legally bound, but the meeting ended in disarray when Somvaru insisted that he was not a man to renege on his word.

> "Shut up," his exasperated son-in-law had finally exploded. "You are not educated. So why do you keep butting in? You understand nothing."
>
> "That's right," said Somvaru, "I am not educated. My father did not educate me. But it is my land. I will sell it to whom I like."
>
> "Look here," the son-in-law shouted. "When you get in a mess you come to me. But you will not listen to what I say. So there is no need to bring all these matters to my house. You solve them in your own home."

At this point Somvaru walked out and it was several weeks before he went back. Though Barle, the son-in-law, was contrite, there was perhaps something self-serving in his manner of expressing it: "An educated man like me should not have spoken in that way to an elder."

Between these two households there are substantial financial flows, and Janaki and her husband are significantly in debt to Somvaru. On most of this money they pay interest of five per cent per month (which is standard between kin). But on one occasion there was a muddle over whether this payment had been made. Both sides insisted that the sum itself was neither here nor there. But Janaki bitterly complained that although she kept a written record, her father could not get it into his head that he must be mistaken. But, as Somvaru saw it, the problem is that "these educated people always think that what they have written is right, and you can never persuade them otherwise."

As the latter represent it, the lack of literacy is more or less synonymous with a lack of "intelligence," suggesting perhaps that "intelligence" is not seen as a source of "natural" inequality, as it is in so much of Western ideology (Béteille 1983). Somvaru is not the only member of the family to suffer from this elision. Since Dukhit's death, there has been a good deal of ill feeling over the attention that Raj Kumar has paid to his widow. Raj Kumar's wife and her sister accused them of having an affair. Though she was completely unwilling to believe the allegation, Janaki was extremely upset. Meena, the widow, had "entrusted the crown" to Raj Kumar at the time of his wedding—which made her "a kind of mother" to him. Though in petty ways Raj Kumar might sometimes seem irresponsible, he was certainly not capable of such shameful behavior. It was all just jealousy on the part of his wife. She is uneducated and "has no intelligence."

Literacy is popularly associated—and not only by literates—with rational understanding (and also more broadly with "civilized" values and behavior); illiterates with the opposite attributes. These stereotypes notwithstanding, Somvaru has always struck me as rather less credulous than the next man—however well lettered. By temperament he is an empiricist, which is perhaps why we get on well. The Girvi *kotval* (village constable) had just told me that on death an unmarried man becomes a *rakshas* (demon). "How does he know?" said Somvaru when I asked him to comment. One day we were discussing the idea that before her departure a bride should be tattooed so that she and her mother may recognize each other in the next world. "Can't they do so without?" I enquired, though I should have known better. "How can I tell?" said Somvaru. "I am only telling you what people say." When Janaki paid over a substantial sum to a charlatan—a failed manufacturer of small bicycle parts—to teach her reflexology, by which she would cure cataracts and cancer, it was Somvaru who said she was gullible. And of Barle's brother, a tailor in the village with a side-line in extracting stones from the bodies of the patients who consult him, Somvaru's kindest comment was that when he was with his *nacha* party he had learned conjuring tricks of that kind. There are, however, limits to Somvaru's down-to-earth pragmatism. Witches are certainly one; and, though there is much duplicity in them, the prognostications of Bhatris (a caste of fortune-tellers and removers of malign planetary influences) are not to be discounted. Both figure in the marital history that follows.

As a *bhandari*, Somvaru presides at Satnami rituals. But if you ask him for exegesis, his standard response is that all sorts of incomprehensible practices have come down from the old people, and he cannot say whether they have any meaning at all. Now the world is "educated," and now they know better. Old ways were generally worse ways, and one of the leitmotifs of his life history is the passage from darkness to light.

Any number of illustrations might be offered, but the story I like best is of the time when Somvaru was engaged in legal warfare with the father of Janaki's first husband. At the height of their dispute, he was introduced to a BSP crane operator who had heard of his woes. The crane operator affected astonishment that he was taking such a long way round, and offered to put him in touch with a *baiga* (exorcist-sorcerer) who, for Rs 5,000, would accept a contract on his enemy's life. Somvaru had paid a deposit, and was given a midnight rendezvous at the Durg cremation ground where the rest of the money would be handed over and the job would be done. His friend Lakhan, and his son Dukhit, went with him, and waiting there sure enough were the crane-operator and the *baiga*—surrounded by magical paraphernalia. The *baiga* had just explained how a "needle-arrow" (*sui-ban*) would fly through the air at his foe when they were set upon by three policemen with *lathis* (metal-tipped staves) who demanded the money that they plainly knew they had, and took their wristwatches too for good measure. Realizing that he had been duped, Somvaru subsequently got his revenge by reporting that he had been robbed of Rs 5,000 at the Uttai cattle market, and identifying the crane operator as the culprit. But the point of this story here is the way that Somvaru now tells it. The way he had acted, he now sees clearly, was completely wrong. "Wrong to try to kill his daughter's father-in-law?" I supposed. "Not that. Wrong to think that it was possible to do so by magical means (*jadu-tona*). In those days we people didn't know better."

Much the same goes for marriage. In his generation, they had no understanding and the merest tiff was sufficient pretext for leaving your spouse. But now he can see that that was not good.

Somvaru and His Wives

In Somvaru's age group, child marriage was common throughout the caste hierarchy. *Shadi* (the wedding proper) would be performed for toddlers, or even for babes-in-arms, though the child-bride would remain with her parents until she was ready for *gauna* (in local dialect, *pathauni*)—at which she was ritually given into the custody of her husband and the marriage consummated. By that time both would be sexually mature, and possibly also experienced. It was in those days almost expected that youngsters would have secret liaisons before their *gauna* was celebrated. In fact, it was sometimes not celebrated at all because one of them had already absconded with somebody else. In principle (there are minor exceptions), a woman can have only one *shadi* ritual, her subsequent secondary unions being only minimally ritualized by "the putting on of bangles" (*churi pehnana*) by her new husband. But if a man takes a *kunvari* (a "virgin" or "unmarried girl") as a subsequent wife, he will go through *shadi* again (see Parry 2001).

Though Somvaru's (one and only) *shadi* was performed when he was still very small, he was probably in his late teens by the time he was joined by his wife. They did not have children (and she never did). But though a woman's failure to conceive quickly is the commonest cause of divorce, Somvaru says that the problem was her habit of chewing tobacco. Janaki tells a different story. Somvaru was always wandering off with his *nacha* party, paid his *shadi-vali* little attention and was never at home. She ran back to her *maike* (her natal home), as is expected of young brides when unhappy. Their husbands are then expected to show their commitment by fetching them back. Somvaru was insufficiently eager; so "she made a new man." They were together for just a year after *gauna*.

Janaki remembers meeting her father's *shadi-vali* much later at the Rajim fair, to which her mother had taken her and the infant Raj Kumar; and she remembers her beauty and kindness. She had clenched her baby brother's tiny fist around a Rs 5 note. Somvaru remembers going with four senior men from his *para* to the village of her new husband to demand *bihati torna*—a payment made "to break the marriage bond." A *panchayat* was summoned and he stood a little way off while his supporters negotiated the sum. He thinks it was Rs 120. Whatever it was, he accepted their decision without demur. He had been advised to do so since that village is famous for witchcraft. He has not seen his *shadi-vali* since, though he once ran into her father who had come for some reason to Girvi. He touched his feet and took him home for a meal. Yes, of course it was awkward, but what else could he do?

Somvaru's second marriage was the one that I learnt about last, and of which he speaks least. Until very recently I had no inkling whether this was because it had no importance for him, or because it still had too much. That I had not is probably significant. Passionate attachment (what Westerners call "love") is not—at least for men of his generation—what marriage is supposed to have been about. But that is not to say that powerful emotions were not sometimes engaged. I have come to suspect that in this case they were.

In search of a new wife, Somvaru enlisted the aid of his father's sister's husband, whom he had met on the road and who did the negotiating for him. They found a young woman whom he fancied. She had been married before but was now "sitting in her *maike*" in what has become one of the most congested slums of the area. She liked the look of him, and a party from her house came to see his. A couple of days later he went with three or four supporters to put on bangles and bring her home. With Somvaru she stayed for a couple of childless years. She had returned to her father's house for the *Tija* festival and from there ran off, at her stepmother's instigation, with the wealthy widower of her deceased sister. What had he done about it? "What was there to do? I went to my in-laws' place (*sasural*) to find out, but by then she had gone to her *bhato* (sister's husband)."

It was said with matter-of-fact resignation, as if it was of no account now, and probably never was. But through his son's wife's father, whose brother is married to another sister of this ex-wife, Somvaru recently got word of her. The intelligence was that she now bitterly rues the day that she listened to her stepmother and left him. To her subsequent husband she had borne five children. So why the regrets? "Because now," as Somvaru characteristically put it, "her livelihood (*guzara*) is so difficult." Not his good looks, sexual prowess or charismatic personality, note, but his ability to provide. His choice of words is significant, even if we should hesitate to infer from it what he thought that she thought and felt. His *samdhi* (son's wife's father) had suggested that he should see her again. But did he want to? "My body," he said, "desires it." Not long after this conversation, he persuaded a mutual friend to take him by motorbike to the village on the edge of the Raipur industrial estate where his ex-wife had remarried. She was away at the house of one of her daughters; her second husband was long dead, the house extremely dilapidated and her sons lived separately from her. Somvaru introduced himself to them as an old acquaintance of their father and came home very subdued. He made no attempt, however, to conceal this visit from his present wife, or from the children, and they teased him about it for days. Despite that, he has returned to the topic several times and is pressing our friend to take him once more.

When he decided to find a third spouse, he again went—as is conventional in such cases—from village to village asking: "Is there any widow or abandoned woman sitting here?" In the village of his mother's brother, he consulted a Bhatri fortune-teller who told him his search would fail. Somvaru ruefully recalls his fury and his stubborn determination to prove the Bhatri's prediction wrong. On the way back through Durg, he met a man called Kanhaiya from a village called Somni that borders on Girvi. Kanhaiya had a separated daughter "sitting" at home, and took Somvaru to see her. The match was made immediately, but he was soon to regret it. The marriage lasted little more than a week.

At the time, Somvaru must have been in his early or mid twenties. He was still in the bullock business. One day he had come home dog-tired from a cattle fair and was sleeping. His new wife had come into the room, loosened her hair and taken off all her clothes. He woke to find her hovering over him, chewing some root and swaying rhythmically from side to side. She was drooling red saliva that sent out sparks as it hit the ground. As he watched them with fascinated horror, he noticed that she was standing on air. He immediately realized that he had married a witch (*tonhi*). Though he was of course terrified, he jumped up, grabbed her by the hair and dragged her into the street so that all the neighbors could see. They threw some clothes over her and packed her out of the village. Somvaru immediately decamped to his married sister's house. Next day the witch's father, Kanhaiya, arrived in Girvi and demanded a *panchayat*. But Somvaru had made himself scarce. Kanhaiya waited three days, and it was only when Somvaru got word that he had gone that he summoned up courage to creep home. He now congratulates himself on his good fortune in discovering her real identity so soon. She subsequently married a schoolteacher from Tirda by whom she had two children. It took the master years to find her out, though he did so in the end.

Even today Somvaru is extremely reluctant to set foot in Somni. On one occasion he had gone with a party of men from their *para* to fetch his classificatory sister, Sanicheri, back to Girvi from her in-laws' for *Tija. Tija* is a festival for which married sisters conventionally return to their *maike*, and for the first *Tija* after marriage they are fetched in style. A whole group goes from her natal village and stays several days before bringing her home. The rule is that while they are there every meal should be taken in a different house of her *sasural's* kin group (a practice known as *pech karna*). In Sanicheri's case, this included the house of Somvaru's witch-wife. She was still with her schoolmaster, and—against his better judgment—Somvaru allowed himself to be persuaded that there was safety in numbers. But he was determined to be vigilant, and as they were about to sit down to eat, he noticed that his *buri sas* (his ex-wife's FeBW) had come to spy out the land. He felt "some doubt," and at the very last moment astutely switched places with Lal Babu. No sooner had they eaten than Lal Babu was taken violently ill and was immediately rushed into hospital in Durg. His formidable father, Ayodhya—for many years one of the big men of their *para*—called a *panchayat* meeting in Somni in which he promised the most terrible consequences unless his son recovered. But it was by only a whisker that Lal Babu escaped with his life.

In the matter of his next marriage, Somvaru agreed to be guided by his sister's husband, who had upbraided him over this last debacle. He quickly identified a good-looking girl from a well-to-do family. Her father—another bullock trader—had thirty acres. Somvaru's sister's husband arranged to bring her for him to see at the Tuesday cattle market in Uttai. She had had two previous unions. Her *shadi-vala* was in the police. Before their *gauna* was celebrated he had taken up with a Ravatin, a woman of Ravat (Grazier) caste, which belongs to the "Hindu" category. She was now living openly with him as his *rakhel* ("kept woman" or "concubine"), and the young bride was beaten by both. She fled to her *maike* and shortly after remarried. But in that marriage, too, she had a co-wife and from there she also ran away, carrying with her an infant daughter, Rukhmin, who had been born of this union. Now already again back in her *maike* for some months, her parents considered—as parents will, for fear of the disgrace she might bring them by getting pregnant without one—that it was time that "she made a new man."

Though she was a very attractive young woman, Somvaru was not at first impressed. Janaki says that that was because his first wife had been so stunning. What Somvaru himself remembers thinking is that a girl from such a well-heeled household would prove expensive, and that he did not like the fashionable earrings she wore. But he was somewhat reassured by her removing them immediately when he said they were not to his taste. And he was completely won over when he asked what she would want from him, and she told him to give her two very cheap saris of a type which the Kostas used to weave (one for herself and one for her mother), plus Rs 60. "How can a girl from such a family be asking for such simple things?" he had wondered. "So I made a bargain at Rs 60 and two saris and came back with another (wife)." The word he chooses to describe this "bargain" (*sauda*) is that used by bullock traders for their deals (though it also has some currency for commercial transactions in general).

In fact, it was not quite so straightforward. Her mother had insisted on a preliminary visit with her daughter, and did not approve. In those days it was a very small house, and she was put out to find it full of *nacha*-party props. It was not a home fit for a daughter of hers. The daughter, however, had different ideas. "She had liked me from the start," Somvaru complacently recalls, and had reminded her mother that "[i]t is I, not you, who will live here." And she got her way, for in all castes which traditionally tolerate divorce it is a clear principle that while "the virgin daughter belongs to the caste *panchayat* (and must therefore do as she's told), the abandoned daughter follows her own disposition." With her she brought Rukhmin, the child of her previous marriage, whom Somvaru has raised as his own—so much so that it took me years to discover that she is not. With her biological father Rukhmin has had no contact at all since her earliest infancy.

By all accounts, the marriage worked well for the first decade or so, and four children were born—a girl, Janaki (b. 1957), followed by three boys, Dukhit (b. 1960), Sukhit (b. 1964) and Raj Kumar (b. 1968). Dukhit is now dead, and was constantly and aggressively drunk during the last years of his life. Sukhit (now a state government paramedical employee in a rather remote village) was given at the age of two to Somvaru's friend, Lakhan, to foster and did not really live at home again until he was fourteen or fifteen, when relations between the two families began to sour. Though I am now well ahead of the story, that relationship has an important bearing on the difficulties that emerged in the marriage.

From Somvaru himself I heard nothing. But Janaki says that the problem started when her father took up with another woman. Her parents began to quarrel violently and weeks went by when they would not speak. Her father was particularly hard and impatient with the children, tying them to a house-post and beating them cruelly when they had been over-boisterous and he was trying to sleep after coming home from his shift. He was always, she claims, too stern with them—though this is hard to credit today when you see him routinely routed by the wheedling ways of his younger daughters and grandchildren. From Janaki, I also had hints that her father's affair led to friction between her mother and her *maike*, with whose family she herself will now have no truck. Her mother's brother's son is a drinker who has squandered his patrimony, and the whole family is completely uneducated.

It was Mangal, a close neighbor, who told me the details which make sense of these last particulars. Somvaru had started a relationship with his wife's elder brother's daughter while she was "sitting" at home in her *maike* (Somavru's *sasural*) after shedding her *shadi-vala* husband. It was a scandalous affair since kinship morality required them to regard each other as father and daughter. After it had gone on for some time, Somvaru had persuaded his friend Lakhan (with whom his second son, Sukhit, was fostered) to take the girl as his fourth wife. But since one of the previous ones was still with him, and since everybody knows that co-wives do not generally get on, the agreement was that Lakhan's new wife would live with her father's sister instead (in Somvaru's house, that is), where Lakhan could easily visit. Moreover, none of Lakhan's three earlier marriages had produced a child, and it was suspected that his house was ill-omened ("had some *totka*"). It therefore made sense for the couple to sleep at Somvaru's. But this arrangement was brought to an abrupt end when it was Somvaru and Lakhan's new wife who were found *in flagrante delicto*. Somvaru was temporarily boycotted and had to feed the whole *para* in penance; and his mistress was forced to move in with her husband. But even after that their relationship continued, the couple were caught red-handed once more and Somvaru had to feed his caste-mates again.

Everybody knows, Mangal added, that Lakhan could never father children, and everybody knows that the only child of his four marriages is really Somvaru's. But who was supposedly doing a favor for whom, and how explicit their understanding, I cannot confidently say. Judging, however, by what I know of Somvaru's attitudes in such matters, I suspect that both men were entirely clear-sighted about the trade-off. For the one it was a solution to the problem of hanging on to an unmarriageable mistress; for the other a solution to the problem of fathering a son.

In May 1975, Somvaru's fourth marriage ended in a tragedy. His wife had gone with a group of co-villagers to excavate earth from a railway embankment in order to provide their fields with new topsoil. The embankment caved in on Somvaru's wife, and her companions ran off in fright. By the time anyone returned to dig her out, she was dead. Janaki in particular was traumatized, and the story of her mother's cremation, of the police investigation and of the compassion shown by one of the officers (whose daughter was Janaki's classmate) is one on which both she and Somvaru repeatedly dwell. Somvaru says that after her death he was initially reluctant to marry again. But Rukhmin was by now with her husband, and Janaki was living in a student hostel. Somvaru found it impossible to do his job in the plant, cultivate his fields, run the household and look after his sons (in particular, Raj Kumar who was just six or seven) without the help of a woman. But before he set out on a new search, he summoned a Bhatri from Somni to whom he gave *chakra dan*—pouring paddy through a large sieve nine times in order "to break the *grah*" (that is, rid himself of evil planetary influences).

Pushpa, his present wife, had borne two boys by her first husband, but both had died in infancy. When the third child turned out to be a girl (who survived), her husband took a new wife. She then went back to her *maike*, where she "sat" for almost five years—suffering all that time, says Somvaru, "in her body" (a reference, I supposed, to sexual and emotional deprivation). Eventually, he himself came to ask for her. Though her father and brother were hostile to start with—his reputation as a "*nacha*-party joker" had preceded him—they were impressed when they came to his house and found that he had a fan and a bullock-cart of his own. Even by that time, they had "nothing" in the villages (though in terms of land Pushpa's family are again quite privileged).

Some months after she had come to him, her *bihata* (her *shadi-vala* husband) had arrived for *bihati torna*. But since she had been moldering in her *maike* for the last five years, Somvaru told him that he had some nerve to turn up after all that time, and sent him away empty-handed. He was back soon enough with a big Satnami leader from Somni, and Somvaru was leaned on. At first they demanded Rs 1,000. He offered Rs 100. They settled at Rs 450 and their agreement was recorded on legal stamp paper.

Sushila, the surviving child of the first marriage, was five when her mother remarried. Her father never came to claim her, nor even enquired after her, and Somvaru brought her up as one of his own and arranged her marriage. They invited her father, but he was too ashamed to show his face, though he did send his son by his second wife "to take a kiss."[10]

By Somvaru, Pushpa had another three daughters. After the third she had an "operation." But, in an otherwise apparently harmonious relationship, her lack of a son still surfaces as a source of domestic dissension. Without one, she worries what will happen to her when Somvaru dies, and she fears that his sons will turn her out of the house. Just before one of my briefer visits to Bhilai, there had been a big row because she had wanted Somvaru to buy her jewelry as security against this eventuality. Somvaru refused, pointing out that his bank account was in their joint names, and that if he died she would get exclusive control of it, as well as a share of the (now sold) land. But Pushpa had not been persuaded, had gone off in a huff to attend her *chacha's* (FyB's) funeral, had refused to accept the money that Somvaru had offered for her expenses (she took the children's Scheduled Caste scholarship money instead), and had still not come back. Somvaru now gloomily supposed that she would stay on for *Tija*—though she had never returned to her *maike* for *Tija* before. On a subsequent trip, I persuaded Somvaru to take me to see the new land he had just bought way out in the country, and several other members of the family came along for the ride. That land is now registered in the names of his three sons. As we wandered through the fields, I casually asked Pushpa whether she would be coming to help with the harvest. She testily told me that it was for those who own the land to work for themselves.

At least for my consumption, however, Somvaru's loyal story is that Pushpa could never be faulted for discriminating between her own children and those of his previous wife; that she has been equally a mother to all, and that though his daughters-in-law may quarrel with each other, they never argue with her. Janaki tells me differently, regularly complaining of her stepmother's "stepmotherly treatment" of her sibling group, and describing her as a "very cunning woman." Now even Somvaru discriminates against them. Compare his indulgence of Pushpa's daughters with the harshness they suffered. At Kavita's age she would not have dared to ask her father for clothes; but Kavita wanders here and there in search of high heels, and goes on hunger strike when they are not bought for her. It is plainly a matter of *maternal* origins. Janaki is equally resentful on Rukhmin's behalf, and the fact that Somvaru is not her biological father is carefully suppressed. Though he actually remains in close contact with Rukhmin's household and has provided it with significant material support, Janaki complains that he neglects her. It is, however, of Raj Kumar that Janaki is most protective. He was just a boy when their mother died, and he who suffered most at their stepmother's hands. She really should look to the future.

Without sons of her own, she ought to consider on whom she will ultimately depend.

Janaki's Tapestry

Somvaru takes pride in Janaki's rise in the world, and a modest amount of the credit. He always said that she could take her studies as far as she would—though in Girvi they mostly said it was pointless, that she would end up cooking like the rest. But on Janaki's account, her father was less supportive than he now makes out and she had a great "struggle" to overcome the obstacles he put in her way. After Class 5, he had refused to let her continue because it meant walking five miles each way to a new school (where she would be the only girl in her class and the only girl from Girvi). It was a childless classificatory uncle, who lived close to the school, who finally persuaded him. She could stay in his house when she needed. But though a frail child, she mostly walked from Girvi—Somvaru paying a Tamrakar (coppersmith) boy to carry her copy-laden satchel and arranging with a Gujarati tea-stall owner near the school to provide her with daily snacks. But it is her mother's support that she now remembers. She would surreptitiously sell small quantities of rice from the household's storage bins to buy her extra exercise books. Later Janaki herself took in sewing to meet her additional expenses. But even on her account, it was Somvaru who provided the main subventions right up to her completion of her MA—at that stage at a level sufficiently generous for her to pass on a small monthly surplus to Dukhit. Even in India, fathers pay and children forget.

Janaki's educational achievements are intimately bound up with her marital tribulations. Her *shadi* was celebrated at the age of fourteen. She blames her father. Others say it was her mother who took the initiative. She had been seriously ill and said she wanted to see her daughter married before she died; and Somvaru claims that by the time he learned of the proposed match he could not honorably refuse it. It was with the son of a man called Dau Lal who used to play the harmonium in Girvi, and who had been impressed by Janaki's striking good looks and obvious intelligence. Dau Lal had property; the educational attainments of his son had been inflated; they were misled into supposing that the grand house in which they were entertained when they went to check out Janaki's future home was his own, and at that time Somvaru had not heard about his unsavory reputation. But even at that stage in her life Janaki seems to have known her mind. She knew that she did not want the marriage, and acquiesced in it only on the clear understanding that she would be allowed to continue her studies, and that her *gauna* would not be performed until she had completed them. It was to turn out to be her variant on Penelope's tapestry.

Though they had this agreement *in writing*, she claims, it was immediately tested. When there is a gap between *shadi* (the marriage proper) and *gauna*—as there almost invariably was in the past—the bride returns home with her attendants (*lokrain*) immediately after the part of the wedding ritual that takes place in the groom's house. But as soon as it was completed, Janaki's *phuphi sas* (HFZ) locked her in a room with the groom. Fortunately he was as nervous as she, and could not take advantage of the situation before she had screamed for rescue. They left her in-laws' village that night, and she never returned (or so she maintains).[11]

By 1975, when her mother died, Janaki was enrolled in the degree college in Durg. She had been deeply attached to her mother and was distraught at her death. But what made it all the more traumatic was that at the cremation her father-in-law proposed that her *gauna* be celebrated immediately after the tenth-day rituals. True, he was silenced at the time by her senior kin; but he was back again on the tenth day to renew his demand—which he urged on the plea that now there was no responsible adult woman left in Somvaru's house to supervise his daughter-in-law. If she were "spoilt"—such things *can* happen when boys and girls study together—"the infamy (*badnami*) will be with us" (i.e. her in-laws). The family protected her once more. The time was not right. See her state. She must be allowed to grieve for her mother and complete her exams. A compromise was reached. Her husband would be sent to stay with Somvaru in Girvi while he took a typing course in the township.

He had other things on his mind, and this arrangement lasted only a week, during which time he pestered Janaki incessantly. She was forced to remind him of the deal—that until she had completed her studies there would be no *gauna*; and before that they should live together "like brother and sister" and there should be no "dirty mischief." He had some difficulty grasping it. One night, when Somvaru had left for his shift, when everybody else had gone to sleep, and when

Janaki was studying under the light outside, he crept up behind her, gagged her mouth with one hand and tried to fondle her breasts with the other. She pushed him off so violently that he fell, and her screams awoke the neighborhood. The next day he left. Within a week, Somvaru had received a lawyer's letter accusing him of willfully conspiring to deprive his son-in-law of his conjugal rights. It was the first salvo in a long legal campaign—during the course of which Somvaru was to employ a sorcerer-assassin to dispose of his rival. But then Dau Lal had taunted him beyond endurance: how would an illiterate fellow like him be able to fight Dau Lal with the law? By the time he had done with him, Somvaru would have had to sell every inch of his land; and—even if he had to dig her corpse out of its grave or fish it out of the village tank—he would bring Janaki to his village for at least four days.

In 1978, the Lower Court sustained Dau Lal's plaint for the implementation of conjugal rights; and Janaki's counter-case for legal separation on the grounds that the marriage had not conformed to the Hindu Marriage Act, and had never been consummated, was dismissed. So, too, was her subsequent appeal to the High Court in Jabalpur, which ordered her to join her husband within the year. Soon after this, however, events were to come to her rescue. Her husband was convicted of raping a girl from his village and sentenced to a year in jail. For Somvaru and Janaki it was a godsend. It not only bought them time, but more importantly provided them with what Indian law recognizes as clear-cut grounds for divorce. Not surprisingly, Dau Lal's son's defense (I know this only from the legal papers Janaki showed me) was that the alleged "victim" had been an agent provocateur acting at the instigation of his in-laws. Though this did not convince the court, the husband's sentence was soon served; and, once out of jail, the demand for *gauna* was renewed.

It was, I think, at this point that Somvaru appears to have lost his nerve—perhaps partly because of the legal costs he was incurring, but principally I suspect because of a swell of gossip about Janaki's romantic attachments. In any event, a date was now fixed. Janaki describes a botched attempt to hang herself from the rafters using her *dopatta* (headscarf) as a noose. The *dopatta* broke. But still Somvaru was unbending. The day came, but Janaki had absconded. A week later word came that she was with her mother's sister's husband. Somvaru went to fetch her, but she refused to return until he had renewed his promise that her *gauna* would not be celebrated until she had done all the studying she desired.

There was perhaps more to it than a single-minded commitment to learning, or even a straightforward dislike of her husband. There was also Barle, who comes from a distant village in Raipur district. He had been married at the age of five and widowed by ten. Now he was a student in the Durg degree college. When Janaki was still at school and living at home with her parents, Barle would regularly come to Girvi with his class-fellow, a nephew of their neighbor Mangal. He was happy to help with her homework and they would spend hours together at Mangal's house. Subsequently, when Janaki herself joined the college and lived in a girl's hostel, Barle's visits caused a scandal. She moved into a rented a room near the Apsara Talkies, but it was much the same story. Barle and his friends would drop by; her husband would arrive and make a scene. The neighbors objected. By now, Barle was enrolled as an MA student in Raipur, and after completing her first degree Janaki joined the same course. But during her first year—and after her husband had provoked a violent fracas in the girl's hostel—she suffered a nervous breakdown and was admitted to BSP's psychiatric unit. As Somvaru somewhat disingenuously puts it, "her mind became 'cracked' from too much study." Restored to health, she enrolled in a BEd course in Bhilai, but at the same time surreptitiously continued her MA studies and took the first-year exam as an external student. She passed both. The following year she returned to Raipur to complete her MA

BA, BEd, MA—Janaki's priority was now a job. BSP had just advertised for secondary teachers. Barle was discouraging. Boys of that age are so rough and uncontrollable, and everybody "knows" that you cannot get such a job without paying a significant bribe. Though he himself had by this time a post in a BSP school, his family circumstances made it impossible for him to help. As for Somvaru, he wanted to know why he had spent all that money on her studies if he now had to part with more to get her employed. She nonetheless attended the interview. Though she never paid one paisa, and though without payment such things are popularly, though I believe entirely inaccurately (Parry 2000) held to be hardly possible, Janaki received her appointment letter within the week. Somehow she got herself assigned to a school in the BSP mining township to which Barle was posted, where she and younger brother—Sukhit—moved into a quarter, with Lal Babu's wife's brother, which was right next door to his. Within a few months she was pregnant. The senior men of the family insisted on an abortion. But Janaki was adamant. Barle had waited for her for six years and now was the time for them to deliver her to the house of her "real" parents-in-law. Their first child was born in early 1983.[12]

In the mean time, the legal warfare continued. Janaki had petitioned for divorce. Dau Lal had tried to get her jailed for bigamously marrying Barle (in a civil ceremony held in 1982), and to get all her possessions auctioned to help with his legal expenses. And he had succeeded in obtaining a maintenance order from the Lower Court requiring her to pay his unemployed son Rs 100 per month from her wages until he remarried. The legal arguments went to and fro. The marriage had never been consummated, said Janaki's lawyers, and should therefore be annulled. A plea premised on a failure to comply with earlier orders of the court could not be admitted, the opposition protested. Her adulterous relations with Barle, and the birth of her illegitimate daughter, meant that no court could find in her favor. Irrelevant, said the court, since when Dau Lal's son had informed it of her confinement, he had expressed the magnanimous hope that she would now come "home" and had thereby condoned her conduct. What in the end it all turned on, however, was the rape conviction. Janaki's divorce was finally granted, and she and Barle have lived together—to all appearances more or less happily—ever after.

"Cold Brains" and Double-Beds

As Janaki tells her story, her emotional engagement with it is obvious. She weeps as she describes her attachment to her mother, is (in private) transparently resentful of her father's new family, gleeful as she recounts some legal ploy that had embarrassed Dau Lal and contemptuous of his son. Though I am sure that there is much of it I still do not know, I am equally sure that but for this deep emotional involvement I would know a great deal less than I do. It is true that she is probably—with some reason—suspicious of Somvaru's discretion, and assumes that I would anyway hear his version. But were she not also so carried away by the telling, I doubt that many important details would have ever been revealed to me. Middle-class propriety would have filtered them out.

Somvaru, by contrast, seems almost detached from the events of his life, and rarely dwells on the emotional aspects of family relationships or opens them up for discussion. He is far more likely to foreground their financial implications, and to offer me minutely detailed accounts of his transactions with his kin. Though he had clearly worried about his son for years, even after Dukhit's suicide he displayed little emotion and had little to say of his feelings. Thinking back on our many conversations, my sense is that for such an articulate man the vocabulary he deploys for describing emotional states is surprisingly restricted. I have certainly often been struck by how little he has ever volunteered, or revealed, about his feelings for any of his wives, or about the breakdown of his earlier marriages. No bitterness or acrimony (though admittedly some relief at having got rid of the witch); but no sense of intimacy, fulfillment or personal loss either.

But perhaps I am struck by his emotional reticence because I am looking in the wrong place to find feeling expressed? Somvaru, as we have seen, tends to "somatize" it, to talk about inner feelings as bodily states. Could it then be that the discourse of emotion is "displaced" into a discourse about physical well being? I do not think so. Apart from the normal complaints of aging, Somvaru continues to enjoy pretty good health and certainly does not dwell on bodily processes or infirmities. Nor, unlike my Banarasi Brahmin informants, does he endlessly deploy physiological metaphors to talk about other things, or cite bodily symptoms as an index of spiritual states (Parry 1985; 1989). Or perhaps, alternatively, I am ignoring the lesson of Abu-Lughod's (1986) study of the poetry which the Bedouin of the Western Desert recite, or—nearer home—the lesson of Raheja and Gold's (1994) analysis of women's oral traditions in rural North India? In both cases, a "counter-hegemonic" discourse that celebrates emotional attachments and a longing for intimacy, runs alongside a dominant discourse that discountenances and even suppresses the expression of them. Could it be that I am attending only to the second of these in Somvaru's story, and failing to listen out for the first? Again, I think not. If it exists, I have found no trace of it.

It is not, I assume, that Somvaru has always managed to remain emotionally indifferent to the women he married; and I suspect—as I have hinted—that the conjugal relationship he is most reticent about continues to touch some chord. It is rather that, as he sees it, "the communion of souls" is not what marriage is about. That he should represent his second wife's reported regrets at having left him as regrets for having failed to see which side her bread was buttered is characteristic. Characteristic, I believe, not just of Somvaru, but of a particular cultural discourse about what marriage is. It is not one to which Janaki would subscribe. In any event, the contrast in the way in which she and her father talk about marriage and its breakdown is striking.

Now I am, of course, conscious that this may be partly a matter of individual personality, and partly of gender—as Kakar's report (1990: chapter 5) on Delhi slum women's dreams of forming a "couple" (*jori*), and Raheja and Gold's discussion (1994: chapter 4) of the hankering after conjugal intimacy that runs through the songs and stories of rural women, would suggest. On the premise that the elderly *ought* to disengage themselves from emotional bonds (however impossible they find that in practice [Lamb 2000]), it might also be supposed that Somvaru's emotional detachment is an expression of cultural attitudes appropriate to his stage in life. I do not, however, believe that it is— partly because I do not believe that for him that kind of disengagement is either a preoccupation or a value; and partly because many young people with little schooling and low-status jobs in the informal economy talk about marriage and its break-up in a very similar way. I should also acknowledge that the personality, gender and age of his interlocutor might be relevant too. Indeed, Somvaru's reticence on such matters in the presence of an *angrez* (English) professor who periodically parachutes in from another world might seem scarcely worthy of note were it not for his remarkable openness about so much else that might seem equally threatening.

These other possibilities notwithstanding, an important part of the explanation for Somvaru's silence has, I suggest, to do with the values and ideology surrounding marriage in his particular milieu. And it is a significant shift in this ideology that explains much of the difference between the way in which he and his daughter view their conjugal lives. We are dealing with historical trends to which different generations are exposed in unequal measure, and with what we might loosely call class positioning.

What is marriage for? The first time Somvaru volunteered an answer to this question was in the context of a discussion of the long gap between *shadi* and *gauna* that was customary in the past, and during which many youngsters (as we have seen) would have secret affairs. So why bother to marry them off so young? Because marriage, Somvaru explained, is "for lifting the weight of virginity"—the weight, that is, that falls on the shoulders of the parents of a girl who have a duty to ensure that she is properly disposed of within the caste while she is still a virgin. What she does after that is of less account. A kissing scene in an old American TV movie elicited a second answer. Chhattisgarhis, he observed, do not go in for kissing on the mouth (nor, because men have the authority, for having women on top during intercourse). But "Kamdev's torments," he mused, are a terrible trouble to men, and that is why marriage is necessary. Why, even at the age of seventy, and though he and his wife sleep separately, his mind turns in "that direction" every three or four days. But some men "have peace in their bodies," he continued, "and don't mind if their wife goes with somebody else. They just say, 'so what?'"

When Somvaru describes somebody as having a "cold brain" (*thanda dimag*) it is a mark of real approbation. Perhaps I should translate his phrase less exotically as "cool headed," but this bland rendering fails to capture its strong connotations of civilized restraint and peaceable amiability. One of his favorite moral tales concerns Pushpa's sister, Suraj, and her husband. The latter returned one day from his shift in the plant to find that Suraj had left him and gone to live with his closest friend. A couple of days later he came home to find that his friend's wife had moved in with him. Nothing was ever said about it between the two men and they continued their friendship as though nothing had happened. That, says Somvaru, is how one should be in such matters—"cold-brained." And it was a "cold-brained" understanding of this sort, I suspect, that existed between Somvaru and Lakhan with regard to the latter's fourth wife. The earlier ethnography suggests plenty of precedents:

> [In Chhattisgarh] marriage ties are of the loosest description, and adultery is scarcely recognized as an offense. A woman may go and live openly with another man and her husband will take her back afterwards. Sometimes, when two men are in the relation of Mahaprasad or nearest friend to each other . . . they will each place his wife at the other's disposal. The Chamars [now Satnamis] justify this carelessness of the fidelity of their wives by the saying, "If my cow wanders and comes home again, shall I not let her into the stall?" (Russell and Hiralal 1916, vol. 2: 412).

But if exclusive proprietary rights in a woman's sexuality were not stressed by the "traditional" ideology of marriage in this area, nor was the idea that marriage had very much to do with intimate companionship, emotional empathy, or shared tastes. It is above all an institutional arrangement for the bearing and raising of children, and for the management of the household economy. It is perhaps to be expected that Somvaru should after so many years look back on his own previous marriages with a degree of philosophical detachment. But the calm neutrality—almost indifference—with which many younger people from the bottom of the working-class heap also talk about marital break-up is striking.

For those, however, who belong to the new aristocracy of labor and for those, like Janaki, who have climbed into the lower echelons of the middle classes—that is, for those with secure BSP jobs, or jobs in other large-scale organized sector factories or in government departments—marriage is rapidly changing its meaning. A woman's sexuality is certainly not for sharing, divorce is increasingly discountenanced, and a new companionate ideology makes the conjugal bond the object of much greater emotional investment. No longer merely a matter of the satisfactory discharge of marital duties, it is increasingly seen as a union between two intimate selves and carries a much heavier emotional freight. In this much at least, Giddens's (1999) recent stress on the new ideological emphasis on the couple and their relationship rings true to my ethnography. In upwardly mobile BSP families in the neighborhoods I studied, suicides triggered by frustrated romantic attachments are now almost an epidemic. While in Somvaru's old-style village house there is no separate space for the couple, Janaki and her husband have a private bedroom, dominated by what in village eyes is almost a pornographic object—a large double-bed.

For this particular instance, though not I think in the general case (Parry 2001), Giddens is also right to identify the growth of intimacy with a new sense of equality between the couple. Janaki addresses Barle with the familiar second person pronoun *tu*; calls him *yaar* ("friend," but something more like the English "mate"), complains to me in his presence that "this *dehati*" ("countryman," but nearer to "backwoodsman") has failed to do this or that, and tells him to get going now if he is going at all. But most striking of all, Janaki and Barle are prepared to bicker—even have flaming (if quickly quenched) rows—in the presence of visitors like myself. In Somvaru's house, by contrast, communication between husband and wife is never in my observation so abrasive. But nor is there very much of it. On a number of occasions I have found myself primly shocked by young upwardly mobile individuals of both sexes who have expressed their disappointment, dislike, or even detestation of a spouse by whom they feel encumbered. It is possible that men of Somvaru's age may have long since come to terms with their regrets and for that reason do not voice them. But I also suspect that those who share his views on marriage may have fewer of them. Conjugal expectations are less exacting, and the spouse who fails to meet them is a good deal easier to be free of.

At least as they *tell* their stories, then, I find a broad contrast between the emotional distance that Somvaru maintains from the events of his life, and Janaki's far more overt and explicit emotional engagement with personal relationships. But the narrower and more specific contrast that I want to emphasize concerns the much greater affective load that the marriage bond bears in the upwardly mobile segment of society to which Janaki belongs. Schooling and the media (TV and Bollywood in particular) have undoubtedly played a significant part in promoting this new ideology of conjugality. But in a town like Bhilai—and thanks in significant measure to the dominant role of public sector employment—so too has the modern industrial urban milieu. What are regarded as the best jobs are mainly public sector ones, and these are in theory—and very largely in practice as well—assigned to *individuals* who have the appropriate paper qualifications, and irrespective of caste and kinship. In such an occupational system, the significance of consanguineal kinship is loosened. The effect—as Parsons (1949) long ago argued—is a trend toward more individuated and isolated conjugal units which are sustained by a source of income independent of other kin.

This tendency is reinforced by the fact that a large proportion of BSP employees live in company quarters in the township, or (like Barle and Janaki) have built their own houses in one of the many new colonies. In neither case is it probable that they will live with the husband's parents and brothers (who have often remained in the village or are employed elsewhere). In such circumstances, the pivot of the household is the conjugal couple. Husbands and wives are increasingly forced on each other's society, and the open expression of emotion between them is not muted or suppressed in the way that it characteristically is in "traditional" joint household where it is seen as a threat to intergenerational hierarchy and a source of division.

Not only are there new possibilities for—and a new ideological stress on—intimacy, but also a new preoccupation with marriage as an expression of status. In Somvaru's generation, and still today in the less upwardly mobile segments of his own immediate family, the casualness with which marriages (both primary and secondary) are contracted and negotiated is breathtaking. That is not unrelated, of course, to the ease with which they are dissolved. But the new stress on the couple and their relationship is accompanied by a new concern that they be properly "matched" and by a new sense of personal failure if the marriage does not work out well. While Somvaru calmly says that "if two people do not like each other, it is better they part," in Janaki's world their parting almost inevitably becomes a matter of bitter and lasting recrimination. It is also increasingly liable to involve the law.

Pramod—now a godlike engineer—is Barle's younger brother's son, but he and Janaki brought him up. An eminently suitable boy, so suitable that it proved extraordinarily difficult to find his match. Many months were devoted to the search. Barle, Janaki, Sukhit and Pramod himself took whole weeks off work; taxis were hired to take them about, and over forty girls were "inspected"—all, of course, graduates. Most were either too tall, too small, too fat, too old, too forward, or too shy. Pramod could "pass" only three. But on further enquiry, one had witchcraft in the family and another an uncle with leukoderma. The choice made itself, but it turned out disastrously. The girl had a lover. Pramod filed for divorce; the girl's family retaliated by registering a case of "dowry torture." Pramod took another wife. The divorce proceedings pending, there were charges of bigamy and a counter-case against the first wife's father for criminal defamation. The sense of betrayal, the imagined sniggers of their colleagues—for weeks and weeks the pitch of emotional intensity in Janaki's house was feverish.

This ready recourse to the law signals, I believe, an important paradox. As conjugality is increasingly seen as a matter of intimacy, it is as it were "privatized." If not just for the couple themselves, it is a matter for only their nearest family—a matter in which the right of the wider caste and kinship group to have any significant say is strongly questioned. With regard to the regulation of marriage, the caste *panchayats* have now lost most of their teeth. These days, "for shame" it is said, hardly anybody goes for *bihati torna* ("to break the marriage bond"), with the result that the termination of a primary union is no longer publicly sanctioned by the wider community. Instead, it is increasingly likely that the couple will arrive in court. At the same time as marriage is "privatized" and ideologically reconfigured as "the union of two souls," the impersonal—but cynically manipulable—judicial apparatus of the state is becoming the ultimate arbiter in "personal life."

While the scrutiny of caste, kin group, and local community has been weakened, the role of the state in the regulation of domestic life has started to be increasingly intrusive.

References

Abu-Lughod, L. 1986. *Veiled Sentiments: Honor and Poetry in a Bedouin Society*. Berkeley: University of California Press.

Babb, L. A. 1972. "The Satnamis: Political Involvement of a Religious Movement." In J.M. Mahar (ed.), *The Untouchables in Contemporary India*, pp. 143–51. Tucson: University of Arizona Press.

Béteille, A. 1983. "The Idea of Natural Inequality." In *The Idea of Natural Inequality and Other Essays*. Delhi: Oxford University Press.

Bloch, Maurice. 1998a. "Internal and External Memory: Different Ways of being in History." In *How We Think They Think: Anthropological Approaches to Cognition, Memory, and Literacy*, pp. 67–84. Oxford: Westview Press.

———. 1998b. "Autobiographical Memory and the Historical Memory of the More Distant Past." In *How We Think They Think: Anthropological Approaches to Cognition, Memory, and Literacy*, pp. 114–27. Oxford: Westview Press.

Dube, S. 1998. *Untouchable Pasts: Religion, Identity, and Power among a Central Indian Community, 1780–1950*. New York: State University of New York Press.

Freeman, J.M. 1979. *Untouchable: An Indian Life History*. Stanford: Stanford University Press.

Giddens, A. 1999. *Runaway World: How Globalisation is Shaping Our World*. London: Profile Books.

Goody, Jack. 1977. *The Domestication of the Savage Mind*. Cambridge: Cambridge University Press.

Kakar, Sudhir. 1990. *Intimate Relations: Exploring Indian Sexuality*. Chicago: Chicago University Press.

Lamb, Sarah. 2000. *White Saris and Sweet Mangoes: Aging, Gender, and Body in North India*. Berkeley: University of California Press.

Metcalf, Barbara. 1995. "Narrating Lives: A Mughal Empress, a French Nabab, a Nationalist Intellectual." *Journal of Asian Studies* 54: 474–80.

Moon, Vasant. 2001. *Growing up Untouchable in India: A Dalit Autobiography* (transl. from Marathi by Gail Omvedt). Oxford: Eowman and Littlefield.

Parry, Jonathan P. 1979. *Caste and Kinship in Kangra*. London: Routledge & Kegan Paul.

————. 1985. "Death and Digestion: The Symbolism and Food and Eating in North Indian Mortuary Rites." *Man* (n.s.) 29: 612–30.

————. 1989. "The End of the Body." In Michel Feher *et al.* (eds), *Fragments for a History of the Human Body*, vol. 2, pp. 490–517. New York: Zone Books.

————. 1994. *Death in Banaras*. Cambridge: Cambridge University Press.

————. 1999a. "Two Cheers for Reservation: The Satnamis and the Steel Plant." In R. Guha and J. Parry (eds), *Institutions and Inequalities: Essays in Honour of Andre Béteille*. New Delhi: Oxford University Press.

————. 1999b. "Lords of Labour: Working and Shirking in Bhilai." In J. Parry, J. Breman and K. Kapadia (eds), *The Worlds of Indian Industrial Labour*. New Delhi: Sage Publications.

————. 2000. " 'The Crisis of Corruption' and 'The Idea of India': A Worm's Eye View." In I. Pardo (ed.), *The Morals of Legitimacy*, pp. 27–55. Oxford: Berghahn Books.

————. 2001. "Ankalu's Errant Wife: Sex, Marriage and Industry in Contemporary Chhattisgarh." *Modern Asian Studies* 35: 783–820.

Parsons, Talcot. 1949. "The Kinship System of the Contemporary United States." In *Essays in Sociological Theory: Pure and Applied*, pp. 233–50. Glencoe, Illinois: The Free Press.

Prakasam, G. 1993. "The Changing Status of a Scheduled Caste in Chhattisgarh, Madhya Pradesh." D.Phil. dissertation, University of Oxford.

Raheja, Gloria G., and Ann G. Gold. 1994. *Listen to the Heron's Words: Reimagining Gender and Kinship in North India*. Berkeley: University of California Press.

Russell, R.V. and R.B. Hiralal. 1916. *The Tribes and Castes of the Central Provinces of India*, 4 vols. London: Macmillan.

Sahlins. Marshall. 1985. *Islands of History*. Chicago: Chicago University Press.

Van Velsen, J. 1967. "The Extended Case Method and Situational Analysis." In A.L. Epstein (ed.), *The Craft of Social Anthropology*, pp.129–49. London: Tavistock Publications.

Viramma, Josiane Racine and Jean-Luc Racine.1997. *Viramma: Life of an Untouchable*. London: Verso.

ACKNOWLEDGMENTS

This chapter is a spin-off from approximately nineteen months' field research, undertaken at various intervals between September 1993 and August 2001. I gratefully acknowledge the support of the Nuffield Foundation, the Economic and Social Science Research Council and the London School of Economics. Special thanks are also due to Ajay T.G. for his invaluable research assistance; and to André Bétéille, Henrike Donner, Chris Fuller, Ram Guha, Sudipta Kaviraj, Filippo Osella and Alpa Shah for their comments on an earlier draft.

Notes

1. A pseudonym, as are all other names in this account. I have, however, tried to preserve something of the flavor of the originals.
2. But it is also true that these shifts were significantly foreshadowed by much earlier work. It is perhaps no coincidence that what Van Velsen (1967) called the "post-structuralist" methods of the Manchester School ("situational analysis" and "the extended case method") also involved the collection of detailed life-history material.
3. For Satnami history and ethnography, see Babb 1972, Dube 1998, and Prakasam 1993; and for the impact of steel plant employment on their social position and place in the contemporary caste hierarchy of the industrial belt, see Parry 1999a.
4. This is a customarily appropriate form of widow remarriage, though it is unusual for another union to intervene before the widow is claimed by her *devar* (HyB).
5. In his own name, Somvaru had in April 2000 nearly Rs 5 lakhs, from which he was getting an income of about Rs 5,000 per month. Since Dukhit was officially deemed to have been killed in "an industrial accident" while on duty, his widow is entitled to draw his basic pay and dearness allowance up to the date at which he would have retired. This amounts to Rs 5,800 per month, out of which she was giving Somvaru Rs 1,500 toward household expenses.
6. I estimate that this probably amounts in total to another Rs 5 lakhs.
7. A detailed account of his transactions over a ten-year period is provided in Parry 1999a.
8. Indian People's Theatre Association, loosely affiliated to the Communist Party of India.
9. On the complete disdain of the young for all forms of agricultural labor, see Parry 1999b.
10. At a certain stage in the wedding ritual, all close relatives "take a kiss."
11. One of her main arguments in the subsequent legal battle was that the marriage had never been consummated, so this was a crucial claim at the time.
12. During the course of one emotional conversation, Janaki revealed that she thinks that her daughter is a reincarnation of her mother. She has a small mark on her nose at the very point where the pick-axe had made a wound on her mother's nose at the time she was buried alive, and has a

mole on her chest in the very same place. At the time of her birth she had greenish marks on her wrists. Her mother was cremated wearing green bangles. She had died on a Monday, the day of the week on which her daughter—and also coincidentally (?) Somvaru—was born. On the assumption that they must have discussed it, I once mentioned this idea to Somvaru. He had never heard it before. It did however elicit his own notion—based on similar evidence—that Raj Kumar is the reincarnation of his father's father's younger brother who brought him up.

Index